BARRON'S

HOW TO PREPARE FOR THE

SAT II

MATH LEVEL IIC

6TH EDITION

Howard P. Dodge
The Wheeler School
Providence, Rhode Island

BARRON'S

All inquiries should be addressed to:
Barron's Educational Series, Inc.
250 Wireless Boulevard
Hauppauge, New York 11788
http://www.barronseduc.com

Library of Congress Catalog Card No. 98-18035

International Standard Book No. 0-7641-0462-4

Library of Congress Cataloging-in-Publication Data

Dodge, Howard P.
     Barron's how to prepare for SAT II : mathematics level IIC / Howard P.
  Dodge.—6th ed.
       p. cm.
     Rev. ed. of : Barron's how to prepare for SAT II.
     Includes index.
     ISBN 0-7641-0462-4
     1. Mathematics—Examinations, questions, etc. 2. College entrance
  achievement tests—United States—Study guides. I. Dodge, Howard
  P. Barron's how to prepare for SAT. II. Title.
  QA43.D57   1998   98-18035
  510'.76—dc20   CIP

PRINTED IN THE UNITED STATES OF AMERICA

9 8 7 6 5 4

CONTENTS

ACKNOWLEDGMENTS

I would like to express my appreciation to my former colleagues in the mathematics department of Choate Rosemary Hall, Wallingford, Connecticut, for the many helpful suggestions and useful problems used throughout this book. Particular thanks are due to Dean Blanchard and Charles Bodine, formerly of St. George's School, Newport, Rhode Island, for their helpful comments on early drafts of this book, and to my son, Laurence, for his careful checking of the solution to each problem.

Finally, I would like to express my thanks to Barron's editors Carole Berglie, Mickey Wright, Jane O'Sullivan, Donna Jones, and Pat Wilson for their suggestions and assistance in preparing the previous editions of this book, and especially to Wendy Sleppin, who has guided me through the preparation of this new edition.

INTRODUCTION

HOW THIS BOOK IS STRUCTURED

This introduction has been designed to help you approach the Mathematics Level IIC Subject Test with confidence. It describes the makeup and content of the test, gives you suggestions that will help you score as high as possible, and answers the questions most often asked by students who take the test. Once you have read through the introduction, you will be ready for the body of the book, which is divided into three parts.

As an accomplished mathematics student who feels prepared for the Level IIC examination, begin your review with Part 1, which is a diagnostic test covering the topics on the Level IIC examination. Answers and explanations are given at the end of the test. Following each solution is a number in square brackets that refers you to a place in this book where that topic is reviewed. If you do not get the correct answer, you can find the proper section in the book either by checking the contents page or by looking at the heading at the top of each page. For example, if you get question 26 wrong, you are referred to [4.4]. On the contents page, you can see that 4.4, "Greatest Integer Function," begins on page 76. Otherwise you could flip through the pages until you come to Chapter 4 and then check the headings on right-hand pages until you reach Section 4.4.

Part 2 is a review of the topics covered by the Level IIC test. You can either read through it in its entirety or refer to it whenever you have difficulty with a problem. This part consists of a discussion of the methods and formulas necessary to solve the many types of problems you will encounter. A fuller explanation of some of the more elementary topics can be found in *Barron's How to Prepare for SAT II: Mathematics Level IC*. Since this is a review, very few derivations of formulas are included. If you are curious about derivations, you should refer to your high school textbooks.

Part 3 contains eight sample Level IIC examinations each consisting of 50 multiple-choice questions. A solution is given for each problem. Also provided is a cross reference in square brackets that refers you to the appropriate review topic.

HOW THE LEVEL IIC TEST IS STRUCTURED

The Mathematics Level IIC test contains 50 multiple-choice questions, each with five possible answers, only one of which is correct. You will have 1 hour to complete the test.

Although the test is aimed at students who have had $3\frac{1}{2}$ or more years of high-school mathematics, it is often taken by those who have had 3 years of strong mathematics courses. Regardless of the amount of mathematics you have completed, remember that this examination is prepared for talented students who have studied trigonometry and elementary functions in detail. If you have such a background, you will be better prepared for this test than for the Mathematics Level IC test, which contains several questions on Euclidean plane geometry, since the material tested will have been covered more recently in your courses.

According to the most recent College Board information, the questions in the Mathematics Level IIC test are divided into five categories. (The percentages given below indicate the approximate weighting of each topic in the examination.)

18% – 1. Algebra
20% – 2. Geometry (coordinate geometry in two or three dimensions, transformations, synthetic geometry in three dimensions, and vectors)
    8% – (a) Solid geometry
    12% – (b) Coordinate geometry
20% – 3. Trigonometry (properties and graphs of the trigonometric functions, inverse trigonometric functions, identities, equations, and inequalities)
24% – 4. Elementary functions
18% – 5. Miscellaneous topics (sequences, series and limits, logic and proof, permutations and combinations, probability and statistics, and number theory)

The topics in the model examinations in this book have been weighted in the same way in order to give you a realistic experience of the breadth you will encounter in the actual examination.

To take the Mathematics Level IIC test, you must have available a scientific calculator. In other words, only students who regularly use calculators in their mathematics classes will be able to take this test.

You may use any calculator you desire, including a graphic calculator, but *not* a computer or a model with a typewriter keyboard. For more information you should consult the most recent College Board bulletin.

To use your calculator most effectively, you must know the precise protocol that it requires to obtain answers.

Three types of questions will be asked:

1. *Active* questions, for which a calculator must be used.

EXAMPLE: Log(sin 0.5) =

(A) 0.48
(B) −2.1
(C) 0.01
(D) −0.32
(E) −0.28

Solution: **D**   Since 0.5 does not have a degree sign (°), make sure that your calculator is in radian mode. If you press the appropriate buttons to make *your* calculator determine the log of sin 0.5, it will display −0.3192788. (Notice that if your calculator was set in degree mode you would have obtained Choice B, −2.1, which would *not* be correct.)

2. *Inactive* questions, for which a calculator is of no use.

EXAMPLE: If a and b represent the legs and c represents the hypotenuse of a right triangle, then tan A =

(A) $\dfrac{a}{b}$

(B) $\dfrac{a}{c}$

(C) $\dfrac{b}{a}$

(D) $\dfrac{b}{c}$

(E) $\dfrac{c}{a}$

Solution: **A**   Since there are no numbers, obviously a calculator cannot be used.

In a right triangle, tan A = $\dfrac{\text{opposite side}}{\text{adjacent side}}$. Since $\angle A$ is opposite side a, tan $A = \dfrac{a}{b}$.

3. *Neutral* questions, for which a calculator may or may not be used.

EXAMPLE: Sin[cos⁻¹(−0.5)] =

(A) 0.5
(B) 0.7
(C) 0.9
(D) −0.9
(E) −0.7

Solution: **C** If you know your trigonometry facts and an approximate value for $\sqrt{3}$, this problem can be done in

your head. Otherwise, you can use your calculator.

Without calculator: Cos⁻¹(−0.5) equals the angle in the second quadrant whose cosine is −0.5. The angle is 120°.

$$\text{Sin } 120° = \frac{\sqrt{3}}{2} \approx 0.866 \approx 0.9.$$

With calculator: With the correct keystrokes the calculator displays 0.866025403.

Active and neutral questions make up approximately 60% of the test.

Thus, if you expect to do well on the Mathematics Level IIC Subject Test, you must have a thorough understanding of the material, a good working knowledge of your calculator, and the ability to recognize when, and when not, to use your calculator.

Although this is an advanced test, there are several relatively elementary questions among the 50 asked. Here are two examples:

1.   **An equation of line ℓ could be**

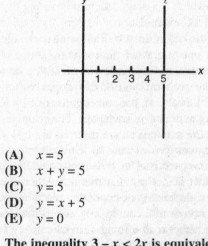

    (A) $x = 5$
    (B) $x + y = 5$
    (C) $y = 5$
    (D) $y = x + 5$
    (E) $y = 0$

2.   **The inequality $3 − x < 2x$ is equivalent to which one of the following?**

    (A) $x > 1$
    (B) $x < 1$
    (C) $x < 3$
    (D) $x > 3$
    (E) $x > \dfrac{3}{2}$

The answer to question 1 is Choice A since x must remain 5 regardless of the value of y. The inequality in question 2 can be transformed into Choice A by adding x to both sides and dividing by 3.

SUGGESTIONS FOR SCORING HIGHER ON THE TEST

There is no quick shortcut method of preparing for SAT II tests. You should plan your review several weeks in advance of the examination and set aside a regular time and place each day for review and practice.

How you should prepare

On the first day you should spend between 1 and 2 hours taking the diagnostic test under simulated testing conditions—quiet with no distractions or disturbances. The results of this test will help you determine the areas you need to work on. Each day thereafter, plan to work on your weaknesses for 20 to 30 minutes until you feel prepared to take the first model test. Again, use the results of the test to pinpoint weak areas and repeat your study schedule.

This preparation will lead to an increase in knowledge, a deeper understanding of the material, and greater confidence when taking the actual Mathematics Level IIC Subject Examination. With such a wide variety of topics covered, no student is expected to have studied every one. Do not be surprised if a few questions seem to make no sense. On one administration of the Math IIC examination, for example, students who earned a raw score between 42 and 50 (out of a possible 50 points) received an 800—the highest possible scaled score.

How the test is scored

Your raw score is determined by the number of correct answers *minus* one-fourth of the number of incorrect answers. This system means that if you do not know how to do a particular problem, you should stop to think before you guess blindly. If you can eliminate only one choice, guessing may not be advisable. If, however, you can eliminate more than one choice and you are guessing at four or more questions, it may be worth the risk. Remember that a raw score of as little as 42 points could give you a perfect 800. Note that this translation varies from year to year, depending on how other students score. One year a raw score of 42 could give you a scaled score of 780, but another year that same 42 could translate to 800. On a recent test given by the College Board, a 20 gave 610, a 30 gave 700, and a 40 gave 780.

How to raise your score

To help you raise your score, the following lists summarize suggestions for math examinations in general, any type of timed examination, and this examination in particular.

Suggestions for any timed examination

- *Budget your time.* Work swiftly: don't linger over difficult questions.
- *Guess intelligently.* Random guessing will probably not raise your score.
- *Read each question carefully.* Answer the question asked, not the one you may have expected.
- *Save the hardest questions for last.*
- *Mark answers clearly and accurately.* Check the numbering of your answer sheet often. Erase cleanly; leave no stray marks. Mark only one answer. You will be marked wrong if two spaces are filled in.

- *Change an answer only if you have a good reason for doing so.* It is usually best not to change on the basis of a hunch or whim.

Suggestions for mathematics examinations in general

- Round off and estimate wherever possible. Minimize calculation.
- Look for the shortcuts that are built into many problems.
- Work in units (hours, ounces, square miles) consistent with those in the answer choices.
- Break down complex word problems and make computations one step at a time.

Suggestions for the Math Level IIC test

- Go through the entire test, doing only the problems that can be solved easily.
- Be aware when and when not to try to use your calculator.
- Go back through the test, doing the problems that seem to be on familiar material but will take a little time to figure out.
- Finally, if there is time, use the five answer choices as a guide (and, if possible, your calculator) to try to figure out the correct answer to the remaining questions, *OR* check the answers to the problems that have previously been completed.
- At each step, be careful to mark the correct space on the answer sheet.

Suggestions for calculator usage

- *Be familiar with your calculator.* Use the calculator that you have been using all year. Don't get a new, fancy calculator for the Math Level IIC test. It will slow you down, and you will not know how to use all of its features.
- *Be familiar with the functions of your calculator.* Make sure you are using the proper mode, especially with the trigonometric and inverse trigonometric functions. Make sure you know how to switch between modes. Make sure you know how to use all the necessary functions.
- *Always check the answer choices.* If they are in terms of whole numbers, fractions, radicals, π, and so on, the problem can usually be solved without using a calculator.
- *Always simplify problems before trying to use your calculator.* Many problems that at first glance appear to require a calculator will not require one after simplification.
- *Avoid lengthy calculations.* Lengthy calculations are never required or expected. Do not get involved with them. There must be an easier way.
- *Never round off results in the middle of a problem.* This could cause your answer to be significantly different from the answer choices.
- *All calculations should be done "within" the calculator.* If you choose to use a calculator, you should never

have to write down intermediate results. This is time-consuming, and there is too much of a chance of miscopying. If you do need to write down intermediate results, it means that you probably have not used your mathematical knowledge to simplify the problem sufficiently.

 Throughout this book this symbol indicates the use of a calculator in solutions and suggestions.

QUESTIONS STUDENTS ASK ABOUT SAT II: SUBJECT TESTS*

What is an SAT II Subject Test?

An SAT II: Subject Test tests your knowledge of a subject and your ability to apply that knowledge. Unlike the SAT I test, an SAT II test is curriculum-based and is intended to measure how much you have learned rather than how much learning ability you have.

How is it used?

Colleges use SAT II: Subject Tests to predict an admission candidate's future success on the level of work typical at that college. Applicants to colleges use the tests to demonstrate their acquired knowledge in subject areas important to their future goals.

Some colleges, especially the most selective schools, have found subject test results to be better predictors of success in related college courses than SAT I scores and, frequently, the high school record. Because grading systems, standards, and course offerings differ among secondary schools, a student's SAT II: Subject Test score may provide the college with more and better information about what the student knows than is available from his or her high school transcript.

Colleges also use SAT II: Subject Test results to place students in appropriate courses after they have been admitted.

High schools use SAT II: Subject Tests to examine the success of their curriculum and to indicate strengths and weaknesses.

Should I take a math SAT II: Subject Test?

Depending on the secondary school you attend and the college to which you apply, you may not have much choice. Most private colleges and many state universities require applicants to take three SAT II: Subject Tests, though often not specifying which ones. According to a counselor at a selective independent secondary school, "Ninety-nine percent of the colleges our students apply to require three achievement [SAT II: Subject] tests, so we ask all of our students to take them regardless of where they apply."

Many secondary school counselors believe that an application is improved by SAT II: Subject Test scores even when a college does not require them, because the tests allow the candidate to demonstrate proficiency in the areas of his or her greatest strength.

Which tests you take will depend on your most successful courses in secondary school and your intended major in college. You should not take an SAT II: Subject Test unless you have been successful in that subject or have made a special effort to prepare for the test (it is best if you satisfy both conditions).

Examine the description of the contents of the Level IIC test on page v to see whether you have studied the topics tested.

Many secondary school counselors believe that the subject tests most helpful to your application are an English test, a math test, and a third test in your best third subject. If you intend to major in a science or in any other math-related field (engineering, economics, etc.), you definitely should take a math SAT II: Subject Test.

How important are SAT II: Subject Tests in college admissions?

College admissions committees generally regard achievement test scores as "confirming" evidence to be compared with high school grades, the level of courses taken, and SAT I scores. Grades (especially because of grade inflation) and courses offered vary greatly from high school to high school (and even from teacher to teacher within the same high school). A grade in "intermediate math," for example, at a selective independent school may represent something entirely different from the same grade in a course of the same name at a small rural public high school.

No other factor on an application is so uniform an assessment of all applicants as a standardized achievement test.

The scores are used not only as a measure of knowledge but also as a means of interpreting the high school record. Low achievement test scores accompanied by high grades, for example, may suggest an inflated grading system. High scores with average grades may mean the applicant is attending a more demanding high school that offers a challenging program to competitive students chosen for special abilities.

In general, test scores are more important if they disagree with the high school record and less important if they agree. They are also more important if they lie outside the range of scores of students normally selected by the college and less important if they fall within this range. And, finally, they are more important if they conflict with the scores on the SAT I than if they confirm these scores.

*Adapted from *How to Prepare for the SAT II: Mathematics Level IC*, 6th Ed., by James J. Rizutto, Barron's Educational Series, Inc., Hauppauge, New York, 1994. Reprinted with permission.

In other words, if the SAT II: Subject Test scores don't say the same thing as the rest of the record, it's the new message that is important. If the new message is positive, it will help. But in the majority of cases, the achievement test scores confirm the rest of the data on the application.

When and where are SAT II: Subject Tests given?

These tests are usually given in the morning of the first Saturday in November, December, May, and June and the last Saturday in January. There are hundreds of test centers around the country. Dates vary from year to year. For other information on dates and test sites, write to the College Board Admission Testing Program for its current schedule.

To whom do I write for information and registration?

Write to:

> College Board SAT Program
> P.O. Box 6200
> Princeton, New Jersey 08541-6200

or call:

> (609) 771-7600.

The College Entrance Examination Board, an association of colleges and secondary schools, is headquartered in New York City. To arrange for testing, use *only* the Princeton address.

What should I bring with me to the test?

You should bring your ticket of admission, some positive form of identification, two or more no. 2 pencils (with erasers, or bring an eraser), a watch (though test centers *should* have clearly visible clocks), and a simple twist-type pencil sharpener (so that you need not waste time walking back and forth to and from a pencil sharpener if your point breaks).

No books, calculators (except for the Math Level IIC Subject Test), rulers, scratch paper, slide rules, compasses, protractors, or other devices are allowed in the examination room.

ACTUAL MATH LEVEL IIC QUESTIONS

This section contains directions and several questions from an actual Math Level IIC test, reprinted with the permission of the Educational Testing Service. These particular questions were chosen to familiarize you with the various types that may appear. They were also chosen because their answers can be found by using unorthodox or "nonroutine" methods or by intelligent guessing—methods that your math teacher may frown upon but that sometimes work

with multiple-choice type questions. Each question is followed by a comment describing such an approach.

Obviously, if you understand a problem and can solve it directly, you should do so. Other methods are suggested only to show you that there is often an alternative way to look for an answer. Although these questions are from past achievement examinations, Problems 4, 5, 7, and 12 may be considered *neutral* questions because a calculator could be useful in finding the answers. See the specific comments following those problems. The directions, questions, and comments follow.

Directions: For each of the following problems, decide which is the best of the choices given. Then blacken the corresponding space on the answer sheet.

Notes: (1) Figures that accompany problems in this test are intended to provide information useful in solving the problems. They are drawn as accurately as possible EXCEPT when it is stated in a specific problem that its figure is not drawn to scale. All figures lie in a plane unless otherwise indicated.

(2) Unless otherwise specified, the domain of a function f is assumed to be the set of all real numbers x for which $f(x)$ is a real number.

1. The set of all ordered pairs (x,y) that satisfy the system $\begin{cases} y = x \\ xy = 1 \end{cases}$ is

    (A) $\{(-1, -1)\}$
    (B) $\{(-1, 1)\}$
    (C) $\{(1, 1)\}$
    (D) $\{(-1, -1), (1, 1)\}$
    (E) $\{(-1, 1), (1, -1)\}$

Comment: An easy, straightforward problem. Just substitute x for y in the second equation: $x^2 = 1$. $x = \pm 1$. Don't jump at Choice B as the answer. Make sure you ANSWER THE QUESTION—ordered pairs for x and y. Correct answer: Choice D.

2. If k is an integer less than zero, which of the following is less than zero?

    (A) $-k$
    (B) $-(-k)$
    (C) $(-k)^2$
    (D) $(k)^2$
    (E) $(-k)^3$

Comment: Try a specific negative integer for k. For example, let $k = -1$, and check the given choices until you find one that answers the question. Choice A: $-(-1) > 0$, Choice B: $-[-(-1)] < 0$. You have found the answer. Go on to the next question.

3. When a certain integer is divided by 5, the remainder is 3. What is the remainder when 4 times that integer is divided by 5?

(A) 0
(B) 1
(C) 2
(D) 3
(E) 4

Comment: Again, try a specific number that satisfies the conditions of the problem. For example, when 8 is divided by 5, the remainder is 3. $4 \cdot 8 = 32$, which, when divided by 5, leaves a remainder of 2. Correct answer: Choice C.

4. Which of the following defines a function that associates a positive integer y with each positive integer x so that x and y have the same tens' digit?

(A) $y = 10x$
(B) $y = 11x$
(C) $y = 100x$
(D) $y = 101x$
(E) $y = 111x$

Comment: This time try a specific two-digit number, for example, 21. Choices A and C can be eliminated since they shift all digits. Simple multiplications of 21 by 11, 101, and 111 lead to the correct answer: Choice D.

Calculator: Use it to make the multiplication easier.

5. The solution set of $\dfrac{(x+1)^2}{x} > 0$ is

(A) the empty set
(B) $\{x \mid x > -1\}$
(C) $\{x \mid x > 0\}$
(D) $\{x \mid x > 1\}$
(E) $\{x \mid x$ is any real number$\}$

Comment: Think about the problem before "diving in" to solve a quadratic inequality. Notice that the numerator is always positive or 0. Therefore, the denominator, x, must also be positive. We must also rule out $x = -1$, which makes the numerator 0. The solution occurs when $x > 0$. Correct answer: Choice C.

Graphing calculator: Plot the graph of $y = \dfrac{(x+1)^2}{x}$ in an $x \in [-10 \times 10]$, $y \in [-10 \times 10]$ window to see that the graph is above the x-axis when $x > 0$.

6. In the figure, the bases of the right prism are equilateral triangles, each with perimeter 30 centimeters. If the altitude of the prism is 10 centimeters, what is the total surface area of the solid in square centimeters?

(A) 100
(B) $\dfrac{250}{\sqrt{3}}$
(C) $100\sqrt{3}$
(D) 300
(E) $50\sqrt{3} + 300$

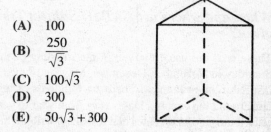

Comment: Since the lateral sides are squares, 10 centimeters on a side, their area is 300. Equilateral triangles have a $\sqrt{3}$ in their area, which must be added to the 300. Choice E must be the correct answer.

7. If $f(x) = \dfrac{1}{x}$, which of the following could be the graph of $y = f(-x)$?

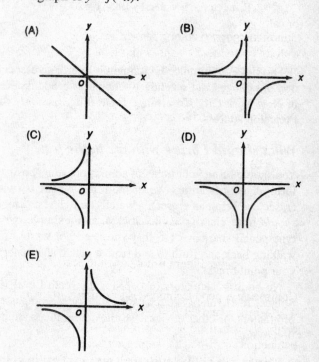

(A)

(B)

(C)

(D)

(E)

Comment: Since $y = f(-x)$ is the mirror image of $y = f(x)$ reflected on the y-axis, and the graph of $f(x) = \dfrac{1}{x}$ looks like the sketch on the following page, the graph of $f(-x)$ must look like Choice B.

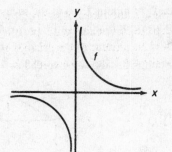

 Graphing calculator: Plot the graph of $y = \dfrac{1}{-x}$ in an $x \in [-10 \times 10], y \in [-10 \times 10]$ window to see that the correct answer is Choice B.

8. If line $y = k$ is tangent to the circle $(x-2)^2 + y^2 = 9$, then $k =$

   (A) -1 or 4
   (B) -3 or 3
   (C) -4 or 1
   (D) -6 or 6
   (E) -9 or 9

Comment: $y = k$ is a horizontal line, tangent to a circle with its center at $(2,0)$ and with radius 3. Therefore, the line is either 3 units above the center or 3 units below the center. Thus, $k = \pm 3$. Correct answer: Choice B.

9. In the figure, if Arcsin x = Arccos x, then $k =$

   (A) x
   (B) x^2
   (C) 1
   (D) $1 - x$
   (E) $\dfrac{1}{x}$

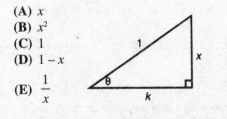

Note: Figure is not drawn to scale

Comment: A good technique is to simplify notation. Let A = Arcsin x and let B = Arccos x. Then the question really states that $\sin A = \cos B$ since both equal x: If the cofunctions of two acute angles are equal, the angles are complementary. But the question also tells us that they are equal. Therefore, $A = B = 45°$, the triangle shown is isosceles, and $x = k$. Correct answer: Choice A.

10. $(-i)^n$ is a negative real number if $n =$

   (A) 21
   (B) 22
   (C) 23
   (D) 24
   (E) 25

Comment: Remember $i^4 = 1$. n must be even for $(-i)^n$ to be a real number. This eliminates Choices A, C, and E. If n is divisible by 4, $(-i)^n = (-1)^n(i)^n = (-1)^n(i)^{4k} = (1)(i^4)^k = (1)(1)^k = (1)(1) = 1$, which eliminates Choice D. Correct answer: Choice B.

11. $\dfrac{(n-1)!}{n!} + \dfrac{(n+1)!}{n!} =$

   (A) $\dfrac{n-1}{n}$

   (B) $\dfrac{n^2+1}{n}$

   (C) $\dfrac{n^2-1}{n}$

   (D) $\dfrac{n+1}{n}$

   (E) $\dfrac{n^2+n+1}{n}$

Comment: If the method of solution is not obvious, try expanding the factorials a bit to see if you can find a clue to the solution.

$$\frac{(n-1)!}{n!} + \frac{(n+1)!}{n!}$$

$$= \frac{(n-1)(n-2)!}{n(n-1)(n-2)!} + \frac{(n+1)(n!)}{n!}$$

$$= \frac{1}{n} + \frac{n+1}{1}$$

$$= \frac{n^2+n+1}{n}$$

Correct answer: Choice E.

12. What is the range of the function defined by $f(x) = \dfrac{1}{x} + 2$?

   (A) all real numbers
   (B) all real numbers except $-\dfrac{1}{2}$
   (C) all real numbers except 0
   (D) all real numbers except 2
   (E) all real numbers between 2 and 3

Comment: It often helps to reduce the problem to a simpler and more manageable one. $f(x) = \dfrac{1}{x}$ is simpler than $f(x) = \dfrac{1}{x} + 2$ but related to it. The graph of $y = \dfrac{1}{x}$ looks like the one on the following page. Its range is all values of y except zero. The graph of $f(x)$ is the same, but it is shifted up 2 units. Therefore, the range of $f(x)$ is all real numbers except 2. Correct answer: Choice D.

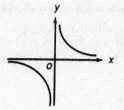

 Graphing calculator: Plot the graph of $y = \dfrac{1}{x} + 2$ in an $x \in [-10 \times 10]$, $y \in [-10 \times 10]$ window to see that there appears to be a horizontal asymptote. Use the Trace function to see that it is at $y = 2$. All other values of y are defined, so the correct answer is Choice D.

13. How many different sets of two parallel edges are there in a cube?

(A) 6
(B) 8
(C) 12
(D) 18
(E) 24

Comment: Draw a sketch of a cube and try to find a pattern. Take one edge, a, and find all edges parallel to it. There are three (b,c,d). Now take b and find all edges parallel to it except a. There are two (c,d). Now take c and find all edges parallel to it except a and b. There is one (d). Thus, for this set of edges, there are six sets of parallel edges. There are also two other sets of edges, (E,F,G,H) and $(1,2,3,4)$. Therefore, there is a total of 18 sets of two parallel edges. Correct answer: Choice D.

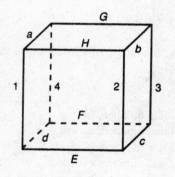

14. The "spread" of a point (x,y) in the rectangular coordinate plane is defined as $|x| + |y|$. Which of the following points has the same spread as $\left(\dfrac{3}{2}, -\dfrac{1}{2}\right)$?

(A) $(-1, 0)$

(B) $\left(0, \dfrac{1}{2}\right)$

(C) $\left(\dfrac{1}{2}, \dfrac{1}{2}\right)$

(D) $(1, -1)$

(E) $(2, 1)$

Comment: Often problems are presented where a new operation (such as spread) is defined. Usually this new operation is just a combination of simple, familiar operations. In this case, the spread is just the sum of absolute values. $\left|\dfrac{3}{2}\right| + \left|-\dfrac{1}{2}\right| = \dfrac{3}{2} + \dfrac{1}{2} = 2$. By inspection the correct answer is Choice D.

15. The least positive integer N for which each of $\dfrac{N}{2}, \dfrac{N}{3}, \dfrac{N}{4}, \dfrac{N}{5}, \dfrac{N}{6}, \dfrac{N}{7}, \dfrac{N}{8}$, and $\dfrac{N}{9}$ is an integer is

(A) $9 \cdot 8 \cdot 7 \cdot 6 \cdot 5 \cdot 4 \cdot 3 \cdot 2$
(B) $9 \cdot 8 \cdot 6 \cdot 5 \cdot 4 \cdot 3 \cdot 2$
(C) $9 \cdot 8 \cdot 7 \cdot 6 \cdot 5$
(D) $9 \cdot 8 \cdot 7 \cdot 5$
(E) $9 \cdot 8 \cdot 7$

Comment: Since all the denominators must divide into N, start with the largest one and work down. 9, 8, 7, and 5 are the needed factors of N. 6, 4, 3, and 2 are not needed because all their factors are already included in 9 and 8. Correct answer: Choice D.

DIAGNOSTIC TEST

PART

ANSWER SHEET FOR DIAGNOSTIC TEST

Determine the correct answer for each question. Then, using a no. 2 pencil, blacken completely the oval containing the letter of your choice.

1. Ⓐ Ⓑ Ⓒ Ⓓ Ⓔ
2. Ⓐ Ⓑ Ⓒ Ⓓ Ⓔ
3. Ⓐ Ⓑ Ⓒ Ⓓ Ⓔ
4. Ⓐ Ⓑ Ⓒ Ⓓ Ⓔ
5. Ⓐ Ⓑ Ⓒ Ⓓ Ⓔ
6. Ⓐ Ⓑ Ⓒ Ⓓ Ⓔ
7. Ⓐ Ⓑ Ⓒ Ⓓ Ⓔ
8. Ⓐ Ⓑ Ⓒ Ⓓ Ⓔ
9. Ⓐ Ⓑ Ⓒ Ⓓ Ⓔ
10. Ⓐ Ⓑ Ⓒ Ⓓ Ⓔ
11. Ⓐ Ⓑ Ⓒ Ⓓ Ⓔ
12. Ⓐ Ⓑ Ⓒ Ⓓ Ⓔ
13. Ⓐ Ⓑ Ⓒ Ⓓ Ⓔ
14. Ⓐ Ⓑ Ⓒ Ⓓ Ⓔ
15. Ⓐ Ⓑ Ⓒ Ⓓ Ⓔ
16. Ⓐ Ⓑ Ⓒ Ⓓ Ⓔ
17. Ⓐ Ⓑ Ⓒ Ⓓ Ⓔ

18. Ⓐ Ⓑ Ⓒ Ⓓ Ⓔ
19. Ⓐ Ⓑ Ⓒ Ⓓ Ⓔ
20. Ⓐ Ⓑ Ⓒ Ⓓ Ⓔ
21. Ⓐ Ⓑ Ⓒ Ⓓ Ⓔ
22. Ⓐ Ⓑ Ⓒ Ⓓ Ⓔ
23. Ⓐ Ⓑ Ⓒ Ⓓ Ⓔ
24. Ⓐ Ⓑ Ⓒ Ⓓ Ⓔ
25. Ⓐ Ⓑ Ⓒ Ⓓ Ⓔ
26. Ⓐ Ⓑ Ⓒ Ⓓ Ⓔ
27. Ⓐ Ⓑ Ⓒ Ⓓ Ⓔ
28. Ⓐ Ⓑ Ⓒ Ⓓ Ⓔ
29. Ⓐ Ⓑ Ⓒ Ⓓ Ⓔ
30. Ⓐ Ⓑ Ⓒ Ⓓ Ⓔ
31. Ⓐ Ⓑ Ⓒ Ⓓ Ⓔ
32. Ⓐ Ⓑ Ⓒ Ⓓ Ⓔ
33. Ⓐ Ⓑ Ⓒ Ⓓ Ⓔ
34. Ⓐ Ⓑ Ⓒ Ⓓ Ⓔ

35. Ⓐ Ⓑ Ⓒ Ⓓ Ⓔ
36. Ⓐ Ⓑ Ⓒ Ⓓ Ⓔ
37. Ⓐ Ⓑ Ⓒ Ⓓ Ⓔ
38. Ⓐ Ⓑ Ⓒ Ⓓ Ⓔ
39. Ⓐ Ⓑ Ⓒ Ⓓ Ⓔ
40. Ⓐ Ⓑ Ⓒ Ⓓ Ⓔ
41. Ⓐ Ⓑ Ⓒ Ⓓ Ⓔ
42. Ⓐ Ⓑ Ⓒ Ⓓ Ⓔ
43. Ⓐ Ⓑ Ⓒ Ⓓ Ⓔ
44. Ⓐ Ⓑ Ⓒ Ⓓ Ⓔ
45. Ⓐ Ⓑ Ⓒ Ⓓ Ⓔ
46. Ⓐ Ⓑ Ⓒ Ⓓ Ⓔ
47. Ⓐ Ⓑ Ⓒ Ⓓ Ⓔ
48. Ⓐ Ⓑ Ⓒ Ⓓ Ⓔ
49. Ⓐ Ⓑ Ⓒ Ⓓ Ⓔ
50. Ⓐ Ⓑ Ⓒ Ⓓ Ⓔ

The diagnostic test is designed to help you pinpoint the weak spots in your background. The answer explanations that follow the test are keyed to sections of the book.

To make the best use of this diagnostic test, set aside between 1 and 2 hours so you will be able to do the whole test at one sitting. Tear out the preceding answer sheet and indicate your answers in the appropriate spaces. Do the problems as if this were a regular testing session. Review the suggestions on page vii.

When finished, check your answers with those at the end of the test. For those that you got wrong, note the sections containing the material that you must review. If you do not fully understand how you arrived at some of the correct answers, you should review those sections also.

Finally, fill out the self-evaluation sheet on page 21 in order to pinpoint the topics that gave you the most difficulty.

50 questions   1 hour

OFFICIAL COLLEGE BOARD DIRECTIONS

Directions: For each of the following problems, decide which is the BEST of the choices given. If the exact numerical value is not one of the choices, select the choice that best approximates this value. Then fill in the corresponding oval on the answer sheet.

Notes: (1) A calculator will be necessary for answering some (but not all) of the questions in this test. For each question you will have to decide whether or not you should use a calculator. The calculator you use must be at least a scientific calculator; programmable calculators and calculators that can display graphs are permitted.

(2) For some questions in this test you may have to decide whether your calculator should be in the radian mode or the degree mode.

(3) Figures that accompany problems in this test are intended to provide information useful in solving the problems. They are drawn as accurately as possible EXCEPT when it is stated in a specific problem that the figure is not drawn to scale. All figures lie in a plane unless otherwise indicated.

(4) Unless otherwise specified, the domain of any function f is assumed to be the set of all real numbers x for which $f(x)$ is a real number.

Reference Information: The following information is for your reference in answering some of the questions in this test.

Volume of a right circular cone with radius r and height h: $V = \frac{1}{3}\pi r^2 h$

Lateral area of a right circular cone with circumference of the base c and slant height ℓ: $S = \frac{1}{2}c\ell$

Volume of a sphere with radius r: $V = \frac{4}{3}\pi r^3$

Surface area of a sphere with radius r: $S = 4\pi r^2$

Volume of a pyramid with base area B and height h: $V = \frac{1}{3}Bh$

---

1. A linear function, f, has a slope of -2. $f(1) = 2$ and $f(2) = q$. Find q.

(A) 0

(B) 4

(C) $\frac{3}{2}$

(D) $\frac{5}{2}$

(E) 3

USE THIS SPACE FOR SCRATCH WORK

GO ON TO THE NEXT PAGE

2. A function is said to be even if $f(x) = f(-x)$. Which of the following is *not* an even function?

(A) $y = |x|$
(B) $y = \sec x$
(C) $y = \log x^2$
(D) $y = x^2 + \sin x$
(E) $y = 3x^4 - 2x^2 + 17$

3. What is the radius of a sphere, with center at the origin, that passes through point $(2,3,4)$?

(A) 3.32
(B) 5.39
(C) 3
(D) 3.31
(E) 5.38

4. If a point (x,y) is in the second quadrant, which of the following must be true?

I. $x < y$
II. $x + y > 0$
III. $\dfrac{x}{y} < 0$

(A) only I
(B) only II
(C) only III
(D) only I and II
(E) only I and III

5. If $f(x) = x^2 - ax$, then $f(a) =$

(A) a
(B) $a^2 - a$
(C) 0
(D) 1
(E) $a - 1$

6. The average of your first three test grades is 78. What grade must you get on your fourth and final test to make your average 80?

(A) 80
(B) 82
(C) 84
(D) 86
(E) 88

7. $\log_7 9 =$

(A) 0.89
(B) 0.95
(C) 1.13
(D) 1.21
(E) 7.61

GO ON TO THE NEXT PAGE

8. If $\log_2 m = x$ and $\log_2 n = y$, then $mn =$

    (A) 2^{x+y}
    (B) 2^{xy}
    (C) 4^{xy}
    (D) 4^{x+y}
    (E) cannot be determined

9. How many integers are there in the solution set of $|x - 2| \le 5$?

    (A) 11
    (B) 0
    (C) an infinite number
    (D) 9
    (E) 7

10. If $f(x) = \sqrt{x^2}$, then $f(x)$ can also be expressed as

    (A) x
    (B) $-x$
    (C) $\pm x$
    (D) $|x|$
    (E) $f(x)$ cannot be determined because x is unknown.

11. The graph of $(x^2 - 1)y = x^2 - 4$ has

    (A) one horizontal and one vertical asymptote
    (B) two vertical but no horizontal asymptotes
    (C) one horizontal and two vertical asymptotes
    (D) two horizontal and two vertical asymptotes
    (E) neither a horizontal nor a vertical asymptote

12. $\displaystyle\lim_{x \to \infty} \left(\frac{3x^2 + 4x - 5}{6x^2 + 3x + 1} \right) =$

    (A) $\dfrac{1}{2}$
    (B) 1
    (C) -5
    (D) $\dfrac{1}{5}$
    (E) This expression is undefined.

13. A linear function has an x-intercept of $\sqrt{3}$ and a y-intercept of $\sqrt{5}$. The graph of the function has a slope of

    (A) 0.77
    (B) -1.29
    (C) 2.24
    (D) 1.29
    (E) -0.77

14. If $f(x) = \sin x$, then $f^{-1}\left(\dfrac{\pi}{4}\right) =$

    (A) 52
    (B) 41
    (C) 0.90
    (D) 0.71
    (E) none of the above

GO ON TO THE NEXT PAGE

15. The plane $2x + 3y - 4z = 5$ intersects the x-axis at $(a,0,0)$, the y-axis at $(0,b,0)$, and the z-axis at $(0,0,c)$. The value of $a + b + c$ is

(A) 5

(B) $\dfrac{35}{12}$

(C) $\dfrac{65}{12}$

(D) 1

(E) 9

16. Given the set of data 1, 1, 2, 2, 2, 3, 3, 4, which one of the following statements is true?

(A) mean ≤ median ≤ mode

(B) median ≤ mean ≤ mode

(C) median ≤ mode ≤ mean

(D) mode ≤ mean ≤ median

(E) The relationship cannot be determined because the median cannot be calculated.

17. If $\dfrac{x - 3y}{x} = 7$, what is the value of $\dfrac{x}{y}$?

(A) $-\dfrac{8}{3}$

(B) -2

(C) $-\dfrac{1}{2}$

(D) $\dfrac{3}{8}$

(E) 2

18. $\dfrac{\sin 120° \cdot \cos \dfrac{2\pi}{3}}{\tan 315°} =$

(A) $\dfrac{\sqrt{3}}{2}$

(B) $-\dfrac{\sqrt{3}}{4}$

(C) $\dfrac{\sqrt{6}}{4}$

(D) $-\dfrac{\sqrt{3}}{2}$

(E) $\dfrac{\sqrt{3}}{4}$

19. If $f(x) = \dfrac{1}{2}x^2 - 8$ is defined when $-4 \le x \le 4$, the maximum value of the graph of $|f(x)|$ is

(A) -8

(B) 0

(C) 8

(D) 4

(E) 2

GO ON TO THE NEXT PAGE

20. If $\tan \theta = \dfrac{2}{3}$, then $\sin \theta =$

(A) $\dfrac{2\sqrt{13}}{13}$

(B) $\pm \dfrac{2\sqrt{13}}{13}$

(C) $\dfrac{3\sqrt{13}}{13}$

(D) $\pm \dfrac{2}{5}$

(E) $\dfrac{2\sqrt{5}}{5}$

21. If a circle has a central angle of 75° that intercepts an arc of length 75 feet, the number of feet in the radius is

(A) 63.7
(B) 57.3
(C) 44.1
(D) 75.0
(E) 28.6

22. The area of a triangle with sides 3, 5, and 7 is

(A) 7.5
(B) 6.5
(C) 3.75
(D) 13.0
(E) 2.4

23. If $f(x) = i$, where i is an integer such that $i \le x < i + 1$, and $g(x) = f(x) - |f(x)|$, what is the maximum value of $g(x)$?

(A) 0
(B) 1
(C) –1
(D) 2
(E) i

24. If $f(x) = \dfrac{1}{\sec x}$, then

(A) $f(x) = f(-x)$

(B) $f(\dfrac{1}{x}) = -f(x)$

(C) $f(-x) = -f(x)$

(D) $f(x) = f(\dfrac{1}{x})$

(E) $f(x) = \dfrac{1}{f(x)}$

GO ON TO THE NEXT PAGE

25. The polar coordinates of a point P are $(2, 240°)$. The Cartesian (rectangular) coordinates of P are

(A) $\left(-1, -\sqrt{3}\right)$

(B) $\left(-1, \sqrt{3}\right)$

(C) $\left(-\sqrt{3}, -1\right)$

(D) $\left(-\sqrt{3}, 1\right)$

(E) none of the above

26. The height of a cone is equal to the radius of its base. The radius of a sphere is equal to the radius of the base of the cone. The ratio of the volume of the *cone* to the volume of the *sphere* is

(A) $\dfrac{1}{3}$

(B) $\dfrac{1}{4}$

(C) $\dfrac{1}{12}$

(D) $\dfrac{1}{1}$

(E) $\dfrac{4}{3}$

27. In how many different ways can the seven letters in the word MINIMUM be arranged, if all the letters are used each time?

(A) 7

(B) 42

(C) 420

(D) 840

(E) 5040

28. From a deck of 52 different cards, how many different hands, each consisting of three cards, can be drawn?

(A) 132,600

(B) 1.3×10^{67}

(C) 22,100

(D) 1.4×10^{10}

(E) 2652

29. What is the probability of getting at least three heads when flipping four coins?

(A) $\dfrac{3}{4}$

(B) $\dfrac{1}{4}$

(C) $\dfrac{7}{16}$

(D) $\dfrac{5}{16}$

(E) $\dfrac{3}{16}$

USE THIS SPACE FOR SCRATCH WORK

GO ON TO THE NEXT PAGE

30. The positive zero of $y = 3x^2 - 4x - 5$ is, to the nearest tenth, equal to

(A) 0.8
(B) 0.7 + 1.1i
(C) 0.7
(D) 2.1
(E) 2.2

31. In the figure, S is the set of all points in the shaded region. Which of the following represents the set consisting of all points $(2x, y)$, where (x, y) is a point in S?

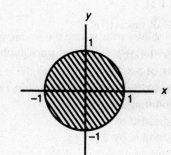

(A)

(B)

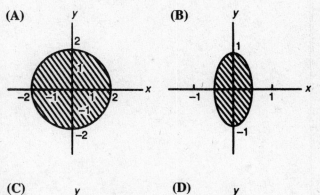

(C)

(D)

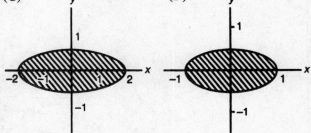

(E)

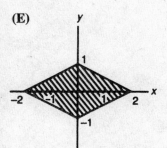

32. If a square prism is inscribed in a right circular cylinder of radius 3 and height 6, the volume inside the cylinder but outside the prism is

(A) 169.6
(B) 3.14
(C) 115.6
(D) 2.14
(E) 61.6

33. If y varies jointly as x, w, and the square of z, what is the effect on w when x, y, and z are doubled?

(A) w is doubled
(B) w is multiplied by 4
(C) w is multiplied by 8
(D) w is divided by 4
(E) w is divided by 2

34. Given the statement "All girls play tennis," which of the following negates this statement?

(A) All boys play tennis.
(B) Some girls play tennis.
(C) All boys do not play tennis.
(D) At least one girl doesn't play tennis.
(E) All girls do not play tennis.

35. 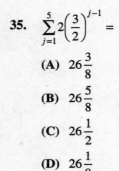 $\displaystyle\sum_{j=1}^{5} 2\left(\frac{3}{2}\right)^{j-1} =$

(A) $26\dfrac{3}{8}$

(B) $26\dfrac{5}{8}$

(C) $26\dfrac{1}{2}$

(D) $26\dfrac{1}{8}$

(E) $26\dfrac{7}{8}$

36. If $f(x) = \dfrac{k}{x}$ for all nonzero real numbers, for what value of k does $f(f(x)) = x$?

(A) only 1
(B) only 0
(C) all real numbers
(D) all real numbers except 0
(E) no real numbers

37. $F(x) = \begin{cases} \dfrac{3x^2 - 3}{x - 1}, & \text{when } x \neq 1 \\ \\ k, & \text{when } x = 1 \end{cases}$

For what value(s) of k is F a continuous function?

(A) 1
(B) 2
(C) 3
(D) 6
(E) no value of k

38. If $f(x,y) = 2x^2 - y^2$ and $g(x) = 2^x$, the value of $g(f(1,2)) =$

(A) 1
(B) 4
(C) $\dfrac{1}{4}$
(D) -4
(E) 0

39. What is the amplitude of the graph of the function $y = \cos^4 x - \sin^4 x$?

(A) $\dfrac{1}{2}$
(B) $\dfrac{\sqrt{2}}{2}$
(C) 1
(D) $1 + \dfrac{\sqrt{2}}{2}$
(E) 2

40. Which of the following could be the equation of the graph in the figure?

I. $y = \sin 4x$
II. $y = \cos\left(4x - \dfrac{\pi}{2}\right)$
III. $y = -\sin(4x + \pi)$

(A) only I
(B) only I and II
(C) only II and III
(D) only II
(E) I, II, and III

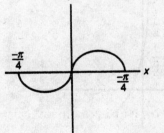

41. If $2 \cdot \sin^2 x - 3 = 3 \cdot \cos x$ and $90° < x < 270°$, the number of values that satisfy the equation is

(A) 0
(B) 1
(C) 2
(D) 3
(E) 4

GO ON TO THE NEXT PAGE

42. If $A = \text{Arctan}\left(-\dfrac{3}{4}\right)$ and $A + B = 315°$, then $B =$

    (A) 278.13°
    (B) 351.87°
    (C) −8.13°
    (D) 171.87°
    (E) 233.13°

43. The units digit of 1567^{93} is

    (A) 1
    (B) 3
    (C) 7
    (D) 9
    (E) none of the above

44. The vertex angle of an isosceles triangle is 35°. The length of the base is 10 centimeters. How many centimeters are in the perimeter?

    (A) 17.4
    (B) 44.9
    (C) 20.2
    (D) 16.6
    (E) 43.3

45. If the graph below represents the function $f(x)$, which of the following could represent the equation of the inverse of f?

    (A) $x = y^2 - 8y - 1$
    (B) $x = y^2 + 11$
    (C) $x = (y - 4)^2 - 3$
    (D) $x = (y + 4)^2 - 3$
    (E) $x = (y + 4)^2 + 3$

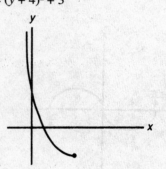

46. The figure below most closely resembles the graph whose equation is

    (A) $r = 2 \cdot \cos 2\theta + 2$
    (B) $r = 4 \cdot \cos \theta$
    (C) $r^2 = 4 \cdot \cos^2 2\theta$
    (D) $r^2 = 4 \cdot \cos 2\theta$
    (E) $r = \sin \theta + 4$

47. If $f(x) = \log_b x$ and $f(2) = 0.231$, the value of b is

    (A) 1.3
    (B) 20.1
    (C) 0.3
    (D) 13.2
    (E) 32.5

48. If $f_{n+1} = f_{n-1} + 2 \cdot f_n$ for $n = 2, 3, 4, \ldots$, and $f_1 = 1$ and $f_2 = 1$, then $f_5 =$

    (A) 7
    (B) 41
    (C) 11
    (D) 21
    (E) 17

49. In a plane, the *homogeneous coordinates* of a point P, whose rectangular coordinates are (x,y), are any three numbers a, b, and c for which $\dfrac{a}{c} = x$ and $\dfrac{b}{c} = y$. If the coordinates of P are $(3,4)$ and a, b, and c are integers, then the sum of a, b, and c could be

    (A) 2
    (B) 5
    (C) 8
    (D) 11
    (E) 14

50. If $[x]$ is defined to represent the greatest integer less than or equal to x, and $f(x) = \left| x - [x] - \dfrac{1}{2} \right|$, what is the period of $f(x)$?

    (A) 1
    (B) $\dfrac{1}{2}$
    (C) 2
    (D) 4
    (E) f is not a periodic function.

ANSWER KEY

1. A	18. E	35. A
2. D	19. C	36. D
3. B	20. B	37. D
4. E	21. B	38. C
5. C	22. B	39. C
6. D	23. A	40. E
7. C	24. A	41. D
8. A	25. A	42. B
9. A	26. B	43. C
10. D	27. C	44. E
11. C	28. C	45. C
12. A	29. D	46. D
13. B	30. D	47. B
14. C	31. C	48. E
15. B	32. E	49. C
16. C	33. D	50. A
17. C	34. D	

ANSWER EXPLANATIONS

The following explanations to questions on the diagnostic test are keyed to the review portions of this book. For example, material covered in Question 1 is reviewed in Sections 1.2 and 2.2. If you had trouble answering any of these questions, be sure to check the review topics indicated.

In these solutions the following notation is used:

- a: active—Calculator use is necessary or, at a minimum, extremely helpful.
- n: neutral—Answers may be found without a calculator, but a calculator may help.
- i: inactive—Calculator use is not helpful and may even be a hindrance.

1. i **A** $f(1) = 2$ means that the line goes through point $(1,2)$. $f(2) = q$ means that the line goes through point $(2,q)$. $-2 =$ slope $= \dfrac{\Delta y}{\Delta x} = \dfrac{q-2}{2-1}$ implies $-2 = \dfrac{q-2}{1}$ and $q = 0$. [2.2, 1.2].

2. n **D** Since $\sin x \neq \sin(-x)$, Choice D is not an even function. [1.4].

 Graphing calculator: Even functions are symmetric about the y-axis. Sketch the graph of each answer to see that Choice D is *not* symmetric about the y-axis.

TIP: Properties of even and odd functions:
Even + even is always an even function.
Odd + odd is always an odd function.
Odd × even is always an odd function.

3. a **B** Since the radius of a sphere is the distance between the center, $(0,0,0)$, and a point on the surface, $(2,3,4)$, use the distance formula in three dimensions to get

$$\sqrt{(2-0)^2 + (3-0)^2 + (4-0)^2} = \sqrt{29}$$

Use your calculator to find $\sqrt{29} \approx 5.39$. [2.2, 5.5].

4. i **E** A point in the second quadrant has a negative x-coordinate and a positive y-coordinate. Therefore, $x < y$, and $\dfrac{x}{y} < 0$ must be true, but $x + y$ can be less than or equal to zero. The correct answer is E. [1.3]

5. i **C** $f(a)$ means to replace x in the formula with an a. Therefore, $f(a) = a^2 - a \cdot a = 0$. [1.2]

6. n **D** Since the average of your first three test grades is 78, each test grade could have been a 78. If x represents your final test grade, the average of the four test grades is $\dfrac{78 + 78 + 78 + x}{4}$, which is to be equal to 80. Therefore, $\dfrac{234 + x}{4} = 80$. $234 + x = 320$. So $x = 86$. [5.8]

7. a **C Calculator:** Use the change-of-base theorem:
$$\log_7 9 = \frac{\log_{10} 9}{\log_{10} 7} \approx \frac{0.9542}{0.8451} \approx 1.13. \ [4.2].$$

8. a **A** Add the two equations: $\log_2 m + \log_2 n = x + y$, which becomes $\log_2 mn = x + y$ (basic property of logs). $2^{x+y} = mn$. [4.2]

9. n **A** x is less than or equal to 5 units from 2. Therefore, $-3 \leq x \leq 7$. [2.5, 4.3].

Alternative Solution: $|x - 2| \leq 5$ means that $-5 \leq x - 2 \leq 5$. Thus, $-3 \leq x < 7$. [2.5, 4.3].

 Graphing calculator: Plot the graph of $y = \text{abs}(x - 2) - 5$ in an $x \in [-10 \times 10]$, $y \in [-10 \times 10]$ window. Use the Trace function to see that it crosses the x-axis at -3 and 7 and is below the x-axis between -3 and 7. Counting from -3 to 7 gives 11 integers.

10. i D $\sqrt{x^2}$ indicates the need for the *positive* square root of x^2. Therefore, $\sqrt{x^2} = x$ if $x \geq 0$ and $\sqrt{x^2} = -x$ if $x < 0$. This is just the definition of absolute value, and so $\sqrt{x^2} = |x|$ is the only answer for all values of x. [4.3].

11. n C $y = \dfrac{x^2 - 4}{x^2 - 1}$. Vertical asymptotes occur when $x = \pm 1$ because the denominator would become zero. Divide both the numerator and the denominator through by x^2. Then, as $x \to \infty$, $y \to 1$, giving one horizontal asymptote when $y = 1$. Therefore, there are one horizontal and two vertical asymptotes. [4.5].

Graphing calculator: Plot the graph of $y = \dfrac{x^2 - 4}{x^2 - 1}$ in an $x \in [-10 \times 10]$, $y \in [-10 \times 10]$ window to see a graph that appears to have one horizontal and two vertical asymptotes.

12. n A Divide numerator and denominator through by x^2. As $x \to \infty$, the fraction $\to \dfrac{3}{6} = \dfrac{1}{2}$. [4.5].

Graphing calculator: Plot the graph of $y = \dfrac{3x^2 + 4x - 5}{6x^2 + 3x + 1}$ in an $x \in [-50 \times 50]$, $y \in [-2 \times 2]$ window. Use the Trace function to see that, as x increases, y seems to approach 0.5, leading to Choice A.

13. a B $y = mx + b$. Use the x-intercept to get $0 = \sqrt{3}m + b$, and the y-intercept to get $\sqrt{5} = 0 \cdot m + b$. Therefore, $0 = \sqrt{3}m + \sqrt{5}$ and $m = -\dfrac{\sqrt{5}}{\sqrt{3}}$.

Use your calculator to get $m \approx -1.29$. [2.2].

14. a C Calculator (in radian mode): Find the value of the inverse sin of $\dfrac{\pi}{4}$, which is approximately 0.90. [3.6].

15. i B Substituting the points into the equation gives $a = \dfrac{5}{2}, b = \dfrac{5}{3}$, and $c = -\dfrac{5}{4}$. [5.5].

16. i C Mode = 2, median $= \dfrac{2 + 2}{2} = 2$, mean $= \dfrac{2 + 6 + 6 + 4}{8} = \dfrac{18}{8} = 2.25$.

Thus, median $\leq$ mode $\leq$ mean. [5.8].

17. n C Multiply $\dfrac{x - 3y}{x} = 7$ through by x to get $x - 3y = 7x$. Combine like terms to get $-3y = 6x$. Divide through by $6y$ so that $\dfrac{x}{y}$ will be on one side of the equals sign. This gives $\dfrac{x}{y} = -\dfrac{3}{6} = -\dfrac{1}{2}$. 2.2

18. n E $\sin 120° = \dfrac{\sqrt{3}}{2}, \cos \dfrac{2\pi}{3} = -\dfrac{1}{2}, \tan 315° = -1$. [3.3]

 Calculator: If you use your calculator, don't forget to switch back and forth between degree and radian mode, *or* change $\dfrac{2\pi}{3}$ to 120° and do all calculations in degrees.

TIP: Any angle greater than 90° has an acute reference angle associated with it, formed by the terminal side of the large angle and the **x-axis**. The reference angle has the same trig function value as the original angle, with the possible exception of the sign. Thus, you need to learn the values of the trig functions for only a handful of special acute angles.

Example: 120° has a reference angle of 60°. Therefore, $|\sin 120°| = |\sin 60°| = \dfrac{\sqrt{3}}{2}$. To remember which functions have which signs in which quadrant, the following statement is helpful:

"**A**ll **S**tudents **T**ake **C**alculus."

All functions are positive in quadrant I.
Sin (and its reciprocal, csc) is positive in quadrant II.
Tan (and its reciprocal, cot) is positive in quadrant III.
Cos (and its reciprocal, sec) is positive in quadrant IV.

Therefore, $\sin 120° = +\dfrac{\sqrt{3}}{2}$.

19. n C f is a parabola symmetric about the y-axis which opens up. $f(-4) = 0, f(0) = -8, f(4) = 0$ are the extreme values. Therefore, the maximum occurs at $|-8| = 8$. [2.3, 4.3].

Graphing calculator: Plot the graph of $y = \text{abs}\left(\dfrac{1}{2}x^2 - 8\right)$ in an $x \in [-4 \times 4]$, $y \in [-10 \times 10]$ window. Use the Trace function to see that the maximum value is 8.

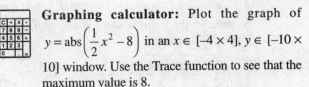

20. n **B** In a right triangle, $\tan\theta = \dfrac{\text{opposite side}}{\text{adjacent side}}$. Draw the right triangle below and use the Pythagorean theorem to compute the hypotenuse. Since in a right triangle $\sin\theta = \dfrac{\text{opposite side}}{\text{hypotenuse}}$, $\sin\theta = \dfrac{2}{\sqrt{13}}$. Since $\tan\theta$ is positive, θ could lie in either quadrant I or quadrant III.

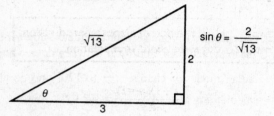

$\sin\theta = \dfrac{2}{\sqrt{13}}$

Therefore, $\sin\theta = \pm\dfrac{2\sqrt{13}}{13}$ since θ could be in quadrant I or III, where $\tan\theta$ is positive. [3.1].

 Calculator: Find the inverse $\tan\left(\dfrac{2}{3}\right)$ in order to get a value for θ (either 33.69° or 0.588 radian). Find $\sin\theta$ to get 0.5547. Evaluate the answer choices to find that $\dfrac{2\sqrt{13}}{13} \approx 0.5547$. Since θ could be in quadrant I or III, the answer is Choice B.

21. a **B** $s = r \cdot \theta^{R}$, $75° = \dfrac{75\pi}{180}$. Therefore, 75 feet $=$ $r \cdot \dfrac{75\pi}{180}$ and $r = \dfrac{180}{\pi}$ feet $\approx \dfrac{180}{3.1416} \approx 57.3$ feet. [3.2]

22. a **B** By the law of cosines, cosine of largest angle $= -\dfrac{1}{2}$. Therefore, largest angle (opposite side 7) $=$ 120°. Area $= \dfrac{1}{2}ab\sin C$. Area $= \dfrac{15\sqrt{3}}{4}$. [3.7].

<u>Alternative Solution</u>: Use Heron's formula, $A = \sqrt{s(s-a)(s-b)(s-c)}$, where a, b, and c are the sides of the triangle and s is one-half the perimeter. Therefore,

$$S = \sqrt{\dfrac{15}{2}\left(\dfrac{9}{2}\right)\left(\dfrac{5}{2}\right)\left(\dfrac{1}{2}\right)} = \dfrac{5\cdot 3}{2\cdot 2}\sqrt{3} = \dfrac{15\sqrt{3}}{4}.$$ [6.5].

 Calculator: After using either of the above methods, evaluate $\dfrac{15\sqrt{3}}{4}$ to find that the answer is about 6.5.

23. n **A** If $i \geq 0$, $f(x) = |f(x)|$ and therefore $g(x) = 0$. If $i < 0$, $|f(x)| = -f(x))$ and therefore $g(x) = 2i$, which is negative. Therefore, maximum $= 0$. [4.4].

 Graphing calculator: Using the greatest integer function and the absolute value function, plot the graph of $y = \text{int}(x) - \text{abs}(\text{int}(x))$ in an $x \in [-10 \times 10]$, $y \in [-10 \times 10]$ window. Use the Trace function to see that the maximum value is at 0.

> **TIP:** Don't get confused and immediately think that $i = \sqrt{-1}$. Read the definition given in the problem.

24. n **A** Sec x is symmetric about the y-axis, and so it is an even function. By definition, $f(x) = f(-x)$. [1.4]

 Calculator: Since there is no sec button on your calculator, you could consider $\cos x$ which equals $\dfrac{1}{\sec x}$. Choose a convenient value of x. For example, use $\dfrac{\pi}{3}$ or 60° whose cosine is $\dfrac{1}{2}$ and secant is 2. Evaluate each of the answer choices to see that only Choice A is true. [3.1]

25. i **A** From the figure $\left(-1, -\sqrt{3}\right)$. [4.7].

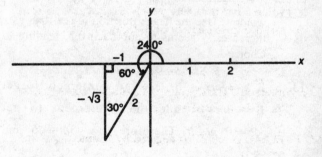

26. i **B** Since $r = h$ in the cone,

$$\dfrac{\text{Volume of cone}}{\text{Volume of sphere}} = \dfrac{\dfrac{1}{3}\pi r^2 h}{\dfrac{4}{3}\pi r^3} = \dfrac{\dfrac{1}{3}\pi r^3}{\dfrac{4}{3}\pi r^3} = \dfrac{1}{4}.$$ [5.5].

27. i **C** Permutation with repetitions is $\dfrac{7!}{3!2!} = 420$. [5.1].

28. a **C** Since the order in which the cards are drawn does not make a difference, this is a combination. $_{52}C_3 = \dfrac{52!}{49! \cdot 3!}$.

Use your calculator to find that the answer is 22,100 [5.1].

29. i D There are 16 outcomes in the sample space. $\binom{4}{3} = 4$ ways to get 3 heads. $\binom{4}{4} = 1$ way to get 4 heads. [5.3].

Alternative Solution: There are $2^4 = 16$ outcomes when flipping 4 coins. List those that contain 3 or 4 heads: HHHT, HHTH, HTHH, THHH, HHHH. Therefore, $P(3$ or 4 heads$) = \dfrac{5}{16}$.

30. a D Using the general quadratic formula, you find that $x = \dfrac{4 \pm \sqrt{16 + 60}}{6} = \dfrac{4 \pm \sqrt{76}}{6}$. The positive zero is $\dfrac{4 + \sqrt{76}}{6}$, which (using your calculator) is approximately 2.1. [2.3].

31. i C Since the y values remain the same but the x values are doubled, the circle is stretched along the x-axis. [5.5].

32. a E Volume of cylinder $= \pi r^2 h = \pi \cdot 9 \cdot 6 = 54\pi$. Volume of square prism $= Bh$, where B is the area of the square base, which is $3\sqrt{2}$ on a side. Thus, $Bh = (3\sqrt{2})^2 \cdot 6 = 112$. Therefore, the desired volume is $54\pi - 108$, which (using your calculator) is approximately 61.6. [5.5].

33. i D $\dfrac{y}{xwz^2} = K$. The doubling of y and x cancel each other out. The doubling of z is squared, and so w has to be divided by 4. [5.6].

34. i D "All G are T" is negated by "Some G are not T." [5.7]

35. n A The terms are $2 + 3 + \dfrac{9}{2} + \dfrac{27}{4} + \dfrac{81}{8} = 26\dfrac{3}{8}$.

Alternative Solution: Since there are only five terms in this series, they can be added easily. However, you should recognize this as a geometric series with first term $= 2$ and ratio $= \dfrac{3}{2}$. Using the formula for the sum of n terms gives

$$S = \dfrac{2 - 2\left(\dfrac{3}{2}\right)^5}{1 - \dfrac{3}{2}} = \dfrac{2 - \dfrac{243}{16}}{-\dfrac{1}{2}}$$

$$= -4 + \dfrac{243}{8} = -4 + 30\dfrac{3}{8} = 26\dfrac{5}{8}. \text{ [5.4].}$$

 Calculator: Evaluate

$$2 \cdot (1.5^0 + 1.5^1 + 1.5^2 + 1.5^3 + 1.5^4)$$

to get 26.375, which equals $26\dfrac{3}{8}$.

36. i D $f(f(x)) = \dfrac{k}{f(x)} = k \div \dfrac{k}{x} = k \cdot \dfrac{x}{k} = x$. Since the k's divide out, k can equal any real number except zero (since you cannot divide by zero). [1.2].

> **TIP:** Always keep an eye out for places where division by zero might occur *throughout* your solution.

37. n D $\dfrac{3x^2 - 3}{x - 1} = \dfrac{3(x+1)(x-1)}{(x-1)} = 3(x+1)$. Since $\lim\limits_{x \to 1} 3(x+1) = 6$, in the top part of the function definition, k must equal 6 when $x = 1$. [4.5, 2.4].

 Graphing Calculator: Plot the graph of $y = \dfrac{3x^2 - 3}{x - 1}$ in an $x \in [-10 \times 10]$, $y \in [-10 \times 10]$ window. Use the Trace function to see that as x gets close to 1, y seems to approach 6, which is Choice D.

38. i C $f(1,2) = 2(1^2) - 2^2 = -2$.

$g(f(1,2)) = g(-2) = 2^{-2} = \dfrac{1}{4}$. [1.2, 1.5, 4.2].

39. n C $\cos^4 x - \sin^4 x = (\cos^2 x + \sin^2 x) \cdot (\cos^2 x - \sin^2 x) = 1 \cdot (\cos 2x)$. Amplitude $= 1$. [3.4].

 Graphing calculator: Plot the graph of $y = \cos^4 x - \sin^4 x$ in an $x \in [-4 \times 4]$, $y \in [-4 \times 4]$ window. Use the Trace function to see that the maximum appears to be about 1 and the minimum about -1. Therefore, the amplitude is 1.

40. n E All three equations have a period of $\dfrac{\pi}{2}$. I: It is a normal sine curve. II: Phase shift $\dfrac{\pi}{8}$; cosine curve fits. III: Phase shift $\dfrac{\pi}{4}$; sine curve shifted and reflected about x-axis; sine curve fits. Therefore, all three are equations of the graph. [3.4]

Graphing calculator (in degree mode): Since $\dfrac{\pi}{4} = 45°$, plot the graph of each function in an $x \in [-45° \times 45°]$, $y \in [-4 \times 4]$ window. All the graphs look like the one in the problem, and so the answer is Choice E.

TIP: When an equation of a periodic function is written in the form $y = A \cdot f(B(x - C)) + D$, $|A|$ = the amplitude, $\dfrac{\text{normal period}}{|B|}$ = the period, C = the horizontal shift of the graph, and D = the vertical shift of the graph.

41. n **D** $2(1 - \cos^2 x) - 3 = 3 \cos x$.

   $2\cos^2 x + 3\cos x + 1 = 0$. $\cos x = -\dfrac{1}{2}$ or -1.

   Therefore, $x = 120°, 240°, 180°$. [3.1].

 Graphing calculator (in degree mode): Plot the graph of $y = 2 \cdot \sin^2 x - 3 - 3 \cdot \cos x$ in an $x \in [90° \times 270°]$, $y \in [-0.2 \times 0.2]$ window to see that it touches the x-axis three times. Thus, the answer is Choice D.

TIP: Here is an example of a problem where the size of the window is very important. A y-range much bigger than $[-0.2 \times 0.2]$ would give ambiguous results. Although using a graphing calculator may seem to be the "easy" way to do the problem, much more time may be required to find an answer than would be needed with just a little thinking and no calculator.

42. a **B Calculator** (in degree mode because the answer choices are in degrees): Evaluate inverse tan (-0.75) to get $-36.73°$ for $\angle A$. Therefore, $B = 315° - (-36.73°) = 351.87°$. [3.6].

43. i **C** When 1567 is multiplied by itself successively, the units digit takes on values of 7, 9, 3, 1, 7, 9, 3, 1, ... Every fourth multiplication ends in 1. Therefore, 1567^{92} ends in 1, and so 1567^{93} ends in a 7. [5.9].

44. a **E** Drop the altitude from the vertex to the base. The altitude bisects both the vertex angle and the base, cutting the triangle into two congruent right triangles. Since $\sin 17.5° = \dfrac{5}{\text{leg}}$, the leg = $\dfrac{5}{\sin 17.5°} \approx \dfrac{5}{0.3007} \approx 16.628$ cm and the perimeter = 43.3 cm. [3.7, 6.3].

45. n **C** If the graph is folded about the line $y = x$ to get the inverse, the graph is one-half of a parabola opening to the right with vertex at a point with negative x-coordinate and positive y-coordinate. Choice A has a negative y-coordinate. Choice C is the only possible answer with vertex at $(-3,4)$. [1.3].

Alternative Solution: If x and y are interchanged in each of the answer choices, one of the choices will be the equation for the given graph. Each choice represents a parabola. Completing the square in Choice A gives $x = (y - 4)^2 - 17$. It can now be seen that the only answer with a positive y-intercept and a vertex in quadrant IV is Choice C. [1.3, 2.3].

 Graphing calculator: Sketch the graphs of the inverses mentioned in the alternative solution. Only A and C are possible solutions. Zoom in on the y-intercept of Choice A to find that it is negative. Therefore, the solution must be Choice C.

46. n **D** By letting $\theta = 0$, Choices A, B, and E can be ruled out because they do not allow the graph to cross the x-axis at ± 2. Plotting a few points rules out Choice C. [4,7].

 Graphing calculator (in polar mode): Sketch the graph of each of the answer choices to see that the correct answer is Choice D.

47. a **B** $f(2) = \log_b 2 = 0.231$. Therefore, $b^{0.231} = 2$, and so $b = 2^{1/0.231}$, which (using your calculator) is approximately 20.1. [4.2].

48. i **E** Let $n = 2$, $f_3 = 3$; then let $n = 3$, $f_4 = 7$; and finally let $n = 4$, $f_5 = 17$. [5.4].

49. i **C** Since $\dfrac{a}{c} = 3$ and $\dfrac{b}{c} = 4$, therefore $a = 3c$ and $b = 4c$. If $c = 1$, then $a = 3$ and $b = 4$. [5.9].

50. n **A** When a few points have been plotted, the graph looks like this. Therefore, the period is 1. [4.4, 4.3].

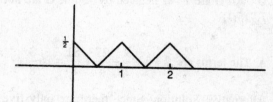

 Graphing calculator: Using the greatest integer function and the absolute value function, plot the graph of $y = \text{abs}\left(x - \text{int}(x) - \dfrac{1}{2}\right)$ in an $x \in [-4 \times 4]$, $y \in [-1 \times 1]$ window. Use the Trace function to see that the period appears to be approximately 1, which indicates that the correct answer is Choice A.

SELF-EVALUATION CHART FOR DIAGNOSTIC TEST

SUBJECT AREA	QUESTIONS	NUMBER OF RIGHT WRONG OMITTED

Mark correct answers with C, wrong answers with X, and omitted answers with O.

Algebra
(9 questions)
Review section

7	8	9	10	11	17	30	33	50
4.2	4.2	2.5	4.3	4.5	2.2	2.3	5.6	4.4

___ ___ ___

Solid geometry
(4 questions)
Review section

3	15	26	32
2.2	5.5	5.5	5.5

___ ___ ___

Coordinate geometry
(6 questions)
Review section

13	24	25	31	46	49
2.3	3.1	4.7	5.5	4.7	5.9

___ ___ ___

Trigonometry
(10 questions)
Review section

14	18	20	21	22	39	40	41	42	44
3.6	3.3	3.1	3.2	3.7	3.4	3.4	3.1	3.6	3.7

___ ___ ___

Functions
(12 questions)
Review section

1	2	4	5	19	23	36	37	38	45	47	48
2.2	1.4	1.3	1.2	2.3	4.4	1.2	4.5	1.2	1.3	4.2	5.4

___ ___ ___

Miscellaneous
(9 questions)
Review section

6	12	16	27	28	29	34	35	43
5.8	4.5	5.8	5.1	5.1	5.3	5.7	5.4	5.9

___ ___ ___

TOTALS   ___ ___ ___

Raw score = (number right) $-\frac{1}{4}$ (number wrong) = _____

Round your raw score to the nearest whole number = _____

Evaluate Your Performance
Diagnostic Test

Rating	Number Right
Excellent	41–50
Very good	33–40
Above average	25–32
Average	15–24
Below average	Below 15

REVIEW OF MAJOR TOPICS

PART

2

NOTE TO THE STUDENT

The mathematics that you need to know in order to be prepared for SAT II: Mathematics Level IIC is the same as that required for the previous Math Level IIC Achievement Test. The only difference is that you *must now use a calculator* on several problems and so you will have to decide whether using a calculator will be helpful in finding the solution to each of the problems with which you are faced. This decision will be an added drain on the limited time you have available to do the problems. Thus, the more familiar you are with your calculator, and the more you have used it in your mathematics courses, the more adept you will be in making the correct choice.

Throughout Part 2, notes indicate, where appropriate, when and how calculators should or should not be used. As you study the material and do the exercises, always try to make your own decision about how you would plan to solve a problem before referring to the annotation or solution.

INTRODUCTION TO FUNCTIONS

CHAPTER

1.1 DEFINITIONS

A *relation* is a set of ordered pairs. A *function* is a relation such that for each first element there is one and only one second element. The set of numbers that make up all first elements of the ordered pairs is called the *domain* of the function, and the resulting set of second elements is called the *range* of the function.

EXAMPLE 1: {(1,2),(3,4),(5,6),(6,1),(2,2)}
This is a function because every ordered pair has a different first element. Domain = {1,2,3,5,6}. Range = {1,2,4,6}.

EXAMPLE 2: $f(x) = 3x + 2$
This is a function because for each value substituted for x there is one and only one value for $f(x)$. Domain = {all real numbers}. Range = {all real numbers}.

EXAMPLE 3: {(1,2),(3,2),(1,4)}
This is a relation but *not* a function because when the first element is 1, the second element can be either 2 or 4. Domain = {1,3}. Range = {2,4}.

EXAMPLE 4: {(x,y):y² = x}
[This should be read, "The set of all ordered pairs (x,y) such that $y^2 = x$."] This is a relation but *not* a function because, for each nonnegative number that is substituted for x, there are two values for y. For example, x = 4, y = +2, or y = –2. Domain = {all nonnegative real numbers}. Range = {all real numbers}.

EXERCISES

1. If {(3,2),(4,2),(3,1),(7,1),(2,3)} is to be a function, which one of the following must be removed from the set?

    (A) (3,2)
    (B) (4,2)
    (C) (2,3)
    (D) (7,1)
    (E) none of the above

2. For $f(x) = 3x^2 + 4$, $g(x) = 2$, and h {(1,1), (2,1), (3,2)},

    (A) f is the only function
    (B) h is the only function
    (C) f and g are the only functions
    (D) g and h are the only functions
    (E) f, g, and h are all functions

3. What value(s) must be excluded from the domain of $f = \left\{ (x,y) : y = \dfrac{x+2}{x-2} \right\}$?

    (A) 2
    (B) –2
    (C) 0
    (D) 2 and –2
    (E) no value

24

1.2 FUNCTION NOTATION

The expressions $f = \{(x,y):y = x^2\}$ and $f(x) = x^2$ both name the same function; f is the rule that pairs any number with its square. Thus, $f(x) = x^2$, $f(a) = a^2$, $f(z) = z^2$ all name the same function. The symbol $f(2)$ is the value of the function f when $x = 2$. Thus, $f(2) = 4$.

If f and g name two functions, the following rules apply:

$$(f + g)(x) = f(x) + g(x)$$
$$(f \cdot g)(x) = f(x) \cdot g(x)$$
$$\frac{f}{g}(x) = \frac{f(x)}{g(x)}$$

if and only if $g(x) \neq 0$

$$(f \circ g)(x) = f(x) \circ g(x) = f(g(x))$$

(this is called the *composition* of functions).

EXAMPLE: If $f(x) = 3x - 2$ and $g(x) = x^2 - 4$, then indicate the function that represents (A) $(f + g)(x)$ (B) $(f - g)(x)$ (C) $(f \cdot g)(x)$ (D) $\dfrac{f}{g}(x)$ (E) $(f \circ g)(x)$ (F) $(g \circ f)(x)$

(A) $(f + g)(x) = f(x) + g(x)$

$$= (3x - 2) + (x^2 - 4) = x^2 + 3x - 6$$

(B) $(f - g)(x) = f(x) - g(x)$

$$= (3x - 2) - (x^2 - 4) = -x^2 + 3x + 2$$

(C) $(f \cdot g)(x) = f(x) \cdot g(x)$

$$= (3x - 2)(x^2 - 4)$$
$$= 3x^3 - 2x^2 - 12x + 8$$

(D) $\dfrac{f}{g}(x) = \dfrac{f(x)}{g(x)} = \dfrac{3x - 2}{x^2 - 4}$ and $x \neq \pm 2$

(E) $(f \circ g)(x) = f(x) \circ g(x)$

$$= f(g(x)) = 3(g(x)) - 2$$
$$= 3(x^2 - 4) - 2 = 3x^2 - 14$$

(F) $(g \circ f)(x) = g(x) \circ f(x)$

$$= g(f(x)) = (f(x))^2 - 4$$
$$= (3x - 2)^2 - 4 = 9x^2 - 12x$$

(Notice that the composition of functions is not commutative.)

EXERCISES

1. If $f(x) = 3x^2 - 2x + 4$, $f(-2) =$

   (A) −2
   (B) 20
   (C) −4
   (D) 12
   (E) −12

2. If $f(x) = 4x - 5$ and $g(x) = 3^x$, then $f(g(2)) =$

   (A) 27
   (B) 9
   (C) 3
   (D) 31
   (E) none of the above

3. If $f(g(x)) = 4x^2 - 8x$ and $f(x) = x^2 - 4$, then $g(x) =$

   (A) $2x - 2$
   (B) x
   (C) $4x$
   (D) $4 - x$
   (E) x^2

4. What values must be excluded from the domain of $\dfrac{f}{g}(x)$ if $f(x) = 3x^2 - 4x + 1$ and $g(x) = 3x^2 - 3$?

   (A) no values
   (B) 0
   (C) 3
   (D) 1
   (E) both ±1

5. If $g(x) = 3x + 2$ and $g(f(x)) = x$, then $f(2) =$

   (A) 2
   (B) 6
   (C) 0
   (D) 8
   (E) 1

6. If $p(x) = 4x - 6$ and $p(a) = 0$, then $a =$

   (A) −6
   (B) 2
   (C) $\dfrac{3}{2}$
   (D) $\dfrac{2}{3}$
   (E) $-\dfrac{3}{2}$

7. If $f(x) = e^x$ and $g(x) = \sin x$, then the value of $f \circ g\left(\sqrt{2}\right)$ is

   (A) −0.8
   (B) −0.01
   (C) 0.34
   (D) 2.7
   (E) 1.8

1.3   INVERSE FUNCTIONS

The *inverse* of a function f, denoted by f^{-1}, is a relation that has the property that $f(x) \circ f^{-1}(x) = f^{-1}(x) \circ f(x) = x$, where f^{-1} is not necessarily a function.

EXAMPLE 1: $f(x) = 3x + 2$. Is $y = \dfrac{x-2}{3}$ the inverse of f?

To answer this question assume that $f^{-1}(x) = \dfrac{x-2}{3}$ and verify that $f(x) \circ f^{-1}(x) = x$.

To verify this, proceed as follows:

$$f(x) \circ f^{-1}(x) = f(f^{-1}(x))$$
$$= f\left(\frac{x-2}{3}\right) = 3\left(\frac{x-2}{3}\right) + 2 = x$$

and

$$f^{-1}(x) \circ f(x) = f^{-1}(f(x)) = f^{-1}(3x+2)$$
$$= \frac{(3x+2)-2}{3} = x.$$

Since $f(x) \circ f^{-1}(x) \circ f^{-1}(x) \circ f(x) = x$, $\dfrac{x-2}{3}$ is the inverse of f.

EXAMPLE 2: $f = \{(1,2),(2,3),(3,2)\}$ Find the inverse.
$$f^{-1} = \{(2,1),(3,2),(2,3)\}$$

To verify this, check $f \circ f^{-1}$ and $f^{-1} \circ f$ term by term.

$f \circ f^{-1} = f(f^{-1}(x))$; when $x = 2, f(f^{-1}(2)) = f(1) = 2$

when $x = 3, f(f^{-1}(3)) = f(2) = 3$

when $x = 2, f(f^{-1}(2)) = f(3) = 2$

Thus, for each x, $f(f^{-1}(x)) = x$.

$f^{-1} \circ f = f^{-1} \circ f(x)$; when $x = 1, f^{-1}(f(1)) = f^{-1}(2) = 1$

when $x = 2, f^{-1}(f(2)) = f^{-1}(3) = 2$

when $x = 3, f^{-1}(f(3)) = f^{-1}(2) = 3$

Thus, for each x, $f^{-1}(f(x)) = x$. In this case f^{-1} is *not* a function.

If the point with coordinates (a,b) belongs to a function f, then the point with coordinates (b,a) belongs to the inverse of f. Because this is true of a function and its inverse, the graph of the inverse is the reflection of the graph of f about the line $y = x$.

EXAMPLE 3: f^{-1} is *not* a function.

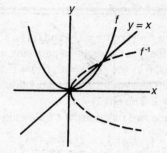

EXAMPLE 4: f^{-1} is a function.

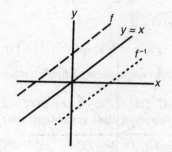

As can be seen from the above examples, if the graph of f is given, the graph of f^{-1} is the image obtained by folding the graph of f about the line $y = x$. Algebraically the equation of the inverse of f can be found by interchanging the variables.

EXAMPLE 5: $f = \{(x,y) : y = 3x + 2\}$. Find f^{-1}.
In order to find f^{-1}, interchange x and y and solve for y: $x = 3y + 2$, which becomes $y = \dfrac{x-2}{3}$. Thus,
$$f^{-1} = \left\{ (x,y) : y = \frac{x-2}{3} \right\}.$$

EXAMPLE 6: $f = \{(x,y) : y = x^2\}$. Find f^{-1}.
Interchange x and y: $x = y^2$.

Solve for y: $y = \pm\sqrt{x}$.

Thus, $f^{-1} = \left\{ (x,y) : y = \pm\sqrt{x} \right\}$, which is *not* a function.

The inverse of any function f can always be made a function by limiting the domain of f. In Example 6 the domain of f could be limited to all nonnegative numbers or all nonpositive numbers. In this way f^{-1} would become either $y = +\sqrt{x}$ or $y = -\sqrt{x}$, both of which are functions.

EXAMPLE 7: $f = \{(x,y) : y = x^2 \text{ and } x \geq 0\}$. Find f^{-1}.
$f^{-1} = \{(x,y) : x = y^2 \text{ and } y \geq 0\}$, which can also be written as
$$f^{-1} = \left\{ (x,y) : y = +\sqrt{x} \right\}.$$

Here f^{-1} is a function.

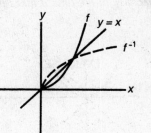

EXAMPLE 8: $f = \{(x,y): y = x^2 \text{ and } x \leq 0\}$. find f^{-1}.

$f^{-1} = \{(x,y): x = y^2 \text{ and } y \leq 0\}$, which can also be written as

$$f^{-1} = \left\{(x,y): y = -\sqrt{x}\right\}.$$

Here f^{-1} is a function.

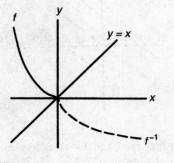

EXERCISES

1. If $f(x) = 2x - 3$, the inverse of f, f^{-1}, could be represented by

    (A) $f^{-1}(x) = 3x - 2$

    (B) $f^{-1}(x) = \dfrac{1}{2x - 3}$

    (C) $f^{-1}(x) = \dfrac{x - 2}{3}$

    (D) $f^{-1}(x) = \dfrac{x + 2}{3}$

    (E) $f^{-1}(x) = \dfrac{x + 3}{2}$

2. If $f(x) = x$, the inverse of f, f^{-1}, could be represented by

    (A) $f^{-1}(x) = x$

    (B) $f^{-1}(x) = 1$

    (C) $f^{-1}(x) = \dfrac{1}{x}$

    (D) $f^{-1}(x) = y$

    (E) f^{-1} does not exist

3. The inverse of $f = \{(1,2),(2,3),(3,4),(4,1),(5,2)\}$ would be a function if the domain of f is limited to

    (A) $\{1,3,5\}$
    (B) $\{1,2,3,4\}$
    (C) $\{1,5\}$
    (D) $\{1,2,4,5\}$
    (E) $\{1,2,3,4,5\}$

4. Which of the following could represent the equation of the inverse of the graph in the figure?

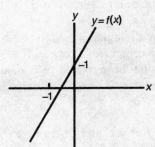

    (A) $y = -2x + 1$

    (B) $y = 2x + 1$

    (C) $y = \dfrac{1}{2}x + 1$

    (D) $y = \dfrac{1}{2}x - 1$

    (E) $y = \dfrac{1}{2}x - \dfrac{1}{2}$

1.4   ODD AND EVEN FUNCTIONS

A function (or a relation) is said to be *even* if it is symmetric about the y-axis. This occurs whenever $f(x) = f(-x)$ for all real numbers x in the domain of f.

EXAMPLE 1: $f(x) = x^2$ and $f(-x) = (-x)^2 = x^2.$

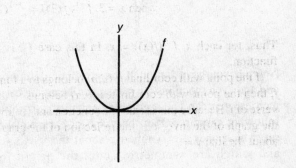

EXAMPLE 2: $f(x) = |x|$ and $f(-x) = |-x| = |-1 \cdot x| = |-1| \cdot |x| = |x|$.

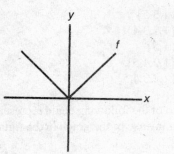

A function (or a relation) is said to be *odd* if it is symmetric about the origin (for example, if the graph looks the same after it has been rotated 180° about the origin). This occurs whenever $f(x) = -f(-x)$ for all real numbers in the domain of f.

EXAMPLE 3: $f(x) = x^3$ and $f(-x) = (-x)^3 = -x^3$. Therefore, $-f(-x) = x^3 = f(x)$.

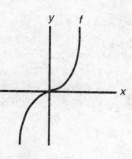

EXAMPLE 4: $f(x) = \dfrac{1}{x}$ and $f(-x) = \dfrac{1}{-x}$.

Therefore, $-f(-x) = \dfrac{1}{x} = f(x)$.

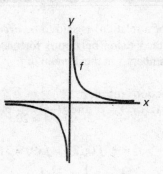

Note: If you have forgotten the algebraic definitions of odd and even functions but remember the geometric symmetries, you can use a graphing calculator to solve the following exercises. Plot the graph of each equation to see which ones are symmetric about the y-axis (even) and which are symmetric about the origin (odd).

• *Using a graphing calculator will give you the correct answer, but because of the time it takes it will not be the best method.*

EXERCISES

1. Which of the following relations are said to be *even*?

   I. $y = 2$
   II. $y = x$
   III. $x^2 + y^2 = 1$

   (A) only I
   (B) only I and II
   (C) only II and III
   (D) only I and III
   (E) I, II, and III

2. Which of the following relations are said to be *odd*?

   I. $y = 2$
   II. $y = x$
   III. $x^2 + y^2 = 1$

   (A) only II
   (B) only I and II
   (C) only I and III
   (D) only II and III
   (E) I, II, and III

3. Which of the following relations are said to be both *odd* and *even*?

   I. $x^2 + y^2 = 1$
   II. $x^2 - y^2 = 0$
   III. $x + y = 0$

   (A) only III
   (B) only I and II
   (C) only I and III
   (D) only II and III
   (E) I, II, and III

4. Which of the following functions is neither *odd* nor *even*?

   (A) $\{(1,2),(4,7),(-1,2),(0,4),(-4,7)\}$
   (B) $\{(1,2),(4,7),(-1,-2),(0,0),(-4,-7)\}$
   (C) $\{(x,y):y = x^3 - 1\}$
   (D) $\{(x,y):y = x^2 - 1\}$
   (E) $f(x) = -x$

1.5 MULTIVARIABLE FUNCTIONS

At times it is necessary or convenient to express a function or relation in terms of more than one variable. For instance, the area of a triangle is expressed in terms of the length of its base, b, and its altitude, h. Thus, in function notation, $A(b,h) = \frac{1}{2}bh$, where b and h are the independent variables.

The formula for the surface area of a rectangular solid expresses the surface area in terms of three independent variables, l, w, and h: $S(l,w,yh) = 2lw + 2lh + 2wh$.

EXAMPLE 1: If $f(x,y,z) = (x + y)(y + z)$, what does $f(1,-2,3) = ?$

Substituting 1 for x, -2 for y, and 3 for z gives

$$f(1,-2,3) = (1 - 2)(-2 + 3) = (-1)(1) = -1.$$

EXAMPLE 2: If $f(x,y) = 2x + 3y - 4$, what does $f(2x,-3y + 1) = ?$

Substituting $2x$ for x and $-3y + 1$ for y gives

$$f(2x,-3y + 1) = 2(2x) + 3(-3y + 1) - 4$$
$$= 4x - 9y - 1.$$

EXAMPLE 3: If $f(x,y) = x^2 + y^2 + y$ and $g(z) = z - 2$, what does $f(2, g(1)) = ?$

Substituting 2 for x and $g(1) = 1 - 2 = -1$ for y gives

$$f(2,g(1)) = 2^2 + (g(1))^2 + g(1)$$
$$= 4 + (-1)^2 + (-1) = 4.$$

EXERCISES

1. If $f(x,y) = 3x + 2y - 8$ and $g(z) = z^2$ for all real numbers x, y, and z, then $f(3,g(4)) =$

   (A) 9
   (B) 33 –
   (C) 81
   (D) 7
   (E) 5

2. If $f(x,y,z) = x^2 + y^2 - 2z$ for all real numbers x, y, and z, then $f(-1,1,-1) =$

   (A) 0
   (B) 2
   (C) 4
   (D) –2
   (E) 1

3. If $f(x,y) = 3x + 2y$ and $g(x,y) = x^2 - y^2$ for all real numbers x and y, then $f(g(1,2)3) =$

   (A) 40
   (B) –3
   (C) 9
   (D) 6
   (E) 3

4. If $f(x,y) = \sqrt{2x^2 - y^2}$ and $g(x) = 2^x$, the value of $g(f(2,1)) =$

   (A) 2.65
   (B) 14.65
   (C) 6.25
   (D) 5.65
   (E) 7.05

ANSWERS AND EXPLANATIONS

In these solutions the following notation is used:

   a: active—Calculator use is necessary or, at a minimum, extremely helpful.

   n: neutral—Answers may be found without a calculator, but a calculator may help.

   i: inactive—Calculator use is not helpful and may even be a hindrance.

Part 1.1 Definitions

1. i **A** Either (3,2) or (3,1), which is not an answer choice, must be removed so that 3 will be paired with only one number.

2. i **E** For each value of x there is only one value for y in each case. Therefore, f, g, and h are all functions.

3. i **A** Since division by zero is forbidden, x cannot equal 2.

Part 1.2 Function Notation

1. i **B** $f(-2) = 3(-2)^2 - 2(-2) + 4 = 20$.

2. i **D** $g(2) = 3^2 = 9$. $f(g(2)) = f(9) = 31$.

3. i **A** To get from $f(x)$ to $f(g(x))$, x^2 must become $4x^2$. Therefore, the answer must contain $2x$ since $(2x)^2 = 4x^2$.

4. i **E** $g(x)$ cannot equal 0. Therefore, $x \neq \pm1$.

5. i **C** Since $f(2)$ implies that $x = 2$, $g(f(2)) = 2$. Therefore, $g(f(2)) = 3(f(2)) + 2 = 2$. Therefore, $f(2) = 0$.

6. i **C** $p(a) = 0$ implies $4a - 6 = 0$.

7. a **D** $f \circ g(\sqrt{2}) = f(g(\sqrt{2})) = f(\sin\sqrt{2}) = e^{\sin\sqrt{2}} \approx e^{0.9878} \approx 2.7$.

Part 1.3 Inverse Functions

1. i **E** If $y = 2x - 3$, the inverse is $x = 2y - 3$, which equals $y = \dfrac{x+3}{2}$.

2. i **A** By definition.

3. i **B** The inverse is $\{(2,1),(3,2),(4,3),(1,4),(2,5)\}$, which is not a function because of $(2,1)$ and $(2,5)$. Therefore, the domain of the original function must lose either 1 or 5.

4. i **E** If this line were reflected about the line $y = x$ to get its inverse, the slope would be less than 1 and the y-intercept would be less than zero. The only possibilities are Choices D and E. Choice D can be excluded because since the x-intercept of $f(x)$ is greater than -1, the y-intercept of its inverse must be greater than -1.

Part 1.4 Odd and Even Functions

1. n **D** Only I and III remain unchanged when reflected about the y-axis.

 Graphing calculator: Plot the graph of each function in an $x \in [-5,5]$, $y \in [-5,5]$ window to see which is (are) symmetric to the y-axis and thus even.

> **TIP:** In order to graph a relation like III, it may be necessary to first solve it for y and then graph both branches, $y = \sqrt{1-x^2}$ and $y = -\sqrt{1-x^2}$.

2. n **D** Only II and III remain unchanged when rotated 180° about the origin.

 Graphing calculator: Plot the graph of each function in an $x \in [-5,5]$, $y \in [-5,5]$ window to see which is (are) symmetric about the origin and thus odd.

3. n **B** Only I and II remain unchanged when reflected about the y-axis or rotated 180° about the origin.

 Graphing calculator: Plot the graph of each function in an $x \in [-5,5]$, $y \in [-5,5]$ window to see which is (are) symmetric to both the origin and the y-axis and thus both odd and even.

4. n **C** This is the only function that does not satisfy one of the two tests.

Graphing calculator: You will have to plot the Choices A and B by hand. Plot the graph of the last three choices in an $x \in [-5,5]$, $y \in [-5,5]$ window until you find the one that is *not* symmetric about either the origin or the y-axis. This is the one that is neither odd nor even.

Part 1.5 Multivariable Functions

1. i **B** $g(4) = 16$. $f(3,16) = 9 + 32 - 8 = 33$.

2. i **C** $f(-1,1,-1) = (-1)^2 + (1)^2 + 2(1)^2 = 4$.

3. i **B** $g(1,2) = 1^2 - 2^2 = -3$. $f(-3,3) = 3(-3) + 2(3) = -3$.

4. a **C** $f(2,1) = \sqrt{2(2^2) - 1^2} = \sqrt{7}$, and so $g(f(2,1)) = g(\sqrt{7}) = 2^{\sqrt{7}} \approx 6.25$ (using your calculator).

POLYNOMIAL FUNCTIONS

CHAPTER 2

2.1 DEFINITIONS

A *polynomial* is an algebraic expression of the form

$$a_n x^n + a_{n-1} x^{n-1} + \cdots + a_1 x + a_0$$

where x is a variable, n is a nonnegative integer, and the coefficients $a_n, a_{n-1}, \ldots, a_1, a_0$ are complex numbers. If the coefficients are all real numbers, the expression is called a real polynomial. If the coefficients are all rational numbers, the expression is called a rational polynomial.

2.2 LINEAR FUNCTIONS

Linear functions are polynomials in which the largest exponent is 1. The graph is always a straight line. Although the general form of the equation is $Ax + By + C = 0$, where A, B, and C are constants, the most useful form occurs when the equation is solved for y. This is known as the *slope-intercept* form and is written $y = mx + b$. The slope of the line is represented by m and is defined to be the ratio of $\dfrac{y_1 - y_2}{x_1 - x_2}$, where (x_1, y_1) and (x_2, y_2) are any two points on the line. The y-intercept is b (the point where the graph crosses the y-axis).

Parallel lines have the same slope. The slopes of two perpendicular lines are negative reciprocals of one another.

EXAMPLE 1: The equation of line l_1 is $y = 2x + 3$, and the equation of line l_2 is $y = 2x - 5$.
These lines are parallel because the slope of each line is 2, and the y-intercepts are different.

EXAMPLE 2: The equation of line l_1 is $y = \dfrac{5}{2} x - 4$, and the equation of line l_2 is $y = -\dfrac{2}{5} x + 9$.
These lines are perpendicular because the slope of l_2, $-\dfrac{2}{5}$, is the negative reciprocal of the slope of l_1, $\dfrac{5}{2}$.

The distance between two points P and Q whose coordinates are (x_1, y_1) and (x_2, y_2) is given by the formula

$$\text{Distance} = \sqrt{(x_1 - x_2)^2 + (y_1 - y_2)^2}$$

and the midpoint, M, of the segment $\overline{PQ}$ has coordinates $\left(\dfrac{x_1 + x_2}{2}, \dfrac{y_1 + y_2}{2} \right)$.

EXAMPLE 3: Given point (2,–3) and point (–5,4). Find the length of $\overline{PQ}$ and the coordinates of the midpoint, **M.**

$$PQ = \sqrt{(2-(-5))^2 + (-3-4)^2} = \sqrt{(7)^2 + (-7)^2}$$

$$= \sqrt{98} = 7\sqrt{2}$$

$$M = \left(\frac{2+(-5)}{2}, \frac{-3+4}{2}\right) = \left(\frac{-3}{2}, \frac{1}{2}\right)$$

The perpendicular distance between a line $Ax + By + C = 0$ and a point $P(x_1, y_1)$ not on the line is given by the formula

$$\text{Distance} = \frac{|Ax_1 + By_1 + C|}{\sqrt{A^2 + B^2}}$$

The angle θ between two lines, l_1 and l_2, can be found by using the formula

$$\text{Tan } \theta = \frac{m_1 - m_2}{1 + m_1 m_2}$$

where m_1 is the slope of l_1, and m_2 is the slope of l_2. If tan $\theta > 0$, θ is the acute angle formed by the two lines. If tan $\theta < 0$, θ is the obtuse angle formed by the two lines.

EXAMPLE 4: Find the distance between the line $3x + 4y = 5$ and the origin.

$$d = \frac{|3 \cdot 0 + 4 \cdot 0 - 5|}{\sqrt{9+16}} = \frac{5}{\sqrt{25}} = 1$$

EXAMPLE 5: Find the acute angle formed by lines $2x + 3y + 5 = 0$ and $3x – 5y + 8 = 0$.
When these two equations are written in the slope-intercept form, the slope of $2x + 3y + 5 = 0$ is found to be $-\frac{2}{3}$ and the slope of $3x – 5y + 8 = 0$ is found to be $\frac{3}{5}$.

$$\text{Tan } \theta = \frac{-\frac{2}{3} - \frac{3}{5}}{1 + \left(-\frac{2}{3}\right)\left(\frac{3}{5}\right)} = \frac{\left(-\frac{2}{3} - \frac{3}{5}\right) \cdot 15}{\left(1 - \frac{2}{5}\right) \cdot 15}$$

$$= \frac{-2 \cdot 5 - 3 \cdot 3}{15 - 2 \cdot 3} = \frac{-10 - 9}{15 - 6} = \frac{-19}{9}$$

Therefore, if θ is acute, $\tan \theta = \frac{19}{9}$, and if θ is obtuse, $\tan \theta = \frac{-19}{9}$. Therefore, $\theta = \text{Tan}^{-1}\left(\frac{19}{9}\right) \approx 64.65°$.

TIP: When using a calculator to find the angle represented by an inverse trig function, always evaluate the positive number to obtain the acute reference angle. You can then easily determine the appropriate angle in the correct quadrant.

EXERCISES

1. The slope of the line through points $A(3,–2)$ and $B(–2,–3)$ is

   (A) –5

   (B) $-\frac{1}{5}$

   (C) $\frac{1}{5}$

   (D) 1

   (E) 5

2. The slope of line $8x + 12y + 5 = 0$ is

   (A) 2

   (B) $\frac{2}{3}$

   (C) 3

   (D) $-\frac{3}{2}$

   (E) $-\frac{2}{3}$

3. The slope of the line perpendicular to line $3x – 5y + 8 = 0$ is

   (A) $\frac{3}{5}$

   (B) $\frac{5}{3}$

   (C) $-\frac{3}{5}$

   (D) $-\frac{5}{3}$

   (E) 3

4. The y-intercept of the line through the two points whose coordinates are (5,–2) and (1,3) is

   (A) $\frac{5}{4}$

   (B) $-\frac{5}{4}$

   (C) 17

   (D) $\frac{17}{4}$

   (E) 7

5. The equation of the perpendicular bisector of the segment joining the points whose coordinates are (1,4) and (–2,3) is

   (A) $3x – 2y + 5 = 0$
   (B) $x – 3y + 2 = 0$
   (C) $3x + y – 2 = 0$
   (D) $x – 3y + 11 = 0$
   (E) $x + 3y – 10 = 0$

6. The length of the segment joining the points with coordinates (–2,4) and (3,–5) is

   (A) 2.8
   (B) 10.3
   (C) 3,7
   (D) 10.0
   (E) none of these

7. The slope of the line parallel to the line whose equation is $2x + 3y = 8$ is

   (A) $\dfrac{2}{3}$

   (B) $-\dfrac{2}{3}$

   (C) -2

   (D) $-\dfrac{3}{2}$

   (E) $\dfrac{3}{2}$

8. If point $P(m,2m)$ is 5 units from the line $12x + 5y = 1$, m could equal

   (A) $\dfrac{43}{11}$

   (B) -3

   (C) $-\dfrac{65}{22}$

   (D) 5

   (E) 3

9. If θ is the angle between lines $2x – 3y + 4 = 0$ and $2x – y – 3 = 0$, θ could equal

   (A) 131°
   (B) 97°
   (C) 76°
   (D) 30°
   (E) 146°

10. The distance between point (2,4) and the line $3x – 7y = 8$ is

    (A) 1.8
    (B) 3.6
    (C) 3.9
    (D) 5.5
    (E) 5.9

11. If the graph of $\pi x + \sqrt{2}y + \sqrt{3} = 0$ is perpendicular to the graph of $ax + 3y + 2 = 0$, then $a =$

    (A) –4.5
    (B) 1.35
    (C) 0.45
    (D) –1.35
    (E) –2.22

12. The lines $3x – 4y + 8 = 0$ and $9x + 6y – 4 = 0$ intersect at point P. One angle formed at point P contains

    (A) 36.9°
    (B) 89.5°
    (C) 56.3°
    (D) 86.8°
    (E) 123.7°

13. If $x + 3y = 6$ and $2x – y = 3$, then $\dfrac{x}{y} =$

    (A) 1.67
    (B) 0.43
    (C) 0.60
    (D) 2.14
    (E) 1.29

14. The distance between line $11x + 7y = 5$ and the origin is

    (A) 0.14
    (B) 0.45
    (C) 1.0
    (D) 1.76
    (E) 0.38

2.3 QUADRATIC FUNCTIONS

Quadratic functions are polynomials in which the largest exponent is 2. The graph is always a parabola. The general form of the equation is $y = ax^2 + bx + c$. If $a > 0$, the parabola opens up and has a minimum value. If $a < 0$, the parabola opens down and has a maximum value. The x-coordinate of the vertex of the parabola is equal to $-\dfrac{b}{2a}$, and the axis of symmetry is the vertical line whose equation is $x = -\dfrac{b}{2a}$.

To find the minimum (or maximum) value of the function, substitute $-\dfrac{b}{2a}$ for x to determine y. Thus, in the general case the coordinates of the vertex are $\left(-\dfrac{b}{2a}, c - \dfrac{b^2}{4a}\right)$ and the minimum (or maximum) value of the function is $c - \dfrac{b^2}{4a}$.

Unless specifically limited, the domain of a quadratic function is all real numbers, and the range is all values of y greater than or equal to the minimum value (or all values of y less than or equal to the maximum value) of the function.

EXAMPLE 1: Determine the coordinates of the vertex and the equation of the axis of symmetry of $y = 3x^2 + 2x - 5$. Does the quadratic function have a minimum or maximum value? If so, what is it?
The equation of the axis of symmetry is

$$x = -\frac{b}{2a} = -\frac{2}{2 \cdot 3} = -\frac{1}{3}$$

and the y-coordinate of the vertex is

$$y = 3\left(-\frac{1}{3}\right)^2 + 2\left(-\frac{1}{3}\right) - 5 = \frac{1}{3} - \frac{2}{3} - 5 = -5\frac{1}{3}$$

The vertex is, therefore, at $\left(-\dfrac{1}{3}, -5\dfrac{1}{3}\right)$.

The function has a minimum value because $a = 3 > 0$.

The minimum value is $-5\dfrac{1}{3}$. The graph of $y = 3x^2 + 2x - 5$ is shown below.

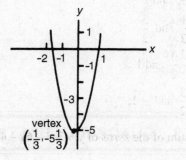

vertex
$\left(-\dfrac{1}{3}, -5\dfrac{1}{3}\right)$

The points where the graph crosses the x-axis are called the *zeros* of the function and occur when $y = 0$. To find the zeros of $y = 3x^2 + 2x - 5$, solve the quadratic equation $3x^2 + 2x - 5 = 0$. The roots of this equation are the zeros of the polynomial. Often the quickest way to do this is to factor the polynomial. However, if it is not

immediately obvious how to do the factoring, substitute the coefficients into the general quadratic formula.

Every quadratic equation can be changed into the form $ax^2 + bx + c = 0$ (if it is not already in that form), which can be solved by completing the square. The solutions are $x = \dfrac{-b \pm \sqrt{b^2 - 4ac}}{2a}$, the *general quadratic formula*. In the case of $3x^2 + 2x - 5 = 0$, factoring is the best method to use; $3x^2 + 2x - 5 = (3x + 5)(x - 1) = 0$. Thus, $3x + 5 = 0$ or $x - 1 = 0$, which leads to $x = -\dfrac{5}{3}$ or 1. The zeros of the polynomials are $-\dfrac{5}{3}$ and 1.

EXAMPLE 2: Find the zeros of $y = 2x^2 + 3x - 4$.
Solve the equation $2x^2 + 3x - 4 = 0$. This does not factor easily. Using the general quadratic formula, where $a = 2$, $b = 3$, and $c = -4$, gives

$$x = \frac{-3 \pm \sqrt{9 + 32}}{4} = \frac{-3 \pm \sqrt{41}}{4}.$$

Thus, the zeros are $\dfrac{-3 + \sqrt{41}}{4}$ and $\dfrac{-3 - \sqrt{41}}{4}$.

Graphing calculator: You could solve this equation by plotting the graph of $y = 2x^2 + 3x - 4$ in an $x \in [-5,5]$, $y \in [-5,5]$ window. Use the Trace and Zoom functions or the Root, Zero, or Solve function to see that the graph crosses the x-axis at approximately -2.35 and 0.85, which are the zeros of the original function.

It is interesting to note that the sum of the two zeros, $\dfrac{-b + \sqrt{b^2 - 4ac}}{2a}$ and $\dfrac{-b - \sqrt{b^2 - 4ac}}{2a}$, equals $-\dfrac{b}{a}$, and their product equals $\dfrac{c}{a}$. This information can be used to check whether the correct zeros have been found. In Example 2, the sum and product of the zeros can be determined by inspection from the equations. Sum $= -\dfrac{3}{2}$ and Product $= \dfrac{-4}{2} = -2$. Adding the zeros $\dfrac{-3 + \sqrt{41}}{4}$ and $\dfrac{-3 - \sqrt{41}}{4}$ gives $\dfrac{-6}{4} = -\dfrac{3}{2}$. Multiplying the zeros $\dfrac{-3 + \sqrt{41}}{4}$ and $\dfrac{-3 - \sqrt{41}}{4}$ gives $\dfrac{9 - 41}{16} = \dfrac{-32}{16} = -2$. Thus, the zeros are correct.

At times it is necessary to determine only the *nature* of the roots of a quadratic equation, not the roots themselves. Because $b^2 - 4ac$ of the general quadratic formula is under the radical, it determines the nature of the roots and is called the *discriminant* of a quadratic equation.

(i) If $b^2 - 4ac = 0$, the two roots become $\dfrac{-b+0}{2a}$ and $\dfrac{-b-0}{2a}$, which are the same, and the graph of the function is tangent to the x-axis.

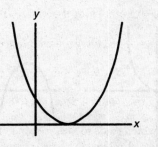

(ii) If $b^2 - 4ac < 0$, there is a negative number under the radical, which gives two complex numbers (of the form $p + qi$ and $p - qi$, where $i = \sqrt{-1}$) as roots, and the graph of the function does not intersect the x-axis.

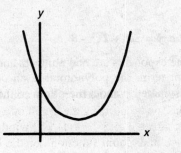

(iii) If $b^2 - 4ac > 0$, there is a positive number under the radical, which gives two different real roots, and the graph of the function intersects the x-axis at two points.

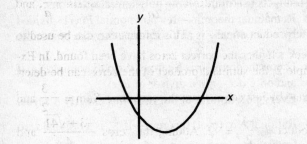

Note: The nature of the roots of any equation can be determined by sketching the graph on a graphing calculator, provided that the correct viewing window is used. For example, if you plot the graph of $y = x^2 - 2x + 1.1$ in an $x \in [-10, 10]$, $y \in [-10, 10]$ window, the graph appears to hit the x-axis. However, if you then use the Zoom function to shrink the window size, you can see that the graph does not touch the x-axis, and thus the nature of the roots is that they consist of two unequal complex roots.

EXERCISES

1. The coordinates of the vertex of the parabola whose equation is $y = 2x^2 + 4x - 5$ are

   (A) $(2, 11)$
   (B) $(-1, -7)$
   (C) $(1, 1)$
   (D) $(-2, -5)$
   (E) $(-4, 11)$

2. The range of the function
   $f = \{(x,y) : y = 5 - 4x - x^2\}$ is

   (A) $\{y : y \leq 0\}$
   (B) $\{y : y \geq -9\}$
   (C) $\{y : y \leq 9\}$
   (D) $\{y : y \geq 0\}$
   (E) $\{y : y \leq 1\}$

3. The equation of the axis of symmetry of the function $y = 2x^2 + 3x - 6$ is

   (A) $x = \dfrac{1}{3}$

   (B) $x = -\dfrac{3}{4}$

   (C) $x = -\dfrac{1}{3}$

   (D) $x = \dfrac{3}{4}$

   (E) $x = -\dfrac{3}{2}$

4. Find the zeros of $y = 2x^2 + x - 6$.

   (A) 3 and 2

   (B) -3 and 2

   (C) $\dfrac{1}{2}$ and $\dfrac{3}{2}$

   (D) $-\dfrac{3}{2}$ and 1

   (E) $\dfrac{3}{2}$ and -2

5. The sum of the zeros of $y = 3x^2 - 6x - 4$ is

   (A) $\dfrac{4}{3}$

   (B) 2

   (C) 6

   (D) -2

   (E) $-\dfrac{4}{3}$

6. $x^2 + 2x + 3 = 0$ has

   (A) two real rational roots
   (B) two real irrational roots
   (C) two equal real roots
   (D) two equal rational roots
   (E) two complex conjugate roots

7. If $f(x) = ax^2 + bx + c$, $f(1.54) = -7.3$, and $g(-1.54) = 7.3$, what is the ratio of a to c?

   (A) $-2.37:1$
   (B) $1.54:1$
   (C) $-0.42:1$
   (D) $-0.21:1$
   (E) $0.73:1$

8. A parabola with a vertical axis has its vertex at the origin and passes through point $(7,7)$. The parabola intersects line $y = 6$ at two points. The length of the segment joining these points is

   (A) 14
   (B) 12
   (C) 13
   (D) 8.6
   (E) 6.5

=====

2.4 HIGHER-DEGREE POLYNOMIAL FUNCTIONS

=====

Polynomial functions of degree greater than two (largest exponent greater than 2) are usually treated together since there are no simple formulas, such as the general quadratic formula, that aid in finding zeros.

Five facts about the graphs of polynomial functions:

(1) They are always continuous curves. (The graph can be drawn without removing the pencil from the paper.)

(2) If the largest exponent is an even number, both ends of the graph leave the coordinate system either at the top or at the bottom:

EXAMPLES:

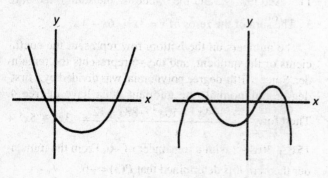

(3) If the largest exponent is an odd number, the ends of the graph leave the coordinate system at opposite ends.

EXAMPLES:

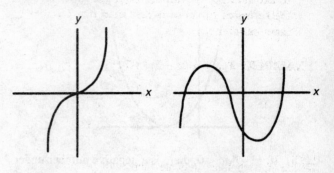

(4) If all the exponents are even numbers, the polynomial is an *even function* and is symmetric about the y-axis.

EXAMPLE: $y = 3x^4 + 2x^2 - 8$

(5) If all the exponents are odd numbers and there is no constant term, the polynomial is an *odd function* and is symmetric about the origin of the coordinate system.

EXAMPLE: $y = 4x^5 + 2x^3 - 3x$

To find the zeros (if possible) of a higher-degree polynomial function, $a_n x^n + a_{n-1} x^{n-1} + \cdots + a_1 x + a_0$, set $y = 0$ and attempt to solve the resulting polynomial equation.

Ten facts useful in solving polynomial equations:

(1) Remainder theorem—If a polynomial $P(x)$ is divided by $x - r$ (where r is any constant), then the remainder is $P(r)$.

(2) Factor theorem—r is a zero of the polynomial $P(x)$ if and only if $x - r$ is a divisor of $P(x)$.

(3) Every polynomial of degree n has exactly n zeros.

(4) Rational zero (root) theorem—If $\dfrac{p}{q}$ is a rational zero (reduced to lowest terms) of a polynomial $P(x)$ with integral coefficients, then p is a factor of a_0 (the constant term) and q is a factor of a_n (the leading coefficient).

(5) If $P(x)$ is a polynomial with rational coefficients, then irrational zeros occur as conjugate pairs. (For example, if $p + \sqrt{q}$ is a zero, then $p - \sqrt{q}$ is also a zero.)

(6) If $P(x)$ is a polynomial with real coefficients, then complex zeros occur as conjugate pairs. (For example, if $p + qi$ is a zero, then $p - qi$ is also a zero.)

(7) Descartes' rule of signs—The number of positive real zeros of a polynomial $P(x)$ either is equal to the number of variations in the sign between terms or is less than that number by an even integer. The number of negative real zeros of $P(x)$ either is equal to the number of variations of the sign between the terms of $P(-x)$ or is less than that number by an even integer.

EXAMPLE: $P(x) = 18x^4 - 2x^3 + 7x^2 + 8x - 5$

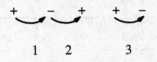

Three sign changes indicate there will be either one or three positive zeros of $P(x)$.

$$P(-x) = 18x^4 + 2x^3 + 7x^2 - 8x - 5$$

One sign change indicates there will be exactly one negative zero of $P(x)$.

(8) Relation between zeros and coefficients—In a polynomial $P(x)$ with zeros $z_1, z_2, z_3, \ldots, z_n$,

$$-\frac{a_{n-1}}{a_n} = \text{sum of the zeros} = z_1 + z_2 + z_3 + \cdots + z_n$$

$$\frac{a_{n-2}}{a_n} = \text{sum of the products of the zeros taken two}$$
$$\text{at a time} = z_1z_2 + z_1z_3 + \cdots + z_1z_n + z_2z_3 + z_2z_4 + \cdots + z_2z_n + \cdots z_{n-1}z_n$$

$$-\frac{a_{n-3}}{a_n} = \text{sum of the products of the zeros taken three}$$
$$\text{at a time} = z_1z_2z_3 + z_1z_2z_4 + \cdots + z_1z_2z_n + z_2z_3z_4 + \cdots + z_2z_3z_n + \cdots + z_{n-2}z_{n-1}z_n$$

$$\vdots$$

$$(-1)^k, \frac{a_0}{a_n} = \text{product of all the zeros} = z_1z_2z_3\cdots z_n, \text{ where } k \text{ is the number of zeros in each product}$$

EXAMPLE: $P(x) = 18x^4 - 2x^3 + 7x^2 + 8x - 5$ has four zeros.

$$z_1 + z_2 + z_3 + z_4 = -\frac{-2}{18} = \frac{1}{9}$$

$$z_1z_2 + z_1z_3 + z_1z_4 + z_2z_3 + z_2z_4 + z_3z_4 = \frac{7}{18}$$

$$z_1z_2z_3 + z_1z_2z_4 + z_1z_3z_4 + z_2z_3z_4 = -\frac{8}{18} = -\frac{4}{9}$$

$$z_1z_2z_3z_4 = \frac{-5}{18}$$

(9) Synthetic division—Synthetic division greatly decreases the amount of work necessary when dividing a polynomial by a divisor of the form $x - r$. The easiest way to learn how to use synthetic division is through examples.

EXAMPLE: Divide $P(x) = 3x^5 - 4x^4 - 15x^2 - 88x - 12$ by $x - 3$.
Write just the coefficients of $P(x)$, inserting a zero for any missing term. Put the value of r to the right of the row of coefficients.

$$
\begin{array}{rrrrrr|r}
3 & -4 & 0 & -15 & -88 & -12 & \underline{3} \\
\downarrow & 9 & 15 & 45 & 90 & 6 & \\
\hline
3 & 5 & 15 & 30 & 2 & -6 = \text{remainder} = P(3) &
\end{array}
$$

Procedure to follow:
1. Bring the first coefficient (3) down to the third row.
2. Multiply the number in the third row (3) by the number on the right (3) and place the product under the -4.
3. Add the -4 and the 9, putting the sum in the third row.
4. Multiply the number in the third row (5) by the number on the right (3) and place the product under the 0.
5. Add the 0 and the 15, putting the sum in the third row.
6. Multiply the number in the third row (15) by the number on the right (3) and place the product under the -15.
7. Add the -15 and the 45, putting the sum in the third row.
8. Multiply the number in the third row (30) by the number on the right (3) and place the product under the -88.
9. Add the -88 and the 90, putting the sum in the third row.
10. Multiply the number in the third row (2) by the number on the right (3) and place the product under the -12.
11. Add the -12 and the 6, putting the sum in the third row.

The numbers on the bottom row represent the coefficients of the quotient, and the -6 represents the remainder. Since a fifth-degree polynomial was divided by a first-degree polynomial, the quotient must have degree 4. Therefore, $\dfrac{3x^5 - 4x^4 - 15x^2 - 88x - 12}{x - 3} = 3x^4 + 5x^3 + 15x^2 + 30x + 2$ with a remainder of -6. From the remainder theorem it is determined that $P(3) = -6$.

EXAMPLE: Divide $P(x) = x^4 + 8$ by $x + 2$.

Since the divisor should be in the form $x - r$, $x + 2$ is changed to $x - (-2)$. In the synthetic division format zeros must be inserted as coefficients for the x^3, x^2, and x terms that are missing.

$$
\begin{array}{rrrrr|r}
1 & 0 & 0 & 0 & 8 & \underline{-2} \\
\downarrow & -2 & 4 & -8 & 16 & \\
\hline
1 & -2 & 4 & -8 & 24 & = P(-2)
\end{array}
$$

Procedure to follow:

1. Bring the first coefficient (1) down to the third row.
2. Multiply the number in the third row by the number on the right (-2) and add the product to the next number in the top row.
3. Repeat step 2 until the third row is filled.

The resulting quotient will be $x^3 - 2x^2 + 4x - 8$ with a remainder of 24. Thus, from the remainder theorem $P(-2) = 24$.

(10) Upper and lower bounds on zeros—If $P(x)$ is divided by $x - r$, where r is a positive number, and if the numbers in the third row of the synthetic division are all positive or zero, there is no zero of the polynomial greater than r. Thus, r is an upper bound of all the zeros.

If $P(x)$ is divided by $x - r$, where r is a negative number, and if all the numbers in the third row of the synthetic division are alternately positive and negative (or zero), there is no zero of the polynomial less than r. Thus, r is a lower bound of all the zeros.

Each of the following examples illustrates one or more of these 10 facts.

EXAMPLE 1: What is the remainder when $3x^3 + 2x^2 - 5x - 8$ is divided by $x + 2$?

Method 1: If $P(x) = 3x^3 + 2x^2 - 5x - 8$, the remainder is given to be $P(-2)$ and $P(-2) = 3(-2)^3 + 2(-2)^2 - 5(-2) - 8 = -24 + 8 + 10 - 8 = -14$. Therefore, the remainder = -14.

 Graphing calculator: Plot the graph of $y = 3x^3 + 2x^2 - 5x - 8$ in an $x \in [-10,10]$, $y \in [-20,20]$ window. Use the Trace and Zoom functions to see that as x approaches the -2, y approaches -14, which is the value of $P(-2)$, the remainder.

Method 2: Using synthetic division:

$$
\begin{array}{rrrr|r}
3 & 2 & -5 & -8 & \underline{-2} \\
\downarrow & -6 & 8 & -6 & \\
\hline
3 & -4 & 3 & -14 & = P(-2)
\end{array}
$$

Therefore, the remainder = -14.

Graphing calculator: Evaluate the function at -2 to find that -14 is the remainder.

EXAMPLE 2: Is $x - 99$ a factor of $P(x) = x^4 - 100x^3 + 97x^2 + 200x - 197$?

If $x - 99$ is a factor, the remainder upon division by $x - 99$ will be zero. It would be tedious to determine whether $P(99) = 0$ directly (as in method 1 above) even if you use your calculator, but synthetic division is quite easy.

$$
\begin{array}{rrrrr|r}
1 & -100 & 97 & 200 & -197 & \underline{99} \\
\downarrow & 99 & -99 & -198 & 198 & \\
\hline
1 & -1 & -2 & 2 & 1 & = P(99)
\end{array}
$$

Therefore, $x - 99$ is not a factor of $P(x)$.

EXAMPLE 3: If $3 + 2i$, 2, and $2 - 3i$ are all zeros of $P(x) = 3x^5 - 36x^4 + 2x^3 - 8x^2 + 9x - 338$, what are the other zeros?

Since $P(x)$ must have five zeros because it is a fifth-degree polynomial, and since complex zeros come in conjugate pairs, the two remaining zeros must be $3 - 2i$ and $2 + 3i$.

EXAMPLE 4: What are all the possible rational zeros of $P(x) = 3x^3 + 2x^2 + 4x - 6$?

Note that this question does not ask what the zeros are, only which rational numbers might be zeros. From the rational root theorem, the rational roots, $\dfrac{p}{q}$, are such that p is a factor of 6 and q is a factor of 3. Thus, $p \in \{\pm 1, \pm 2, \pm 3, \pm 6,\}$ and $q \in \{\pm 1, \pm 3\}$. Forming all possible fractions gives $\dfrac{p}{q} \in \left\{ \pm 1, \pm 2, \pm 3, \pm 6, \pm \dfrac{1}{3}, \pm \dfrac{2}{3} \right\}$.

Thus, these 12 numbers are the only possible rational numbers that could be zeros of $P(x)$. It could turn out that none of them actually is a zero, meaning that the three zeros are irrational and/or complex numbers.

EXAMPLE 5: How many positive real zeros and how many negative real zeros could you expect to find for the polynomial $P(x) = 3x^3 + 2x^2 + 4x - 6$?

Since there is only one sign change in $P(x)$, there is exactly one positive real zero.

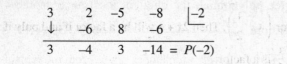

$$P(-x) = -3x^3 + 2x^2 - 4x - 6$$

Since there are two sign changes in $P(-x)$, there will be either two negative real zeros or no negative real zero. Since $P(x)$ is a third-degree polynomial and has three zeros, there will be either one positive real zero and two negative real zeros, or one positive real zero and two complex conjugate zeros.

Graphing calculator: Plot the graph of $y = 3x^3 + 2x^2 + 4x - 6$ in an $x \in [-10,10]$, $y \in [-10,10]$ window to see that there is only one positive real and zero negative real zeros. (Zoom out a couple of times to make sure that the curve does not cross the x-axis outside your viewing window.)

EXAMPLE 6: What is the smallest positive integer that is an upper bound of the zeros of $P(x) = 3x^3 + 2x^2 + 4x - 6$?

Use synthetic division, dividing by successive integers:

$$
\begin{array}{rrrr|l}
3 & 2 & 4 & -6 & \underline{1} \\
\downarrow & 3 & 5 & 9 & \\
\hline
3 & 5 & 9 & 3 & = P(1)
\end{array}
$$

Since all the numbers in the third row are positive, there are no zeros greater than 1. Therefore, 1 is the smallest positive integer that is an upper bound for the zeros of $P(x)$.

 Graphing calculator: Plot the graph of $y = 3x^3 + 2x^2 + 4x - 6$ in an $x \in [-10,10]$, $y \in [-10,10]$ window. Use the Trace and Zoom functions to see that the graph crosses the positive x-axis only once, just to the left of 1.

EXAMPLE 7: Find the zeros of $P(x) = x^6 - x^5 - 4x^4 - x^3 + 5x^2 + 8x + 4$.

The only possible rational zeros are ± 1, ± 2, ± 4. By Descartes' rule of signs there are two or no positive real zero and four, two, or no negative real zero. Using synthetic division, divide by $x - 1$:

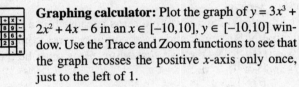

$$
\begin{array}{rrrrrrr|l}
1 & -1 & -4 & -1 & 5 & 8 & 4 & \underline{1} \\
\downarrow & 1 & 0 & -4 & -5 & 0 & 8 & \\
\hline
1 & 0 & -4 & -5 & 0 & 8 & 12 & = P(1)
\end{array}
$$

Thus, $x - 1$ is not a factor of $P(x)$ and 1 is not a zero. Divide by $x - 2$.

$$
\begin{array}{rrrrrrr|l}
1 & -1 & -4 & -1 & 5 & 8 & 4 & \underline{-2} \\
\downarrow & 2 & 2 & -4 & -10 & -10 & -4 & \\
\hline
1 & 1 & -2 & -5 & -5 & -2 & 0 & = P(2)
\end{array}
$$

Thus, $x - 2$ is a factor, and 2 is a zero. $P(x)$ can be factored into $(x - 2)Q_1(x)$, where $Q_1(x) = x^5 + x^4 - 2x^3 - 5x^2 - 5x - 2$, using the numbers in the third row of the synthetic division. Since all future factors of $P(x)$ must also be factors of $Q_1(x)$, it is sufficient to search for factors (and zeros) of $Q_1(x)$. Since $Q_1(x) = x^5 + x^4 - 2x^3 + 5x^2 - 5x - 2$ was obtained from a polynomial of higher degree, it is called a *depressed equation*. Continuing the synthetic division by dividing $Q_1(x)$ by $x - 2$:

$$
\begin{array}{rrrrrr|l}
1 & 1 & -2 & -5 & -5 & -2 & \underline{2} \\
\downarrow & 2 & 6 & 8 & 6 & 2 & \\
\hline
1 & 3 & 4 & 3 & 1 & 0 & = Q_1(2) = P(2)
\end{array}
$$

we find that both positive zeros of $P(x)$ are 2, and 2 is said to be a *double zero* or a *zero of multiplicity* 2. In factored form $P(x) = (x - 2)^2(x^4 + 3x^3 + 4x^2 + 3x + 1)$. Descartes' rule of signs indicates that there are no more positive zeros.

Attempting to find negative zeros, divide $Q_2(x) = x^4 + 3x^3 + 4x^2 + 3x + 1$ by $x + 1$.

$$
\begin{array}{rrrrr|l}
1 & 3 & 4 & 3 & 1 & \underline{-1} \\
\downarrow & -1 & -2 & -2 & -1 & \\
\hline
1 & 2 & 2 & 1 & 0 & = Q_2(-1) = P(-1)
\end{array}
$$

Thus, $x + 1$ is a factor, and -1 is a zero. Continuing the synthetic division by dividing $Q_3(x) = x^3 + 2x^2 + 2x + 1$ by $x + 1$:

$$
\begin{array}{rrrr|l}
1 & 2 & 2 & 1 & \underline{-1} \\
\downarrow & -1 & -1 & -1 & \\
\hline
1 & 1 & 1 & 0 & = Q_3(-1) = P(-1)
\end{array}
$$

we find that -1 is also a zero of multiplicity 2. In factored form, $P(x) = (x - 2)^2(x + 1)^2(x^2 + x + 1)$. Since the final quotient is a second-degree polynomial, its zeros can be found by using the general quadratic formula; $x^2 + x + 1 = 0$, where $a = 1$, $b = 1$, and $c = 1$. Therefore,

$$x = \frac{-1 \pm \sqrt{1 - 4}}{2} = \frac{-1 \pm i\sqrt{3}}{2}$$

and the entire list of zeros of $P(x) = x^6 - x^5 - 4x^4 - x^3 + 5x^2 + 8x + 4$ is $2, 2, -1, -1, \dfrac{-1 + i\sqrt{3}}{2}$, and $\dfrac{-1 - i\sqrt{3}}{2}$.

 Note: You could use your graphing calculator to see that -1 and 2 are both even multiple zeros (because the Trace and Zoom functions show that the graph is tangent to the x-axis at -1 and 2). But, you would have to use both of the procedures described in this solution to find the two complex zeros.

EXAMPLE 8: Is $2x + 1$ a factor of $P(x) = 2x^3 + 3x^2 - 3x - 2$?

Since $2x + 1$ is not in the form $x - r$, it appears that synthetic division cannot be used. However, if $2x + 1$ is written as $2\left(x + \dfrac{1}{2}\right)$, synthetic division can be used with the factor $\left(x + \dfrac{1}{2}\right)$. Then $2x + 1$ will be a factor if and only if $x + \dfrac{1}{2}$ is a factor:

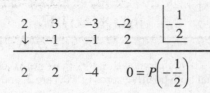

$$
\begin{array}{rrrr|r}
2 & 3 & -3 & -2 & -\dfrac{1}{2} \\
\downarrow & -1 & -1 & 2 & \\
\hline
2 & 2 & -4 & 0 = P\left(-\dfrac{1}{2}\right)
\end{array}
$$

Thus, both $2x + 1$ and $x + \dfrac{1}{2}$ are factors of $P(x)$. To find other factors the third row of the synthetic division must be divided by the 2 that was factored out of the original divisor. In factored form, $P(x) = \left(x + \dfrac{1}{2}\right)(2x^2 + 2x - 4) = (2x + 1)(x^2 + x - 2)$. This quadratic factor can itself be factored into $(x + 2)(x - 1)$. Thus, $P(x) = (2x + 1)(x + 2)(x - 1)$.

Graphing calculator: Plot the graph of $y = 2x^3 + 3x^2 - 3x - 2$ in an $x \in [-10,10]$, $y \in [-10,10]$ window. Use the Trace and Zoom functions to see that as x approaches $\dfrac{1}{2}$, y approaches 0. Therefore $2x + 1$ is a factor of $P(x)$.

Graphing calculator: <u>Alternative Solution:</u> Evaluate the function at $-\dfrac{1}{2}$ to find that the remainder is 0. Therefore, $2x + 1$ is a factor of $P(x)$.

EXERCISES

1. The graph of $P(x) = 3x^5 + 5x^3 - 8x + 2$ can cross the x-axis in no more than r points. What is the value of r?

    (A) 0
    (B) 1
    (C) 2
    (D) 3
    (E) 5

2. Between which two consecutive integers is there a zero of $P(x) = 28x^3 - 11x^2 + 15x - 28$?

    (A) –2 and –1
    (B) –1 and 0
    (C) 0 and 1
    (D) 1 and 2
    (E) 2 and 3

3. $P(x) = ax^4 + x^3 - bx^2 - 4x + c$. If $P(x)$ increases without bound as x increases without bound, then, as x decreases without bound, $P(x)$

    (A) increases without bound
    (B) decreases without bound
    (C) approaches zero from above the x-axis
    (D) approaches zero from below the x-axis
    (E) cannot be determined

4. Which of the following is an odd function?

    I. $f(x) = 3x^3 + 5$
    II. $g(x) = 4x^6 + 2x^4 - 3x^2$
    III. $h(x) = 7x^5 - 8x^3 + 12x$

    (A) only I
    (B) only II
    (C) only III
    (D) only I and II
    (E) only I and III

Note: Use a graphing calculator to graph each choice in order to see which is (are) symmetric to the origin. •*Using a graphing calculator will give you the correct answer, but because of the time it takes it will not be the best method.*

5. Using the rational root theorem, how many possible rational roots are there for $2x^4 + 4x^3 - 6x^2 + 15x - 12 = 0$?

    (A) 8
    (B) 4
    (C) 16
    (D) 12
    (E) 6

6. How many positive real zeros would you expect to find for the polynomial function $P(x) = 3x^4 - 2x^2 - 12$?

    (A) 0
    (B) 2 or 0
    (C) 1
    (D) 3 or 1
    (E) 4 or 2 or 0

Note: Use a graphing calculator to graph the function in order to see how many times it crosses the positive x-axis. • *Using a graphing calculator will give you the correct answer, but because of the time it takes it will not be the best method.*

7. If both $x - 1$ and $x - 2$ are factors of $x^3 - 3x^2 + 2x - 4b$, then b must be

    (A) 0
    (B) 1
    (C) 2
    (D) 3
    (E) 4

8. If i is a root of $x^4 + 2x^3 - 3x^2 + 2x - 4 = 0$, what are the real roots?

   (A) ± 2

   (B) $1, -4$

   (C) $-1 \pm \sqrt{5}$

   (D) $1 \pm \sqrt{5}$

   (E) $-1, 4$

9. How many positive real roots does $x^4 + x^3 - 3x^2 - 3x = 0$ have?

   (A) 0

   (B) 1

   (C) 2

   (D) 3

   (E) 4

   Note: Use a graphing calculator to graph the function in order to see how many times it crosses the positive x-axis. •*Using a graphing calculator will give you the correct answer, but because of the time it takes it will not be the best method.*

10. The sum of the zeros of $P(x) = 8x^3 - 2x^2 + 3$ is

    (A) 2

    (B) $-\dfrac{3}{8}$

    (C) $-\dfrac{1}{4}$

    (D) $\dfrac{3}{8}$

    (E) $\dfrac{1}{4}$

11. If $3x^3 - 9x^2 + Kx - 12$ is divisible by $x - 3$, then it is also divisible by

    (A) $3x^2 - x + 4$

    (B) $3x^2 - 4$

    (C) $3x^2 + 4$

    (D) $3x - 4$

    (E) $3x + 4$

12. Write the equation of lowest degree with real coefficients if two of its roots are -1 and $1 + i$.

    (A) $x^3 + x^2 + 2 = 0$

    (B) $x^3 - x^2 - 2 = 0$

    (C) $x^3 - x + 2 = 0$

    (D) $x^3 - x^2 + 2 = 0$

    (E) none of the above

2.5 INEQUALITIES

Given any algebraic expression $f(x)$, there are exactly three situations that can exist:

   (1) for some values of x, $f(x) < 0$;
   (2) for some values of x, $f(x) = 0$;
   (3) for some values of x, $f(x) > 0$.

If all three of these sets of numbers are indicated on a number line, the set of values that satisfy $f(x) < 0$ is always separated from the set of values that satisfy $f(x) > 0$ by the values of x that satisfy $f(x) = 0$.

 Note: In the following example and in Exercises 1 and 3, after converting the function to the form $f(x) < 0$, use a graphing calculator to graph $f(x)$. Use the Zoom function to see where the function is below the x-axis.

EXAMPLE: Find the set of values for x that satisfies $x^2 - 3x - 4 < 0$.

Consider the associated equation:

$$x^2 - 3x - 4 = 0$$

Factoring gives

$$(x - 4)(x + 1) = 0$$
$$x - 4 = 0 \text{ or } x + 1 = 0$$

Therefore, $x = 4$ or $x = -1$.

$$-2 \quad -1 \quad 0 \quad 1 \quad 2 \quad 3 \quad 4 \quad 5$$

These two points, -1 and 4, separate the set of x-values that satisfy $x^2 - 3x - 4 < 0$ from the set of x-values that satisfy $x^2 - 3x - 4 > 0$. The correct region can be determined by direct substitution of a number for x from each of the three regions indicated on the number line into the original inequality.

Let $x = -2$: $x^2 - 3x - 4 = 4 + 6 - 4 > 0$.
Let $x = 0$: $x^2 - 3x - 4 = 0 + 0 - 4 < 0$.
Let $x = 5$: $x^2 - 3x - 4 = 25 - 15 - 4 > 0$.

Therefore, the region that contains zero is the only one that satisfies $x^2 - 3x - 4 < 0$, and the solution set is $\{x - 1 < x < 4\}$. The graph of this solution set on a number line is indicated below.

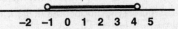

$$-2 \quad -1 \quad 0 \quad 1 \quad 2 \quad 3 \quad 4 \quad 5$$

Although this may seem to be a rather roundabout method of solution, it does have the advantage of working for all types of inequalities. No special rules for special cases must be remembered.

EXERCISES

1. Which of the following is equivalent to $3x^3 - x < 2$?

   (A) $-\dfrac{3}{2} < x < 1$

   (B) $-1 < x < \dfrac{2}{3}$

   (C) $-\dfrac{2}{3} < x < 1$

   (D) $-1 < x < \dfrac{3}{2}$

   (E) $x < -\dfrac{2}{3}$ or $x > 1$

2. If $3 < x < 7$ and $-12 < y < -6$, what are all possible values of xy?

   (A) $-72 < xy < -21$
   (B) $-84 < xy < -18$
   (C) $-42 < xy < -36$
   (D) $-84 < xy < -36$
   (E) $-36 < xy < -42$

3. The number of integers that satisfy the inequality $x^2 + 48 < 16x$ is

   (A) 0
   (B) 4
   (C) 7
   (D) an infinite number
   (E) none of the above

ANSWERS AND EXPLANATIONS

In these solutions the following notation is used:

   a: active—Calculator use is necessary or, at a minimum, extremely helpful.

   n: neutral—Answers may be found without a calculator, but a calculator may help.

   i: inactive—Calculator use is not helpful and may even be a hindrance.

Part 2.2 Linear Functions

1. i **C** Slope $= \dfrac{-3-(-2)}{-2-3} = \dfrac{1}{5}$.

2. i **E** $y = -\dfrac{2}{3}x - \dfrac{5}{12}$. The slope is $-\dfrac{2}{3}$.

3. i **D** $y = \dfrac{3}{5}x + \dfrac{8}{5}$. The slope of the given line is $\dfrac{3}{5}$.
   The slope of a perpendicular line is $-\dfrac{5}{3}$.

4. n **D** If (x,y) represents any point on the line, the slope =

   $$\frac{y-3}{x-1} = \frac{-2-3}{5-1}.$$

   Therefore $y = -\dfrac{5}{4}x + \dfrac{17}{4}$. The y-intercept $= \dfrac{17}{4}$.

    Graphing calculator: Plot the segment that passes between $(5,-2)$ and $(1,3)$. Move the cursor to the point on the y-axis where it appears that an extension of the segment would cross. The value of y at that point is approximately 4. Only Choice D is close to 4.

5. i **C** The slope of the line is $\dfrac{3-4}{-2-1} = \dfrac{1}{3}$. Therefore, the slope of a perpendicular line is -3. The midpoint of the segment is $\left(\dfrac{1-2}{2}, \dfrac{4+3}{2}\right) =$

   $\left(\dfrac{1}{2}, \dfrac{7}{2}\right)$. The equation of the line is $\dfrac{\left(y - \dfrac{7}{2}\right)}{\left(x - \dfrac{1}{2}\right)} = 3$,

   and so $3x + y - 2 = 0$.

6. a **B** Length $=$
   $$\sqrt{(3+2)^2 + (-5-4)^2} = \sqrt{25+81} = \sqrt{106} \approx 10.3$$

7. i **B** $y = -\dfrac{2}{3}x + \dfrac{8}{3}$. Therefore, the slope of a parallel line $= -\dfrac{2}{3}$.

8. n **E** Distance $= \dfrac{|12(m) + 5(2m) - 1|}{\sqrt{144+25}} = 5.$

   $|22m - 1| = 65;\ 22m - 1 = 65$ or $-22m + 1 = 65.$

   Therefore, $m = 3$ or $-\dfrac{32}{11}$.

9. a **D** The slope of the first line is $\dfrac{2}{3}$. The slope of the second line is 2.

   $$\tan \theta = \frac{2 - \dfrac{2}{3}}{1 + \dfrac{4}{3}} = \frac{4}{7}.$$

   Therefore, $\theta = \tan^{-1}\left(\dfrac{4}{7}\right) \approx 30°$.

10. a **C** Distance $= \dfrac{|3 \cdot 2 - 7 \cdot 4 - 8|}{\sqrt{3^2 + (-7)^2}} = \dfrac{|-30|}{\sqrt{58}} \approx 3.9.$

11. a **D** The slope of the first line is $-\dfrac{\pi}{\sqrt{2}}$, and the slope of the second line is $-\dfrac{a}{3}$. To be perpendicular, $-\dfrac{\pi}{\sqrt{2}} = \dfrac{3}{a}$. $a = \dfrac{-3\sqrt{2}}{\pi} \approx -1.35$.

12. a **D** The two lines and the x-axis form a triangle.

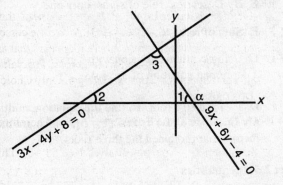

The slope of a line equals the tangent of the angle α formed by the line and the positive x-axis. Thus, $\tan \angle 2 = \dfrac{3}{4}$, which implies that $\angle 2 = \mathrm{Tan}^{-1}\left(\dfrac{3}{4}\right) \approx 36.9°$. Since $\tan \angle \alpha = -\dfrac{3}{2}$, $\tan \angle 1 = \dfrac{3}{2}$, which implies that $\angle 1 = \mathrm{Tan}^{-1}\left(\dfrac{3}{2}\right) \approx 56.3°$. Therefore, $\angle 3 = 180° - 36.9° - 56.3° = 86.8°$.

13. a **A** Multiply the second equation by -2 and add to the first equation to get $-3x + 5y = 0$. Then $3x = 5y$, $\dfrac{x}{y} = \dfrac{5}{3} \approx 1.67$. [5.9].

14. a **E** $d = \dfrac{|ax_0 + by_0 + c|}{\sqrt{a^2 + b^2}} = \dfrac{|11(0) + 7(0) - 5|}{\sqrt{11^2 + 7^2}}$

$= \dfrac{5}{\sqrt{121 + 49}} = \dfrac{5}{\sqrt{170}} \approx 0.38$. [2.2].

Part 2.3 Quadratic Functions

1. n **B** Complete the square. Then $y = 2(x^2 + 2x + 1) - 5 - 2 = 2(x + 1)^2 - 7$. The coordinates of the vertex are $(-1,-7)$.

 Graphing calculator: Plot the graph of $y = 2x^2 + 4x - 5$ in an $x \in [-10,10]$, $y \in [-10,10]$ window. Use the Trace and Zoom functions or the Min function to see that the vertex is approximately at the point $(-1,-7)$.

2. n **C** Complete the square. Then $y = -1(x^2 + 4x + 4) + 5 + 4 = -1(x + 2)^2 + 9$. This is a parabola with the vertex at $(-2,9)$ which opens down. Therefore, the range is $\{y : y \le 9\}$.

 Graphing calculator: Plot the graph of $y = 5 - 4x - x^2$ in an $x \in [-10,10]$, $y \in [-10,10]$ window. Use the Trace and Zoom functions or the Max function to see that the maximum value of y is approximately 9. Therefore, the range is Choice C.

3. n **B** Complete the square. Then

$$y = 2\left(x^2 + \dfrac{3}{2}x + \dfrac{9}{16}\right) - 6 - \dfrac{9}{8} = 2\left(x + \dfrac{3}{4}\right)^2 - \dfrac{57}{8}.$$

This equation of the axis of symmetry is $x + \dfrac{3}{4} = 0$.

 Graphing calculator: Plot the graph of $y = 2x^2 + 3x - 6$ in an $x \in [-10,10]$, $y \in [-10,10]$ window. Use the Trace and Zoom functions or the Min function to see that the x value at the vertex is approximately 0.75. Therefore, the axis of symmetry is Choice B.

4. n **E** $2x^2 + x - 6 = (2x - 3)(x + 2) = 0$. The zeros are $\dfrac{3}{2}$ and -2.

Graphing calculator: Plot the graph of $y = 2x^2 + x - 6$ in an $x \in [-10,10]$, $y \in [-10,10]$ window. Use the Trace and Zoom functions or the Root, Zero, or Solve function to see that the graph crosses the x-axis at approximately $-\dfrac{3}{2}$ and 2. Therefore, the zeros are given in Choice E.

5. n **B** Sum of zeros $= -\dfrac{b}{a} = -\dfrac{-6}{3} = 2$

Graphing calculator: Plot the graph of $y = 3x^2 - 6x - 4$ in an $x \in [-10,10]$, $y \in [-10,10]$ window. Use the Trace and Zoom functions or the Root, Zero, or Solve function to see that the graph crosses the x-axis at approximately -0.5 and 2.5. Therefore, the sum of the zeros is 2.

6. n **E** From the discriminant $b^2 - 4ac = 4 - 4 \cdot 1 \cdot 3 = -8 < 0$.

Graphing calculator: Plot the graph of $y = x^2 + 2x + 3$ in an $x \in [-10,10]$, $y \in [-10,10]$ window. Since the graph does not cross the x-axis, there are no real roots. Therefore, the answer is Choice E.

7. a **C** Substitute 1.54 for x to get $f(1.54) = (1.54)^2a + 1.54b + c = -7.3$ and substitute -1.54 for x to get $f(-1.54) = (-1.54)^2a - 1.54b + c = 7.3$. Add these two equations to get $4.7432a + 2c = 0$. Divide each term by $4.7432c$ to get $\dfrac{a}{c} + \dfrac{2}{4.7432} = 0$. Therefore, $\dfrac{a}{c} \approx \dfrac{-0.42}{1}$.

8. a **C** The equation of a vertical parabola with its vertex at the origin has the form $y = ax^2$. Substitute (7,7) for x and y to find $a = \frac{1}{7}$. When $y = 6$, $x^2 = 42$. Therefore, $x = \pm\sqrt{42}$, and the segment $= 2\sqrt{42} \approx 13$.

Part 2.4 Higher-Degree Polynomial Functions

1. n **D** By Descartes' rule of signs, there can be two or zero positive real root and one negative real root, for a maximum of three.

 Graphing calculator: Plot the graph of $y = 3x^5 + 5x^3 - 8x + 2$ in an $x \in [-10,10]$, $y \in [-10,10]$ window. Use the Trace and Zoom functions to see that the graph crosses the x-axis at three different points.

2. n **C** $P(0) = -28$ $P(1) = 4$; therefore, Choice C is correct.

Graphing calculator: Plot the graph of $y = 28x^3 - 11x^2 + 15x - 28$ in an $x \in [-10,10]$, $y \in [-10,10]$ window. Use the Trace and Zoom functions to see that the graph crosses the x-axis at approximately 0.95. Therefore, Choice C is correct.

3. i **A** Since the degree of the polynomial is an even number, both ends of the graph go off in the same direction. Since $P(x)$ increases without bound as x increases without bound, $P(x)$ also increases without bound as x decreases without bound.

4. n **C** Since $h(x) = -h(-x)$, it is the only odd function.

5. i **C** Rational roots have the form $\frac{p}{q}$, where p is a factor of 12 and q is a factor of 2. $\frac{p}{q} \in \left\{ \pm 12, \pm 6, \pm 4, \pm 3, \pm 2, \pm 1, \pm\frac{3}{2}, \pm\frac{1}{2} \right\}$. The total is 16.

6. n **C** By Descartes' rule of signs, only one.

7. i **A** Sum of the roots $= 3$. Since 1 and 2 are roots, the third root is 0. Product of the roots $= 4b$. Therefore, $b = 0$.

Alternative Solution: Since $x - 1$ is a factor, $P(1) = 1^3 - 3 \cdot 1^2 + 2 \cdot 1 - 4b = 0$. Therefore, $b = 0$.

8. i **C** Using synthetic division with i and $-i$ results in a depressed equation of $x^2 + 2x - 4 = 0$ whose roots are $-1 \pm \sqrt{5}$.

9. n **B** By Descartes' rule of signs, only one.

10. i **E** Sum of roots $= -\frac{b}{a} = \frac{2}{8} = \frac{1}{4}$.

11. i **C** Using synthetic division with 3 gives $K = 4$ and a depressed equation of $3x^2 + 4$.

12. i **D** $1 - i$ is also a root. To find the equation, multiply $(x + 1)[x - (1 + i)][x - (1 - i)]$, which are the factors that produced the three roots.

Part 2.5 Inequalities

1. n **C** $3x^2 - x - 2 = (3x + 2)(x - 1) = 0$ when $x = -\frac{2}{3}$ or 1. Numbers between these satisfy the original inequality.

 Graphing calculator: Plot the graph of $y = 3x^2 - x - 2$ in an $x \in [-10,10]$, $y \in [-10,10]$ window. Use the Trace and Zoom functions to see that the graph crosses the x-axis at approximately -0.7 and 1 and is below the x-axis between those two points. Therefore, Choice C is the answer.

2. i **B** The smallest number possible is -84, and the largest is -18.

3. n **C** $x^2 - 16x + 48 = (x - 4)(x - 12) = 0$, when $x = 4$ or 12. Numbers between these satisfy the original inequality.

Graphing calculator: Plot the graph of $y = x^2 - 16x + 48$ in an $x \in [-10,10]$, $y \in [-10,10]$ window. Use the Trace and Zoom functions to see that the graph crosses the x-axis at 4 and 12 and is below the x-axis between these two points. Therefore, there are seven integer values of x that satisfy the inequality.

TRIGONOMETRIC FUNCTIONS

CHAPTER

3

3.1 DEFINITIONS

The general definitions of the six trigonometric functions are obtained from an angle placed in standard position on a rectangular coordinate system. When an angle θ is placed so that its vertex is at the origin, its initial side is along the positive x-axis, and its terminal side is anywhere on the coordinate system, it is said to be in *standard position*. The angle is given a positive value if it is measured in a counterclockwise direction from the initial side to the terminal side, and a negative value if it is measured in a clockwise direction.

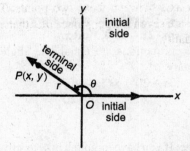

Let $P(x,y)$ be any point on the terminal side of the angle, and let r represent the distance between O and P. The six trigonometric functions are defined to be:

$$\sin \theta = \frac{\text{ordinate of } P}{OP} = \frac{y}{r}$$

$$\cos \theta = \frac{\text{abscissa of } P}{OP} = \frac{x}{r}$$

$$\tan \theta = \frac{\text{ordinate of } P}{\text{abscissa of } P} = \frac{y}{x}$$

$$\cot \theta = \frac{\text{abscissa of } P}{\text{ordinate of } P} = \frac{x}{y}$$

$$\sec \theta = \frac{OP}{\text{abscissa of } P} = \frac{r}{x}$$

$$\csc \theta = \frac{OP}{\text{ordinate of } P} = \frac{r}{y}$$

Sine and cosine, tangent and cotangent, and secant and cosecant are *cofunctions*. From these definitions it follows that:

$$\sin \theta \cdot \csc \theta = 1 \qquad \tan \theta = \frac{\sin \theta}{\cos \theta}$$

$$\cos \theta \cdot \sec \theta = 1 \qquad \cot \theta = \frac{\cos \theta}{\sin \theta}$$

$$\tan \theta \cdot \cot \theta = 1$$

The distance OP is always positive, and the ordinate and abscissa of P are positive or negative depending on which quadrant the terminal side of $\angle \theta$ lies in. The signs

45

of the trigonometric functions are indicated in the following table.

Quadrant	I	II	III	IV
Function: sin θ, csc θ	+	+	−	−
cos θ, sec θ	+	−	−	+
tan θ, cot θ	+	−	+	−

Each angle θ whose terminal side lies in quadrant II, III, or IV has associated with it two acute angles called *reference angles*. Angle α is the acute angle formed by the x-axis and the terminal side. Angle β is the acute angle formed by the y-axis and the terminal side.

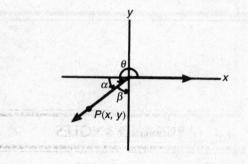

Any function of $\angle\theta = \pm$ the same function of $\angle\alpha$, and any function of $\angle\theta = \pm$ the cofunction of $\angle\beta$. The sign is determined by the quadrant in which the terminal side lies.

EXAMPLE 1: Express sin 320° in terms of $\angle\alpha$ and $\angle\beta$.

$$\alpha = 360° - 320° = 40°$$
$$\beta = 320° - 270° = 50°$$

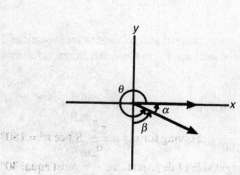

Since the sine is negative in quadrant IV, sin 320° = −sin 40° = −cos 50°.

EXAMPLE 2: Express cot 200° in terms of $\angle\alpha$ and $\angle\beta$.

$$\alpha = 200° - 180° = 20°$$
$$\beta = 270° - 200° = 70°$$

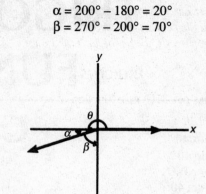

Since the cotangent is positive in quadrant III, cot 200° = cot 20° = tan 70°.

EXAMPLE 3: Express cos 130° in terms of $\angle\alpha$ and $\angle\beta$.

$$\alpha = 180° - 130° = 50°$$
$$\beta = 130° - 90° = 40°$$

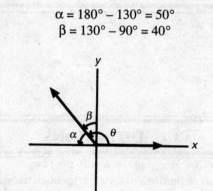

Since the cosine is negative in quadrant II, cos 130° = −cos 50° = −sin 40°.

These examples indicate that any function of α = the cofunction of β and that α and β are *complementary* angles because their sum is 90°. A very useful property is obtained from this observation: *Cofunctions of complementary angles are equal.*

EXAMPLE 4: If both the angles are acute and sin $(3x + 20°) = $ cos $(2x − 40°)$, find x.
Since these cofunctions are equal, the angles must be complementary.

Therefore, $(3x + 20°) + (2x − 40°) = 90°$
$$5x - 20° = 90°$$
$$x = 22°$$

Note: If you have forgotten how to solve the equation in Example 4, you can use a graphing calculator to sketch the graphs of $y = \sin(3x + 20°)$ and $y = \cos(2x − 40°)$ in an $x \in [0°, 90°]$, $y \in [-1,1]$

window. Use the Trace and Zoom functions or the Intersect function to find the value of *x* where they intersect. •*Using a graphing calculator will give you the correct answer, but because of the time it takes it will not be the best method.*

EXERCISES

1. Express cos 320° as a function of an angle between 0° and 45°.

   (A) cos 40°
   (B) sin 40°
   (C) −cos 40°
   (D) −sin 40°
   (E) none of the above

2. If point $P(-5,12)$ lies on the terminal side of $\angle\theta$ in standard position, sin θ =

   (A) $\dfrac{-5}{12}$

   (B) $\dfrac{12}{13}$

   (C) $\dfrac{-5}{13}$

   (D) $\dfrac{12}{5}$

   (E) $-\dfrac{12}{13}$

3. If sec $\theta = -\dfrac{5}{4}$ and sin $\theta > 0$, then tan θ =

   (A) $\dfrac{4}{3}$

   (B) $\dfrac{3}{4}$

   (C) $-\dfrac{4}{3}$

   (D) $-\dfrac{3}{4}$

   (E) none of the above

4. If *x* is an angle in quadrant III and tan $(x - 30°)$ = cot *x*, find *x*.

   (A) 210°
   (B) 240°
   (C) 225°
   (D) 60°
   (E) none of the above

Note: If you have forgotten how to solve the equation, you can use a graphing calculator to sketch the graphs of $y = \tan(x - 30°)$ and $y = \dfrac{1}{\tan x}$ in an

$x \in [180°, 270°]$, $y \in [-10,10]$ window. Use the Trace and Zoom functions or the Intersect function to find the value of *x* where they intersect. •*Using a graphing calculator will give you the correct answer, but because of the time it takes it will not be the best method.*

5. If $90° < \alpha < 180°$ and $270° < \beta < 360°$, then which of the following *cannot* be true?

   (A) sin α = sin β
   (B) tan α = sin β
   (C) tan α = tan β
   (D) sin α = cos β
   (E) sec α = csc β

6. Expressed as a function of an acute angle, cos 310° + cos 190° =

   (A) −cos 40°
   (B) cos 70°
   (C) −cos 50°
   (D) sin 20°
   (E) −cos 70°

3.2 ARCS AND ANGLES

Although the degree is the chief unit used to measure an angle in elementary mathematics courses, the radian has several advantages in more advanced mathematics. Degrees and radians are related by this equation: $\pi^R = 180°$.

EXAMPLE 1: In each of the following, convert the degrees to radians or the radians to degrees. (If no unit of measurement is indicated, radians are assumed.)

(A) 30°

(B) 270°

(C) $\dfrac{\pi^R}{4}$

(D) $\dfrac{17\pi}{3}$

(E) 24

(A) $\dfrac{x^R}{30°} = \dfrac{\pi^R}{180°}$. Solving for *x*, $x = \dfrac{\pi^R}{6}$. Since $\pi^R = 180°$ on the right side of the equation, $\dfrac{\pi^R}{6}$ must equal 30° on the left side of the equation.

(B) $\dfrac{x^R}{270°} = \dfrac{\pi^R}{180°}$. $x = \dfrac{3\pi^R}{2}$.

(C) $\dfrac{\dfrac{\pi}{4}}{x^\circ} = \dfrac{\pi^R}{180^\circ}.\ x = 45^\circ$

(D) $\dfrac{\dfrac{17\pi}{3}}{x^\circ} = \dfrac{\pi^R}{180^\circ}.\ x = 1020^\circ$

(E) $\dfrac{24}{x^\circ} = \dfrac{\pi^R}{180^\circ}.\ x = \left(\dfrac{4320}{\pi}\right)^\circ$

  Note: Most scientific calculators have a DRG ▶ button, which converts angle measures from one unit to another. To go from radians to degrees, put your calculator in radian mode, enter the angle, and then push the DRG ▶ button until you are in degree mode. When going from degree to radian mode, some experimentation is often necessary if the result is to be in terms of π.

In a circle of radius r inches with an arc subtended by a central angle of θ^R, two important formulas can be derived. The length of the arc, s, is equal to $r\theta$, and the area of the sector, AOB, is equal to $\dfrac{1}{2}r^2\theta$.

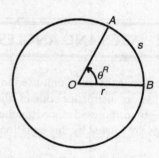

EXAMPLE 2: Find the area of the sector and the length of the arc subtended by a central angle of $\dfrac{2\pi}{3}$ radians in a circle whose radius is 6 inches.

$s = r\theta$ $\qquad\qquad A = \dfrac{1}{2}r^2\theta$

$s = 6 \cdot \dfrac{2\pi}{3} = 4\pi$ inches $\qquad A = \dfrac{1}{2}\cdot 36 \cdot \dfrac{2\pi}{3} = 12\pi$ square inches

EXAMPLE 3: In a circle of radius 8 inches, find the area of the sector whose arc length is 6π inches.

$s = r\theta$ $\qquad\qquad A = \dfrac{1}{2}r^2\theta$

$6\pi = 8\theta$ $\qquad\quad A = \dfrac{1}{2}\cdot 64 \cdot \dfrac{3\pi}{4} = 24\pi$ square inches

$\theta = \dfrac{3\pi^R}{4}$

EXAMPLE 4: Find the length of the radius of a circle in which a central angle of 60° subtends an arc of length 8π inches.

The 60° angle must be converted to radians:

$$\dfrac{x^R}{60^\circ} = \dfrac{\pi^R}{180^\circ}$$

Therefore, $\qquad\qquad x = \dfrac{\pi}{3}$

Also, $\qquad\qquad s = r\theta$

$\qquad\qquad\qquad 8\pi = r \cdot \dfrac{\pi}{3}$

$\qquad\qquad\qquad r = 24$ inches

EXERCISES

1. An angle of 30 radians is equal to how many degrees?

   (A) $\dfrac{\pi}{6}$

   (B) $\dfrac{30}{\pi}$

   (C) $\dfrac{5400}{\pi}$

   (D) $\dfrac{540}{\pi}$

   (E) $\dfrac{\pi}{30}$

2. If a sector of a circle has an arc length of 2π inches and an area of 6π square inches, what is the length of the radius of the circle?

   (A) 1
   (B) 2
   (C) 3
   (D) 6
   (E) 12

3. If a circle has a circumference of 16 inches, the area of a sector with a central angle of 4.7 radians is

   (A) 48
   (B) 12
   (C) 10
   (D) 15
   (E) 25

4. A central angle of 40° in a circle of radius 1 inch intercepts an arc whose length is s. Find s.

(A) 1.4
(B) 40
(C) 0.7
(D) 2.0
(E) 3.0

5. The pendulum on a clock swings through an angle of 25°, and the tip sweeps out an arc of 12 inches. How long is the pendulum?

(A) 43.2 inches
(B) 27.5 inches
(C) 86.4 inches
(D) 1.67 inches
(E) 13.8 inches

3.3 SPECIAL ANGLES

Although most of the values of the trigonometric functions are difficult to determine (and are usually obtained from your calculator), values of functions involving angles that are multiples of $\frac{\pi}{6}, \frac{\pi}{4}, \frac{\pi}{3}$, or $\frac{\pi}{2}$ are easy to find. Any angle that is a multiple of $\frac{\pi}{2}$ is known as a *quadrantal* angle because, in standard position, its terminal side lies on one of the axes between quadrants. Any function of a quadrantal angle is easily determined because one of the coordinates of point P on the terminal side is zero.

	0	$\frac{\pi}{2}$	π	$\frac{3\pi}{2}$	2
sine	0	1	0	−1	0
cosine	1	0	−1	0	1
tangent	0	und	0	und	0
cotangent	und	0	und	0	und
secant	1	und	−1	und	1
cosecant	und	1	und	−1	und

In the table above, "und" means that the function is undefined because the definition of the function necessitates division by zero.

Any function of an odd multiple of $\frac{\pi}{4} = \pm$ that function of any other odd multiple of $\frac{\pi}{4}$. (The sign is determined by the quadrant in which the terminal side of the angle lies.)

Any function of $k \cdot \frac{\pi}{6}$ (where k is not a multiple or factor of 6) $= \pm$ that function of any other similar multiple of $\frac{\pi}{6}$.

Any function of $k \cdot \frac{\pi}{3}$ (where k is not a multiple or factor of 3) $= \pm$ that function of any other similar multiple of $\frac{\pi}{3}$.

Because of these properties it is necessary only to learn the values of the trigonometric functions of $\frac{\pi}{4}, \frac{\pi}{6}$, and $\frac{\pi}{3}$ and then to attach a + or −, depending on the quadrant in which the terminal side of the angle lies.

	$\frac{\pi}{6}$ or 30°	$\frac{\pi}{4}$ or 45°	$\frac{\pi}{3}$ or 60°
sine	$\frac{1}{2}$	$\frac{\sqrt{2}}{2}$	$\frac{\sqrt{3}}{2}$
cosine	$\frac{\sqrt{3}}{2}$	$\frac{\sqrt{2}}{2}$	$\frac{1}{2}$
tangent	$\frac{\sqrt{3}}{3}$	1	$\sqrt{3}$
cotangent	$\sqrt{3}$	1	$\frac{\sqrt{3}}{2}$
secant	$\frac{2\sqrt{3}}{2}$	$\sqrt{2}$	2
cosecant	2	$\sqrt{2}$	$\frac{2\sqrt{3}}{3}$

Notice that several of these functions contain $\sqrt{2}$ and $\sqrt{3}$. If you were to use your calculator to find cos 30°, for instance, it would be approximately equal to 0.866. In order to find the *exact value* of cos 30°, $\left(\frac{\sqrt{3}}{2}\right)$, from 0.866 ..., just *square* 0.866 ... to get 0.75, which equals $\frac{3}{4}$. Taking the *square root* of this gives $\frac{\sqrt{3}}{2}$.

EXAMPLE: What is the exact value of each of the following?

(A) $\cos 0$

(B) $\csc \dfrac{3\pi}{2}$

Note: Since $\csc$ is not on your calculator, you must use the fact that $\csc \dfrac{3\pi}{2} = \dfrac{1}{\sin \dfrac{3\pi}{2}} = \dfrac{1}{1} = 1$.

Similarly, you must use $\dfrac{1}{\cos \theta}$ to find $\sec \theta$

and $\dfrac{1}{\tan \theta}$ to find $\cot \theta$.

(C) $\cos \dfrac{7\pi}{6}$

(D) $\tan \dfrac{5\pi}{4}$

(E) $\sec \dfrac{3\pi}{4}$

(F) $\sin 300°$
(G) $\cos (-390°)$
(H) $\cot 60°$
(I) $\tan (-45°)$

Note: Use the methods in the two previous notes to practice using your calculator to do this type of problem.

Procedures are as follows:

(A) From the first table on page 49, $\cos 0 = 1$.

(B) $\dfrac{3\pi}{2}$ is a quadrantal angle with its terminal side along the negative y-axis. Therefore, $P(0, -r)$, where $OP = r$. $\csc \dfrac{3\pi}{2} = \dfrac{r}{-r} = -1$. (Or, from the first table on page 49, $\csc \dfrac{3\pi}{2} = -1$.)

(C) $\dfrac{7\pi}{6}$ is a multiple of $\dfrac{\pi}{6}$, and so $\cos \dfrac{7\pi}{6} = \pm \cos \dfrac{\pi}{6} = \pm \dfrac{\sqrt{3}}{2}$. Since the terminal side of $\dfrac{7\pi}{6}$ is in quadrant III, $\cos \dfrac{7\pi}{6} = -\dfrac{\sqrt{3}}{2}$.

(D) $\dfrac{5\pi}{4}$ is a multiple of $\dfrac{\pi}{4}$, and its terminal side lies in quadrant III. Therefore, $\tan \dfrac{5\pi}{4}$ is positive, and $\tan \dfrac{5\pi}{4} = \tan \dfrac{\pi}{4} = 1$.

(E) $\dfrac{3\pi}{4}$ is a multiple of $\dfrac{\pi}{4}$, and its terminal side lies in quadrant II. Therefore, $\sec \dfrac{3\pi}{4}$ is negative, and $\sec \dfrac{3\pi}{4} = -\sec \dfrac{\pi}{4} = -\sqrt{2}$.

(F) $300° = \dfrac{5\pi}{3}$, which is a multiple of $\dfrac{\pi}{3}$, and its terminal side lies in quadrant IV. Therefore, $\sin 300°$ is negative, and $\sin 300° = \sin \dfrac{5\pi}{3} = -\sin \dfrac{\pi}{3} = -\dfrac{\sqrt{3}}{2}$.

(G) $-390° = -\dfrac{13\pi}{6}$, which is a multiple of $\dfrac{\pi}{6}$, and its terminal side lies in quadrant IV. Therefore, $\cos (-390°)$ is positive, and $\cos (-390°) = \cos\left(-\dfrac{13\pi}{6}\right) = \cos \dfrac{\pi}{6} = \dfrac{\sqrt{3}}{2}$.

(H) $60° = \dfrac{\pi}{3}$. Therefore, $\cot 60° = \cot \dfrac{\pi}{3} = \dfrac{\sqrt{3}}{3}$.

(I) $-45° = -\dfrac{\pi}{4}$, which is a multiple of $\dfrac{\pi}{4}$, and its terminal side lies in quadrant IV. Therefore, $\tan (-45°)$ is negative, and $\tan (-45°) = \tan\left(-\dfrac{\pi}{4}\right) = -\tan \dfrac{\pi}{4} = -1$.

EXERCISES

1. Tan $(-60°)$ equals

    (A) $-\tan 30°$
    (B) $\cot 30°$
    (C) $-\tan 60°$
    (D) $-\cot 60°$
    (E) $\tan 60°$

2. Tan $(-135°) + \cot 315°$ equals

    (A) 1
    (B) 2
    (C) -1
    (D) -2
    (E) 0

3. $\cos \pi - \sin 570° - \csc\left(-\dfrac{\pi}{2}\right) + \sec 0°$ equals

    (A) 1
    (B) $1\dfrac{1}{2}$
    (C) $-1\dfrac{1}{2}$
    (D) 0
    (E) $-\dfrac{1}{2}$

4. Sec $\dfrac{11\pi}{6} \cdot \tan \dfrac{2\pi}{3} \cdot \sin \dfrac{7\pi}{4}$ equals

(A) -1

(B) $\sqrt{2}$

(C) $\dfrac{\sqrt{6}}{3}$

(D) $-\sqrt{2}$

(E) $-\dfrac{\sqrt{6}}{3}$

5. Sin 300° equals

(A) cos 60°

(B) sin 120°

(C) cos 240°

(D) sin 240°

(E) cos 120°

3.4 GRAPHS

Since the values of all the trigonometric functions repeat themselves at regular intervals, and, for some number p, $f(x) = f(x + p)$ for all numbers x, these functions are called *periodic functions*. The smallest positive value of p for which this property holds is called the *period* of the function.

The sine, cosine, secant, and cosecant have periods of 2π, and the tangent and cotangent have periods of π. The graphs of the six trigonometric functions, shown below, demonstrate that the tangent and cotangent repeat on intervals of length π and that the others repeat on intervals of length 2π.

From the graphs or from the table of values at the right it is possible to determine the domain and range of each of the six trigonometric functions.

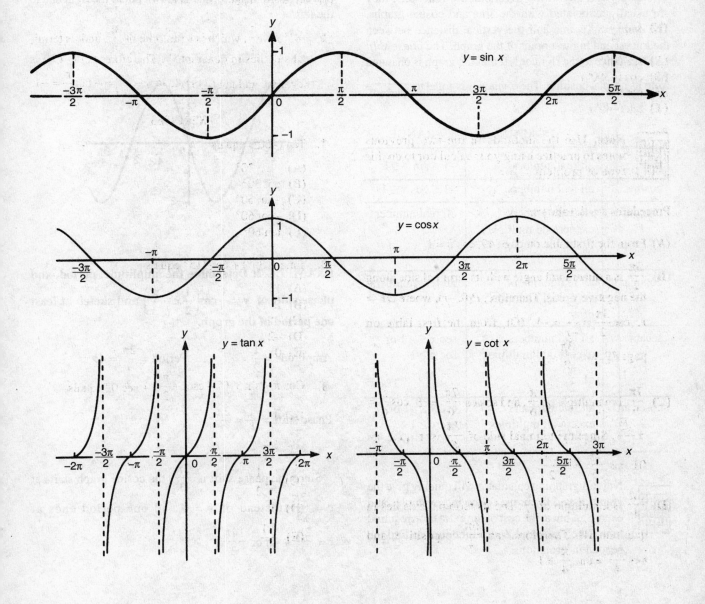

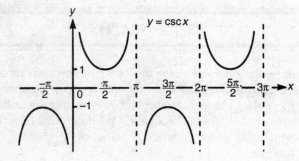

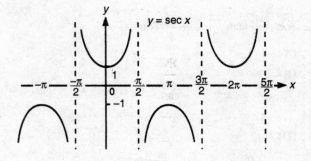

The general form of a trigonometric function, f, is given to be $y = A \cdot f(Bx + C)$, where $|A|$ is the amplitude, $\dfrac{\text{normal period of } f}{B}$ is the period of the graph, and $-\dfrac{C}{B}$ is the phase shift. Although the amplitude is associated with only the sine and cosine, the period and phase shift can be associated with any of the trigonometric functions; they are usually associated with the sine and cosine graphs. The *amplitude* is one-half the vertical distance between the lowest and highest point of the graph. The *phase shift* is the distance to the right or left that the graph is changed from its normal position. The *frequency* is equal to $\dfrac{1}{\text{period}}$.

		DOMAIN	RANGE
sine		all real numbers	$-1 \le \sin x \le 1$
cosine		all real numbers	$-1 \le \cos x \le 1$
tangent		all real numbers except odd multiples of $\dfrac{\pi}{2}$	all real numbers
cotangent		all real numbers except all multiples of π	all real numbers
secant		all real numbers except odd multiples of $\dfrac{\pi}{2}$	$\sec x \le -1$ or $\sec x \ge 1$
cosecant		all real numbers except all multiples of π	$\csc x \le -1$ or $\csc x \ge 1$

Note: A graphing calculator will quickly give the graphs asked for in the following examples and exercises, but at the cost of the extra time required to use the Trace and Zoom functions to find the needed information.

EXAMPLE 1: Determine the amplitude, period, and phase shift of $y = 2\sin 2x$ and sketch at least one period of the graph.

Amplitude = 2   Period = $\dfrac{2\pi}{2} = \pi$ Phase shift = 0

Since the phase shift is zero, the sine graph starts at its normal position, $(0,0)$, and is drawn out to the right and to the left.

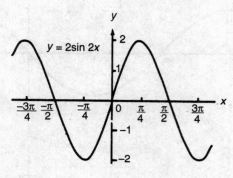

EXAMPLE 2: Determine the amplitude, period, and phase shift of $y = \dfrac{1}{2}\cos\left(\dfrac{1}{2}x - \dfrac{\pi}{3}\right)$ and sketch at least one period of the graph.

Amplitude = $\dfrac{1}{2}$ Period = $\dfrac{2\pi}{\dfrac{1}{2}} = 4\pi$

Phase shift = $\dfrac{\dfrac{\pi}{3}}{\dfrac{1}{2}} = \dfrac{2\pi}{3}$

Since the phase shift is $\dfrac{2\pi}{3}$, the cosine graph starts at $x = \dfrac{2\pi}{3}$ instead of $x = 0$ and one period ends at $x = \dfrac{2\pi}{3} + 4\pi$ or $\dfrac{14\pi}{3}$.

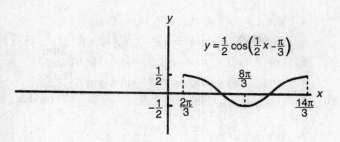

$$y = \frac{1}{2}\cos\left(\frac{1}{2}x - \frac{\pi}{3}\right)$$

EXAMPLE 3: Determine the amplitude, period, and phase shift of $y = -2\sin(\pi x + 3\pi)$ and sketch at least one period of the graph.

Amplitude = 2 $\qquad$ Period $= \dfrac{2\pi}{\pi} = 2$

Phase shift $= -\dfrac{3\pi}{\pi} = -3$

Since the phase shift is −3, the sine graph starts at $x = -3$ instead of $x = 0$, and one period ends at −3 + 2 or $x = -1$. The graph can continue to the right and to the left for as many periods as desired. Since the coefficient of the sine is negative, the graph starts down as x increases from −3, instead of up as a normal sine graph does.

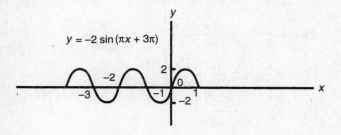

$$y = -2\sin(\pi x + 3\pi)$$

EXERCISES

1. In the figure, part of the graph of $y = \sin 2x$ is shown. What are the coordinates of point P?

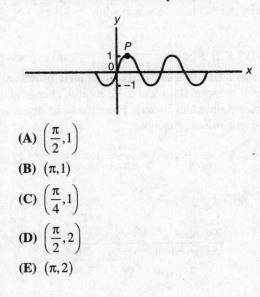

(A) $\left(\dfrac{\pi}{2}, 1\right)$

(B) $(\pi, 1)$

(C) $\left(\dfrac{\pi}{4}, 1\right)$

(D) $\left(\dfrac{\pi}{2}, 2\right)$

(E) $(\pi, 2)$

2. The figure below could be a portion of the graph whose equation is

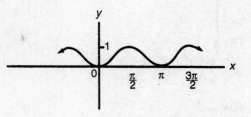

(A) $y - 1 = \sin x \cdot \cos x$
(B) $y \sec x = 1$
(C) $2y + 1 = \sin 2x$
(D) $2y + 1 = \cos 2x$
(E) $1 - 2y = \cos 2x$

3. As θ increases from $\dfrac{\pi}{4}$ to $\dfrac{5\pi}{4}$, the value of $4\cos\dfrac{1}{2}\theta$

(A) increases, and then decreases
(B) decreases, and then increases
(C) decreases throughout
(D) increases throughout
(E) decreases, increases, and then decreases again

4. The function $f(x) = \sqrt{3}\cos x + \sin x$ has an amplitude of

(A) $\sqrt{3}$

(B) $\sqrt{3} + 1$

(C) 2

(D) $2\sqrt{3}$

(E) $\dfrac{\sqrt{3} + 1}{2}$

5. For what value of P is the period of the function $y = \dfrac{1}{3}\cos Px$ equal to $\dfrac{2\pi}{3}$?

(A) $\dfrac{1}{3}$

(B) 2

(C) 3

(D) 6

(E) $\dfrac{2}{3}$

6. If $0 \le x \le \dfrac{\pi}{2}$, what is the maximum value of the function $f(x) = \sin \dfrac{1}{3} x$?

(A) 0

(B) 1

(C) $\dfrac{1}{3}$

(D) $\dfrac{1}{2}$

(E) $\dfrac{\sqrt{3}}{2}$

7. If the graph in the figure below has an equation of the form $y = \sin (Mx + N)$, what is the value of N?

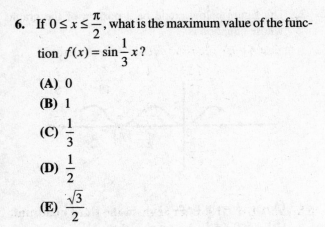

(A) π

(B) $-\pi$

(C) $-\dfrac{1}{2}$

(D) $\dfrac{\pi}{2}$

(E) -1

3.5 IDENTITIES, EQUATIONS, AND INEQUALITIES

Many of the problems involving trigonometry depend on several formulas that can be used with any angle as long as the value of the function is not undefined. A list of the most frequently used formulas follows:

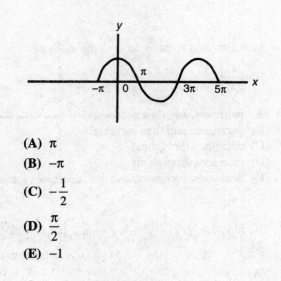

1. $\sin^2 x + \cos^2 x = 1$

2. $\tan^2 x + 1 = \sec^2 x$ }Pythagorean identities

3. $\cot^2 x + 1 = \csc^2 x$

4. $\sin(A + B) = \sin A \cdot \cos B + \cos A \cdot \sin B$

5. $\sin(A - B) = \sin A \cdot \cos B - \cos A \cdot \sin B$

6. $\cos(A + B) = \cos A \cdot \cos B - \sin A \cdot \sin B$

7. $\cos(A - B) = \cos A \cdot \cos B + \sin A \cdot \sin B$ }Sum and difference formulas

8. $\tan(A + B) = \dfrac{\tan A + \tan B}{1 - \tan A \cdot \tan B}$

9. $\tan(A - B) = \dfrac{\tan A - \tan B}{1 + \tan A \cdot \tan B}$

10. $\sin 2A = 2 \sin A \cdot \cos A$

11. $\cos 2A = \cos^2 A - \sin^2 A$

12. $ = 2 \cos^2 A - 1$ }Double-angle formulas

13. $ = 1 - 2 \sin^2 A$

14. $\tan 2A = \dfrac{2 \tan A}{1 - \tan^2 A}$

A few other formulas are rarely used on the Math Level IIC examination but may be helpful:

15. $\sin \dfrac{1}{2} A = \pm \sqrt{\dfrac{1 - \cos A}{2}}$

16. $\cos \dfrac{1}{2} A = \pm \sqrt{\dfrac{1 + \cos A}{2}}$

17. $\tan \dfrac{1}{2} A = \pm \sqrt{\dfrac{1 - \cos A}{1 + \cos A}}$ }Half-angle formulas

18. $\phantom{\tan \dfrac{1}{2} A} = \dfrac{1 - \cos A}{\sin A}$

19. $\phantom{\tan \dfrac{1}{2} A} = \dfrac{\sin A}{1 + \cos}$

The correct sign for Formulas 15 through 17 is determined by the quadrant in which angle $\dfrac{1}{2} A$ lies.

EXAMPLE 1: Simplify $\dfrac{\csc A}{\cot A + \tan A}$ **and express the answer in terms of a single trigonometric function.**

If none of the formulas seem to be helpful, change all the functions to sines and cosines. From the basic definitions of the trigonometric functions,

$$\csc A = \dfrac{1}{\sin A}, \cot A = \dfrac{\cos A}{\sin A}, \tan A = \dfrac{\sin A}{\cos A}.$$

Therefore,

$$\dfrac{\csc A}{\cot A + \tan A} = \dfrac{\dfrac{1}{\sin A}}{\dfrac{\cos A}{\sin A} + \dfrac{\sin A}{\cos A}}.$$

When the numerator and the denominator of the complex fraction are multiplied by the lowest common denominator of the three "little" denominators, $\sin A \cdot \cos A$, the fraction becomes

$$\frac{\dfrac{1}{\sin A} \cdot \sin A \cdot \cos A}{\left(\dfrac{\cos A}{\sin A} + \dfrac{\sin A}{\cos A}\right) \cdot \sin A \cdot \cos A} = \frac{\cos A}{\cos^2 A + \sin^2 A}$$

$$= \frac{\cos A}{1}.$$

by Formula 1. Therefore,

$$\frac{\csc A}{\cot A + \tan A} = \cos A.$$

EXAMPLE 2: Express sin $4x$ in terms of sin x and cos x.

Sin $4x$ = sin $2(2x)$. Let $A = 2x$ and use Formula 10.
Sin $4x$ = sin $2A$ = $2\sin A \cdot \cos A$ = $2\sin 2x \cdot \cos 2x$. Using Formulas 10 and 11 gives

$$\sin 4x = 2(2\sin x \cdot \cos x) \cdot (\cos^2 x - \sin^2 x)$$
$$= 4 \sin x \cdot \cos^3 x - 4 \sin^3 x \cdot \cos x.$$

Note: In Examples 3, 4, and 5, you can use a scientific calculator to determine the values of A, B, and θ and then find the answer to the problem. However, be sure you compute an angle in the proper quadrant.

EXAMPLE 3: If tan $A = \dfrac{5}{12}$ and sin $B = \dfrac{3}{5}$, where A and B are acute angles, find the value of cos $(A + B)$.

From the basic definitions of the trigonometric functions and the Pythagorean theorem, $\sin A = \dfrac{5}{13}$, $\cos A = \dfrac{12}{13}$, and $\cos B = \dfrac{4}{5}$.

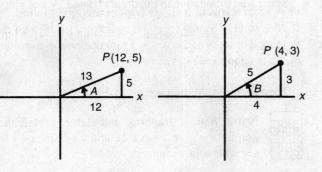

Therefore, using Formula 6 gives

$$\cos(A + B) = \cos A \cdot \cos B - \sin A \cdot \sin B$$

$$= \frac{12}{13} \cdot \frac{4}{5} - \frac{5}{13} \cdot \frac{3}{5}$$

$$= \frac{48}{65} - \frac{15}{65}$$

$$= \frac{33}{65}.$$

EXAMPLE 4: If A is an angle in the third quadrant, B is an angle in the second quadrant, $\tan A = \dfrac{3}{4}$, and $\tan B = -\dfrac{1}{2}$, in which quadrant does angle $(A + B)$ lie?

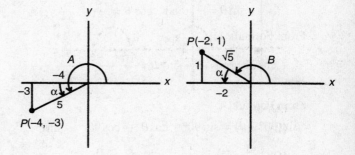

Since $180° < A < 270°$ and $90° < B < 180°$, therefore $270° < A + B < 450°$, meaning that angle $(A + B)$ must lie in quadrant I or IV. Since the sine is positive in quadrant I and negative in quadrant IV, the value of $\sin(A + B)$ determines the correct quadrant. From the basic definitions of the trigonometric functions and the Pythagorean theorem, $\sin A = -\dfrac{3}{5}$, $\cos A = -\dfrac{4}{5}$, $\sin B = \dfrac{\sqrt{5}}{5}$, and $\cos B = \dfrac{-2\sqrt{5}}{5}$. From Formula 4,

$$\sin(A + B) = \sin A \cdot \cos B + \cos A \cdot \sin B$$

$$= \frac{-3}{5} \cdot \frac{-2\sqrt{5}}{5} + \frac{-4}{5} \cdot \frac{\sqrt{5}}{5}$$

$$= \frac{6\sqrt{5}}{25} - \frac{4\sqrt{5}}{25}$$

$$= \frac{2\sqrt{5}}{25} \quad > 0$$

Therefore, angle $(A + B)$ lies in quadrant I.

EXAMPLE 5: Find the value of $\cos 2\theta - \sin(90° + \theta)$ if $\tan \theta = -\dfrac{3}{4}$ and $\sin\theta$ is positive.

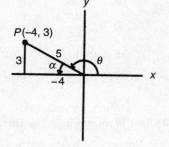

Since $\tan \theta < 0$ and $\sin \theta > 0$, the terminal side of angle θ must lie in quadrant II. From the basic definitions of the trigonometric functions and the Pythagorean theorem,

$$\sin\theta = \frac{3}{5} \quad \text{and} \quad \cos\theta = \frac{-4}{5}.$$

From Formula 11,

$$\cos 2\theta = \cos^2 \theta - \sin^2 \theta = \frac{16}{25} - \frac{9}{25} = \frac{7}{25}.$$

From Formula 4,

$$\sin(90° + \theta) = \sin 90° \cdot \cos \theta + \cos 90° \cdot \sin \theta$$
$$= 1 \cdot \frac{-4}{5} + 0 \cdot -\frac{4}{5}$$

Therefore,

$$\cos 2\theta - \sin(90° + \theta) = \frac{7}{25} - \left(\frac{-4}{5}\right) = \frac{7}{25} + \frac{4}{5} = \frac{27}{25}.$$

EXAMPLE 6: If $\sin \theta = a$, find the value of $\sin 2\theta$ in terms of a.

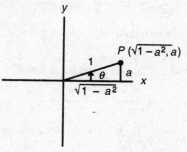

Choose θ to be an angle in any quadrant. (It can be chosen in quadrant I for convenience and without any loss of generality.) From the basic definitions of the trigonometric functions and the Pythagorean theorem, the coordinates of P are $\left(\sqrt{1 - a^2}, a\right)$. From Formula 10, $\sin 2\theta =$

$2 \sin \theta \cdot \cos \theta = 2 \cdot a \cdot \sqrt{1 - a^2}$.

EXAMPLE 7: If $\cos 23° = z$, find the value of $\cos 46°$ in terms of z.

Since $46 = 2(23)$, Formula 12 can be used: $\cos 2A = 2 \cos^2 A - 1$. $\cos 46° = \cos 2(23°) = 2 \cos^2 23° - 1 = 2(\cos 23°)^2 - 1 = 2z^2 - 1$.

 Note: In Examples 8–14, solutions can be found by sketching the graph(s) in the indicated domain(s) and then using the Trace and Zoom functions or the Intersect function.

EXAMPLE 8: Solve $\sin 2x = 3 \sin x$ for x, where $0 \le x < 2\pi$.

Use Formula 10 to convert each term into a function of x only.

$$2 \sin x \cdot \cos x = 3 \sin x$$
$$2 \sin x \cdot \cos x - 3 \sin x = 0$$

Use the distributive property to factor $\sin x$ out of each term:

$$\sin x(2 \cos x - 3) = 0$$

Therefore, $\sin x = 0$ or $2 \cos x - 3 = 0$. The second equation implies that $\cos x = \dfrac{3}{2}$, which is impossible because the range of cosine $= \{y: -1 \le y \le 1\}$. Therefore, $\sin x = 0$ contributes the only roots of the original equation. $\sin x = 0$, when $x = 0, \pi$.

 Note: With a graphing calculator, sketch the graphs of $y = \sin 2x$ and $y = 3 \sin x$ to see where they intersect.

EXAMPLE 9: Solve $\sin x + \cos 2x = 4 \sin^2 x - 1$ for all values of x such that $0 \le x < 2\pi$.

Use Formula 13 to convert every term to $\sin x$. The equation becomes $2 \sin x + 1 - 2 \sin^2 x = 2 \sin^2 x - 1$. Then

$$4 \sin^2 x - 2 \sin x - 2 = 0$$
$$2 \sin^2 x - \sin x - 1 = 0$$
$$(2 \sin x + 1)(\sin x - 1) = 0$$
$$2 \sin x + 1 = 0 \text{ or } \sin x - 1 = 0$$
$$\sin x = -\frac{1}{2} \text{ or } \sin x = 1.$$

Since sine is negative in quadrants III and IV and since $\sin \dfrac{\pi}{6} = \dfrac{1}{2}$, $\sin x = -\dfrac{1}{2}$ when $x = \dfrac{7\pi}{6}$ and $\dfrac{11\pi}{6}$. Also, $\sin x = 1$ when $x = \dfrac{\pi}{2}$.

Therefore, the solution set $= \left\{\dfrac{\pi}{2}, \dfrac{7\pi}{6}, \dfrac{11\pi}{6}\right\}$.

 Note: With a graphing calculator, sketch the graphs of $y = \sin x + \cos 2x$ and $y = 4 \sin^2 x - 1$ to see where they intersect.

EXAMPLE 10: Solve $\tan 3x$ for all values of x such that $0° \le x < 360°$.

Tan $3x$ is positive when angle $3x$ is in quadrants I and III.

Therefore, $3x = \dfrac{\pi}{4} = 45°$ or $3x = \dfrac{5\pi}{4} = 225°$. However, to find all values of x such that $0° \le x < 360°$, two angles coterminal with 45° and 225° must also be found for values of $3x$. Since $3x = 45°, 45° + 360°, 45° + 720°,$ or $3x = 225°, 225° + 360°, 225° + 720°,$ therefore, if $3x = 45°, 225°, 405°, 585°, 765°,$ or $945°,$ then $x = 15°, 75°, 135°, 195°, 255°,$ or $315°$.

In this type of problem make sure that enough coterminal angles are chosen to determine all values of x. If n is the coefficient of x (in this problem it is 3), $n - 1$ angles coterminal to the principal values are necessary.

EXAMPLE 11: Solve $\sin x = \sqrt{3} \cos x$ for all values of x such that $0 \le x < 2\pi$.

Method 1: Since a solution is not obtained when $\cos x = 0$, it is possible to divide both sides of the equation by $\cos x$.

$\dfrac{\sin x}{\cos x} = \sqrt{3}$, which becomes $\tan x = \sqrt{3}$

$\tan x = \sqrt{3}$ when $x = \dfrac{\pi}{3}$ or $\dfrac{4\pi}{3}$

Method 2: Square both sides of the equation and use Formula 1.

$$\sin^2 x = 3 \cos^2 x$$
$$\sin^2 x = 3(1 - \sin^2 x) = 3 - 3 \sin^2 x$$
$$4 \sin^2 x = 3$$
$$\sin^2 x = \frac{3}{4}$$
$$\sin x = \pm \frac{\sqrt{3}}{2}$$

Therefore,

$$x = \frac{\pi}{3}, \frac{2\pi}{3}, \frac{4\pi}{3}, \frac{5\pi}{3}$$

This method has introduced extra roots into the solution set, as the squaring of both sides of any equation is apt to do. If the four roots are checked in the original equation, only $\dfrac{\pi}{3}$ and $\dfrac{4\pi}{3}$ obtained above will be found to be solutions.

Thus, the solution set obtained by either method is $\left\{ \dfrac{\pi}{4}, \dfrac{4\pi}{3} \right\}$.

 Note: With a graphing calculator, sketch the graphs of $y = \sin x$ and $y = \sqrt{3} \cos x$ to see where they intersect.

EXAMPLE 12: Solve $\sin x \cdot \sin 40° - \cos x \cdot \cos 40° = \dfrac{1}{2}$ for all values of x such that $0° \le x < 360°$.

When this equation is multiplied through by -1, the left side is similar to the right side of Formula 6. From Formula 6, $\cos (x + 40°) = \cos x \cdot \cos 40° - \sin x \cdot \sin 40°$.

Thus, this equation becomes $\cos (x + 40°) = -\dfrac{1}{2}$. Since $\cos \dfrac{2\pi}{3} = \cos \dfrac{4\pi}{3} = -\dfrac{1}{2}, \dfrac{2\pi}{3} = 120°,$ and $\dfrac{4\pi}{3} = 240°, x + 40° = 120°$ or $x + 40° = 240°$. Solving for x, the solution set is $\{80°, 200°\}$.

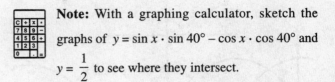 **Note:** With a graphing calculator, sketch the graphs of $y = \sin x \cdot \sin 40° - \cos x \cdot \cos 40°$ and $y = \dfrac{1}{2}$ to see where they intersect.

EXAMPLE 13: Solve $\sqrt{3} \cos x - \sin x = 2$ for all values of x such that $0 \le x < 2\pi$.

Method 1: Divide the equation through by 2, obtaining $\dfrac{\sqrt{3}}{2} \cos x - \dfrac{1}{2} \sin x = 1$. Since $\sin \dfrac{\pi}{3} = \dfrac{\sqrt{3}}{2}$ and $\cos \dfrac{\pi}{3} = \dfrac{1}{2}$, the equation becomes $\sin \dfrac{\pi}{3} \cdot \cos x - \cos \dfrac{\pi}{3} \cdot \sin x = 1$. Using Formula 5, the equation becomes $\sin \left(\dfrac{\pi}{3} - x \right) = 1$.

Therefore, $\dfrac{\pi}{3} - x = \dfrac{\pi}{2}$ and $x = \dfrac{\pi}{3} - \dfrac{\pi}{2} = -\dfrac{\pi}{6}$, which is not in the range $0 \le x < 2\pi$. Add 2π to this angle to find a coterminal angle within this range: $-\dfrac{\pi}{6} + 2\pi = \dfrac{11\pi}{6}$.

Therefore, the solution set has only one member: $\left\{ \dfrac{11\pi}{6} \right\}$.

Method 2: Add $\sin x$ to both sides of the equation and then square each side, obtaining:

$$(\sqrt{3} \cos x)^2 = (2 + \sin x)^2$$
$$3 \cos^2 x = 4 + 4 \sin x + \sin^2 x$$

Using a form of Formula 1 ($\cos^2 x = 1 - \sin^2 x$) and setting everything equal to zero gives

$$3(1 - \sin^2 x) = 4 + 4 \sin x + \sin^2 x$$
$$3 - 3 \sin^2 x = 4 + 4 \sin x + \sin^2 x$$
$$4 \sin^2 x + 4 \sin x + 1 = 0$$
$$(2 \sin x + 1)^2 = 0$$
$$\sin x = -\frac{1}{2}$$

Note: With a graphing calculator, sketch the graphs of $y = \sqrt{3} \cos x - \sin x$ and $y = 2$ to see where they intersect.

EXAMPLE 14: For what values of *x* between 0 and 2π is sin *x* < cos *x*?

Sketch the graphs of *y* = sin *x* and *y* = cos *x* on the same set of axes between 0 and 2π. Observe where the graph of *y* = sin *x* is below the graph of *y* = cos *x* (the sections indicated with xxxxx).

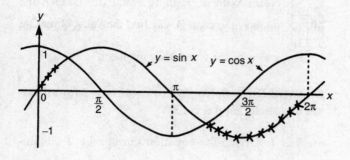

To find the points of intersection of the two graphs solve the equation

$$\sin x = \cos x$$

$$\frac{\sin x}{\cos x} = 1$$

$$\tan x = 1$$

$$x = \frac{\pi}{4} \text{ and } \frac{5\pi}{4}$$

Therefore, the set of *x* values that solve the inequality is

$$0 < x < \frac{\pi}{4} \text{ or } \frac{5\pi}{4} < x < 2\pi.$$

 Note: With a graphing calculator, sketch the graphs of *y* = sin *x* and *y* = cos *x* to see where the graph of sin *x* is below the graph of cos *x*. Then use the Trace and Zoom functions to see approximately where the graphs intersect.

EXERCISES

Note: Each of the following problems can, and probably should, be done without a calculator. A graphing calculator will quickly give the graphs of the functions mentioned in the exercises, but at the cost of the extra time required to use the Trace and Zoom functions to find the needed information.

1. Solve cos 2*x* + cos *x* + 1 = 0 when 0 ≤ *x* < 2π. The solutions set is

(A) $\left\{\dfrac{\pi}{3}, \dfrac{\pi}{2}, \dfrac{3\pi}{2}, \dfrac{5\pi}{3}\right\}$

(B) $\left\{\dfrac{2\pi}{3}, \dfrac{4\pi}{3}\right\}$

(C) $\left\{\dfrac{\pi}{2}, \dfrac{3\pi}{2}\right\}$

(D) $\left\{\dfrac{\pi}{2}, \dfrac{2\pi}{3}, \dfrac{4\pi}{3}, \dfrac{3\pi}{2}\right\}$

(E) $\left\{\dfrac{\pi}{3}, \dfrac{5\pi}{3}\right\}$

2. Which of the following is the solution set of $\sin\theta \cdot \cos\theta = \dfrac{1}{4}$ when 0° ≤ θ < 360°?

(A) {30°, 150°}
(B) {30°, 150°, 210°, 330°}
(C) {15°, 75°}
(D) {15°, 75°, 195°, 225°}
(E) {60°, 300°}

3. How many positive values of *x* ≤ 2π make tan 4*x* = $\sqrt{3}$?

(A) 0
(B) 1
(C) 2
(D) 4
(E) 8

4. If $\cos\theta = \dfrac{3}{5}$, tan 2θ equals

(A) $\dfrac{24}{7}$

(B) $-\dfrac{24}{7}$

(C) $\dfrac{24}{5}$

(D) $-\dfrac{24}{5}$

(E) $\pm\dfrac{24}{7}$

5. Solve the equation $\cos 2\theta = -\sin \theta$ for all positive values of $\theta < 2\pi$. Here, θ equals

(A) $\dfrac{\pi}{2}, \dfrac{7\pi}{6}, \dfrac{11\pi}{6}$

(B) $\dfrac{\pi}{2}, \dfrac{7\pi}{6}, \dfrac{3\pi}{2}, \dfrac{11\pi}{6}$

(C) $\dfrac{\pi}{6}, \dfrac{\pi}{2}, \dfrac{5\pi}{6}$

(D) $\dfrac{\pi}{6}, \dfrac{\pi}{2}, \dfrac{5\pi}{6}, \dfrac{3\pi}{2}$

(E) $\dfrac{\pi}{2}$

6. If $\sin 37° = z$, then $\sin 74°$ equals

(A) $2z\sqrt{1 - z^2}$

(B) $2z^2 + 1$

(C) $2z$

(D) $2z^2 - 1$

(E) $\dfrac{z}{\sqrt{1 - z^2}}$

7. $\mathrm{Cot}(A + B)$ equals

(A) $\dfrac{\cot A \cdot \cos B + 1}{\cot A - \cot B}$

(B) $\dfrac{\cot A \cdot \cot B - 1}{\cot A + \cot B}$

(C) $\dfrac{\tan A - \tan B}{1 - \tan A \cdot \tan B}$

(D) $\dfrac{1 + \tan A \cdot \tan B}{\tan A - \tan B}$

(E) $\dfrac{\cot A \cdot \cot B + 1}{\cot B - \cot A}$

8. $\dfrac{\tan 140° + \tan 70°}{1 - \tan 140° \cdot \tan 70°}$ equals

(A) $-\sqrt{3}$

(B) $\dfrac{\sqrt{3}}{3}$

(C) $\dfrac{\sqrt{3}}{1 - \sqrt{3}}$

(D) $\sqrt{3}$

(E) $\dfrac{3 - \sqrt{3}}{3}$

9. Which of the following is equal to $\cos^4 40° - \sin^4 40°$?

(A) $\cos 80°$

(B) $\sin 80°$

(C) 0

(D) 1

(E) none of the above

10. If $\sin A = \dfrac{2}{3}$ and $\cos A < 0$, find the value of $\tan 2A$.

(A) $\dfrac{4\sqrt{5}}{5}$

(B) $-4\sqrt{5}$

(C) $-\dfrac{4\sqrt{5}}{9}$

(D) $\dfrac{4\sqrt{5}}{9}$

(E) $4\sqrt{5}$

11. What values of x satisfy the inequality $\sin 2x < \sin x$ so that $0 \le x \le 2\pi$?

(A) $\dfrac{\pi}{3} < x < \dfrac{5\pi}{3}$

(B) $0 < x < \dfrac{\pi}{3}$ or $\dfrac{5\pi}{3} < x < 2\pi$

(C) $\dfrac{2\pi}{3} < x < 2\pi$

(D) $\dfrac{\pi}{3} < x < \pi$ or $\dfrac{5\pi}{3} < x < 2\pi$

(E) $0 < x < \dfrac{\pi}{3}$ or $\pi < x < \dfrac{5\pi}{3}$

3.6 INVERSE FUNCTIONS

If the graph of any trigonometric function $f(x)$ is reflected about the line $y = x$ (see Section 1.3), the graph of the inverse of that trigonometric function, $f^{-1}(x)$, results. In every case the resulting graph is *not* the graph of a function. To obtain a function, the range of the inverse relation must be severely limited. The particular range of each inverse trigonometric function is accepted by convention. The ranges of the inverse functions are as follows:

$-\dfrac{\pi}{2} \le \mathrm{Sin}^{-1}x$ or $\mathrm{Arcsin}\, x \le \dfrac{\pi}{2}$

$0 \le \mathrm{Cos}^{-1}x$ or $\mathrm{Arccos}\, x \le \pi$

$-\dfrac{\pi}{2} < \mathrm{Tan}^{-1}x$ or $\mathrm{Arctan}\, x < \dfrac{\pi}{2}$

$0 < \mathrm{Cot}^{-1}x$ or $\mathrm{Arccot}\, x < \pi$

$0 \le \mathrm{Sec}^{-1}x$ or $\mathrm{Arcsec}\, x \le \pi$ and $\mathrm{Sec}^{-1}x \ne \dfrac{\pi}{2}$

$-\dfrac{\pi}{2} \le \mathrm{Csc}^{-1}x$ or $\mathrm{Arccsc}\, x \le \dfrac{\pi}{2}$ and $\mathrm{Csc}^{-1}x \ne 0$

The last three inverse functions are rarely used. The inverse trigonometric functions are used to represent angles that cannot be expressed in any other way without the help of tables or a calculator. It is important to understand that each inverse trigonometric function represents an angle.

Note: To use your calculator to find $\mathrm{Arccot}\, x$, use $\mathrm{Tan}^{-1}\dfrac{1}{x}$. To find $\mathrm{Arcsec}\, x$, use $\mathrm{Cos}^{-1}\dfrac{1}{x}$. To find $\mathrm{Arccsc}\, x$, use $\sin\dfrac{1}{x}$.

EXAMPLE 1: Express each of the following in simpler form:

(A) $\mathrm{Sin}^{-1}\dfrac{\sqrt{3}}{2}$

(B) $\mathrm{Arccos}\left(-\dfrac{\sqrt{2}}{2}\right)$

(C) $\mathrm{Arctan}(-1)$

(D) $\mathrm{Arccot}\sqrt{3}$

(E) $\mathrm{Sec}^{-1}\sqrt{2}$

(F) $\mathrm{Csc}^{-1}(-2)$

Referring to the ranges of the inverse trigonometric functions:

(A) $\mathrm{Sin}^{-1}\dfrac{\sqrt{3}}{2} = \theta$. Find the principal value of θ (the angle that is in the range of $\mathrm{Sin}^{-1}\, x$) such that $\sin\theta = \dfrac{\sqrt{3}}{2}$. Since $\sin\theta > 0$, θ must be in quadrant I, $\theta = \dfrac{\pi}{3}$.

(B) $\mathrm{Arccos}\left(-\dfrac{\sqrt{2}}{2}\right) = \theta$. Find the principal value of θ such that $\cos\theta = -\dfrac{\sqrt{2}}{2}$. Since $\cos\theta < 0$, θ must be in quadrant II, $\theta = \dfrac{3\pi}{4}$.

(C) $\mathrm{Arctan}(-1) = \theta$. Find the principal value of θ such that $\tan\theta = -1$. Since $\tan\theta < 0$, θ must be in quadrant IV and $-\dfrac{\pi}{2} < \mathrm{Arctan}\, x < \dfrac{\pi}{2}$; $\theta = -\dfrac{\pi}{4}$.

(D) $\mathrm{Arccot}\sqrt{3} = \theta$. Find the principal value of θ such that $\cot\theta = \sqrt{3}$. Since $\cot\theta > 0$, θ must be in quadrant I; $\theta = \dfrac{\pi}{6}$.

(E) $\mathrm{Sec}^{-1}\sqrt{2} = \theta$. Find the principal value of θ such that $\sec\theta = \sqrt{2}$. Since $\sec\theta > 0$, θ must be in quadrant I; $\theta = \dfrac{\pi}{4}$.

(F) $\mathrm{Csc}^{-1}(-2) = \theta$. Find the principal value of θ such that $\csc\theta = -2$. Since $\csc\theta < 0$, θ must be in quadrant IV and $-\dfrac{\pi}{2} \le \mathrm{Csc}^{-1}x \le \dfrac{\pi}{2}$; $\theta = -\dfrac{\pi}{6}$.

Note: Examples 2–4 can be evaluated directly using a calculator.

EXAMPLE 2: Evaluate $\sin\left(\mathrm{Arccos}\dfrac{3}{5}\right)$.

Let $\mathrm{Arccos}\dfrac{3}{5} = \theta$. The problem now becomes "Evaluate $\sin\theta$ when $\cos\theta = \dfrac{3}{5}$ and θ is in quadrant I." From the basic definitions of the trigonometric functions and the Pythagorean theorem, $\sin\theta = \dfrac{4}{5}$.

Therefore, $\sin\left(\mathrm{Arccos}\dfrac{3}{5}\right) = \dfrac{4}{5}$.

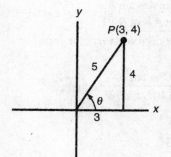

EXAMPLE 3: Evaluate

$$\cos\left[\mathrm{Arcsin}\left(-\dfrac{3}{5}\right) + \mathrm{Arccos}\dfrac{5}{13}\right].$$

Let $\mathrm{Arcsin}\left(-\dfrac{3}{5}\right) = \alpha$ and $\mathrm{Arccos}\dfrac{5}{13} = \beta$. The problem now becomes "Evaluate $\cos(\alpha + \beta)$ when $\sin\alpha = -\dfrac{3}{5}$ and

α is in quadrant IV, and $\cos\beta = \dfrac{5}{13}$ and β is in quadrant I." From the basic definitions of sine and cosine and the Pythagorean theorem, $\cos\alpha = \dfrac{4}{5}$ and $\sin\beta = \dfrac{12}{13}$.

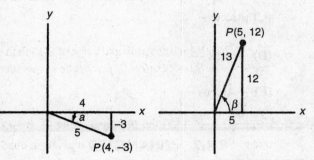

From Formula 6,

$$\cos(\alpha+\beta) = \cos\alpha \cdot \cos\beta - \sin\alpha \cdot \sin\beta$$
$$= \frac{4}{5} \cdot \frac{5}{13} - \left(-\frac{3}{5}\right) \cdot \frac{12}{13}$$
$$= \frac{20}{65} + \frac{36}{65} = \frac{56}{65}$$

Therefore, $\cos\left[\text{Arcsin}\left(-\dfrac{3}{5}\right) + \text{Arccos}\dfrac{5}{13}\right] = \dfrac{56}{65}$.

EXAMPLE 4: Evaluate $\sin\left[2\,\text{Arctan}\left(-\dfrac{8}{15}\right)\right]$.

Let $\theta = \text{Arctan}\left(-\dfrac{8}{15}\right)$. The problem now becomes "Evaluate $\sin 2\theta$ when $\tan\theta = -\dfrac{8}{15}$ and θ is in quadrant IV." From the basic definitions of the trigonometric functions and the Pythagorean theorem, $\sin\theta = -\dfrac{8}{17}$ and $\cos\theta = \dfrac{15}{17}$.

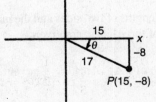

From Formula 10,

$$\sin 2\theta = 2\sin\theta \cdot \cos\theta = 2\left(-\frac{8}{17}\right) \cdot \left(\frac{15}{17}\right) = -\frac{240}{289}.$$

Therefore, $\sin\left[2\,\text{Arctan}\left(-\dfrac{8}{15}\right)\right] = \dfrac{240}{289}$.

EXAMPLE 5: Solve $3\sin^2\theta + 10\sin\theta - 8 = 0$ for all values of θ such that $0 \le \theta < 2\pi$.

The equation $3\sin^2\theta + 10\sin\theta - 8 = 0$ factors into $(3\sin\theta - 2)(\sin\theta + 4) = 0$, which leads to $3\sin\theta - 2 = 0$ or $\sin\theta + 4 = 0$. Thus, $\sin\theta = \dfrac{2}{3}$ or $\sin\theta = -4$. Since -4 is not in the range of the sine function, the second factor gives no solutions. $\sin\theta = \dfrac{2}{3}$ implies that $\theta = \text{Sin}^{-1}\left(\dfrac{2}{3}\right) \approx 41.81°$. Since $\sin\theta > 0$, it is necessary to find angles in quadrants I and II. In quadrant I, $\theta \approx 41.81°$. The quadrant II angle that has the same reference angles as $41.81°$ is $180° - 41.81° \approx 138.19°$. Therefore, the solution set $= \{41.81°, 138.19°\}$.

EXERCISES

1. Solve for x: $\text{Arccos}(2x^2 - 2x) = \dfrac{2\pi}{3}$.

   (A) $\pm\dfrac{1}{2}$

   (B) $\dfrac{1}{2}$

   (C) $-\dfrac{1}{2}$

   (D) $\dfrac{\pi}{3}$

   (E) 0

2. $\text{Arcsin}\left(\sin\dfrac{7\pi}{6}\right) =$

   (A) $-\dfrac{1}{2}$

   (B) $\dfrac{\pi}{6}$

   (C) $\dfrac{7\pi}{6}$

   (D) $-\dfrac{\pi}{6}$

   (E) $\dfrac{1}{2}$

3. Which of the following is (are) true?
   I. $\text{Arcsin}\,1 + \text{Arcsin}(-1) = 0$
   II. $\text{Cos}^{-1}(1) + \text{Cos}^{-1}(-1) = 0$
   III. $\text{Arccos}\,x = \text{Arccos}(-x)$ for all values of x in the domain of Arccos.

   (A) only I
   (B) only II
   (C) only III
   (D) only I and II
   (E) only II and III

4. Express in terms of an inverse trigonometric function the angle that a diagonal of a cube makes with the base of the cube.

(A) $\text{Arcsin} \dfrac{\sqrt{2}}{2}$

(B) $\text{Arcsin} \dfrac{\sqrt{3}}{3}$

(C) $\text{Arccos} \dfrac{\sqrt{6}}{2}$

(D) $\text{Arccos} \dfrac{\sqrt{3}}{3}$

(E) $\text{Arctan} \sqrt{2}$

5. $\text{Tan}\left[\text{Arcsin}\left(-\dfrac{3}{5} \right) \right]$ equals

(A) $\dfrac{3}{4}$

(B) $-\dfrac{3}{4}$

(C) $\dfrac{4}{3}$

(D) $-\dfrac{4}{3}$

(E) $-\dfrac{4}{5}$

6. When only principal values are used, $\text{Arcsin}\left(-\dfrac{5}{13} \right) + \text{Arccos}\left(-\dfrac{3}{5} \right)$ represents an angle lying in which quadrant?

(A) I
(B) II
(C) III
(D) IV
(E) I or II

7. Which of the following is not defined?

(A) $\text{Arcsin} \dfrac{1}{9}$

(B) $\text{Arccos}\left(-\dfrac{4}{3} \right)$

(C) $\text{Arctan} \dfrac{11}{12}$

(D) $\text{Arccot}(-4)$

(E) $\text{Arcsec } 3\pi$

8. Which of the following is a solution of $\cos 3x = \dfrac{1}{2}$?

(A) $60°$

(B) $\dfrac{5\pi}{3}$

(C) $\text{Arccos} \dfrac{1}{6}$

(D) $\text{Arccos} \dfrac{\sqrt{3}}{2}$

(E) $\dfrac{1}{3} \text{Arccos} \dfrac{1}{2}$

3.7   TRIANGLES

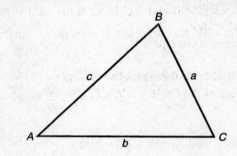

The final topic in trigonometry concerns the relationship between the angles and sides of a triangle that is *not* a right triangle. Depending on which of the sides and angles of the triangle are supplied, the following formulas are helpful. In $\triangle ABC$

Law of sines : $\dfrac{\sin A}{a} = \dfrac{\sin B}{b} = \dfrac{\sin C}{c}$

used when the lengths of two sides and the value of the angle opposite one, or two angles and the length of one side are given.

Law of cosines :
$$a^2 = b^2 + c^2 - 2bc \cdot \cos A$$
$$b^2 = a^2 + c^2 - 2ac \cdot \cos B$$
$$c^2 = a^2 + b^2 - 2ab \cdot \cos C$$

used when the lengths of two sides and the included angle, or the lengths of three sides, are given.

Area of a $\triangle$:
$$\text{Area} = \dfrac{1}{2} bc \cdot \sin A$$
$$\text{Area} = \dfrac{1}{2} ac \cdot \sin B$$
$$\text{Area} = \dfrac{1}{2} ab \cdot \sin C$$

used when two sides and the included angle are given.

EXAMPLE 1: Find the number of degrees in the largest angle of a triangle whose sides are 3, 5, and 7.

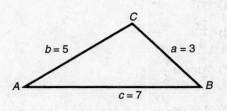

The largest angle is opposite the longest side. Use the law of cosines:

$$c^2 = a^2 + b^2 - 2ab \cdot \cos C$$
$$49 = 9 + 25 - 30 \cdot \cos C$$

Therefore, $\cos C = -\dfrac{15}{30} = -\dfrac{1}{2}$.

Since $\cos C < 0$ and $\angle C$ is an angle of a triangle, $90° < \angle C < 180°$.

Therefore, $\angle C = 120°$.

EXAMPLE 2: Find the number of degrees in the other two angles of $\triangle ABC$ if $c = 75\sqrt{2}$, $b = 150$, and $\angle C = 30°$.

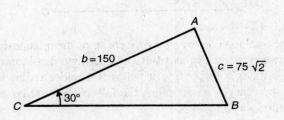

Use the law of sines:

$$\frac{75\sqrt{2}}{\sin 30°} = \frac{150}{\sin B}$$

$$75\sqrt{2} \cdot \sin B = 150 \cdot \sin 30°$$

$$\sin B = \frac{150 \cdot \dfrac{1}{2}}{75\sqrt{2}} = \frac{75}{75\sqrt{2}} = \frac{1}{\sqrt{2}} = \frac{\sqrt{2}}{2}$$

Therefore, $\angle B = 45°$ or $135°$; $\angle A = 105°$ or $15°$ since there are $180°$ in the sum of the three angles of a triangle.

EXAMPLE 3: Find the area of $\triangle ABC$ if $a = 180$ inches, $b = 150$ inches, and $\angle C = 30°$.

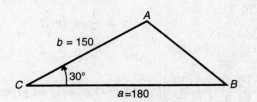

$$\text{Area} = \frac{1}{2} ab \cdot \sin C$$
$$= \frac{1}{2} \cdot 180 \cdot 150 \cdot \sin 30°$$
$$= \frac{1}{2} \cdot 180 \cdot 150 \cdot \frac{1}{2}$$
$$= 90 \cdot 75 = 675 \text{ square inches.}$$

If the length of two sides of a triangle and the angle opposite one of those sides are given, it is possible that two triangles, one triangle, or no triangle can be constructed with the data. This is called the *ambiguous* case. If the length of sides a and b and the value of $\angle A$ are given, the length of side b determines the number of triangles that can be constructed.

Case 1: If $\angle A > 90°$ and $a \leq b$, no triangle can be formed because side a would not reach the base line. If $a > b$, one obtuse triangle can be drawn.

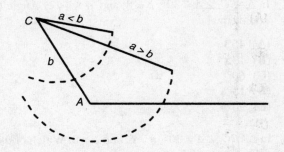

Let the length of the altitude from C to the base line be h. From the basic definition of sine, $\sin A = \dfrac{h}{b}$, and thus, $h = b \cdot \sin A$.

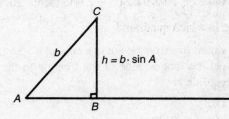

Case 2: If $\angle A < 90°$ and side $a < b \cdot \sin A$, no triangle can be formed. If $a = b \cdot \sin A$, one triangle can be formed. If $a > b$, there also will be only one triangle. If, on the other hand, $b \cdot \sin A < a < b$, two triangles can be formed.

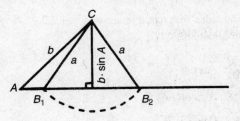

If a compass is opened the length of side a and a circle is drawn with center at C, the circle will cut the baseline at two points, B_1 and B_2. Thus, $\triangle AB_1C$ satisfies the conditions of the problem, as does $\triangle AB_2C$.

EXAMPLE 1: How many triangles can be formed if $a = 24$, $b = 31$, and $\angle A = 30°$?

Because $\angle A < 90°$, $b \cdot \sin A = 31 \cdot \sin 30° = 31 \cdot \dfrac{1}{2} = 15\dfrac{1}{2}$. Since $b \cdot \sin A < a < b$, there are two triangles.

EXAMPLE 2: How many triangles can be formed if $a = 24$, $b = 32$, and $\angle A = 150°$?

Since $\angle A > 90°$ and $a < b$, no triangle can be formed.

EXERCISES

1. In $\triangle ABC$, $\angle A = 30°$, $b = 8$, and $a = 4\sqrt{2}$. Angle C could equal

   (A) 45°
   (B) 135°
   (C) 60°
   (D) 15°
   (E) 90°

2. In $\triangle ABC$, $\angle A = 30°$, $a = 6$, and $c = 8$. Which of the following must be true?

   (A) $0° < \angle C < 90°$
   (B) $90° < \angle C < 180°$
   (C) $45° < \angle C < 135°$
   (D) $0° < \angle C < 45°$ or $90° < \angle C < 135°$
   (E) $0° < \angle C < 45°$ or $130° < \angle C < 180°$

3. The angles of a triangle are in a ratio of $8 : 3 : 1$. The ratio of the longest side of the triangle to the next longest side is

   (A) $\sqrt{6} : 2$
   (B) $8 : 3$
   (C) $\sqrt{3} : 1$
   (D) $8 : 5$
   (E) $2\sqrt{2} : \sqrt{3}$

4. The sides of a triangle are in a ratio of $4 : 5 : 6$. The smallest angle is

   (A) 82°
   (B) 69°
   (C) 56°
   (D) 41°
   (E) 27°

5. Find the length of the longer diagonal of a parallelogram if the sides are 6 inches and 8 inches and the smaller angle is 60°.

   (A) 8
   (B) 11
   (C) 12
   (D) 7
   (E) 17

6. What are all values of side a in the figure below such that two triangles can be constructed?

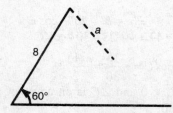

   (A) $a > 4\sqrt{3}$
   (B) $a > 8$
   (C) $a = 4\sqrt{3}$
   (D) $4\sqrt{3} < a < 8$
   (E) $8 < a < 8\sqrt{3}$

7. In $\triangle ABC$, $\angle B = 30°$, $\angle C = 105°$, and $b = 10$. The length of side a equals

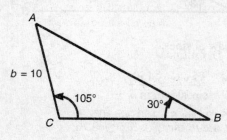

   (A) 7
   (B) 17
   (C) 9
   (D) 10
   (E) 14

8. The area of $\triangle ABC$, $= 24\sqrt{3}$, side $a = 6$, and side $b = 16$. The value of $\angle C$ is

   (A) 30°
   (B) 30° or 150°
   (C) 60°
   (D) 60° or 120°
   (E) none of the above

9. The area of $\triangle ABC = 12\sqrt{3}$, side $a = 6$, and side $b = 8$. Side $c =$

(A) $2\sqrt{37}$

(B) $2\sqrt{13}$

(C) $2\sqrt{37}$ or $2\sqrt{13}$

(D) 10

(E) 10 or 12

10. Given the following data, which can form two triangles?

   I. $\angle C = 30°$, $c = 8$, $b = 12$

  II. $\angle B = 45°$, $a = 12\sqrt{2}$, $b = 15\sqrt{2}$

 III. $\angle C = 60°$, $b = 12$, $c = 5\sqrt{3}$

(A) only I

(B) only II

(C) only III

(D) only I and II

(E) only I and III

ANSWERS AND EXPLANATIONS

In these solutions the following notation is used:

  a: active — Calculator use is necessary or, at a minimum, extremely helpful.

  n: neutral — Answers may be found without a calculator, but a calculator may help.

  i: inactive — Calculator use is not helpful and may even be a hindrance.

Part 3.1 Definitions

1. n **A** Reference angle is 40°. Cosine in quadrant IV is positive.

 Calculator: Cos 320° ≈ 0.766. Check each of the answer choices to see that cos 40° ≈ 0.766.

2. i **B** See corresponding figure. Therefore, sin $\theta = \dfrac{12}{13}$.

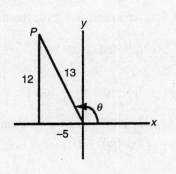

3. i **D** Angle θ is in quadrant II since sec < 0 and sin > 0. Therefore, $\tan \theta = \dfrac{3}{-4} = \dfrac{-3}{4}$.

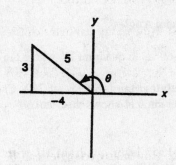

4. i **B** Cofunctions of complementary angles are equal. $x - 30 + x = 90$ finds a reference angle of 60° for x. The angle in quadrant III that has a reference angle of 60° is 240°.

5. i **A** Angle α is in quadrant II, and sin α is positive. Angle β is in quadrant IV, and sin β is negative.

6. a **E** Put your calculator in degree mode, $\cos 310° + \cos 190° \approx 0.643 + (-0.985) \approx -0.342$. Checking the answer choices show that $-\cos 70° \approx -0.342$.

Part 3.2 Arcs and Angles

1. n **C** $\dfrac{30}{\pi} = \dfrac{x}{180°}$. Therefore, $x = \dfrac{5400°}{\pi}$.

Calculator: Put your calculator in radian mode. Input 30 and press the DRG ▶ key to get degree mode that gives 1719° approximately. Answer choice C looks like the only possibility. Verify this by evaluating $\dfrac{5400}{\pi}$ to get 1719° approximately.

2. i **D** $s = r\theta$. $2\pi = r\theta$. $A = \dfrac{1}{2}r^2\theta$.

$6\pi = \dfrac{1}{2}r^2\theta = \dfrac{1}{2}r(r\theta) = \dfrac{1}{2}r(2\pi)$. $r = 6$.

3. a **D** $C = 2\pi r = 16$. $r = \dfrac{8}{\pi} \approx 2.55$.

$A = \dfrac{1}{2}r^2\theta \approx \dfrac{1}{2}(2.55)^2 \cdot 4.7 \approx 15$.

4. a **C** $40° = \dfrac{2\pi^R}{9} \approx 0.7$ radians.

$s = r\theta \approx 1 \cdot 0.7 \approx 0.7$.

5. a B Change 25° to 0.436 radian $\left(0.436 = \dfrac{25}{180}\pi\right)$.

$s = r\theta$, and so $12 = r(0.436)$ and $r = 27.5$ inches

Part 3.3 Special Angles

1. n C –60° is in quadrant IV, where tan < 0.

Calculator: tan (–60°) ≈ –1.732. Checking the answer choices shows that –tan 60° ≈ –1.732.

2. n E –135° is in quadrant III with reference angle 45°. Tan > 0 is in quadrant III. Therefore tan(–135°) = 1. Reference angle for 315° is 45°. Cot < 0 is in quadrant IV. Therefore, cot 315° = –1. 1 + (–1) = 0.

Calculator: $\tan(-135°) + \dfrac{1}{\tan 315°} = 1 + \dfrac{1}{-1} = 0.$

3. n B The terms equal, in order, $-1,\ -\dfrac{1}{2},\ -1,\ 1.$

$-1 - \left(-\dfrac{1}{2}\right) - (-1) + 1 = \dfrac{3}{2}.$

Calculator: Put your calculator in radian mode:

$$\cos \pi - \dfrac{1}{\sin\left(-\dfrac{\pi}{2}\right)} = -1 - \dfrac{1}{-1} = 0.$$

Put your calculator in degree mode:

$$-\sin 570° + \dfrac{1}{\cos 0°} = \dfrac{1}{2} + \dfrac{1}{1} = \dfrac{3}{2}.$$

Therefore, $0 + \dfrac{3}{2}$ gives Choice B.

4. n B The terms equal, in order, $\dfrac{2\sqrt{3}}{3},\ \dfrac{-\sqrt{3}}{1},\ \dfrac{-\sqrt{2}}{2}.$

Calculator : $\dfrac{1}{\cos \dfrac{11\pi}{6}} \cdot \tan \dfrac{2\pi}{3} \cdot \sin \dfrac{7\pi}{4} =$

$\dfrac{1}{0.866} \cdot (-1.732) \cdot (-0.707) \approx 1.414 \approx \sqrt{2}.$

5. n D $\sin 300° = \dfrac{-\sqrt{3}}{2}$. Choices A and B are ruled out because they are positive. Choices C and E are ruled out because they are cosines with the same reference angle (60°) as sin 300°.

Calculator: sin 300° ≈ –0.866. Checking the answer choices shows that sin 240° ≈ –0.866. Therefore, the correct answer is Choice D.

Part 3.4 Graphs

1. n C Period = $\dfrac{2\pi}{2} = \pi$. Point P is $\dfrac{1}{4}$ of the way through the period. Amplitude is 1 because the coefficient of sin is 1. Therefore, point P is at $\left(\dfrac{1}{4}\pi, 1\right)$.

Graphing calculator: Put your calculator in radian mode and plot the graph of $y = \sin 2x$ in an $x \in$ [–2,2], $y \in$ [–2,2] window. Use the Trace and Zoom functions or the Max function to see that the coordinates of point P are approximately (0.78,1), which leads to Choice C.

2. n E Amplitude = $\dfrac{1}{2}$. Period = π. Graph shifted $\dfrac{1}{2}$ unit up. Graph looks like a cosine graph reflected about x-axis and shifted up $\dfrac{1}{2}$ unit.

Graphing calculator: Plot the graph of each of the choices in an $x \in$ [–2π, 2π], $y \in$ [–2,2] window to find that Choice E is the correct answer.

3. n C Graph has amplitude of 4 and period of 4π.

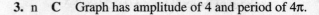
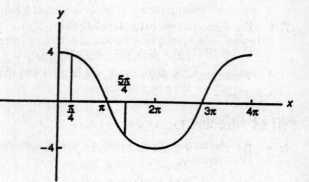

Graphing calculator: Put your calculator in degree mode. Plot the graph of $y = 4\cos\dfrac{1}{2}x$ in an $x \in$ [45°,225°], $y \in$ [–5,5] window $\left(\text{since } \dfrac{\pi}{4} = 45° \text{ and } \dfrac{5\pi}{4} = 225°\right)$ in order to see that the graph decreases throughout the domain.

4. n C Multiply and divide by 2.

$$f(x) = 2\left(\dfrac{\sqrt{3}}{2}\cos x + \dfrac{1}{2}\sin x\right)$$
$$= 2(\sin 60° \cos x + \cos 60° \sin x)$$
$$= 2\sin(60° + x).$$

Therefore, the amplitude is 2 because the coefficient is 2.

 Graphing calculator: Plot the graph of $y = \sqrt{3} \cos x + \sin x$ in an $x \in [-360°,360°]$, $y \in [-2,2]$ window. Use the Trace and Zoom functions or the Max and Min functions to see that the maximum point is approximately 2 and the minimum point is approximately -2. Therefore, the amplitude is $\frac{2-(-2)}{2} = 2$.

5. i C Period $= \frac{2\pi}{P} = \frac{2\pi}{3}$.

6. n D Period $= 6\pi$. Curve reaches its maximum when $x = \frac{6\pi}{4}$, which is not in the allowable set of x values. Therefore, maximum is reached when $x = \frac{\pi}{2}$. Maximum $= \sin\frac{1}{3} \cdot \frac{\pi}{2} = \frac{1}{2}$.

 Graphing calculator: Plot the graph of $y = \sin\frac{x}{3}$ in an $x \in [0°,90°]$, $y \in [-2,2]$ window. Use the Trace and Zoom functions to see that the maximum value is approximately 0.5 at the right-hand end of the interval.

7. i D Period $= \frac{2\pi}{M} = 4\pi$ (from the figure). $M = \frac{1}{2}$. Phase shift for a sine curve in the figure is $-\pi$. Therefore, $\frac{1}{2}x + N = 0$ when $x = -\pi$. Therefore, $N = \frac{\pi}{2}$.

Part 3.5 Identities, Equations, and Inequalities

1. n D $\cos 2x = 2\cos^2 x - 1$. The equation becomes
$$2\cos^2 x + \cos x = 0.$$
$$(2\cos x + 1)\cos x = 0.$$

 Graphing calculator: Put your calculator in radian mode and plot the graph of $y = \cos 2x + \cos x + 1$ in an $x \in [0,2\pi]$, $y \in [-2,2]$ window to see that it crosses the x-axis at 4 points. Use the Trace and Zoom functions or the Root, Zero, or Solve function to see that Choice D is the correct answer.

2. n D $2\sin\theta \cdot \cos\theta = \frac{1}{2}$ becomes $\sin 2\theta = \frac{1}{2}$. $2\theta = 30°, 150°, 390°, 510°$. $\theta = 15°, 75°, 195°, 225°$.

Graphing calculator: Put your calculator in degree mode and plot the graphs of $y = \sin x \cdot \cos x$ and $y = 0.25$ in an $x \in [0°,360°]$, $y \in [-2,2]$ window. The graphs intersect at 4 points. Use the Trace and Zoom functions or the Intersect function to see that Choice D is the correct answer.

3. n E $4x = 60°, 240°, 420°, 600°, 780°, 960°, 1140°, 1320°. x = 15°, 60°, 105°, 150°, 195°, 240°, 285°, 330°$.

 Graphing calculator: Put your calculator in degree mode and plot the graphs of $y = \sin 4x$ and $y = \sqrt{3}$ in an $x \in [0°,360°]$, $y \in [-3,3]$ window. The graphs intersect in 8 points.

Note: If your calculator appears to put in the asymptotes that occur at odd multiples of $22\frac{1}{2}^°$, don't count their intersections with $y = \sqrt{3}$ as solutions.

4. n E $\text{Tan } 2\theta = \frac{2\tan\theta}{1-\tan^2\theta} = \frac{2\left(\frac{4}{3}\right)}{1-\left(\frac{16}{9}\right)}$. Since θ can be in quadrant I or IV, $\tan 2\theta = \pm\frac{24}{7}$.

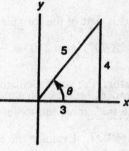

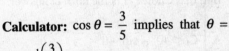 **Calculator:** $\cos\theta = \frac{3}{5}$ implies that $\theta = \text{Cos}^{-1}\left(\frac{3}{5}\right) \approx 53.13°$. Since $\cos\theta$ is also positive in quadrant IV, θ could also $\approx 306.87°$. Therefore, $\tan 2(53.13°) \approx -3.429$. $\text{Tan } 2(306.87) \approx 3.429$. The only possible answer choice given is $\pm\frac{24}{7}$. Verify that it is approximately equal to ± 3.429.

5. n A $1 - 2\sin^2\theta = -\sin\theta$. $2\sin^2\theta - \sin\theta - 1 = 0$. $(2\sin\theta + 1)(\sin\theta - 1) = 0$. $\sin\theta = -\frac{1}{2}$ or $\sin\theta = 1$.

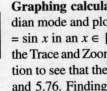 **Graphing calculator:** Put your calculator in radian mode and plot the graphs of $y = \cos 2x$ and $y = \sin x$ in an $x \in [0,2\pi]$, $y \in [-2,2]$ window. Use the Trace and Zoom functions or the Intersect function to see that they intersect when $x \approx 1.57, 3.67$, and 5.76. Finding approximate values of the answer choices indicates that Choice A is the correct answer.

6. i **A** Since $\sin 74° = \sin 2(37°)$, Formula 10 can be used: $\sin 2A = 2 \sin A \cdot \cos A$. $\sin 74° = 2 \sin 37° \cdot \cos 37°$. From the figure, $\cos 37° = \sqrt{1 - z^2}$. Therefore, $\sin 74° = 2z\sqrt{1 - z^2}$.

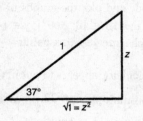

7. i **B** $\cot(A + B) = \dfrac{1}{\tan(A + B)}$

$$= \dfrac{1 - \tan A \cdot \tan B}{\tan A + \tan B}$$

$$= \dfrac{1 - \dfrac{1}{\cot A \cdot \cot B}}{\dfrac{1}{\cot A} + \dfrac{1}{\cot B}}$$

8. n **B** This is part of the formula for $\tan(A + B) = \tan(140° + 70°) = \tan 210° = \dfrac{\sqrt{3}}{3}$.

Calculator: Put your calculator in degree mode. Evaluate the expression to get $\dfrac{-0.839 + 2.75}{1 - (-2.31)} \approx \dfrac{1.91}{3.31} \approx +0.577$. Evaluate the answer choices to find that Choice B is the correct answer.

9. n **A** $\cos^4 40° - \sin^4 40°$
$= (\cos^2 40° + \sin^2 40°)(\cos^2 40° - \sin^2 40°)$
$= 1[\cos 2(40°)] = \cos 80°$.

Calculator: $\cos^4 40° - \sin^4 40° \approx 0.344^4 - 0.177^4 \approx 0.174$. Evaluate the answer choices to find that Choice A is the correct answer.

10. n **B** A is in quadrant II.

$$\tan 2A = \dfrac{2 \tan A}{1 - \tan^2 A} = \dfrac{2\left(-\dfrac{2}{\sqrt{5}}\right)}{1 - \dfrac{4}{5}} = -4\sqrt{5}.$$

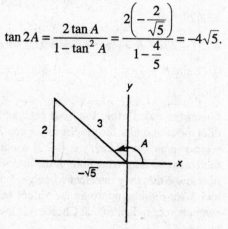

Calculator: $\sin A = \dfrac{2}{3}$ implies that $A = \sin^{-1}\left(\dfrac{2}{3}\right) \approx 41.81°$. Since $\cos A$ is negative, $\angle A$ is in quadrant II. Thus, A must be approximately $138.2°$. Therefore, $\tan 2A \approx -8.9$. Evaluate the answer choices to find that Choice B is the correct answer.

11. n **D** To find the answer to $\sin 2x < \sin x$, solve the associated equation, $\sin 2x = \sin x$. $\sin 2x - \sin x = 2\sin x \cdot \cos x - \sin x = \sin x(2\cos x - 1) = 0$. $\sin x = 0$ or $\cos x = \dfrac{1}{2}$. So $x = 0, \dfrac{\pi}{3}, \pi, \dfrac{5\pi}{3}, 2\pi$. The only regions where inequality is satisfied are $\dfrac{\pi}{3} < x < \pi$ or $\dfrac{5\pi}{3} < x < 2\pi$.

Graphing calculator: Put your calculator in radian mode. Plot the graphs of $y = \sin 2x$ and $y = \sin x$ in an $x \in [0, 2\pi]$, $y \in [-2, 2]$ window to see that there are two regions where the graph of $y = \sin 2x$ is below the graph of $y = \sin x$. Use the Trace and Zoom functions to see that Choice D is the correct answer.

Part 3.6 Inverse Functions

1. i **B** $2x^2 - 2x = \cos \dfrac{2\pi}{3} = -\dfrac{1}{2}$. $4x^2 - 4x + 1 = 0$. $(2x - 1)^2 = 0$. Therefore, $x = \dfrac{1}{2}$.

2. n **D** $\sin \dfrac{7\pi}{6} = -\dfrac{1}{2}$. $\arcsin\left(-\dfrac{1}{2}\right)$ is an angle in quadrant IV.

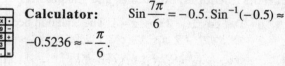

Calculator: $\sin \dfrac{7\pi}{6} = -0.5$. $\sin^{-1}(-0.5) \approx -0.5236 \approx -\dfrac{\pi}{6}$.

Note: The answer is not the "obvious" choice, $\dfrac{7\pi}{6}$, because $-\dfrac{\pi}{2} \leq \sin^{-1} x \leq \dfrac{\pi}{2}$.

3. n **A** $\arcsin 1 = \dfrac{\pi}{2}$ and $\arcsin(-1) = -\dfrac{\pi}{2}$; I is true. $\arccos 1 = 0$ and $\arccos(-1) = \pi$; II is false. Since Arccos is defined in quadrants I and II, III is false.

Calculator: $\sin^{-1} 1 + \sin^{-1}(-1) \approx 1.57 + (-1.57) = 0$. Thus, I is true. $\cos^{-1} 1 + \cos^{-1}(-1) = 0 + \pi \neq 0$. Thus, II is false. Choose any value for x, say 0.5. $\cos^{-1} 0.5 \approx 1.05$. $\cos^{-1}(-0.5) \approx 2.09$. Therefore, III is false since there is at least one value of x for which $\cos^{-1} x \neq \cos^{-1} -x$. Therefore, Choice A is the correct answer.

4. i **B** If the side of a cube is 1, its diagonal $= \sqrt{3}$ and the diagonal of the base is $\sqrt{2}$. Therefore, $\theta = \text{Arcsin} \dfrac{\sqrt{3}}{3}$.

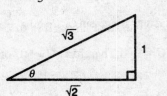

5. n **B** Let $\theta = \text{Arcsin}\left(-\dfrac{3}{5}\right)$. $\sin \theta = -\dfrac{3}{5}$. Therefore, $\tan \theta = -\dfrac{3}{4}$.

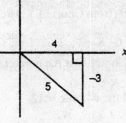

 Calculator: $\text{Sin}^{-1}\left(-\dfrac{3}{5}\right) \approx -36.87°$. Therefore, $\tan(-36.87°) = -\dfrac{3}{4}$.

6. n **B** Let $A = \text{Arcsin}\left(-\dfrac{5}{13}\right)$ and $B = \text{Arccos}\left(-\dfrac{3}{5}\right)$. Since $-90° \le A \le 0°$ and $90° \le B \le 180°$, $0° \le A + B \le 180°$. Since cosine has different signs in quadrants I and II, evaluate:

$$\cos(A + B) = \dfrac{12}{13} \cdot \dfrac{-3}{5} - \dfrac{-5}{13} \cdot \dfrac{4}{5} = \dfrac{-16}{65} < 0.$$

Therefore, $A + B$ is in quadrant II.

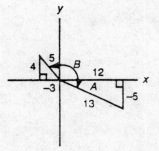

Calculator: $\text{Sin}^{-1}\left(-\dfrac{5}{13}\right) + \text{Cos}^{-1}\left(-\dfrac{3}{5}\right) \approx -22.62°$ $+ 126.87° \approx 104.25°$. Therefore, Choice B is the correct answer.

7. n **B** $-1 \le \cos \theta \le 1$. Thus, Choice B is not defined.

Calculator: Evaluate the answer choices to see that B is undefined.

8. i **E** $3x = \text{Arccos}\left(\dfrac{1}{2}\right)$, and so $x = \dfrac{1}{3} \text{Arccos}\left(\dfrac{1}{2}\right)$.

Part 3.7 Triangles

1. i **D** Law of sines: $\dfrac{\sin B}{8} = \dfrac{\frac{1}{2}}{4\sqrt{2}}$. $\sin B = \dfrac{\sqrt{2}}{2}$. $B = 45°$ or $135°$. Therefore, $C = 105°$ or $15°$.

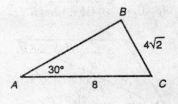

2. n **E** Law of sines: $\dfrac{\sin C}{8} = \dfrac{\frac{1}{2}}{6}$. $\sin C = \dfrac{2}{3} \approx 0.67$.

$\sin 45° = \dfrac{\sqrt{2}}{2} \approx 0.7$. Since sine is an increasing function in quadrant I, $0° \le C \le 45°$. Angles in quadrant II greater than $135°$ use these values of C as reference angles.

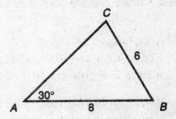

 Calculator: From the law of sines, $\sin C = \dfrac{2}{3}$, which implies that $C = \text{Sin}^{-1}\left(\dfrac{2}{3}\right) \approx 41.8°$ if C is acute, or $180° - 41.8° \approx 138.2°$ if C is obtuse. Therefore, Choice E is the correct answer.

3. n **A** The angles are $15°$, $45°$, and $120°$. Let c be the longest side and b the next longest. $\dfrac{\sin 120°}{c} = \dfrac{\sin 45°}{b}$.

$$\dfrac{c}{b} = \dfrac{\sin 120°}{\sin 45°} = \dfrac{\frac{\sqrt{3}}{2}}{\frac{\sqrt{2}}{2}} = \dfrac{\sqrt{6}}{2}.$$

Calculator: From above $\dfrac{c}{b} = \dfrac{\sin 120°}{\sin 45°} \approx$ $\dfrac{0.866}{0.707} \approx 1.22$. Evaluate the answer choices to see that $\dfrac{\sqrt{6}}{2} \approx 1.22$. Therefore, Choice A is the correct answer.

4. a **D** Use the law of cosines. Let the sides be 4, 5, and 6. $16 = 25 + 36 - 60 \cos A$. $\cos A = \dfrac{45}{60} = \dfrac{3}{4}$, which implies that $A = \cos^{-1}(0.75) \approx 41°$.

5. a **C** Law of cosines: $d^2 = 36 + 64 - 96 \cos 120°$. $d^2 = 148$. Therefore, $d \approx 12$.

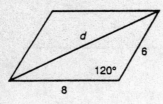

6. i **D** Altitude to base = $8 \sin 60° = 4\sqrt{3}$. Therefore, $4\sqrt{3} < a < 8$.

7. a **E** $A = 45°$. Law of sines: $\dfrac{\sin 45°}{a} = \dfrac{\sin 30°}{10}$. Therefore, $a = 10\sqrt{2} \approx 14$.

8. n **D** Area $= \dfrac{1}{2} ab \sin C$. $24\sqrt{3} = \dfrac{1}{2} \cdot 6 \cdot 16 \sin C$. $\sin C = \dfrac{\sqrt{3}}{2}$. Therefore, $C = 60°$ or $120°$.

9. n **C** Area $= \dfrac{1}{2} ab \sin C$. $12\sqrt{3} = \dfrac{1}{2} \cdot 6 \cdot 8 \sin C$. $\sin C = \dfrac{\sqrt{3}}{2}$. $C = 60°$ or $120°$. Use law of cosines with 60° and then with 120°.

Note: At this point in the solution you know there have to be two values for C. Therefore, the answer must be Choice C or E. If $C = 10$ (from Choice E), ABC is a right triangle with area $= \dfrac{1}{2} \cdot 6 \cdot 8 = 24$. Therefore, Choice E is not the answer, and so Choice C is the correct answer.

10. n **A** In I the altitude $= 12 \cdot \dfrac{1}{2} = 6$, $6 < c < 12$, and so 2 triangles. In II $b > 12\sqrt{2}$, so only 1 triangle. In III the altitude $= 12 \cdot \dfrac{\sqrt{3}}{2} > 5\sqrt{3}$, so no triangle.

MISCELLANEOUS RELATIONS AND FUNCTIONS

CHAPTER

4

4.1 CONIC SECTIONS

The general quadratic equation in two variables has the form $Ax^2 + Bxy + Cy^2 + Dx + Ey + F = 0$, where A, B, and C are not all zero. Depending on the values of the coefficients A, B, and C, the equation represents a circle, a parabola, a hyperbola, an ellipse, or a degenerate case of one of these (e.g., a point, a line, two parallel lines, two intersecting lines, or no graph at all).

If the graph is not a degenerate case, the following indicates which conic section the equation represents:

If $B^2 - 4AC < 0$ and $A = C$, the graph is a circle.
If $B^2 - 4AC < 0$ and $A \neq C$, the graph is an ellipse.
If $B^2 - 4AC = 0$, the graph is a parabola.
If $B^2 - 4AC > 0$, the graph is a hyperbola.

Most of the conic sections encountered on the Level II examination will not have an xy-term (i.e., $B = 0$). This term causes the graph to be rotated so that a major axis of symmetry is not parallel to either the x- or the y-axis. The general quadratic equation in two variables can be changed into a more useful form by completing the square separately on the x's and separately on the y's. After the square has been completed and, for convenience, the letters used as constants have been changed, the equation becomes:

(a) for a circle, $(x - h)^2 + (y - k)^2 = r^2$, where (h,k) are the coordinates of the center and r is the radius of the circle.

(b) for an ellipse, if $C > A$, $\dfrac{(x-h)^2}{a^2} + \dfrac{(y-k)^2}{b^2} = 1$, where (h,k) are the coordinates of the center and the major axis is parallel to the x-axis (Figure a), If $C < A$, $\dfrac{(x-h)^2}{b^2} + \dfrac{(y-k)^2}{a^2} = 1$, where (h,k) are the coordinates of the center and the major axis is parallel to the y-axis (Figure b).

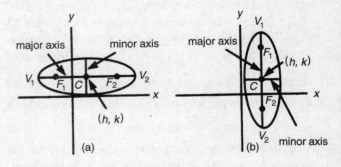

In both cases the length of the *major axis* is $2a$ and the length of the *minor axis* is $2b$.

(c) for a parabola, if $C = 0$, $(x - h)^2 = 4p(y - k)$ (Figure a). If $A = 0$, $(y - k)^2 = 4p(x - h)$ (Figure b). In both cases (h,k) are the coordinates of the vertex and p is the directed distance from the vertex to the focus.

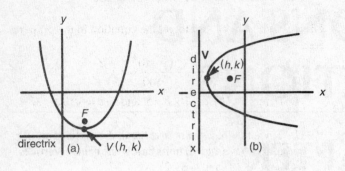

(d) for a hyperbola, $\dfrac{(x-h)^2}{a^2} - \dfrac{(y-k)^2}{b^2} = 1$, where (h,k) are the coordinates of the center, and the graph opens to the side (Figure a). If the graph opens up and down, the equation is $\dfrac{(y-k)^2}{a^2} - \dfrac{(y-h)^2}{b^2} = 1$, where (h,k) are the coordinates of the center (Figure b).

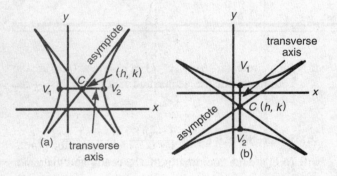

In both cases the length of the *transverse axis* is $2a$, and the length of the *conjugate axis* is $2b$.

An *ellipse* is the set of points in a plane such that the sum of the distances from each point to two fixed points, called *foci,* is a constant equal to $2a$ in the formula on page 71. The distance between the center and a focus is called c and is equal to $\sqrt{a^2 - b^2}$. The *eccentricity* of an ellipse is always less than 1 and is equal to $\dfrac{c}{a}$. The chord through a focus perpendicular to the major axis is called a *latus rectum* and is $\dfrac{2b^2}{a}$ units long.

A *parabola* is the set of points in a plane such that the distance from each point to a fixed point, called the *focus,* is equal to the distance to a fixed line, called the *directrix.* The *eccentricity* is always equal to 1. The chord through the focus perpendicular to the axis of symmetry is called the *latus rectum* and is $4p$ units long.

A *hyperbola* is the set of points in a plane such that the absolute value of the difference of the distances from each point to two fixed points, called *foci,* is a constant equal to $2a$ in the formula previously stated. The distance between the center and a focus is called c and is equal to $\sqrt{a^2 + b^2}$. The *eccentricity* of a hyperbola is always greater than 1 and is equal to $\dfrac{c}{a}$. Every hyperbola has associated with it two lines, called *asymptotes,* that intersect at the center. In general, an asymptote is a line that a curve approaches, but never quite touches, as one or both variables become increasingly larger or smaller. If the hyperbola opens to the side, the slopes of the two asymptotes are $\pm\dfrac{b}{a}$. If the hyperbola opens up and down, the slopes of the two asymptotes are $\pm\dfrac{a}{b}$. The chord through a focus perpendicular to the transverse axis is called a *latus rectum* and is equal to $\dfrac{2b^2}{a}$ units.

The equation $xy = k$, where k is a constant, is the equation of a *rectangular hyperbola* whose asymptotes are the x- and y-axes. If $k > 0$, the branches of the hyperbola lie in quadrants I and III. If $k < 0$, the branches lie in quadrants II and IV.

EXAMPLE 1: Each of the following is an equation of a conic section. State which one and find, if they exist: (I) the coordinates of the center, (II) the coordinates of the vertices, (III) the coordinates of the foci, (IV) the eccentricity, (V) the equations of the asymptotes. Also, sketch the graph.

(A) $9x^2 - 16y^2 - 18x + 96y + 9 = 0$
(B) $4x^2 + 4y^2 - 12x - 20y - 2 = 0$
(C) $4x^2 + y^2 + 24x - 16y = 0$
(D) $y^2 + 6x - 8y + 4 = 0$

In all cases $B = 0$.

(A) $B^2 - 4AC = 0 - 4 \cdot 9 \cdot (-16) > 0$, which means the graph will be a hyperbola. To complete the square, group the x-terms and the y-terms. Factor out of each group the coefficient of the quadratic term:

$$9(x^2 - 2x \quad) - 16(y^2 - 6y \quad) + 9 = 0$$

A perfect trinomial square is obtained within both parentheses by taking one-half of the coefficient of the linear term, squaring it, and adding it to the existing polynomial. A similar amount must be added to the right side of the equation.

$$9(x^2 - 2x + 1) - 16(y^2 - 6y + 9) + 9 = 9 \cdot 1 - 16 \cdot 9$$
$$9(x - 1)^2 - 16(y - 3)^2 = -144$$

Divide each term by -144 to get the equation in the proper form: $\dfrac{(y-3)^2}{9} - \dfrac{(x-1)^2}{16} = 1$.

  I. Center $(1,3)$. $a = 3$, $b = 4$, and so $c = \sqrt{9+16} = 5$.

  II. The vertices are 3 units above and 3 units below the center. Vertices are $(1,6)$ and $(1,0)$.

  III. The foci are 5 units above and 5 units below the center. Foci are $(1,8)$ and $(1,-2)$.

  IV. Eccentricity $= \dfrac{c}{a} = \dfrac{5}{3}$.

  V. The slopes of the asymptotes are $\pm\dfrac{a}{b} = \pm\dfrac{3}{4}$. The asymptotes pass through the center $(1,3)$. Therefore, the equations of the asymptotes are $y - 3 = \pm\dfrac{3}{4}(x-1)$.

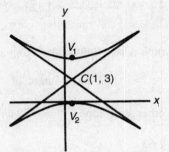

(B) $B^2 - 4AC = 0 - 4 \cdot 4 \cdot 4 < 0$ and $A = C = 4$, which means the graph will be a circle. Divide through by 4, group the x-terms together, group the y-terms together, and complete the square.

$$\left(x^2 - 3x + \frac{9}{4}\right) + \left(y^2 - 5y + \frac{25}{4}\right) - \frac{2}{4} = \frac{9}{4} + \frac{25}{4}$$

$$\left(x - \frac{3}{2}\right)^2 + \left(y - \frac{5}{2}\right)^2 = 9$$

  I. Center $\left(\dfrac{3}{2}, \dfrac{5}{2}\right)$. Radius = 3. None of the other items is defined.

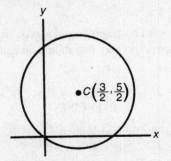

(C) $B^2 - 4AC = 0 - 4 \cdot 4 \cdot 1 < 0$ and $A \neq C$, which means the graph will be an ellipse. Group the x-terms, group the y-terms, and factor out of each group the coefficient of the quadratic term:

$$(x^2 + 6x \qquad) + 1(y^2 - 16y \qquad) = 0$$

Complete the square and add similar amounts to both sides of the equation:

$$4(x^2 + 6x + 9) + 1(y^2 - 16y + 64) = 4 \cdot 9 + 1 \cdot 64$$
$$4(x + 3)^2 + (y - 8)^2 = 100$$

Divide each term by 100 to get the equation in the proper form:

$$\frac{(x+3)^2}{25} + \frac{(y-8)^2}{100} = 1$$

  I. Center $(-3,8)$. $a = 10$, $b = 5$, and so $c = \sqrt{100 - 25} = \sqrt{75} = 5\sqrt{3}$.

  II. Since the major axis is vertical, the vertices are 10 units above and 10 units below the center. Vertices are $(-3,18)$ and $(-3,-2)$.

  III. The foci are $5\sqrt{3}$ units above and $5\sqrt{3}$ units below the center. Foci are $(-3,8 + 5\sqrt{3})$ and $(-3,8 - 5\sqrt{3})$.

  IV. Eccentricity $= \dfrac{c}{a} = \dfrac{5\sqrt{3}}{10} = \dfrac{\sqrt{3}}{2}$.

  V. There are no asymptotes.

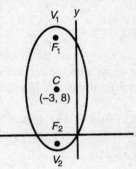

(D) $B^2 - 4AC = 0 - 4 \cdot 0 \cdot 1 = 0$, which means the graph will be a parabola. Group the y-terms and complete the square.

$$(y^2 - 8y + 16) = -6x - 4 + 16$$
$$(y - 4)^2 = -6(x - 2)$$

  I. No center.

  II. Vertex is $(2,4)$.

  III. $4p = -6$, and so $p = -\dfrac{3}{2}$. Since the y-term is squared, the parabola opens to the side. Thus, the focus is $\dfrac{3}{2}$ units to the left of the vertex. Focus $\left(\dfrac{1}{2}, 4\right)$.

  IV. Eccentricity = 1.

  V. No asymptotes.

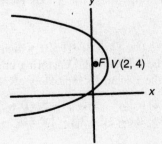

EXAMPLE 2: Find the equation of the hyperbola with center at (3,–4), eccentricity 4, and conjugate axis of length 6.

Two cases are possible: $\dfrac{(x-3)^2}{a^2} - \dfrac{(y+4)^2}{b^2} = 1$ and $\dfrac{(y+4)^2}{a^2} - \dfrac{(x-3)^2}{b^2} = 1$.

Eccentricity $= \dfrac{c}{a} = 4$. Thus, $c = 4a$.

Conjugate axis $= 2b = 6$. Thus, $b = 3$.

In the case of a hyperbola,

$$c^2 = a^2 + b^2$$
$$(4a)^2 = a^2 + 9$$
$$16a^2 = a^2 + 9$$
$$15a^2 = 9$$
$$a^2 = \frac{9}{15}$$

Therefore, the equation becomes:

$$\frac{15(x-3)^2}{9} - \frac{(y+4)^2}{9} = 1 \text{ or } \frac{15(y+4)^2}{9} - \frac{(x-3)^2}{9} = 1.$$

The *degenerate case* occurs when one of the variables drops out, or the terms with the variables equal zero, or a negative number after the square has been completed.

EXAMPLE 3: What is the graph of each of the following?

(A) $x^2 + y^2 - 4x + 2y + 5 = 0$
(B) $xy = 0$
(C) $2x^2 - 3y^2 + 8x + 6y + 5 = 0$
(D) $3x^2 + 4y^2 - 6x - 16y + 19 = 0$
(E) $x^2 + y^2 + 5 = 0$

(A) $B^2 - 4AC = 0 - 4 \cdot 1 \cdot 1 < 0$ and $A = C$, which indicates the graph should be a circle. Completing the square on the x's and y's separately gives:

$$(x^2 - 4x + 4) + (y^2 + 2y + 1) + 5 = 0 + 4 + 1$$
$$(x - 2)^2 + (y + 1)^2 = 0$$

This is a circle with center (2,–1) and radius zero; thus, a degenerate case. The graph is the single point (2,–1).

(B) $xy = 0$ if and only if $x = 0$ or $y = 0$. Thus, the graph is two intersecting lines: the x-axis $(y = 0)$ and the y-axis $(x = 0)$.

(C) $B^2 - 4AC = 0 - 4 \cdot 2 \cdot (-3) > 0$, which indicates the graph should be a hyperbola. Factoring and completing the square on the x's and y's separately gives:

$$2(x^2 + 4x + 4) - 3(y^2 - 2y + 1) + 5 = 0 + 2 \cdot 4 - 3 \cdot 1$$
$$2(x + 2)^2 - 3(y - 1)^2 = 0$$

Since the right side of the equation is zero and the left side is the difference between two perfect squares, the left side of the equation can be factored and simplified.

$$\left[\sqrt{2}(x+2) + \sqrt{3}(y-1)\right] \cdot \left[\sqrt{2}(x+2) - \sqrt{3}(y-1)\right] = 0$$
$$\left[\sqrt{2}x + 2\sqrt{2} + \sqrt{3}y - \sqrt{3}\right] = 0$$

or

$$\left[\sqrt{2}x + 2\sqrt{2} - \sqrt{3}y + \sqrt{3}\right] = 0$$
$$y = -\frac{\sqrt{2}}{\sqrt{3}}x + \frac{\sqrt{3} - 2\sqrt{2}}{\sqrt{3}} \approx -0.82x - 0.63$$

or

$$y = \frac{\sqrt{2}}{\sqrt{3}}x + \frac{\sqrt{3} + 2\sqrt{2}}{\sqrt{3}} \approx 0.82x + 2.63$$

Thus, the graph is two lines intersecting at (–2,1), one with slope $-\dfrac{\sqrt{2}}{\sqrt{3}} \approx -0.82$ and y-intercept $\dfrac{\sqrt{3} - 2\sqrt{2}}{\sqrt{3}} \approx$ –0.63 and the other with slope $\dfrac{\sqrt{2}}{\sqrt{3}} \approx 0.82$ and y-intercept $\dfrac{\sqrt{3} + 2\sqrt{2}}{\sqrt{3}} \approx 2.63$.

(D) $B^2 - 4AC = 0 - 4 \cdot 3 \cdot 4 < 0$ and $A \neq C$, which indicates the graph should be an ellipse. Factoring and completing the square on the x's and y's separately gives:

$$3(x^2 - 2x + 1) + 4(y^2 - 4y + 4) + 19 = 0 + 3 \cdot 1 + 4 \cdot 4$$
$$3(x - 1)^2 + 4(y - 2)^2 = 0$$

Since $3(x - 1)^2 \geq 0$ and $4(y - 2)^2 \geq 0$, the only point that satisfies the equation is (1,2), which makes each term on the left side of the equation equal to zero. The graph is the one point (1,2).

(E) $x^2 + y^2 = -5$. The graph does not exist since $x^2 \geq 0$ and $y^2 \geq 0$ and there is no way that their sum can equal –5.

EXERCISES

1. Which of the following are the coordinates of a focus of $5x^2 + 4y^2 - 20x + 8y + 4 = 0$?

    (A) (1, –1)
    (B) (2, –1)
    (C) (3, –1)
    (D) (2, –2)
    (E) (–2, 1)

2. If the graphs of $x^2 + y^2 = 4$ and $xy = 1$ are drawn on the same set of axes, how many points will they have in common?

(A) 0
(B) 2
(C) 4
(D) 1
(E) 3

3. The graph of $(x - 2)^2 = 4y$ has a

(A) vertex at (4,2)
(B) focus at (2,0)
(C) directrix $y = -1$
(D) latus rectum 2 units in length
(E) none of these

4. Which of the following is an asymptote of $3x^2 - 4y^2 - 12 = 0$?

(A) $y = \dfrac{4}{3}x$

(B) $y = -\dfrac{2}{\sqrt{3}}$

(C) $y = -\dfrac{3}{4}x$

(D) $y = \dfrac{\sqrt{3}}{2}x$

(E) $y = \dfrac{2\sqrt{3}}{3}x$

5. The graph of $x^2 = (2y + 3)^2$ is

(A) a circle
(B) an ellipse
(C) a hyperbola
(D) a point
(E) two intersecting lines

6. The area bounded by the curve $y = \sqrt{4 - x^2}$ and the x-axis is

(A) 4π
(B) 8π
(C) 16π
(D) 2π
(E) π

7. Which of the following is the equation of the circle with center at the origin and tangent to the line with equation $3x - 7y = 29$?

(A) $x^2 + y^2 = 12$
(B) $2x^2 + 2y^2 = 29$
(C) $x^2 + y^2 = 15$
(D) $3x^2 + 3y^2 = 40$
(E) $x^2 + y^2 = 10$

8. An equilateral triangle is inscribed in the circle whose equation is $x^2 + 2x + y^2 - 4y = 0$. The length of the side of the triangle is

(A) 5
(B) 1.9
(C) 2.2
(D) 3.9
(E) 4.5

4.2 EXPONENTIAL AND LOGARITHMIC FUNCTIONS

The basic properties of exponents and logarithms and the fact that the exponential function and the logarithmic function are inverses lead to many interesting problems.

The basic exponential properties:

For all positive real numbers x and y, and all real numbers a and b:

$$x^a \cdot x^b = x^{a+b} \qquad x^0 = 1$$
$$\frac{x^a}{x^b} = x^{a-b} \qquad x^{-a} = \frac{1}{x^a}$$
$$\left(x^a\right)^b = x^{ab} \qquad x^a \cdot y^a = (xy)^a$$

The basic logarithmic properties:

For all positive real numbers a, b, p, and q, and all real numbers x, where $a \neq 1$ and $b \neq 1$:

$$\log_b(p \cdot q) = \log_b p + \log_b q \qquad \log_b 1 = 0 \qquad b^{\log_b p} = p$$
$$\log_b\left(\frac{p}{q}\right) = \log_b p - \log_b q \qquad \log_b b = 1$$
$$\log_b\left(p^x\right) = x \cdot \log_b p \qquad\qquad \log_b p = \frac{\log_a p}{\log_a b}$$

The basic property that relates the exponential and logarithmic functions is:

For all real numbers x, and all positive real numbers b and N,

$$\log_b N = x \text{ is equivalent to } b^x = N.$$

EXAMPLE 1: Simplify $x^{n-1} \cdot x^{2n} \cdot \left(x^{2-n}\right)^2$

This is equal to $x^{n-1} \cdot x^{2n} \cdot x^{4-2n} = x^{n-1+2n+4-2n} = x^{n+3}$.

EXAMPLE 2: Simplify $\dfrac{3^{n-2} \cdot 9^{2-n}}{3^{2-n}}$.

In order to combine exponents using the properties above, the base of each factor must be the same.

$$\frac{3^{n-2} \cdot 9^{2-n}}{3^{2-n}} = \frac{3^{n-2} \cdot (3^2)^{2-n}}{3^{2-n}} = \frac{3^{n-2} \cdot 3^{4-2n}}{3^{2-n}}$$
$$= 3^{n-2+4-2n-(2-n)} = 3^0 = 1$$

Note: Examples 3 and 4 can be easily evaluated with a calculator.

EXAMPLE 3: If $\log_{10} 23 = z$, what does $\log_{10} 2300$ equal?

$\log_{10} 2300 = \log_{10} 23 \cdot 100 = \log_{10} 23 + \log_{10} 100 = z + \log_{10} 10^2 =$

$$z + 2 \cdot \log_{10} 10 = z + 2$$

EXAMPLE 4: If $\log_{10} 2 = a$ and $\log_{10} 3 = b$, find the value of $\log_{10} 15$.

$\log_{10} 15 = \log_{10} (3 \cdot 5) = \log_{10} 3 + \log_{10} \left(\dfrac{10}{2}\right) = \log_{10} 3 + \log_{10} 10 - \log_{10} 2 = b + 1 - a.$

EXAMPLE 5: Solve for x: $\log(x + 5) = \log x + \log 5$.
(When no base is indicated, any arbitrary base can be used. If you plan to use your calculator, you should use base 10.)

$$\log x + \log 5 = \log 5 \cdot x$$

Therefore, $\log(x + 5) = \log(5x)$, which is true only when:

$$x + 5 = 5x$$
$$5 = 4x$$
$$x = \frac{5}{4}$$

Note: If a log problem has a base other than 10 or e, use the change-of-base theorem to convert the base into either 10 or e.

EXAMPLE 6: Evaluate $\log_{27} \sqrt{54} - \log_{27} \sqrt{6}$.

$\log_{27} \sqrt{54} - \log_{27} \sqrt{6} = \log_{27} \left(\dfrac{\sqrt{54}}{\sqrt{6}}\right)$

$$= \log_{27} \sqrt{9} = \log_{27} 3 = x$$

The last equality implies that

$$27^x = 3$$
$$(3^3)^x = 3$$
$$3^{3x} = 3^1$$

Therefore, $3x = 1$ and $x = \dfrac{1}{3}$.

Thus, $\log_{27} \sqrt{54} - \log_{27} \sqrt{6} = \dfrac{1}{3}$.

<u>Alternative Solution:</u>

$$\log_{27} \sqrt{54} = \frac{\log_{10} \sqrt{54}}{\log_{10} 27} \approx \frac{0.866}{1.431} \approx 0.605$$

$$\log_{27} \sqrt{6} = \frac{\log_{10} \sqrt{6}}{\log_{10} 27} \approx \frac{0.389}{1.431} \approx 0.272$$

Therefore, $\log_{27} \sqrt{54} - \log_{27} \sqrt{6} \approx 0.333 \approx \dfrac{1}{3}$.

EXAMPLE 7: Evaluate $\log_8 2 - \log_6 216 + \log_{81} 3 - \log_5 (625)^{1/3}$.

Since each term has a different base, the terms must be evaluated separately.

Let $\log_8 2 = x$. This implies that

$$8^x = 2$$
$$(2^3)^x = 2$$
$$2^{3x} = 2^1$$

Therefore, $3x = 1$ and $x = \dfrac{1}{3}$.

Let $\log_6 216 = y$. This implies that

$$6^y = 216$$
$$6^y = 6^3$$

Therefore, $y = 3$.

Let $\log_3 81 = z$. This implies that

$$3^z = 81$$
$$3^z = 3^4$$

Therefore, $z = 4$.

$\log_5 (625)^{1/3} = \dfrac{1}{3} \cdot \log_5 625$. Let $\log_5 625 = w$. This implies that

$$5^w = 625$$
$$5^w = 5^4$$

Therefore, $w = 4$. Thus, $\log_5 (625)^{1/3} = \dfrac{1}{3} \cdot 4 = \dfrac{4}{3}$. Putting the four parts together, we find that the original expression is equal to $\dfrac{1}{3} - 3 + 4 - \dfrac{4}{3} = 0$.

The graphs of all exponential functions $y = b^x$ have roughly the same shape and pass through point $(0,1)$. If $b > 1$, the graph increases as x increases and approaches the x-axis as an asymptote as x decreases. The amount of curvature becomes greater as the value of b is made greater. If $0 < b < 1$, the graph increases as x decreases and approaches the x-axis as an asymptote as x increases. The amount of curvature becomes greater as the value of b is made smaller.

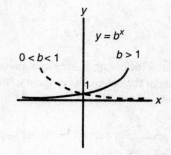

The graphs of all logarithmic functions $y = \log_b x$ have roughly the same shape and pass through point $(1,0)$. If

$b > 1$, the graph increases as x increases and approaches the y-axis as an asymptote as x approaches zero. The amount of curvature becomes greater as the value of b is made greater. If $0 < b < 1$, the graph decreases as x increases and approaches the y-axis as an asymptote as x approaches zero. The amount of curvature becomes greater as the value of b is made smaller.

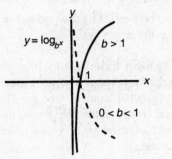

EXERCISES

1. If $x^a \cdot (x^{a+1})^a \cdot (x^a)^{1-a} = x^k$, then $k =$

(A) $2a + 1$
(B) $a + a^2$
(C) $3a$
(D) $3a + 1$
(E) $a^3 + a$

2. If $\log_8 3 = x \cdot \log_2 3$, then $x =$

(A) 4
(B) $\log_4 3$
(C) 3
(D) $\dfrac{1}{3}$
(E) $\log_8 9$

3. If $\log_{10} m = \dfrac{1}{2}$, then $\log_{10} 10m^2 =$

(A) 2.5
(B) 2
(C) 100
(D) 10.25
(E) 3

4. If $\log_b 5 = a$, $\log_b 2.5 = c$, and $5^x = 2.5$, then $x =$

(A) ac
(B) $\dfrac{c}{a}$
(C) $a + c$
(D) $c - a$
(E) The value of x cannot be determined from the information given.

5. If $f(x) = \log_2 x$, then $f\!\left(\dfrac{2}{x}\right) + f(x) =$

(A) $\log\!\left(\dfrac{2}{x}\right) + \log_2 x$
(B) 1
(C) $\log_2\!\left(\dfrac{2 + x^2}{x}\right)$
(D) $\log_2\!\left(\dfrac{2}{x}\right) \cdot \log_2 x$
(E) 0

6. If $\log_b(xy) < 0$, which of the following must be true?

(A) $xy < 0$
(B) $xy < 1$
(C) $xy > 1$
(D) $xy > 0$
(E) none of the above

7. If $\log_2 m = \sqrt{7}$ and $\log_7 n = \sqrt{2}$, $mn =$

(A) 98
(B) 2
(C) 1
(D) 96
(E) 103

8. If $f(x, y) = \dfrac{\log x}{\log y}$, $f(e, \pi) =$

(A) 2.01
(B) 0.50
(C) -1.73
(D) 0.87
(E) -0.37

9. $\log_7 5 =$

(A) 1.2
(B) 1.1
(C) 0.9
(D) 0.8
(E) -0.7

10. $\left(\sqrt[3]{2}\right)\left(\sqrt[5]{4}\right)\left(\sqrt[9]{8}\right) =$

(A) 1.9
(B) 2.0
(C) 2.1
(D) 2.3
(E) 2.5

11. If $300 is invested at 3%, compounded continuously, how long (to the nearest year) will it take for the money to double? (If P is the amount invested, the formula for the amount, A, that is available after t years is $A = Pe^{0.03t}$.)

(A) 26
(B) 25
(C) 24
(D) 23
(E) 22

4.3 ABSOLUTE VALUE

The absolute value of x (written as $|x|$) is defined as follows:

if $x \geq 0$, then $|x| = x$;

if $x < 0$, then $|x| = -x$ (note that $-x$ is a positive number);

$|x| \geq 0$ for all values of x.

 Note: The abs function on a graphing calculator can quickly provide the graphs asked for in most of these examples and exercises. Use the Trace and Zoom functions to find the needed information.

EXAMPLE 1: If $|x - 3| = 2$, find x.

Absolute value problems can always be solved by using the definition to restate the problem in two parts.

Part 1: If $x - 3 \geq 0$, then $|x - 3| = x - 3$. Thus,
$$x - 3 = 2$$
$$x = 5$$

Notice that both conditions, $x - 3 \geq 0$ and $x = 5$, must be satisfied. They are in this case.

Part 2: If $x - 3 < 0$, then $|x - 3| = -(x - 3) = -x + 3$. Thus,
$$-x + 3 = 2$$
$$x = 1$$

Both conditions, $x - 3 < 0$ and $x = 1$, are satisfied. The solution set is $\{1,5\}$.

EXAMPLE 2: If $|3x + 5| = 2x + 3$, find x.

Part 1: If $3x + 5 \geq 0$, then $|3x + 5| = 3x + 5$. Thus,
$$3x + 5 = 2x + 3$$
$$x = -2$$

Both conditions, $x \geq -\dfrac{5}{3}$ and $x = -2$, are not satisfied, and so no solution is supplied by this part.

Part 2: If $3x + 5 < 0$, then $|3x + 5| = -(3x + 5) = -3x - 5$. Thus,
$$-3x - 5 = 2x + 3$$
$$-5x = 8$$
$$x = -\frac{8}{5}$$

Both conditions, $x < -\dfrac{5}{3}$ and $x = -\dfrac{8}{5}$, are not satisfied, so no solution is supplied by this part either. Therefore the solution set is the empty set, $\emptyset$.

 Graphing calculator: Plot the graphs of $y = \text{abs}(3x + 5)$ and $y = 2x + 3$ in an $x \in [-10, 10]$, $y \in [-10, 10]$ window. Use the Trace and Zoom functions to see that the graphs do not intersect. Therefore, there are no values of x that satisfy the equation.

EXAMPLE 3: Find all values of x such that $|2x + 3| \geq 5$.

Consider the equality $|2x + 3| = 5$, which is associated with this inequality. Using the definition of absolute value gives the following:

If $2x + 3 \geq 0$, then $2x + 3 = 5$.

Thus, $x \geq -\dfrac{3}{2}$ and $x = 1$.

If $2x + 3 < 0$, then $-(2x + 3) = 5$.

Thus, $x < -\dfrac{3}{2}$ and $x = -4$.

The solution set of the equality is $\{1, -4\}$. Consider the regions of a number line indicated by these two numbers.

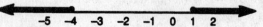

If $x = -5$, then $|2x + 3| = 7 \geq 5$.   *True.*
If $x = 0$, then $|2x + 3| = 3 \leq 5$.   *True.*
If $x = 2$, then $|2x + 3| = 7 \geq 5$.   *False.*

Therefore, the set of numbers that satisfies the original inequality, $|2x + 3| \geq 5$, is $\{x : x \leq -4 \text{ or } x \geq 1\}$. The graph of this solution set on a number line is indicated below.

 Graphing calculator: Plot the graphs of $y = \text{abs}(2x + 3)$ and $y = 5$ in an $x \in [-10, 10]$, $y \in [-10, 10]$ window. Use the Trace and Zoom functions to see that the graph of $y = \text{abs}(2x + 3)$ is below or on the graph of $y = 5$ when $x \leq -4$ or $x \geq 1$.

Note: A graphing calculator will not be much use in this problem unless you are very ingenious.

Hint: Try to find a function that has several of the properties of the given function, $f(x)$. (For example, try $y = -x(x - 2)(x + 3)$ in an $x \in [-2,2]$, $y \in [-10,10]$ window even though it doesn't look much like $f(x)$.) Whatever happens to the graph of this function when you plot the graph of (A) and (B) will also happen to the graph of $f(x)$.

EXAMPLE 4: If the graph of $f(x)$ is shown below, sketch the graph of (A) $|f(x)|$ (B) $f(|x|)$.

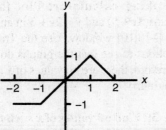

(A) Since $|f(x)| \geq 0$, by the definition of absolute value, the graph cannot have any points below the x-axis. If $f(x) < 0$, then $|f(x)| = -f(x)$. Thus, all points below the x-axis are reflected about the x-axis, and all points above the x-axis remain unchanged.

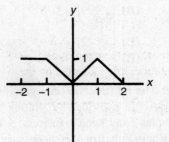

(B) Since the absolute value of x is taken before the function value is found, and since $|x| = -x$ when $x < 0$, any negative value of x will graph the same y-values as the corresponding positive values of x. Thus, the graph to the left of the y-axis will be a reflection of the graph to the right of the y-axis.

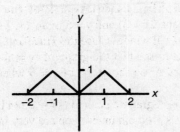

EXAMPLE 5: If $f(x) = |x + 1| - 1$, what is the minimum value of $f(x)$?
Since $|x + 1| \geq 0$, its smallest value is 0. Therefore, the smallest value of $f(x)$ is $0 - 1 = -1$. The graph of $f(x)$ is indicated below.

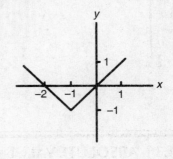

EXERCISES

1. $|2x - 1| = 4x + 5$ has how many numbers in its solution set?

   (A) 0
   (B) 1
   (C) 2
   (D) an infinite number
   (E) none of the above

2. Which of the following is equivalent to $1 \leq |x - 2| \leq 4$?

   (A) $3 \leq x \leq 6$
   (B) $x \leq 1$ or $x \geq 3$
   (C) $1 \leq x \leq 3$
   (D) $x \leq -2$ or $x \geq 6$
   (E) $-2 \leq x \leq 1$ or $3 \leq x \leq 6$

3. The area bound by the relation $|x| + |y| = 2$ is

   (A) 8
   (B) 1
   (C) 2
   (D) 4
   (E) There is no finite area.

4. Given a function, $f(x)$, such that $f(x) = f(|x|)$. Which one of the following could be the graph of $f(x)$?

   (A)

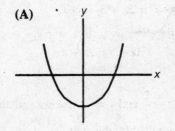

(B)

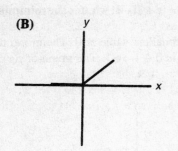

(C)

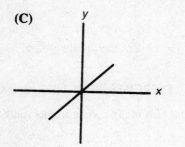

(D)

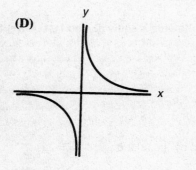

(E)

5. The figure shows the graph of which one of the following?

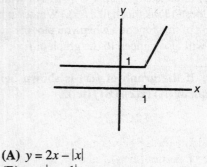

(A) $y = 2x - |x|$
(B) $y = |x - 1| + x$
(C) $y = |2x - 1|$
(D) $y = |x + 1| - x$
(E) $y = 2|x| - |x|$

4.4   GREATEST INTEGER FUNCTION

The greatest integer function, denoted by $[x]$, pairs with each real number x the greatest integer contained in x. In symbols, where i represents an integer: $f(x) = i$, where $i \le x < i + 1$.

EXAMPLE 1:   (A) $[3.2] = 3$
(B) $[1.999] = 1$
(C) $[5] = 5$
(D) $[-3.12] = -4$
(E) $[-0.123] = -1$.

Note: The int function on a graphing calculator can quickly provide the graphs asked for in Examples 2 and 3 and in Exercise 3. Use the Trace and Zoom functions, if necessary, to find the needed information.

EXAMPLE 2: Sketch the graph of $f(x) = [x]$.

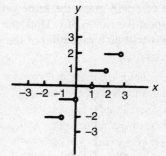

EXAMPLE 3: What is the range of $f(x) = \left[\dfrac{[x]}{x}\right]$.

If x is not an integer, $[x] < x$. Therefore, $\dfrac{[x]}{x}$ represents a

decimal between 0 and 1, and $\left[\dfrac{[x]}{x}\right] = 0$. If x is an integer,

$[x] = x$, and $\left[\dfrac{[x]}{x}\right] = \left[\dfrac{x}{x}\right] = [1] = 1$. Therefore, the range is

$\{0, 1\}$.

EXERCISES

1. If the postal rate for first-class mail is 32 cents for the first ounce or portion thereof and 23 cents for each additional ounce or portion thereof, then the cost in cents of first-class postage for a letter weighing N ounces is always

   (A) $32 + [N - 1] \cdot 23$
   (B) $[N - 32] \cdot 23$
   (C) $32 + [N] \cdot 23$
   (D) $1 + [N] \cdot 23$
   (E) none of the above

2. If $f(x) = i$, where i is an integer such that $i \le x < i + 1$, the range of $f(x)$ is

   (A) the set of all real numbers
   (B) the set of all positive integers
   (C) the set of all integers
   (D) the set of all negative integers
   (E) the set of all nonnegative real numbers

3. If $f(x) = [2x] - 4x$ with domain $0 \le x \le 2$, then $f(x)$ can also be written as

   (A) $2x$
   (B) $-x$
   (C) $-2x$
   (D) $x^2 - 4x$
   (E) none of the above

4.5   RATIONAL FUNCTIONS

F is a rational function if and only if $F(x) = \dfrac{p(x)}{q(x)}$, where $p(x)$ and $q(x)$ are both polynomial functions and $q(x)$ is not zero. As a general rule, the graphs of rational functions are not continuous (i.e., they have holes, or sections of the graphs are separated from other sections by asymptotes). A point of discontinuity occurs at any value of x that would cause $q(x)$ to become zero.

If $p(x)$ and $q(x)$ can be factored so that $F(x)$ can be reduced, removing the factors that caused the discontinuities, the graph will contain only holes. If the factors that caused the discontinuities cannot be removed, asymptotes will occur.

Note: A graphing calculator can quickly provide the graphs asked for in most of the following examples and exercises. Use the Trace and Zoom functions to find the needed information. (Be aware, however, that a calculator rarely shows a hole in a graph and often draws in what appears to be asymptotes that are not part of the function's graph.)

EXAMPLE 1: Sketch the graph of $F(x) = \dfrac{x^2 - 1}{x + 1}$.

There is a discontinuity at $x = -1$ since this value would cause division by zero. The fraction $\dfrac{x^2 - 1}{x + 1} = \dfrac{(x - 1)(x + 1)}{(x + 1)} = (x - 1)$, and so the graph of $F(x)$ is the same as the graph of $y = x - 1$ except for a hole at $x = -1$.

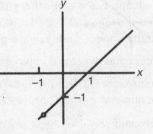

EXAMPLE 2: Sketch the graph of $F(x) = \dfrac{1}{x - 2}$.

Since this fraction cannot be reduced, and $x = 2$ would cause division by zero, a vertical asymptote occurs when $x = 2$. This is true because, as x approaches very close to 2, $F(x)$ gets either extremely large or extremely small. As x becomes extremely large or extremely small, $f(x)$ gets closer and closer to zero. This means that a horizontal asymptote occurs when $y = 0$. Plotting a few points indicates that the graph looks like the figure below.

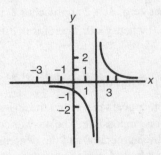

A more compact way of expressing the preceding statements about x approaching 2 or x getting extremely large follows: The statement $\lim\limits_{x \to \infty} f(x) = 0$ is read as "the limit of $f(x)$ is zero as x increases without bound (or as x approaches infinity)." $\lim\limits_{x \to 2^-} f(x) = -\infty$ is read as "the limit of $f(x)$ decreases without bound (or tends to negative infinity) as x approaches 2 from the negative side."

EXAMPLE 3: What does $\lim\limits_{x\to 1}\dfrac{x^2-1}{x+1}$ **equal?**

Since $\dfrac{x^2-1}{x+1}$ reduces to $x-1$,

$$\lim_{x\to 1}\frac{x^2-1}{x+1}=\lim_{x\to 1}x-1=0.$$

EXAMPLE 4: What does $\lim\limits_{x\to 2^+}3x+5$ **equal?**

Since "problems" occur only when division by zero appears imminent, this example is extremely easy. As x gets closer and closer to 2, $3x+5$ seems to be approaching closer and closer to 11. Therefore, $\lim\limits_{x\to 2^+}3x+5=11$.

EXAMPLE 5: What does $\lim\limits_{x\to 2}\left(\dfrac{3x+5}{x-2}\right)$ **equal?**

The denominator does not factor out, and so the graph of this rational function has a vertical asymptote. As x approaches 2 from above (i.e., 2.1, 2.01, 2.001, . . .), the numerator and denominator both remain positive and so $\dfrac{3x+5}{x-2}$ gets larger and larger and approaches positive infinity. As x approaches 2 from below (i.e., 1.9, 1.99, 1.999, . . .), the numerator is still positive, but the denominator is negative and so $\dfrac{3x+5}{x-2}$ gets smaller and smaller and approaches negative infinity. Thus, $\lim\limits_{x\to 2^-}\dfrac{3x+5}{x-2}$ does not exist since $\lim\limits_{x\to 2^-}\dfrac{3x+5}{x-2}$ and $\lim\limits_{x\to 2^+}\dfrac{3x+5}{x-2}=+\infty$, which are not the same.

EXAMPLE 6: If $f(x)=\begin{cases}3x+2 & \text{when }x\neq 0\\0 & \text{when }x=0\end{cases}$, **what does** $\lim\limits_{x\to 0}f(x)$ **equal?**

As x approaches zero, $3x+2$ approaches 2, in spite of the fact that $f(x)=0$ when $x=0$. Therefore, $\lim\limits_{x\to 0}f(x)=2$.

EXAMPLE 7: What does $\lim\limits_{x\to\infty}\left(\dfrac{3x^2+4x+2}{2x^2+x-5}\right)$ **equal?**

At first glance it appears that either the answer is obvious or the problem is impossible. The answer could be 1 because, if both the numerator and the denominator are increasing without bound, their quotient must approach 1. On the other hand, no matter how large a number is substituted for x, the numerator and the denominator are never the same.

This is, in fact, a rather easy problem to solve. The method used most often is to divide both the numerator and the denominator through by the variable raised to its highest exponent in the problem. In this case divide through by x^2.

$$\lim_{x\to\infty}\left(\frac{3x^2+4x+2}{2x^2+x-5}\right)=\lim_{x\to\infty}\left(\frac{3+\dfrac{4}{x}+\dfrac{2}{x^2}}{2+\dfrac{1}{x}-\dfrac{5}{x^2}}\right).$$

Now, as $x\to\infty,\dfrac{4}{x},\dfrac{2}{x^2},\dfrac{1}{x}$, and $\dfrac{5}{x^2}$, each approaches zero. Thus, the entire fraction approaches $\dfrac{3+0+0}{2+0-0}=\dfrac{3}{2}$.

Therefore, $\lim\limits_{x\to\infty}\left(\dfrac{3x^2+4x+2}{2x^2+x-5}\right)=\dfrac{3}{2}$.

EXERCISES

1. To be continuous at $x=1$, the value of $\dfrac{x^4-1}{x^3-1}$ must be defined to be equal to

   (A) $\dfrac{4}{3}$

   (B) 0

   (C) 1

   (D) 4

   (E) −1

2. If $f(x)=\begin{cases}\dfrac{3x^2+2x}{x} & \text{when }x\neq 0\\k & \text{when }x=0\end{cases}$, what must the value of k be equal to in order for $f(x)$ to be a continuous function?

   (A) 0

   (B) 2

   (C) $-\dfrac{2}{3}$

   (D) $-\dfrac{3}{2}$

   (E) No value of k can make $f(x)$ a continuous function.

3. $\lim\limits_{x\to 2}\left(\dfrac{x^3-8}{x^4-16}\right)=$

   (A) $\dfrac{3}{8}$

   (B) $\dfrac{1}{2}$

   (C) $\dfrac{4}{7}$

   (D) 0

   (E) This expression is undefined.

4. $\lim\limits_{x \to \infty}\left(\dfrac{5x^2 - 2}{3x^2 + 8}\right) =$

(A) ∞

(B) $\dfrac{3}{11}$

(C) $\dfrac{5}{3}$

(D) $-\dfrac{1}{4}$

(E) 0

5. Which of the following is the equation of an asymptote of $y = \dfrac{3x^2 - 2x - 1}{9x^2 - 1}$?

(A) $x = -\dfrac{1}{3}$

(B) $y = \dfrac{1}{3}$

(C) $x = 1$

(D) $y = 1$

(E) $y = -\dfrac{1}{3}$

4.6 PARAMETRIC EQUATIONS

At times it is convenient to express a relationship between x and y in terms of a third variable. This third variable is called a *parameter*, and the equations are called *parametric equations*.

EXAMPLE 1: $\begin{cases} x = 3t + 4 \\ y = t - 5 \end{cases}$ are parametric equations with a parameter t.

As different values are substituted for the parameter, ordered pairs of points, (x,y), represent points on the graph. At times it is possible to eliminate the parameter and to rewrite the equation in familiar xy-form. When eliminating the parameter, it is necessary to be aware of the fact that the resulting equation may consist of points not on the graph of the original set of equations.

EXAMPLE 2: $\begin{cases} x = t^2 \\ y = 3t^2 + 1 \end{cases}$. **Eliminate the parameter and sketch the graph.**

Substituting x for t^2 in the second equation results in $y = 3x + 1$, which is the equation of a straight line with a slope of 3 and a y-intercept of 1. However, the original parametric equations indicate that $x \geq 0$ and $y \geq 1$ since t^2 cannot be negative. Thus, the proper way to indicate this set of points without the parameter is as follows: $y = 3x + 1$ and $x \geq 0$. The graph is the ray indicated in the figure.

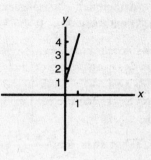

 Note: With the calculator in parametric mode and a sufficiently wide range for the parameter, t, a graphing calculator can show whether there are any restrictions on the extent of the graph.

EXAMPLE 3: Sketch the graph of the parametric equations $\begin{cases} x = 4\cos\theta \\ y = 3\sin\theta \end{cases}$.

It is possible to eliminate the parameter, θ, by dividing the first equation by 4 and the second equation by 3, squaring each, and then adding the equations together.

$$\left(\frac{x}{4}\right)^2 = \cos^2\theta \quad \text{and} \quad \left(\frac{y}{3}\right)^2 = \sin^2\theta$$

$$\frac{x^2}{16} + \frac{y^2}{9} = \cos^2\theta + \sin^2\theta = 1$$

Here, $\dfrac{x^2}{16} + \dfrac{y^2}{9} = 1$ is the equation of an ellipse with its center at the origin, $a = 4$, and $b = 3$. Since $-1 \leq \cos\theta \leq 1$ and $-1 \leq \sin\theta \leq 1$, $-4 \leq x \leq 4$ and $-3 \leq y \leq 3$ from the two parametric equations. In this case the parametric equations do not limit the graph obtained by removing the parameter.

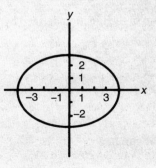

EXAMPLE 4: Sketch the graph of the parametric equations $\begin{cases} x = 2(\theta - \sin \theta) \\ y = 2(1 - \cos \theta) \end{cases}$.

In this case it would be extremely difficult to eliminate the parameter. To sketch the graph it will be necessary to choose values of θ and to determine x and y directly. To keep the work to a minimum, choose values of θ that have easily found sines and cosines.

θ	0	$\frac{\pi}{6}$	$\frac{\pi}{3}$	$\frac{\pi}{2}$	$\frac{2\pi}{3}$	$\frac{5\pi}{6}$	π
x	0	0.05	0.36	1.1	2.5	4.2	6.3
y	0	0.27	1	2	3	3.7	4

θ	$\frac{7\pi}{6}$	$\frac{4\pi}{3}$	$\frac{3\pi}{2}$	$\frac{5\pi}{3}$	$\frac{11\pi}{6}$	2π
x	8.3	10.1	11.4	12.2	12.5	12.6
y	3.7	3	2	1	0.27	0

The figure shows one period of the graph, which is called a *cycloid*.

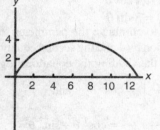

 Graphing calculator: Put your calculator in parametric mode and plot the graph of $x_T = 2(T - \sin T)$ and $y_T = 2(1 - \cos T)$ in a $T \in [0, 2\pi]$, $x \in [-15, 15]$, $y \in [-5, 5]$ window to see that the graph is one arc of a cycloid. If the T window and the x window are expanded, more arcs will appear.

EXERCISES

1. The domain of the function defined by the parametric equations $\begin{cases} x = t^2 + t \\ y = t^2 - t \end{cases}$ is

   (A) $\{x : x \geq 0\}$
   (B) $\left\{x : x \geq -\frac{1}{4}\right\}$
   (C) all real numbers
   (D) $\{x : x \geq -1\}$
   (E) $\{x : x \leq 1\}$

2. The graph of $\begin{cases} x = \sin^2 t \\ y = 2\cos t \end{cases}$ is a

   (A) straight line
   (B) line segment
   (C) parabola
   (D) portion of a parabola
   (E) semicircle

3. Which of the following is (are) a pair of parametric equations that represent a circle?

   I. $\begin{cases} x = \sin\theta \\ y = \cos\theta \end{cases}$

   II. $\begin{cases} x = t \\ y = \sqrt{1 - t^2} \end{cases}$

   III. $\begin{cases} x = \sqrt{s} \\ y = \sqrt{1 - s} \end{cases}$

   (A) only I
   (B) only II
   (C) only III
   (D) only II and III
   (E) I, II, and III

4.7 POLAR COORDINATES

Although the most common way to represent a point in a plane is in terms of its distance from two perpendicular axes, there are several other ways. One such way is in terms of the distance of the point from the origin and the angle between the positive x-axis and the ray emanating from the origin going through the point.

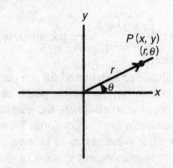

In the figure, the regular rectangular coordinates of P are (x, y) and the *polar coordinates* are (r, θ).

Since $\sin\theta = \dfrac{y}{r}$ and $\cos\theta = \dfrac{x}{r}$, there is an easy relationship between rectangular and polar coordinates:

$x = r \cdot \cos\theta$
$y = r \cdot \sin\theta$
$x^2 + y^2 = r^2$, using the Pythagorean theorem.

Unlike the case involving rectangular coordinates, each point in the plane can be named by an infinite number of polar coordinates.

EXAMPLE 1: $(2,30°)$, $(2,390°)$, $(2,-330°)$, $(-2,210°)$, $(-2,-150°)$ all name the same point.

In general, a point in the plane represented by (r, θ) can also be represented by $(r, \theta + 2\pi n)$ or $[-r, \theta + (2n - 1)\pi]$, where n is an integer.

EXAMPLE 2: Express point P, whose rectangular coordinates are $\left(3, 3\sqrt{3}\right)$, in terms of polar coordinates.

$$r^2 = x^2 + y^2 = 9 + 27 = 36$$
$$r = 6$$
$$r \cdot \cos \theta = x$$
$$\cos \theta = \frac{3}{6} = \frac{1}{2}$$

Therefore, $\theta = 60°$, and the coordinates of P are $(6, 60°)$.

EXAMPLE 3: Without sketching, describe the graphs

of (A) $r = 2$ and (B) $r = \dfrac{1}{\sin \theta}$.

(A) $r^2 = x^2 + y^2$
$r = 2$

Therefore, $x^2 + y^2 = 4$, which is the equation of a circle whose center is at the origin and whose radius is 2.

(B) $r \cdot \sin \theta = x$
$$r = \frac{1}{\sin \theta}$$
Therefore, $x = 1$.

Thus, $r = \dfrac{1}{\sin \theta}$ is the equation of a vertical line one unit to the right of the y-axis.

Since the complex number $a + bi$ can be represented by point $P(a,b)$ on a coordinate plane, it can also be represented in terms of polar coordinates. Thus, $a = r \cdot \cos \theta$ and $b = r \cdot \sin \theta$. Therefore,

$$a + bi = r \cdot \cos \theta + i \cdot r \cdot \sin \theta = r(\cos \theta + i \cdot \sin \theta).$$

This last statement is often abbreviated as $r \cdot \text{cis } \theta$.

There are several useful formulas for manipulating complex numbers when they are written in polar form, which is sometimes called "trigonometric form." If $z_1 = r_1(\cos \theta_1 + i \cdot \sin \theta_1)$ and $z_2 = r_2(\cos \theta_2 + i \cdot \sin \theta_2)$, then

1. $z_1 \cdot z_2 = r_1 r_2 \left[\cos(\theta_1 + \theta_2) + i \cdot \sin(\theta_1 + \theta_2)\right]$ or

$$z_1 \cdot z_2 = r_1 r_2 \text{ cis}(\theta_1 + \theta_2)$$

2. $\dfrac{z_1}{z_2} = \dfrac{r_1}{r_2}\left[\cos(\theta_1 - \theta_2) + i \cdot \sin(\theta_1 - \theta_2)\right]$ or

$$\frac{z_1}{z_2} = \frac{r_1}{r_2} \text{ cis}(\theta_1 - \theta_2)$$

De Moivre's theorem states that

3. $(z_1)^n = (r_1)^n(\cos n\theta_1 + i \cdot \sin n\theta_1)$ or

$(z_1)^n = (r_1)^n \text{ cis } n\theta_1$, where n is any positive integer.

The periodicity of the trigonometric functions allows the use of De Moivre's theorem to find the nth roots of any complex number.

4. $(z_1)^{1/n} = (r_1)^{1/n}\left(\cos \dfrac{\theta_1 + 2\pi k}{n} + i \cdot \sin \dfrac{\theta_1 + 2\pi k}{n}\right)$ or

$(z_1)^{1/n} = (r_1)^{1/n} \text{ cis } \dfrac{\theta_1 + 2\pi k}{n}$, where k is an integer taking on values from 0 to $n - 1$.

EXAMPLE 4: Using the polar form, find the value of $\dfrac{2 + 2i}{\sqrt{3} - 3i}$.

For the numerator, $r^2 = x^2 + y^2 = 4 + 4 = 8$. Therefore, $r = 2\sqrt{2}$. $r \cdot \cos \theta = x$. $\cos \theta = \dfrac{2}{2\sqrt{2}} = \dfrac{\sqrt{2}}{2}$. Therefore, $\theta = 45°$.

Thus, $2 + 2i = 2\sqrt{2} \text{ cis } 45°$.
For the denominator, $r^2 = x^2 + y^2 = 3 + 9 = 12$. Therefore, $r = 2\sqrt{3}$. $r \cdot \cos \theta = x$.

$$\cos \theta = \frac{\sqrt{3}}{2\sqrt{3}} = \frac{1}{2} \quad \text{and} \quad \sin \theta = \frac{-3}{2\sqrt{3}} = \frac{-\sqrt{3}}{2}$$

Therefore, θ is in quadrant IV and $\theta = -60°$ or $300°$.

Thus, $\sqrt{3} + 3i = 2\sqrt{3} \text{ cis }(-60°)$.

$$\frac{2 + 2i}{\sqrt{3} - 3i} = \frac{2\sqrt{2} \text{ cis } 45°}{2\sqrt{3} \text{ cis }(-60°)}$$

$$= \frac{\sqrt{2}}{\sqrt{3}} \text{ cis}[45 - (-60°)]° = \frac{\sqrt{6}}{3} \text{ cis}(105°)$$

EXAMPLE 5: If $z = 2 \text{ cis } \dfrac{\pi}{9}$, what does z^5 equal?

$z^5 = 2^5 \text{ cis}\left(5 \cdot \dfrac{\pi}{9}\right) = 32 \text{ cis } \dfrac{5\pi}{9}$, using De Moivre's theorem.

EXAMPLE 6: Find the three cube roots of *i*.

The complex number *i* is represented on the rectangular coordinate system by the point with coordinates (0,1). Therefore, the polar form of *i* is $1\left(\cos\dfrac{\pi}{2} + i\cdot\sin\dfrac{\pi}{2}\right)$ or $\text{cis}\,\dfrac{\pi}{2}$. Since the cube roots are desired, *i* must be represented by $\text{cis}\left(\dfrac{\pi}{2} + 2k\pi\right)$, where $k = 0,1,2$.

$$\sqrt[3]{i} = 1^{1/3}\,\text{cis}\,\frac{1}{3}\left(\frac{\pi}{2} + 2k\pi\right),\ \text{where } k = 0,1,2$$

$$\sqrt[3]{i} = \text{cis}\left(\frac{\pi}{6} + \frac{2k\pi}{3}\right),\ \text{where } k = 0,1,2$$

$$\sqrt[3]{i} = \text{cis}\,\frac{\pi}{6}$$

or

$$\sqrt[3]{i} = \text{cis}\left(\frac{\pi}{6} + \frac{2k\pi}{3}\right) = \text{cis}\,\frac{5\pi}{6}$$

or

$$\sqrt[3]{i} = \text{cis}\left(\frac{\pi}{6} + \frac{4\pi}{3}\right) = \text{cis}\,\frac{9\pi}{6} = \text{cis}\,\frac{3\pi}{2}.$$

Note: Polar graphs can be drawn by putting your graphing calculator in parametric mode. If $r = f(\theta)$, let $x_t = f(t)\cdot\cos t$ and $y_t = f(t)\cdot\sin t$.

EXERCISES

1. A point has polar coordinate (2,60°). The same point can be represented by

   (A) (−2,240°)
   (B) (2,240°)
   (C) (−2,60°)
   (D) (2,−60°)
   (E) (2,−240°)

2. The graph of $r = \cos\theta$ intersects the graph of $r = \sin 2\theta$ at points

   (A) $\left(\dfrac{\sqrt{3}}{2},\dfrac{\pi}{6}\right), \left(\dfrac{\sqrt{3}}{2},\dfrac{5\pi}{6}\right)$, and $\left(0,\dfrac{\pi}{2}\right)$

   (B) $\left(\dfrac{\sqrt{3}}{2},\dfrac{\pi}{6}\right)$ and $\left(\dfrac{\sqrt{3}}{2},\dfrac{11\pi}{6}\right)$

   (C) $\left(\dfrac{\sqrt{3}}{2},\dfrac{\pi}{3}\right)$ and $\left(-\dfrac{\sqrt{3}}{2},\dfrac{\pi}{3}\right)$

   (D) $\left(\dfrac{\sqrt{3}}{2},\dfrac{\pi}{6}\right), \left(0,\dfrac{\pi}{2}\right)$, and $\left(-\dfrac{\sqrt{3}}{2},\dfrac{5\pi}{6}\right)$

   (E) only (0,0)

3. An equation in rectangular form equivalent to $r^2 = 36\sec 2\theta$ is

   (A) $x^2 - y^2 = 36$
   (B) $(x - y)^2 = 36$
   (C) $x^4 - y^4 = 36$
   (D) $xy = 36$
   (E) $y = 6$

4. If $-2 - 2i\sqrt{3}$ is divided by $-1 + i\sqrt{3}$, the quotient, in trigonometric form is

   (A) $1(\cos 240° + i\cdot\sin 240°)$
   (B) $2(\cos 120° + i\cdot\sin 120°)$
   (C) $2(\cos 135° + i\cdot\sin 135°)$
   (D) $2(\cos 150° + i\cdot\sin 150°)$
   (E) $2(\cos 210° + i\cdot\sin 210°)$

5. If $A = 2(\cos 20° + i\cdot\sin 20°)$ and $B = 3(\cos 40° + i\cdot\sin 40°)$, product $AB =$

   (A) 6 cis 20°
   (B) 6 cis 60°
   (C) 5 cis 20°
   (D) 5 cis 60°
   (E) $5(\cos 80° + i\cdot\sin 80°)$

6. $\sqrt[6]{4\sqrt{3} + 4i} =$

   (A) $\sqrt{2}\left(\cos\dfrac{\pi}{36} - i\cdot\sin\dfrac{\pi}{36}\right)$

   (B) $\sqrt{2}\,\text{cis}\,\dfrac{25\pi}{36}$

   (C) $\sqrt{8}\,\text{cis}\,\dfrac{25\pi}{36}$

   (D) $\sqrt{2}\left(\cos\dfrac{13\pi}{36} - i\cdot\sin\dfrac{13\pi}{36}\right)$

   (E) $\sqrt{8}\,\text{cis}\,\dfrac{13\pi}{36}$

7. The polar coordinates of a point P are (2,200°). The Cartesian (rectangular) coordinates of P are

   (A) (−1.88,−0.68)
   (B) (−0.68,−1.88)
   (C) (−0.34,−0.94)
   (D) (−0.94,−0.34)
   (E) (−0.47,−0.17)

ANSWERS AND EXPLANATIONS

In these solutions the following notation is used:

a: active—Calculator use is necessary or, at a minimum, extremely helpful.

n: neutral—Answers can be found without a calculator, but a calculator may help.

i: inactive—Calculator use is not helpful and may even be a hindrance.

Part 4.1 Conic Sections

1. i   D Complete the squares: $5(x^2 - 4x + 4) + 4(y^2 + 2y + 1) = -4 + 20 + 4$. $5(x-2)^2 + 4(y+1)^2 = 20$. $\dfrac{(x-2)^2}{4} + \dfrac{(y+1)^2}{5} = 1$. $a^2 = 5$, $b^2 = 4$, and so $c^2 = 1$. Therefore, the foci are 1 unit above and below the center, which is at $(2,-1)$.

2. n   C See the figure below.

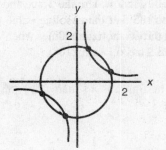

Graphing calculator: Solve the first equation for y and plot the graphs of $y = \sqrt{4 - x^2}$, $y = -\sqrt{4 - x^2}$, and $y = \dfrac{1}{x}$ in an $x \in [-5,5]$, $y \in [-5,5]$ window. The graphs intersect at four points.

3. n   C Vertex is at $(2,0)$, focus is at $(2,1)$, directrix is $y = -1$.

Graphing calculator: Plot the graph of $y = \dfrac{1}{4}(x - 2)^2$ in an $x \in [-10,10]$, $y \in [-10,10]$ window. Use the Trace and Zoom functions to see that the vertex is at $(2,0)$. If the equation were expanded, the coefficient of x^2 would be $\dfrac{1}{4}$. Therefore, the focus would be 1 unit above the vertex, $(2,1)$, and the directrix would be 1 unit below the vertex, $y = -1$. Therefore, the answer is Choice C.

4. i   D $\dfrac{x^2}{4} - \dfrac{y^2}{3} = 1$. Asymptotes $y = \pm\dfrac{\sqrt{3}}{2}x$.

5. i   E $x^2 - (2y + 3)^2 = 0$ factors into $(x - 2y - 3)(x + 2y + 3) = 0$, which breaks into $x - 2y - 3 = 0$ or $x + 2y + 3 = 0$. These are the equations of two intersecting lines.

6. i   D This is the equation of a semicircle with radius 2. $A = \dfrac{1}{2}\pi r^2 = 2\pi$.

7. a   B Distance $= \dfrac{|3\cdot 0 - 7\cdot 0 - 29|}{\sqrt{3^2 + 7^2}} = \dfrac{29}{\sqrt{58}} \approx 3.808$. Therefore, $r^2 = 14.5$. Choice B can be written as $x^2 + y^2 = 14.5$.

8. a   D $x^2 + 2x + 1 + y^2 - 4y + 4 = 0 + 1 + 4$. $(x + 1)^2 + (y - 2)^2 = 5$. Therefore, radius $= \sqrt{5}$. The center is at the centroid of the triangle, which is two-thirds of the distance from the vertex to the midpoint of the opposite side. Therefore, the radius is two-thirds of the altitude (h): $\sqrt{5} = \dfrac{2}{3}h$. $h = 1.5\sqrt{5}$. Triangle AMC is a 30-60-90 triangle so $AC = 2\left(1.5\sqrt{5}\right) \div \sqrt{3} \approx \dfrac{6.708}{1.732} \approx 3.9$.

Alternative Solution: Since $\triangle ABC$ is an equilateral triangle, arc $AB = 120°$. Central angle $\angle AOB = 120°$, OM is an altitude, and $\angle AOM = 60°$. Thus, $\triangle AOM$ is a 30-60-90 triangle. Therefore, $AM = \dfrac{\sqrt{5}}{2}\sqrt{3}$ and $AB = \sqrt{15} \approx 3.9$.

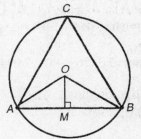

Part 4.2 Exponential and Logarithmic Functions

1. i   C $x^a \cdot x^{a^2 + a} \cdot x^{a - a^2} = x^{a + a^2 + a + a - a^2} = x^{3a}$.

2. n   D Let $\log_8 3 = y$ and $\log_2 3^x = y$. $8^y = 3$. $2^{3y} = 3$. $2^y = 3^{1/3}$. From the second equation $2^y = 3x$. Therefore, $3^x = 3^{1/3}$, and so $x = \dfrac{1}{3}$.

Calculator: $\text{Log}_8\, 3 = \dfrac{\log_{10} 3}{\log_{10} 8} \approx \dfrac{0.477}{0.903} \approx 0.528$. $\log_2 3 \approx \dfrac{\log_{10} 3}{\log_{10} 2} \approx \dfrac{0.477}{0.301} \approx 1.58$. Thus, the equation becomes $0.528 = 1.58x$ and $x \approx 0.333 \approx \dfrac{1}{3}$.

3. n   B $\mathrm{Log}_{10}(10m^2) = \log_{10} 10 + 2\log_{10} m = 1 + 2 \cdot \frac{1}{2} = 2.$

Calculator: $\mathrm{Log}_{10} m = \frac{1}{2}$ implies that $m = 10^{1/2} \approx 3.16$. Therefore, $\log_{10}(10m^2) = \log_{10} 10(3.16)^2 = \log_{10} 100 = 2.$

4. i   B $b^a = 5$, $b^c = 2.5 = 5^x$, using the relationship between logs and exponents: $b^{ax} = 5^x = b^c$. Therefore, $ax = c$ and $x = \frac{c}{a}$.

5. i   B $f\left(\frac{2}{x}\right) + f(x) = \log_2\left(\frac{2}{x}\right) + \log_2 x$
$$= \log_2 2 - \log_2 x + \log_2 x = 1.$$

6. i   E   If $b > 1$, Choice B is the answer. If $b < 1$, Choice C is the answer. Since no restriction was put on b, however, the correct answer is Choice E.

7. i   A   Converting the log expressions to exponential expressions gives $m = 2^{\sqrt{7}}$ and $n = 7^{\sqrt{2}}$. Therefore, $mn = 2^{\sqrt{7}} \cdot 7^{\sqrt{2}} \approx 6.2582 \cdot 15.673 \approx 98.$

8. a   D $f(e, \pi) = \frac{\log e}{\log \pi} \approx \frac{0.434}{0.497} \approx 0.87.$

9. a   D $\log_7 5 = \frac{\log_{10} 5}{\log_{10} 7} \approx \frac{0.699}{0.845} \approx 0.8.$

10. a   C $\left(2^{1/3}\right)\left(4^{1/5}\right)\left(8^{1/9}\right) = \left(2^{1/3}\right)\left(2^{2/5}\right)\left(2^{3/9}\right) = 2^{(1/3 + 2/5 + 1/3)} = 2^{16/15} \approx 2^{1.0667} \approx 2.1.$

Calculator: $2 x^y (16 \div 15) = 2.094588 \approx 2.1$

<u>Alternative Solution:</u> $\sqrt[3]{2} \cdot \sqrt[5]{4} \cdot \sqrt[9]{8} \approx (1.2599)(1.3195)(1.2599) \approx 2.1.$

11. a   D   Substitute in $A = Pe^{0.03t}$ to get $600 = 300e^{0.03t}$. Simplify to get $2 = e^{0.03t}$. Then take $\ln$ of both sides to get $\ln 2 = 0.03t$ and $t = \frac{\ln 2}{0.03}$. Use your calculator to find that t is approximately 23.

Part 4.3 Absolute Value

1. n   B   If $2x - 1 \geq 0$, the equation becomes $2x - 1 = 4x + 5$ and $x = -3$. However, $2x - 1 \geq 0$ implies $x \geq \frac{1}{2}$, and so -3 does not work. If $2x - 1 < 0$, the equation becomes $-2x + 1 = 4x + 5$ and $x = -\frac{2}{3}$. Since $2x - 1 < 0$ implies that $x < \frac{1}{2}$, $x = -\frac{2}{3}$ is the only root.

Graphing calculator: Plot the graphs of $y = \mathrm{abs}(2x - 1)$ and $y = 4x + 5$ in an $x \in [-10, 10]$, $y \in [-10, 10]$ window to see that the graphs intersect at only one point.

2. n   E   Here, x must be more than 1 unit from 2 but less than 4 units from 2 (including 1 and 4).

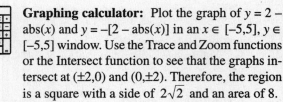

Graphing calculator: Plot the graphs of $y = 1$, $y = \mathrm{abs}(x - 2)$, and $y = 4$ in an $x \in [-10, 10]$, $y \in [-10, 10]$ window. Use the Trace and Zoom functions to see that the absolute value graph is between the two horizontal lines when $-2 \leq x \leq 1$ or when $3 \leq x \leq 6$.

3. n   A   The figure is a square $2\sqrt{2}$ on a side. The area is 8.

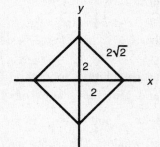

Graphing calculator: Plot the graph of $y = 2 - \mathrm{abs}(x)$ and $y = -[2 - \mathrm{abs}(x)]$ in an $x \in [-5, 5]$, $y \in [-5, 5]$ window. Use the Trace and Zoom functions or the Intersect function to see that the graphs intersect at $(\pm 2, 0)$ and $(0, \pm 2)$. Therefore, the region is a square with a side of $2\sqrt{2}$ and an area of 8.

4. i   A   Since $f(x)$ must $= f(|x|)$, the graph must be symmetric about the y-axis. The only graph meeting this requirement is Choice A.

5. n   B   Since the point where a major change takes place is at $(1, 1)$, the statement in the absolute value should equal zero when $x = 1$. This occurs only in Choice B.

Graphing calculator: Plot the graphs of each of the answer choices in an $x \in [-10, 10]$, $y \in [-10, 10]$ window to see that Choice B is the correct answer.

Part 4.4 Greatest Integer Function

1. i   C   If $N < 1$, the value should be 32; and if $1 \leq N < 2$, the value should be 55. The only answer that satisfies this is Choice C.

2. i **C** Since $f(x)$ = an integer by definition, the answer is Choice C.

3. n **E** Plotting a few numbers between 0 and 2 leads to a rather steep line going down to the right.

x	0	0.4	0.5	0.6	0.9	1	1.1
$f(x)$	0	–1.6	–1	–1.4	–2.6	–2	–2.4

Part 4.5 Rational Functions

1. n **A** Factor and reduce: $\dfrac{(x-1)(x+1)(x^2+1)}{(x-1)(x^2+x+1)}$.

Substitute 1 for x and the fraction equals $\dfrac{4}{3}$.

Graphing calculator: Plot the graph of $y = \dfrac{x^4-1}{x^3-1}$ in an $x \in [-10,10]$, $y \in [-10,10]$ window. Use the Trace and Zoom functions to see that y approaches 1.3333 as x approaches 1. Therefore Choice A is the correct answer.

2. n **B** Factor and reduce the fraction, which becomes $3x + 2$. As x approaches zero, this approaches 2.

Graphing calculator: Plot the graph of $y = \dfrac{3x^2+2x}{x}$ in an $x \in [-10,10]$, $y \in [-10,10]$ window. Use the Trace and Zoom functions to see that y approaches 2 as x approaches 0.

3. n **A** Factor and reduce $\dfrac{(x-2)(x^2+2x+4)}{(x-2)(x+2)(x^2+4)}$.

Substitute 2 for x and the fraction equals $\dfrac{3}{8}$.

Graphing calculator: Plot the graph of $y = \dfrac{x^3-8}{x^4-16}$ in an $x \in [-10,10]$, $y \in [-10,10]$ window. Use the Trace and Zoom functions to see that y approaches 0.375 as x approaches 2. Therefore, Choice A is the correct answer.

4. n **C** Divide numerator and denominator through by x^2. As $x \to \infty$, the fraction approaches $\dfrac{5}{3}$.

Graphing calculator: Plot the graph of $y = \dfrac{5x^2-2}{3x^2+8}$ in an $x \in [-10,10]$, $y \in [-10,10]$ window. Use the Trace and Zoom functions to see that y approaches 1.666 as x approaches ∞. Therefore, Choice C is the correct answer.

5. n **B** Factor and reduce $\dfrac{(3x+1)(3x-1)}{(3x+1)(x-1)}$. Therefore one asymptote is $3x - 1 = 0$ or $x = \dfrac{1}{3}$. As $x \to \infty$, $y \to \dfrac{1}{3}$. Therefore $y = \dfrac{1}{3}$.

Graphing calculator: Plot the graph of $y = \dfrac{3x^2-2x-1}{9x^2-1}$ in an $x \in [-1,1]$, $y \in [-10,10]$ window. Use the Trace and Zoom functions to see that as x passes from 0.32 to 0.34, y jumps from the positive branch of the curve to the negative branch. Therefore, the asymptote occurs at $x = \dfrac{1}{3}$.

Part 4.6 Parametric Equations

1. n **B** Complete the square on the x equation: $x = \left(t^2 + t + \dfrac{1}{4}\right) - \dfrac{1}{4} = \left(t + \dfrac{1}{2}\right)^2 - \dfrac{1}{4}$. This represents a parabola that opens up with vertex at $\left(-\dfrac{1}{2}, -\dfrac{1}{4}\right)$. Therefore, $x \geq -\dfrac{1}{4}$.

Graphing calculator: Put your calculator in parametric mode and plot the graph of $x_T = (T^2 + T)$ and $y_T = T^2 - T$ in a $T \in [-2,2]$, $x \in [-3,3]$, $y \in [-3,3]$ window. Use the Trace and Zoom functions near zero to see that the minimum x value is approximately –0.25. Therefore, the domain is all $x \geq -\dfrac{1}{4}$.

2. n **D** $\dfrac{y}{2} = \cos t$. So $\dfrac{y^2}{4} = \cos^2 t$. Adding this to $x = \sin^2 t$ gives $\dfrac{y^2}{4} + x = \cos^2 t + \sin^2 t = 1$. Since $0 \leq x \leq 1$ because $0 \leq \sin^2 t \leq 1$, this can only be a portion of the parabola given by the equation $y^2 + 4x = 4$.

Graphing calculator: Put your calculator in parametric mode and plot the graph of $x_T = (\sin T)^2$ and $y_T = 2 \cos T$ in a $T \in [0,2\pi]$, $x \in [-3,3]$, $y \in [-3,3]$ window. Use the Trace and Zoom functions to see that the curve is a portion of a parabola (and not a semicircle).

3. n **A** Removing the parameter in I by squaring and adding gives $x^2 + y^2 = 1$, which is a circle of radius 1. Substituting x for t in the y equation of II and squaring gives $x^2 + y^2 = 1$, but $y \geq 0$ so this is only a semicircle. Squaring and substituting x^2 for s in the y equation of III gives $x^2 + y^2 = 1$, but $x \geq 0$ and so this is only a semicircle.

Graphing calculator: Put your calculator in parametric mode and plot the graphs of each of the selections in order to see that only selection 1 represents a circle.

Part 4.7 Polar Coordinates

1. i A The angle must be either coterminal with 60° or 180° away. If coterminal, r must equal 2. No such points are given. 180° away gives +240° or –60°. In either case r must equal –2.

2. n D Set the two equations equal and use the double-angle formula:
$\cos \theta = 2 \sin \theta \cdot \cos \theta$.
$2 \sin \theta \cdot \cos \theta - \cos \theta = 0$.

Then $\cos \theta (2 \sin \theta - 1) = 0$, and so $\cos \theta = 0$ or $\sin \theta = \dfrac{1}{2}$.

 Graphing calculator: Put your calculator in parametric mode (and, if it is available, polar notation). Plot the graphs of $x_{1T} = (\cos T)(\cos T)$, $y_{1T} = (\sin T)(\cos T)$ and $x_{2T} = (\cos T)(\sin 2T)$, $y_{2T} = (\sin T)(\sin 2T)$ in a $T \in [0,2\pi]$, $x \in [-2,2]$, $y \in [-2,2]$ window. The graphs intersect in 3 points, the origin and two others. Use the Trace and Zoom functions to see that the correct answer is Choice D.

3. n A $\operatorname{Sec} 2\theta = \dfrac{1}{\cos 2\theta} = \dfrac{1}{2\cos^2 \theta - 1}$. Substituting in $r^2 = \dfrac{36}{2\cos^2 \theta - 1}$ gives $r^2 = \dfrac{36}{2 \cdot \dfrac{x^2}{r^2} - 1}$.

$r^2 = \dfrac{36r^2}{2x^2 - r^2}$. Dividing by r^2 gives $1 = \dfrac{36}{2x^2 - x^2 - y^2}$. Thus, $x^2 - y^2 = 36$.

Graphing calculator: Put your calculator in parametric mode. Plot the graph of
$$x_T = (\cos T)\left(\sqrt{\dfrac{36}{\cos 2T}}\right),\ y_T = (\sin T)\left(\sqrt{\dfrac{36}{\cos 2T}}\right)$$
in a $T \in [0,2\pi]$, $x \in [-10,10]$, $y \in [-10,10]$ window. The graph appears to be a hyperbola cutting the x-axis at 6. Therefore, the correct answer is Choice A.

4. i B $-2 - 2\sqrt{3}\, i = 4 \operatorname{cis} 240°$

$-1 + \sqrt{3}\, i = 2 \operatorname{cis} 120°$

$\dfrac{-2 - 2\sqrt{3}\, i}{-1 + \sqrt{3}\, i} = \dfrac{4}{2} \operatorname{cis}(240° - 120°)$

$= 2 \operatorname{cis} 120°$.

5. i B $AB = 2 \cdot 3 \operatorname{cis}(20° + 40°) = 6 \operatorname{cis} 60°$.

6. n B $4\sqrt{3} + 4i = 8 \operatorname{cis} \dfrac{\pi}{6}$. The sixth root of this $=$ $\sqrt{2} \operatorname{cis} \dfrac{1}{6}\left(\dfrac{\pi}{6} + 2\pi k\right)$, where $k = 0, 1, 2, 3, 4, 5$.

7. a A Put your calculator in degree mode. Since $x = r \cdot \cos \theta$, $x = 2 \cdot \cos 200° \approx -1.88$, and since $y = r \cdot \sin \theta$, $x = 2 \cdot \sin 200° \approx -0.68$. Therefore, the coordinates are (–1.88, –0.68).

MISCELLANEOUS TOPICS

CHAPTER

5

5.1 PERMUTATIONS AND COMBINATIONS

Any arrangement of the elements of a set in a definite order is called a *permutation*. If all n elements of a set are to be arranged, there are $n!$ (read as "n factorial") ways to arrange them; $n! = n(n-1)(n-2)\ldots 3 \cdot 2 \cdot 1$.

EXAMPLE 1: (A) $5! = 5 \cdot 4 \cdot 3 \cdot 2 \cdot 1 = 120$
(B) $3! = 3 \cdot 2 \cdot 1 = 6$

If only r elements of a set that contains n elements are to be arranged, there are $\dfrac{n!}{(n-r)!}$ arrangements.
$_nP_r = P(n,r) =$ the number of permutations of n elements taken r at a time. Therefore, $_nP_r = \dfrac{n!}{(n-r)!}$.

EXAMPLE 2: Evaluate each of the following:
(A) $_4P_4$ (B) $_7P_2$ (C) $_7P_5$.

(A) $_4P_4$ means "the number of permutations of four elements taken four at a time." From the original definition, this is equal to $4! = 4 \cdot 3 \cdot 2 \cdot 1 = 24$. From the definition of $_nP_r$, $P = \dfrac{4!}{(4-4)!} = \dfrac{4!}{0!}$. This will equal 24 if and only if 0! is defined to equal 1. In fact, 0! is *always* defined to equal 1. Therefore, using either definition, $_4P_4 = 24$.

(B) $_7P_2 = \dfrac{7!}{(7-2)!} = \dfrac{7 \cdot 6 \cdot 5 \cdot 4 \cdot 3 \cdot 2 \cdot 1}{5 \cdot 4 \cdot 3 \cdot 2 \cdot 1} = 7 \cdot 6 = 42$

(C) $_7P_5 = \dfrac{7!}{(7-5)!} = \dfrac{7 \cdot 6 \cdot 5 \cdot 4 \cdot 3 \cdot 2 \cdot 1}{2 \cdot 1}$
$= 7 \cdot 6 \cdot 5 \cdot 4 \cdot 3 = 2520$

Note: It is important to be aware that the definition of $_nP_r = \dfrac{n!}{(n-r)!}$ always allows many factors to divide out. If n is large, your calculator will not be able to handle $n!$. For example, $_{70}P_5$ cannot be evaluated by pressing the buttons $70n! + 65n! =$ because 70! is too big, and you will get an error message. In this problem you have to simplify the fraction to obtain $_{70}P_{65} = 70 \cdot 69 \cdot 68 \cdot 67 \cdot 66 = 1,452,361,680.$

EXAMPLE 3: How many four-digit lottery numbers can be drawn with no repetition of digits?

Method 1: This is a permutation problem:

$_{10}P_4 = \dfrac{10!}{(10-4)!}$
$= \dfrac{10!}{6!} = \dfrac{10 \cdot 9 \cdot 8 \cdot 7 \cdot 6 \cdot 5 \cdot 4 \cdot 3 \cdot 2 \cdot 1}{6 \cdot 5 \cdot 4 \cdot 3 \cdot 2 \cdot 1}$
$= 10 \cdot 9 \cdot 8 \cdot 7 = 5040$

Method 2: Consider putting the digits in a grid.

Any one of the 10 digits can be put in the first space. That leaves only 9 digits for the second space, only 8 for the third, and only 7 for the fourth. Thus, there are $10 \cdot 9 \cdot 8 \cdot 7 = 5040$ different lottery numbers.

EXAMPLE 4: In a club with 15 members, one member is to be chosen president, one secretary, and one treasurer. How many different slates of candidates can be chosen?

Method 1: The president can be any one of 15 people. After he or she is chosen, there are 14 remaining members from whom to choose the secretary and then only 13 members from whom to choose the treasurer. Therefore, there can be $15 \cdot 14 \cdot 13 = 2730$ different slates of candidates.

Method 2: This is a permutation problem:

$$_{15}P_3 = \frac{15!}{(15-3)!} = \frac{15!}{12!} = 15 \cdot 14 \cdot 13 = 2730$$

different slates of candidates.

In all these problems, the answer was obtained by taking the largest r factors of $n!$.

EXAMPLE 5: Evaluate: (A) $_8P_3$, (B) $_5P_5$, (C) $_{12}P_2$.

(A) $_8P_3 = 8 \cdot 7 \cdot 6 = 336$
(B) $_5P_5 = 5 \cdot 4 \cdot 3 \cdot 2 \cdot 1 = 120$
(C) $_{12}P_2 = 12 \cdot 11 = 132$

If the n elements of a set are to be arranged in a circle, they can be so arranged in $\frac{n!}{n}$ or $(n-1)!$ ways. There are fewer such permutations because there is no beginning to a circle as there is with a line.

EXAMPLE 6: How many ways can six people be seated at a round table?

This is a circular permutation, and so there are $(6-1)! = 5! = 120$ ways.

If the circular arrangement can be viewed from either side or turned over like a bracelet, there are one-half as many permutations. Therefore, the number of permutations is $\frac{(n-1)!}{2}$.

If the n elements of a set are not all different, several permutations will appear to be the same. To take care of this repetition, the formula for a permutation of n things where there are a of one kind and b of another kind is

$$\frac{n!}{a!b!}.$$

EXAMPLE 7: How many permutations of the letters in the word TATTLETALE are there?

Of the 10 letters, there are 4 T's, 2 E's, 2 L's, and 2 A's.
Therefore, the number of permutations is

$$\frac{10!}{4!2!2!2!} = \frac{10 \cdot 9 \cdot 8 \cdot 7 \cdot 6 \cdot 5 \cdot 4 \cdot 3 \cdot 2 \cdot 1}{4 \cdot 3 \cdot 2 \cdot 1 \cdot 2 \cdot 1 \cdot 2 \cdot 1 \cdot 2 \cdot 1} = 6300.$$

If a definite order in the grouping of the elements of a set is *not* necessary, the grouping is called a *combination*. The number of combinations of n things taken r at a time is denoted by $_nC_r$ or $C(n,r)$ or $\binom{n}{r}$.

$$\binom{n}{r} = \frac{_nP_r}{r!} = \frac{\text{the product of the largest } r \text{ factors of } n!}{r!}$$

Note: Most permutation and combination problems can be solved by using the $_nP_r$ or $_nC_r$ function on your calculator.

EXAMPLE 8: Set $A = \{a,b,c,d\}$. (A) List all the permutations of the elements of A taken two at a time. (B) List all the combinations of the elements of A taken two at a time.

(A) $_4P_2 = 4 \cdot 3 = 12$. There should be 12 items in the permutation.

$$\left.\begin{array}{llll} ab & ba & ca & da \\ ac & bc & cb & db \\ ad & bd & cd & dc \end{array}\right\} \begin{array}{l}\text{The permutations of } A \\ \text{taken 2 at a time.}\end{array}$$

(B) $\binom{4}{2} = \frac{4 \cdot 3}{2 \cdot 1} = 6$. There should be 6 items in the combination.

$$\left.\begin{array}{lll} ab & & \\ ac & bc & \\ ad & bd & cd \end{array}\right\} \begin{array}{l}\text{The combinations of } A \\ \text{taken 2 at a time.}\end{array}$$

EXAMPLE 9: Evaluate (A) $\binom{9}{3}$, (B) $\binom{9}{2}$, (C) $\binom{8}{2}$, (D) $\binom{8}{2}$.

(A) $\binom{9}{3} = \frac{9 \cdot 8 \cdot 7}{3 \cdot 2 \cdot 1} = 84$

(B) $\binom{9}{6} = \frac{9 \cdot 8 \cdot 7 \cdot 6 \cdot 5 \cdot 4}{6 \cdot 5 \cdot 4 \cdot 3 \cdot 2 \cdot 1} = 84$

(C) $\binom{8}{2} = \frac{8 \cdot 7}{2 \cdot 1} = 28$

(D) $\binom{8}{6} = \frac{8 \cdot 7 \cdot 6 \cdot 5 \cdot 4 \cdot 3}{6 \cdot 5 \cdot 4 \cdot 3 \cdot 2 \cdot 1} = 28$

In this example, the answers to (A) and (B) are the same, and the answers to (C) and (D) are the same. The bottom numbers in (A) and (B), 3 and 6, add up to the top number, 9, and the bottom numbers in (C) and (D), 2 and 6, add up to the top number, 8. There was much less work to do when the bottom number was the smaller of the two numbers. In general, $\binom{n}{r} = \binom{n}{n-r}$.

EXAMPLE 10: From a deck of 52 cards, how many different piles of 50 cards can be selected?

This is a combination problem. Evaluate $\binom{52}{50}$. Since, $\binom{52}{50} = \binom{52}{2}$, it is easier to evaluate $\binom{52}{2}$, which is equal to $\frac{52 \cdot 51}{2 \cdot 1} = 1326$ different piles.

EXAMPLE 11: From a deck of 52 cards, in how many ways can a hand of 13 cards be dealt so that it contains 4 hearts and 9 spades?

Since there are 13 cards of each suit, 4 of 13 hearts and 9 of 13 spades must be selected.

$$\binom{13}{4} = \frac{13 \cdot 12 \cdot 11 \cdot 10}{4 \cdot 3 \cdot 2 \cdot 1} = 715 \quad \text{and} \quad \binom{13}{9} = \binom{13}{4} = 715.$$

Therefore, the number of ways this hand can be chosen is the product $(715)(715) = 511,225$.

EXERCISES

1. $\dfrac{(5+3)!}{5! + 3!} =$
   (A) 1
   (B) 56
   (C) 320
   (D) 8
   (E) 5040

2. Frisbees come in 5 models, 8 colors, and 3 sizes. How many Frisbees must the local dealer have on hand in order to have one of each kind available?
   (A) 24
   (B) 120
   (C) 16
   (D) 39
   (E) 55

3. A craftsperson has six different kinds of seashells. How many different bracelets can be constructed if only four shells are to be used in any one bracelet?
   (A) 90
   (B) 45
   (C) 60
   (D) 360
   (E) 180

4. How many different arrangements of the letters in the word RADAR are possible?
   (A) 120
   (B) 6
   (C) 30
   (D) 60
   (E) 20

5. If a person is dealt two cards from a 52-card deck, how many different hands are possible if order is not important?
   (A) 104
   (B) 13
   (C) 1326
   (D) 103
   (E) 2652

6. If $\binom{6}{x} = \binom{4}{x}$, then $x =$
   (A) 5
   (B) 4
   (C) 11
   (D) 0
   (E) 1

7. How many odd numbers of three digits each can be formed from the digits 2, 4, 6, and 7 if repetition of digits is permitted?
   (A) 6
   (B) 27
   (C) 24
   (D) 16
   (E) 256

8. Given eight points in a plane, no three of which are colinear. How many lines do the points determine?
   (A) 16
   (B) 64
   (C) 28
   (D) 7
   (E) 36

5.2 BINOMIAL THEOREM

Expanding a binomial, $(a + b)^n$, where n is a natural number, is a tedious operation for large values of n. The binomial theorem simplifies the work. For reference, consider the expansion for the first few values of n:

$$(a+b)^1 = a+b$$
$$(a+b)^2 = a^2 + 2ab + b^2$$
$$(a+b)^3 = a^3 + 3a^2b + 3ab^2 + b^3$$
$$(a+b)^4 = a^4 + 4a^3b + 6a^2b^2 + 4ab^3 + b^4$$
$$\vdots \qquad \vdots$$

Observations: There are $n + 1$ terms in each expansion.
The sum of the exponents in each term equals n.
The exponent of b is 1 less than the number of the term.
The coefficient of each term equals $\binom{n}{\text{either exponent}}$

EXAMPLE 1: What is the coefficient of the second term of $(a + b)^4$?
The coefficient of the second term of $(a + b)^4$ is equal to $\binom{4}{1}$ or $\binom{4}{3}$, where 1 is the exponent of b and 3 is the exponent of a. The first exponent in each case is 1. Using the fourth observation above, we can express the first coefficient as $\binom{n}{n}$ or $\binom{n}{0}$.
Therefore, $\binom{n}{n} = \binom{n}{0} = 1$.

EXAMPLE 2: What is the third term of $(a + b)^{10}$?
The exponent of b is $3 - 1$ or 2.
The exponent of a must be 8 because the sum of the exponents, 8 and 2, must equal 10.
The coefficient is $\binom{10}{8} = \binom{10}{2} = \frac{10 \cdot 9}{2 \cdot 1} = 45$.
Therefore, the third term is $45a^8b^2$.

EXAMPLE 3: What is the middle term of $(a - b)^8$?
$(a - b)^8 = [a + (-b)]^8$. There are nine terms. The middle term is the fifth term. The exponent of $(-b)$ is $5 - 1$ or 4. The exponent of a is 4. The coefficient of the middle term is $\binom{8}{4} = \frac{8 \cdot 7 \cdot 6 \cdot 5}{4 \cdot 3 \cdot 2 \cdot 1} = 70$.
Therefore, the middle term is $70a^4b^4$.

EXAMPLE 4: What is the fourth term of $(a - 2b)^{12}$?
$(a - 2b)^{12} = [a + (-2b)]^{12}$. The exponent of $(-2b)$ is 3. The exponent of a is 9. The coefficient is $\binom{12}{3} = \frac{12 \cdot 11 \cdot 10}{3 \cdot 2 \cdot 1} = 220$.
The fourth term is $220a^9(-2b)^3 = 220a^9(-8b^3) = -1760a^9b^3$.

The binomial theorem method of expanding $(a + b)^n$ can be enlarged to include any real-number exponent, n, since the exponent of b is always a nonnegative integer. Although the terminology of combinations is no longer

meaningful, the symbolism is still useful. When n is a non-negative integer (greater than or equal to 3),
$$\binom{n}{3} = \frac{n(n-1)(n-2)}{3 \cdot 2 \cdot 1}.$$
Extending this process to any real number, n, gives the correct result.

EXAMPLE 5: Give the first three terms of $(a + b)^{-3}$.
The exponent of b must be 1 less than the number of the term, and the sum of the exponents must equal -3.
Thus, the expansion is
$$\binom{-3}{0}a^{-3} + \binom{-3}{1}a^{-4}b + \binom{-3}{2}a^{-5}b^2 + \cdots$$
$$= 1a^{-3} + \frac{-3}{1}a^{-4}b + \frac{(-3)(-4)}{2 \cdot 1}a^{-5}b^2 + \cdots$$
$$+ a^{-3} - 3a^{-4}b + 6a^{-5}b^2 - \cdots$$

EXAMPLE 6: Give the first four terms of $(a + b)^{1/2}$.
The exponent of b must be 1 less than the number of the term, and the sum of the exponents must equal $\frac{1}{2}$.
Thus, the expansion is
$$\binom{1/2}{0}a^{1/2} + \binom{1/2}{1}a^{-1/2}b + \binom{1/2}{2}a^{-3/2}b^2$$
$$+ \binom{1/2}{3}a^{-5/2}b^3 + \cdots$$
$$= 1a^{1/2} + \frac{1}{2}a^{-1/2}b + \frac{\frac{1}{2}\left(-\frac{1}{2}\right)}{2 \cdot 1}a^{-3/2}b^2$$
$$+ \frac{\frac{1}{2}\left(-\frac{1}{2}\right)\left(-\frac{3}{2}\right)}{3 \cdot 2 \cdot 1}a^{-5/2}b^3 + \cdots$$
$$= a^{1/2} + \frac{1}{2}a^{-1/2}b - \frac{1}{8}a^{-3/2}b^2 + \frac{1}{8}a^{-5/2}b^3 + \cdots$$

EXAMPLE 7: In the expansion $(a + b)^n$, the rth term is equal to the $(r + 1)$st term when a is 3 times as large as b. What is the relationship between n and r?

The r th term $= \binom{n}{r-1} \cdot a^{n-r+1} \cdot b^{r-1}$
$$= \binom{n}{r-1} \cdot (3b)^{n-r+1} \cdot b^{r-1}$$
$$= \binom{n}{r-1} \cdot 3^{n-r+1} \cdot b^n.$$

The $(r + 1)$st term $= \binom{n}{r} \cdot a^{n-r} \cdot b^r$
$$= \binom{n}{r} \cdot (3b)^{n-r} \cdot b^r$$
$$= \binom{n}{r} \cdot 3^{n-r} \cdot b^n.$$

Therefore,

$$\binom{n}{r-1} \cdot 3 \cdot 3^{n-r} \cdot b^n = \binom{n}{r} \cdot 3^{n-r} \cdot b^n$$

which, when simplified, is

$$\binom{n}{r-1} \cdot 3 = \binom{n}{r}.$$

Expanding gives

$$3 \cdot \frac{n!}{(r-1)!(n-r+1)!} = \frac{n!}{r!(n-r)!}.$$

Dividing out factors and simplifying, we have

$$3 \cdot \frac{1}{n-r+1} = \frac{1}{r}$$

which gives

$$3r = n - r + 1 \quad \text{or} \quad n = 4r - 1.$$

EXERCISES

1. The middle term of $\left(\dfrac{1}{x} - x\right)^{10}$ is

   (A) -126
   (B) 126
   (C) -252
   (D) $252x^5$
   (E) none of these

2. The seventh term of $\left(a^3 - \dfrac{1}{a}\right)^8$ is

   (A) $28a^6$
   (B) $28a^{-6}$
   (C) 28
   (D) $8a^5$
   (E) $8a^{-5}$

3. What is the coefficient of x^{17} in the expansion of $x^5(1 - x^2)^{12}$?

   (A) $12,376$
   (B) -924
   (C) $-12,376$
   (D) -6188
   (E) 924

4. The coefficient of the third term of $(8x - y)^{1/3}$, after simplification, is

   (A) $-\dfrac{1}{9}$

   (B) $-\dfrac{1}{288}$

   (C) $\dfrac{5}{81}$

   (D) $\dfrac{5}{2592}$

   (E) $-\dfrac{1}{576}$

5.3 PROBABILITY

The probability of an event happening is a number defined to be the number of ways the event can happen successfully divided by the total number of ways the event can happen.

EXAMPLE 1: What is the probability of getting a head when a coin is flipped?
A coin can fall in one of two ways, heads or tails, and each is equally likely.

$$P(\text{head}) = \frac{\text{number of ways a head can come up}}{\text{total number of ways the coin can fall}}$$

$$= \frac{1}{2}.$$

EXAMPLE 2: What is the probability of getting a 3 when one die is thrown?
A die can fall with any one of six different numbers showing, and there is only one way a 3 can show.

$$P(3) = \frac{\text{number of ways a 3 can come up}}{\text{total number of ways the die can fall}} = \frac{1}{6}.$$

EXAMPLE 3: What is the probability of getting a sum of 7 when two dice are thrown?
Since it is not obvious how many different throws will produce a sum of 7, or how many different ways the two dice will land, it will be useful to consider all the possible outcomes. The set of all outcomes of an experiment is called the *sample space* of the experiment. In order to keep track of the elements of the sample space in this experiment, let the first die be green and the second die be red. Since the green die can fall in one of six ways, and the red die can fall in one of six ways, there should be $6 \cdot 6$ or 36 elements in the sample space. The elements of the sample space are as follows:

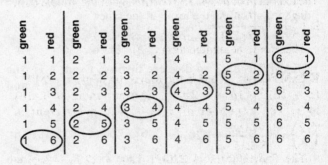

The circled elements of the sample space are those whose sum is 7.

$$P(7) = \frac{\text{number of successes}}{\text{total number}} = \frac{6}{36} = \frac{1}{6}.$$

The probability, p, of any event is a number such that $0 \leq p \leq 1$. If $p = 0$, the event cannot happen. If $p = 1$, the event is sure to happen.

EXAMPLE 4: (A) What is the probability of getting a 7 when one die is thrown? (B) What is the probability of getting a number less than 12 when one die is thrown?

(A) $P(7) = 0$ since a single die has only numbers 1 through 6 on its faces.

(B) $P(\# < 12) = 1$ since any face number is less than 12.

The *odds* in favor of an event happening are defined to be the probability of the event happening successfully divided by the probability of the event not happening successfully.

EXAMPLE 5: What are the odds in favor of getting a number greater than 2 when one die is thrown?

$P(\# > 2) = \dfrac{4}{6} = \dfrac{2}{3}$ and $P(\# \not> 2) = \dfrac{2}{6} = \dfrac{1}{3}$. Therefore, the odds in favor of a number greater than

$2 = \dfrac{P(\# > 2)}{P(\# \not> 2)} = \dfrac{\frac{2}{3}}{\frac{1}{3}} = \dfrac{2}{1}$ or $2:1$.

Independent events are events that have no effect on one another. Two events are defined to be independent if and only if $P(A \cap B) = P(A) \cdot P(B)$, where $A \cap B$ means the intersection of the two sets A and B. If two events are not independent, they are said to be *dependent*.

EXAMPLE 6: If two fair coins are flipped, what is the probability of getting two heads?

Since the flip of each coin has no effect on the outcome of any other coin, these are independent events.

$$P(HH) = P(H) \cdot P(H) = \frac{1}{2} \cdot \frac{1}{2} = \frac{1}{4}.$$

EXAMPLE 7: When two dice are thrown, what is the probability of getting two 5s?

These are independent events because the result of one die does not affect the result of the other.

$$P(\text{two 5s}) = P(5) \cdot P(5) = \frac{1}{6} \cdot \frac{1}{6} = \frac{1}{36}$$

EXAMPLE 8: Two dice are thrown. Event A is "the sum of 7." Event B is "at least one die is a 6." Are A and B independent?

From the chart in Example 3, $A = \{(1,6), (6,1), (2,5), (5,2), (3,4), (4,3)\}$ and $B = \{(1,6), (2,6), (3,6), (4,6), (5,6), (6,6), (6,1), (6,2), (6,3), (6,4), (6,5)\}$. Therefore, $P(A) = \dfrac{1}{6}$ and $P(B) = \dfrac{11}{36}$. $A \cap B = \{(1,6)(6,1)\}$. Therefore, $P(A \cap B) = \dfrac{2}{36} = \dfrac{1}{18}$. $P(A) \cdot P(B) = \dfrac{11}{216} \neq \dfrac{1}{18}$. Therefore, $P(A \cap B) \neq P(A) \cdot P(B)$, and so events A and B are dependent.

EXAMPLE 9: If the probability that John will buy a certain product is $\dfrac{3}{5}$, that Bill will buy that product is $\dfrac{2}{3}$, and that Sue will buy that product is $\dfrac{1}{4}$, what is the probability that at least one of them will buy the product?

Since the purchase by any one of the people does not affect the purchase by anyone else, these events are independent. The best way to approach this problem is to consider the probability that none of them buys the product.

Let A = the event "John does not buy the product."
Let B = the event "Bill does not buy the product."
Let C = the event "Sue does not buy the product."

$$P(A) = 1 - \frac{3}{5} = \frac{2}{5}; \quad P(B) = 1 - \frac{2}{3} = \frac{1}{3}$$
$$P(C) = 1 - \frac{1}{4} = \frac{3}{4}$$

The probability that none of them buys the product =

$P(A \cap B \cap C) = P(A) \cdot P(B) \cdot P(C) = \dfrac{2}{5} \cdot \dfrac{1}{3} \cdot \dfrac{3}{4} = \dfrac{1}{10}$.

Therefore, the probability that at least one of them buys the product is $1 - \dfrac{1}{10} = \dfrac{9}{10}$.

In general, the probability of event A happening or event B happening or both happening is equal to the sum of $P(A)$ and $P(B)$ less the probability of both happening. In symbols, $P(A \cup B) = P(A) + P(B) - P(A \cap B)$, where $A \cup B$ means the union of sets A and B. If $P(A \cap B) = 0$, the events are said to be *mutually exclusive*.

EXAMPLE 10: What is the probability of drawing a spade or a king from a deck of 52 cards?

Let A = the event "drawing a spade."
Let B = the event "drawing a king."

Since there are 13 spades and 4 kings in a deck of cards,

$$P(A) = \frac{13}{52} = \frac{1}{4}; \quad P(B) = \frac{4}{52} = \frac{1}{13}$$

$P(A \cap B) = P(\text{drawing the king of spades}) = \dfrac{1}{52}$

$P(A \cup B) = P(A) + P(B) - P(A \cap B)$

$= \dfrac{13}{52} + \dfrac{4}{52} - \dfrac{1}{52} = \dfrac{16}{52} = \dfrac{4}{13}$.

These events are *not* mutually exclusive.

EXAMPLE 11: In a throw of two dice, what is the probability of getting a sum of 7 or 11?

Let A = the event "throwing a sum of 7."
Let B = the event "throwing a sum of 11."

$P(A \cap B) = 0$, and so these events *are* mutually exclusive.

$P(A \cup B) = P(A) + P(B)$. From the chart in Example 3,

$$P(A) = \frac{6}{36} \quad \text{and} \quad P(B) = \frac{2}{36}.$$

Therefore,

$$P(A \cup B) = \frac{6}{36} + \frac{2}{36} = \frac{8}{36} = \frac{2}{9}.$$

EXERCISES

1. With the throw of two dice, what is the probability that the sum will be a prime number?

   (A) $\dfrac{7}{18}$

   (B) $\dfrac{5}{11}$

   (C) $\dfrac{5}{12}$

   (D) $\dfrac{4}{11}$

   (E) $\dfrac{1}{2}$

2. If a coin is flipped and one die is thrown, what is the probability of getting either a head or a 4?

   (A) $\dfrac{2}{3}$

   (B) $\dfrac{5}{12}$

   (C) $\dfrac{1}{12}$

   (D) $\dfrac{7}{12}$

   (E) $\dfrac{1}{3}$

3. Three cards are drawn from an ordinary deck of 52 cards. Each card is replaced in the deck before the next card is drawn. What is the probability that at least one of the cards will be a spade?

   (A) $\dfrac{3}{8}$

   (B) $\dfrac{3}{4}$

   (C) $\dfrac{3}{52}$

   (D) $\dfrac{9}{64}$

   (E) $\dfrac{37}{64}$

4. A coin is tossed three times. Let A = {three heads occur} and B = {at least one head occurs}. What is $P(A \cup B)$?

   (A) $\dfrac{1}{8}$

   (B) $\dfrac{1}{4}$

   (C) $\dfrac{1}{2}$

   (D) $\dfrac{3}{4}$

   (E) $\dfrac{7}{8}$

5. A class has 12 boys and 4 girls. If three students are selected at random from the class, what is the probability that all will be boys?

   (A) $\dfrac{1}{55}$

   (B) $\dfrac{1}{3}$

   (C) $\dfrac{1}{4}$

   (D) $\dfrac{11}{15}$

   (E) $\dfrac{11}{28}$

6. A red box contains eight items, of which three are defective, and a blue box contains five items, of which two are defective. An item is drawn at random from each box. What is the probability that both items will be nondefective?

   (A) $\dfrac{17}{20}$

   (B) $\dfrac{3}{8}$

   (C) $\dfrac{8}{13}$

   (D) $\dfrac{3}{20}$

   (E) $\dfrac{5}{13}$

7. A hotel has five single rooms available, for which six men and three women apply. What is the probability that the rooms will be rented to three men and two women?

(A) $\dfrac{5}{8}$

(B) $\dfrac{10}{21}$

(C) $\dfrac{23}{112}$

(D) $\dfrac{5}{9}$

(E) $\dfrac{97}{251}$

8. Of all the articles in a box, 80% are satisfactory, while 20% are not. The probability of obtaining exactly five good items out of eight randomly selected articles is

(A) 0.800
(B) 0.003
(C) 0.147
(D) 0.013
(E) 0.132

5.4 SEQUENCES AND SERIES

A *sequence* is a function with a domain consisting of the natural numbers in order. A *series* is the sum of the terms of a sequence.

EXAMPLE 1: Give an example of (A) an infinite sequence of numbers, (B) a finite sequence of numbers, (C) an infinite series of numbers.

(A) $\dfrac{1}{2}, \dfrac{1}{3}, \dfrac{1}{4}, \dfrac{1}{5}, \ldots, \dfrac{1}{n+1}, \ldots$, is an *infinite* sequence of numbers with $t_1 = \dfrac{1}{2}$, $t_2 = \dfrac{1}{3}$, $t_3 = \dfrac{1}{4}$, $t_4 = \dfrac{1}{5}$, and $t_n = \dfrac{1}{n+1}$.

(B) $2, 4, 6, \ldots, 20$ is a *finite* sequence of numbers with $t_1 = 2$, $t_2 = 4$, $t_3 = 6$, $t_{10} = 20$.

(C) $\dfrac{1}{2} + \dfrac{1}{4} + \dfrac{1}{8} + \dfrac{1}{16} + \cdots + \dfrac{1}{2^n} + \cdots$ is an infinite series of numbers.

EXAMPLE 2: If $t_n = \dfrac{2n}{n+1}$, find the first five terms of the sequence.

When 1, 2, 3, 4, and 5 are substituted for n, $t_1 = \dfrac{2}{2} = 1, t_2 = \dfrac{4}{3}, \ t_3 = \dfrac{6}{4} = \dfrac{3}{2}, t_4 = \dfrac{8}{5}$, and $t_5 = \dfrac{10}{6} = \dfrac{5}{3}$.

The first five terms are $1, \dfrac{4}{3}, \dfrac{3}{2}, \dfrac{8}{5}, \dfrac{5}{3}$.

EXAMPLE 3: If $a_1 = 2$ and $a_n = \dfrac{a_{n-1}}{2}$, find the first five terms of the sequence.

Since every term is expressed with respect to the immediately preceding term, this is called a *recursion formula*.

$$a_1 = 2, \ a_2 = \dfrac{a_1}{2} = \dfrac{2}{2} = 1,$$

$$a_3 = \dfrac{a_2}{2} = \dfrac{1}{2}, \ a_4 = \dfrac{a_3}{2} = \dfrac{\frac{1}{2}}{2} = \dfrac{1}{4},$$

$$a_5 = \dfrac{a_4}{2} = \dfrac{\frac{1}{4}}{2} = \dfrac{1}{8}.$$

Therefore, the first five terms are $2, 1, \dfrac{1}{2}, \dfrac{1}{4}, \dfrac{1}{8}$.

A series can be abbreviated by using the Greek letter sigma, Σ, to represent the summation of several terms.

EXAMPLE 4: (A) Express the series $2 + 4 + 6 + \cdots + 20$ in sigma notation. (B) Evaluate $\sum_{k=0}^{5} k^2$.

(A) The series $2 + 4 + 6 + \cdots + 20 = \sum_{i=1}^{10} 2i = 110$.

(B) $\sum_{k=0}^{5} k^2 = 0^2 + 1^2 + 2^2 + 3^2 + 4^2 + 5^2 = 0 + 1 + 4 + 9 + 16 + 25 = 55$.

One of the most common sequences studied at this level is an *arithmetic sequence* (or *arithmetic progression*). Each term differs from the preceding term by a common difference. In general, an arithmetic sequence is denoted by

$$t_1, t_1 + d, t_1 + 2d, t_1 + 3d, \ldots, t_1 + (n-1)d$$

where d is the common difference and $t_n = t_1 + (n-1)d$. The sum of n terms of the series constructed from an arithmetic sequence is given by the formula

$$S_n = \dfrac{n}{2}(t_1 + t_n) \quad \text{or} \quad S_n = \dfrac{n}{2}[2t_1 + (n-1)d]$$

EXAMPLE 5: **(A) Find the 28th term of the arithmetic sequence 2, 5, 8, ... (B) Express the 28 terms of the series of this sequence using sigma notation. (C) Find the sum of the first 28 terms of the series.**

(A) $t_n = t_1 + (n-1)d$

$t_{28} = 2 + 27 \cdot 3 = 83$

(B) $\displaystyle\sum_{k=0}^{27}(3k+2)$ or $\displaystyle\sum_{j=1}^{28}(3j-1)$

(C) $S_n = \dfrac{n}{2}(t_1 + t_n)$

$S_{28} = \dfrac{28}{2}(2+83) = 14 \cdot 85 = 1190$

EXAMPLE 6: **If $t_8 = 4$ and $t_{12} = -2$, find the first three terms of the arithmetic sequence.**

$$t_n = t_1 + (n-1)d$$
$$t_8 = 4 = t_1 + 7d$$
$$t_{12} = -2 = t_1 + 11d$$

To solve these two equations for d, subtract the equations.

$$-6 = 4d$$
$$d = -\frac{3}{2}$$

Substituting in the first equation gives $4 = t_1 + 7\left(-\dfrac{3}{2}\right)$.

Thus,

$$t_1 = 4 + \frac{21}{2} = \frac{29}{2}$$

$$t_2 = \frac{29}{2} + \left(-\frac{3}{2}\right) = \frac{26}{2} = 13$$

$$t_3 = \frac{29}{2} + 2\left(-\frac{3}{2}\right) = \frac{23}{2}$$

The first three terms are $\dfrac{29}{2}, 13, \dfrac{23}{2}$.

EXAMPLE 7: **In an arithmetic series, if $S_n = 3n^2 + 2n$, find the first three terms.**

When $n = 1$, $S_1 = t_1$. Therefore, $t_1 = 3(1)^2 + 2 \cdot 1 = 5$.

$$S_2 = t_1 + t_2 = 3(2)^2 + 2 \cdot 2 = 16$$
$$5 + t_2 = 16$$
$$t_2 = 11$$

Therefore, $d = 6$, which leads to a third term of 17. Thus, the first three terms are 5, 11, 17.

The terms falling between two given terms of an arithmetic sequence are called *arithmetic means*. If there is only one arithmetic mean between two given terms, it is called the *average* of the two terms.

EXAMPLE 8: **Insert three arithmetic means between 1 and 9.**

$$1, m_1, m_2, m_3, 9$$
$$t_1, t_2, \ t_3, \ t_4, \ t_5$$

Since $t_1 = 1$ and $t_5 = t_1 + (5-1)d = 9$,
$$1 + 4d = 9$$
$$4d = 8$$
$$d = 2$$

Therefore, the three arithmetic means are 3, 5, and 7.

Another very common sequence studied at this level is a *geometric sequence* (or *geometric progression*). The ratio of any two successive terms is equal to a constant, r, called the *common ratio*. In general, a geometric sequence is denoted by

$$t_1, t_1 r, t_1 r^2, \ldots, t_1 r^{n-1}, \quad \text{where } t_n = t_1 r^{n-1}.$$

The sum of n terms of a series constructed from a geometric sequence is given by

$$S_n = \frac{t_1(1-r^n)}{1-r}.$$

EXAMPLE 9: **(A) Find the seventh term of the geometric sequence 1, 2, 4, . . ., and (B) the sum of the first seven terms.**

(A) $r = \dfrac{t_2}{t_1} = \dfrac{2}{1} = 2;\ t_7 = t_1 r^{7-1};\ t_7 = 1 \cdot 2^6 = 64$

(B) $S_7 = \dfrac{1(1-2^7)}{1-2} = \dfrac{1-128}{-1} = 127$

EXAMPLE 10: **The first term of a geometric sequence is 64, and the common ratio is $\dfrac{1}{4}$. For what value of n is $t_n = \dfrac{1}{4}$?**

$$t_n = t_1 r^{n-1};\ \frac{1}{4} = 64\left(\frac{1}{4}\right)^{n-1}$$

$$\frac{1}{4} = 4^3\left(\frac{1}{4}\right)^{n-1};\ \frac{1}{4} = \left(\frac{1}{4}\right)^{-3}\cdot\left(\frac{1}{4}\right)^{n-1}$$

$$\frac{1}{4} = \left(\frac{1}{4}\right)^{-3+n-1};\ \left(\frac{1}{4}\right)^{1} = \left(\frac{1}{4}\right)^{n-4}$$

Therefore, $1 = n - 4$ and $n = 5$.

In a geometric sequence, if $|r| < 1$, the sum of the series approaches a limit as n approaches infinity. In the formula

$S_n = \dfrac{t_1(1-r^n)}{1-r}$, if $|r| < 1$, the term $r^n \to 0$ as $n \to \infty$.

Therefore, as long as $|r| < 1$, $\displaystyle\lim_{n \to \infty} S_n = \dfrac{t_1}{1-r}$.

EXAMPLE 11: Evaluate (A) $\displaystyle\lim_{n\to\infty}\sum_{k=1}^{n}\frac{1}{2^k}$ and

(B) $\displaystyle\sum_{j=0}^{\infty}(-3)^{-j}$.

Both problems ask the same question: Find the limit of the sum of the geometric series as $n \to \infty$.

(A) When the first few terms, $\dfrac{1}{2}+\dfrac{1}{4}+\dfrac{1}{8}+\cdots$, are listed,

it can be seen that the common ratio is $r=\dfrac{1}{2}$. Therefore,

$$\lim_{n\to\infty}S_n=\frac{\dfrac{1}{2}}{1-\dfrac{1}{2}}=1.$$

(B) When the first few terms, $\dfrac{1}{1}-\dfrac{1}{3}+\dfrac{1}{9}-\cdots$, are listed,

it can be seen that the common ratio is $r=-\dfrac{1}{3}$. Therefore,

$$\lim_{n\to\infty}S_n=\frac{1}{1-\left(-\dfrac{1}{3}\right)}=\frac{1}{\dfrac{4}{3}}=\frac{3}{4}.$$

EXAMPLE 12: Find the exact value of the repeating decimal 0.4545 . . . .

This can be represented by a geometric series, $0.45 + 0.0045 + 0.000045 + \cdots$, with $t_1 = 0.45$ and $r = 0.01$.
Since $|r| < 1$,

$$\lim_{n\to\infty}S_n=\frac{0.45}{1-0.01}=\frac{0.45}{0.99}=\frac{45}{99}=\frac{5}{11}.$$

The terms falling between two given terms of a geometric sequence are called *geometric means*. If there is only one geometric mean between two given terms, it is called the *mean proportional* of the two terms.

EXAMPLE 13: Insert five geometric means between $\dfrac{1}{8}$ and 8.

$$\frac{1}{8},\, m_1,\, m_2,\, m_3,\, m_4,\, m_5,\, 8$$
$$t_1,\, t_2,\, t_3,\, t_4,\, t_5,\, t_6,\, t_7$$

Since $t_1=\dfrac{1}{8}$ and $t_7=t_1 r^{n-1}=8$,

$$\frac{1}{8}r^6=8$$
$$r^6=64$$
$$r=\pm(64)^{1/6}=\pm(2^6)^{1/6}=\pm2.$$

Thus, there are two sets of geometric means.

	m_1	m_2	m_3	m_4	m_5
If $r=+2$,	$\dfrac{1}{4}$	$\dfrac{1}{2}$	1	2	4
If $r=-2$,	$-\dfrac{1}{4}$	$\dfrac{1}{2}$	-1	2	-4

EXAMPLE 14: Given the sequence 2, x, y, 9, if the first three terms form an arithmetic sequence and the last three terms form a geometric sequence, find x and y.

From the arithmetic sequence $\begin{cases}x=2+d\\y=2+2d\end{cases}$, substitute to eliminate d.

$$y=2+2(x-2)$$
$$y=2+2x-4$$
$$*y=2x-2$$

From the geometric sequence $\begin{cases}9=yr\\y=xr\end{cases}$, substitute to eliminate r.

$$9=y\cdot\frac{y}{x}$$
$$*\,9x=y^2$$

Use the two equations with the * to eliminate y:

$$9x=(2x-2)^2$$
$$9x=4x^2-8x+4$$
$$4x^2-17x+4=0$$
$$(4x-1)(x-4)=0$$
$$4x-1=0\quad\text{or}\quad x-4=0$$

Thus, $x=\dfrac{1}{4}$ or 4.

Substitute in $y=2x-2$:

$$\text{if } x=\frac{1}{4},\, y=-\frac{3}{2}$$
$$\text{if } x=4,\ \ y=6.$$

EXERCISES

1. If $a_1 = 3$ and $a_n = n + a_{n-1}$, the sum of the first five terms is

    (A) 30
    (B) 17
    (C) 42
    (D) 45
    (E) 68

2. If x, y, and z are three consecutive terms in an arithmetic sequence, which one of the following is true?

    (A) $y=\dfrac{1}{2}(x+z)$

    (B) $y=\sqrt{xz}$

    (C) $y=\sqrt{x+z}$

    (D) $y=z+x$

    (E) $z=\dfrac{1}{2}(x+y)$

3. If the repeating decimal $0.237\overline{37}$ ... is written as a fraction in lowest terms, the sum of the numerator and denominator is

(A) 245
(B) 1237
(C) 16
(D) 47
(E) 334

4. The first three terms of a geometric sequence are $\sqrt[4]{3}, \sqrt[8]{3}, 1$. The fourth term is

(A) $\sqrt[16]{3}$

(B) $\dfrac{1}{\sqrt[16]{3}}$

(C) $\dfrac{1}{\sqrt[8]{3}}$

(D) $\dfrac{1}{\sqrt[4]{3}}$

(E) $\sqrt[32]{3}$

5. By how much does the arithmetic mean between 1 and 25 exceed the positive geometric mean between 1 and 25?

(A) 5
(B) about 7.1
(C) 8
(D) 12.9
(E) 18

6. Let S_n equal the sum of all the prime numbers less than or equal to n. What is the largest value for n for which $S_n \leq 100$?

(A) 23
(B) 14
(C) 29
(D) 10
(E) 28

7. The units digit of $\displaystyle\sum_{i=1}^{10} i!$ is

(A) 0
(B) 3
(C) 5
(D) 7
(E) 9

8. $\displaystyle\sum_{k=1}^{100} (-1)^k \cdot k =$

(A) 4950
(B) 100
(C) 5050
(D) 50
(E) 0

9. In a geometric series $S_\infty = \dfrac{2}{3}$ and $t_1 = \dfrac{2}{7}$. What is r?

(A) $\dfrac{2}{3}$

(B) $-\dfrac{4}{7}$

(C) $\dfrac{2}{7}$

(D) $\dfrac{4}{7}$

(E) $-\dfrac{2}{7}$

5.5 GEOMETRY

This section contains miscellaneous topics from geometry not already covered that are likely to appear on the Math Level IIC examination.

Transformations: In a plane, a transformation slides, rotates, or stretches a geometric figure from one position to another. If point (x,y) lies on a graph and is transformed into point (x',y'), the formula for sliding (called a *translation*) is of the form

$$\begin{cases} x' = x + r \\ y' = y + s \end{cases}.$$

The formula for stretching is of the form

$$\begin{cases} x' = hx \\ y' = kx \end{cases}.$$

The formula for rotating is beyond the scope of this book.

EXAMPLE 1: Given the equation $y = x^2 + 4x + 6$, find the equation obtained by performing the translation

$$\begin{cases} x' = x + 2 \\ y' = y - 2 \end{cases}.$$

Solving the translation equations for x and y and substituting gives

$$y' + 2 = (x' - 2)^2 + 4(x' - 2) + 6$$

$$y' + 2 = (x')^2 - 4x' + 4 + 4x' - 8 + 6$$

$$y' = (x')^2$$

EXAMPLE 2: **If the graph of $f(x)$ is given in the figure, what does the graph of $f(2x - 3)$ look like?**

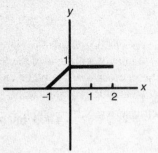

To avoid confusion, let x in $f(2x - 3)$ be called x'. When $2x' - 3$ replaces the original x, the transformation relating the original graph to the desired graph is $x = 2x' - 3$. Therefore, $x' = \dfrac{x+3}{2}$. When the graph is used to find y and this equation to is used find x', it is possible to obtain points on the desired graph.

When $x = -1, y = 0$ and $x' = 1$.

When $x = 0, y = 1$ and $x' = \dfrac{3}{2}$.

When $x = 1, y = 1$ and $x' = 2$.

When $x = 2, y = 1$ and $x' = \dfrac{5}{2}$.

When points (x',y) are graphed, the following figure is obtained:

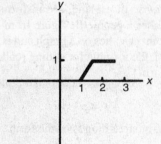

EXAMPLE 3: The shaded region in the figure is acted on by the transformation T, which transforms any point into point $(x, x+y)$. What is this figure transformed into?

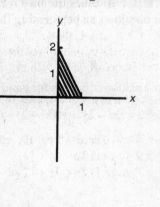

Taking points on the border of the shaded region and transforming them by T gives an idea of the shape of the new region.

$(0,0) \overset{T}{\to} (0,0)$ $\left(\dfrac{1}{4},\dfrac{3}{2}\right) \overset{T}{\to} \left(\dfrac{1}{4},\dfrac{7}{4}\right)$ $\left(\dfrac{3}{4},0\right) \overset{T}{\to} \left(\dfrac{3}{4},\dfrac{3}{4}\right)$

$(0,1) \overset{T}{\to} (0,1)$ $\left(\dfrac{1}{2},0\right) \overset{T}{\to} \left(\dfrac{1}{2},\dfrac{1}{2}\right)$ $\left(\dfrac{3}{4},\dfrac{1}{2}\right) \overset{T}{\to} \left(\dfrac{3}{4},\dfrac{5}{4}\right)$

$(0,2) \overset{T}{\to} (0,2)$ $\left(\dfrac{1}{4},0\right) \overset{T}{\to} \left(\dfrac{1}{4},\dfrac{1}{4}\right)$ $\left(\dfrac{1}{2},1\right) \overset{T}{\to} \left(\dfrac{1}{2},\dfrac{3}{2}\right)$

$(1,0) \overset{T}{\to} (1,1)$

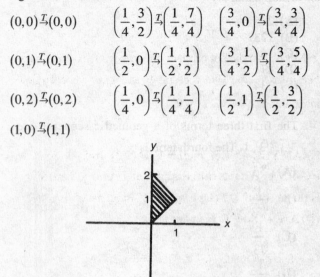

Vectors: A vector in a plane is defined to be an ordered pair of real numbers. A vector in space is defined as an ordered triple of real numbers. On a coordinate system, a vector is usually represented by an arrow whose initial point is the original and whose terminal point is at the ordered pair (or triple) that named the vector. Vector quantities always have a magnitude or *norm* (the length of the arrow) and direction (the angle the arrow makes with the positive x-axis).

All properties of two-dimensional vectors can be extended to three-dimensional vectors. We will express the properties in terms of two-dimensional vectors for convenience. If vector $\vec{V}$ is designated by (v_1,v_2) and vector $\vec{U}$ is designated by (u_1,u_2), vector $\overrightarrow{U + V}$ is designated by $(u_1 + v_1, u_2 + v_2)$ and called the *resultant* of $\vec{U}$ and $\vec{V}$. Vector $-\vec{V}$ has the same magnitude as $\vec{V}$ but has a direction opposite that of $\vec{V}$.

Every vector $\vec{V}$ can be expressed in terms of any other two (three) nonparallel vectors. In many instances unit vectors parallel to the x- and y-axes are used. If vector $\vec{i} = (1,0)$ and vector $\vec{j} = (0,1)$ [and, in three dimensions, $\vec{k} = (0,0,1)$], any vector $\vec{V} = ai + bj$, where a and b are real numbers. A unit vector parallel to $\vec{V}$ can be determined by dividing $\vec{V}$ by its norm, denoted by $\|\vec{V}\|$ and equal to $\sqrt{(v_1)^2 + (v_2)^2}$.

It is possible to determine algebraically whether two vectors are perpendicular by defining the *dot product* or *inner product* of two vectors, $\vec{V}(v_1, v_2)$ and $\vec{U}(u_1, u_2)$.

$$\vec{V} \cdot \vec{U} = v_1 u_1 + v_2 u_2$$

Notice that the dot product of two vectors is a *real number*, not a vector. Two vectors, $\vec{V}$ and $\vec{U}$, are perpendicular if and only if $\vec{V} \cdot \vec{U} = 0$.

EXAMPLE 4: Let vector $\vec{V}$ = (2,3) and vector $\vec{U}$ = (6,–4). (A) What is the resultant of $\vec{U}$ and $\vec{V}$? (B) What is the norm of $\vec{U}$? (C) Express $\vec{V}$ in terms of $\vec{i}$ and $\vec{j}$. (D) Are $\vec{U}$ and $\vec{V}$ perpendicular?

(A) The resultant, $\overrightarrow{U + V}$, equals $(6 + 2, -4 + 3) = (8, -1)$.

(B) The norm of $\vec{U}$, $\|\vec{U}\| = \sqrt{36 + 16} = \sqrt{52} = 2\sqrt{13}$.

(C) $\vec{V} = 2\vec{i} + 3\vec{j}$. To verify this, use the definitions of $\vec{i}$ and $\vec{j}$. $\vec{V} = 2(1,0) + 3(0,1) = (2,0) + (0,3) = (2,3) = \vec{V}$.

(D) $\vec{U} \cdot \vec{V} = 6 \cdot 2 + (-4) \cdot 3 = 12 - 12 = 0$. Therefore, $\vec{U}$ and $\vec{V}$ are perpendicular because the dot product is equal to zero.

EXAMPLE 5: If $\vec{U}$ = (–1,4) and the resultant of $\vec{U}$ and $\vec{V}$ is (4,5), find $\vec{V}$.

Let $\vec{V} = (v_1, v_2)$. The resultant $\overrightarrow{U + V} = (-1,4) + (v_1, v_2) = (4,5)$. Therefore, $(-1 + v_1, 4 + v_2) = (4,5)$, which implies that $-1 + v_1 = 4$ and $4 + v_2 = 5$. Thus, $v_1 = 5$ and $v_2 = 1$. $\vec{V} = (5,1)$.

EXAMPLE 6: Express vector $\vec{V}$ = (3,–7) as a linear combination of (i.e., in terms of) vectors $\vec{U}$ = (–6,8) and $\vec{W}$ = (9,–13).

This question requires that two real numbers, a and b, be found such that $\vec{V} = a\vec{U} + b\vec{W}$.

$$\vec{V} = (3, -7) = a(-6,8) + b(9, -13)$$
$$(3, -7) = (-6a, 8a) + (9b, -13b)$$
$$(3, -7) = (-6a + 9b, 8a - 13b)$$

Therefore, $3 = 6a + 9b$ and $-7 = 8a - 13b$.

Solving these two equations simultaneously gives $a = 4$ and $b = 3$.

Thus, $\vec{V} = 4\vec{U} + 3\vec{W}$.

Three-Dimensional Coordinate Geometry: In three dimensions, the equation of a plane is of the form $Ax + By + Cz + D = 0$. The intercepts of the plane can be found by setting two of the variables equal to zero.

Let $y = z = 0$, and $x = -\dfrac{D}{A}$. The x-intercept occurs at point $\left(-\dfrac{D}{A}, 0, 0\right)$.

Let $x = z = 0$, and $y = -\dfrac{D}{B}$. The y-intercept occurs at point $\left(0, -\dfrac{D}{B}, 0\right)$.

Let $x = y = 0$, and $z = -\dfrac{D}{C}$. The z-intercept occurs at point $\left(0, 0, -\dfrac{D}{C}\right)$.

The line that is the intersection of the plane and one of the coordinate planes is called a *trace*. The equation of the xy-trace is obtained by setting $z = 0$ in the equation of the plane. The xy-trace is the line whose equation is $Ax + By + D = 0$.

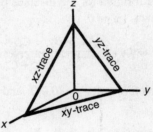

In three dimensions the equation of a line must be expressed as a set of three parametric equations:

$$x = x_0 + c_1 d$$
$$y = y_0 + c_2 d$$
$$z = z_0 + c_3 d$$

where d is the parameter, (x_0, y_0, z_0) are the coordinates of any point on the line, and c_1, c_2, and c_3 are called *direction numbers*. If (x_1, y_1, z_1) are the coordinates of any other point on the line, one set of values for the direction numbers is $c_1 = x_1 - x_0$, $c_2 = y_1 - y_0$, and $c_3 = z_1 - z_0$.

If $(c_1)^2 + (c_2)^2 + (c_3)^2 = 1$, then c_1, c_2, c_3 are called *direction cosines* and are the cosines of the three angles that the line makes with the positive x-, y-, and z-axes.

EXAMPLE 7: What are the traces of the plane with the equation $3x + 2y - 4z = 12$?

Set $z = 0$. The xy-trace is $3x + 2y = 12$.
Set $y = 0$. The xz-trace is $3x - 4z = 12$.
Set $x = 0$. The yz-trace is $2y - 4z = 12$.

EXAMPLE 8: (A) Find an equation of the line passing through the points whose coordinates are (1,2,3) and (4,–2,6). (B) Find the direction cosines of the line.

(A) Let $(x_0, y_0, z_0) = (1,2,3)$. $c_1 = 4 - 1 = 3$, $c_2 = -2 - 2 = -4$, and $c_3 = 6 - 3 = 3$. One set of equations for the line is

$$x = 1 + 3d$$
$$y = 2 - 4d$$
$$z = 3 + 3d$$

(B) To find direction cosines, it is necessary to find the distance between the two points used to determine the direction numbers.

$$\text{Distance} = \sqrt{(4-1)^2 + (-2-2)^2 + (6-3)^2}$$
$$= \sqrt{3^2 + (-4)^2 + 3^2} = \sqrt{9 + 16 + 9} = \sqrt{34}.$$

With direction numbers 3, –4, and 3, the direction cosines become $\dfrac{3}{\sqrt{34}}$, $\dfrac{-4}{\sqrt{34}}$, and $\dfrac{3}{\sqrt{34}}$.

EXAMPLE 9: How far is the plane whose equation is $3x + 4y - 5z + 12 = 0$ from the origin?

Extending the formula for the distance between a point and a line to a formula for the distance between a point and a plane gives

$$\text{Distance} = \frac{|Ax_1 + By_1 + Cz_1 + D|}{\sqrt{A^2 + B^2 + C^2}}$$

In this problem $(x_1, y_1, z_1) = (0,0,0)$ and $A = 3$, $B = 4$, $C = -5$.

$$\text{Distance} = \frac{|3 \cdot 0 + 4 \cdot 0 - 5 \cdot 0 + 12|}{\sqrt{3^2 + 4^2 + (-5)^2}} = \frac{|12|}{\sqrt{9 + 16 + 25}}$$
$$= \frac{12}{\sqrt{50}} = \frac{12}{5\sqrt{2}} = \frac{6\sqrt{2}}{5} \approx 1.697$$

Solid Figures: A solid of revolution is obtained by taking a plane figure and rotating it about some line in the plane that does not intersect the figure to form a solid figure.

EXAMPLE 10: If the segment of line $y = -2x + 2$, which lies in quadrant I (Fig. a) is rotated about the y-axis, a cone is formed (Fig. b). What is the volume of the cone?

$$V = \frac{1}{3}\pi r^2 h$$
$$V = \frac{1}{3}\pi \cdot 1^2 \cdot 2 = \frac{2\pi}{3}$$

Many three-dimensional problems involve situations where it is necessary to picture the solid figures and their relationships to one another.

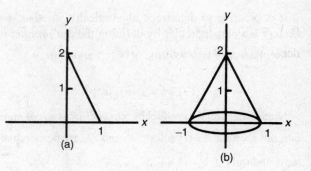
(a)   (b)

EXAMPLE 11: What figure is formed by the set of points at a fixed distance, d, from a line and at the same time $2d$ units from a point, P, on the line?

The set of points d units from the line is a cylinder of radius d, with the line as the central axis of the cylinder. The set of points $2d$ units from P is a sphere with center P and radius $2d$. Since the radius of the sphere is greater than that of the cylinder, the set of points satisfying the conditions is the intersection of the cylinder piercing the sphere. This intersection consists of two parallel circles with centers on the line, perpendicular to the line, and equidistant from the fixed point P.

EXAMPLE 12: In Example 11, how far apart are the two parallel circles?

A partial picture of the situation is shown below.

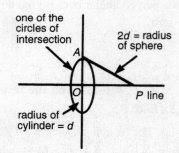

Distance OP is one-half the distance between the circles, and it is a side of a right triangle whose other two sides are known. Using the Pythagorean theorem gives

$$\overline{OP}^2 + d^2 = (2d)^2$$
$$\overline{OP}^2 = 4d^2 - d^2$$

Therefore, $OP = \sqrt{3}d$.

The distance between the circles is $2\sqrt{3}d$.

EXAMPLE 13: A cone is inscribed in a cylinder. What is the ratio of the volume of the cone to the volume of the cylinder?

The radius of the base and the heights of the cone and the cylinder are equal. The formula for the volume of the cone is $V_1 = \frac{1}{3}\pi r^2 h$. The formula for the volume of the cylinder is $V_2 = \pi r^2 h$. Therefore,

$$\frac{V_1}{V_2} = \frac{\frac{1}{3}\pi r^2 h}{\pi r^2 h} = \frac{\frac{1}{3}}{1} = \frac{1}{3}.$$

EXERCISES

1. In the figure, the graph of $f(x)$ has two transformations performed on it. First it is rotated 180° about the origin, and then it is reflected about the x-axis. Which of the choices below is the function expression of the resulting curve?

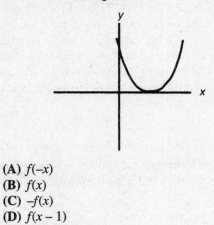

(A) $f(-x)$
(B) $f(x)$
(C) $-f(x)$
(D) $f(x-1)$
(E) none of these

2. If (x,y) represents a point on the graph of $y = x + 2$, which of the following could be a portion of the graph of the set of points $\left(x, \sqrt{y}\right)$?

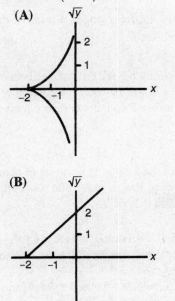

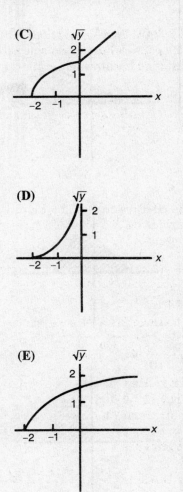

3. In the figure, S is the set of points in the shaded region. Which of the choices below represents the set of all points $(x + y, y)$, where (x,y) is a point in S?

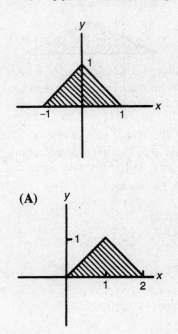

(B)

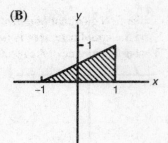

(C)

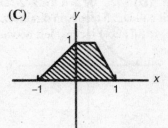

(D)

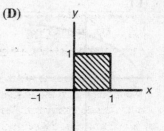

(E)

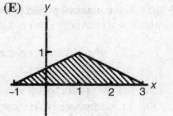

4. If $\vec{V} = 2\vec{i} + 3\vec{j}$ and $\vec{U} = \vec{i} - 5\vec{j}$, the resultant vector

of $2\vec{U} + 3\vec{V}$ equals

(A) $3\vec{i} - 2\vec{j}$

(B) $5\vec{i} + \vec{j}$

(C) $7\vec{i} - 9\vec{j}$

(D) $8\vec{i} - \vec{j}$

(E) $2\vec{i} + 3\vec{j}$

5. A unit vector perpendicular to vector $\vec{V} = (3, -4)$ is

(A) $(4, 3)$

(B) $\left(\dfrac{3}{5}, \dfrac{4}{5}\right)$

(C) $\left(-\dfrac{3}{5}, -\dfrac{4}{5}\right)$

(D) $\left(-\dfrac{4}{5}, -\dfrac{3}{5}\right)$

(E) $\left(-\dfrac{4}{5}, \dfrac{3}{5}\right)$

6. The plane $2x + 3y - 4z = 5$ intersects the x-axis at the point where the x-coordinate is

(A) 2

(B) 2.5

(C) $1\dfrac{2}{3}$

(D) -1.25

(E) 5

7. The distance between two points in space, $P_1(x, -1, -1)$ and $P_2(3, -3, 1)$, is 3. Find the possible values of x.

(A) only 1 and 2

(B) only 2 and 3

(C) only -2 and -3

(D) only 2 and 4

(E) only -2 and -4

8. Which of the following is a trace of the plane $3x + 5y - 7z + 8 = 0$?

(A) $3x + 5y = 8$

(B) $3x + 7z + 8 = 0$

(C) $5y - 7z = 8$

(D) $7z + 3x = 8$

(E) $7z - 5y = 8$

9. Which of the following is the set of parametric equations for the line in space that passes through points $(2, 4, 1)$ and $(-1, 5, 2)$?

(A) $x = -1 + 2d, y = 5 + 4d, z = 2 + d$

(B) $x = -1 + d, y = 5 - d, z = 2 - d$

(C) $x = 2 - d, y = 4 + 5d, z = 1 + 2d$

(D) $x = 2 - 3d, y = 4 + d, z = 1 + d$

(E) $x = 2 + d, y = 4 + 9d, z = 1 + 3d$

10. If the portion of the graph of $x^2 + y^2 = 4$ that lies in quadrant I is revolved around the x-axis, the volume of the resulting figure is

(A) 3.1
(B) 6.3
(C) 12.6
(D) 16.8
(E) 33.5

11. A right circular cone whose base radius is 12 is inscribed in a sphere of radius 13. What is the volume of the cone?

(A) 720π

(B) $\dfrac{2197\pi}{3}$

(C) 864π
(D) 1440π
(E) 2592π

12. Given a right circular cylinder such that the volume has the same numerical value as the total surface area. The smallest integral value for the radius of the cylinder is

(A) 1
(B) 2
(C) 3
(D) 4
(E) This value cannot be determined.

13. A square pyramid is inscribed in a cylinder whose base radius is 4 and height is 9. What is the volume of the pyramid?

(A) 48
(B) 144
(C) 288
(D) 96
(E) 108

14. The set of points in space equidistant from two fixed points is

(A) one point
(B) one line
(C) a plane
(D) a hyperbola
(E) none of the above

15. What is the length of the xz-trace, between the positive x-axis and the positive z-axis, of the plane whose equation is $2x + 3y + 4z = 7$?

(A) 2.3
(B) 3.9
(C) 4.2
(D) 2.9
(E) 4.6

16. The region in the first quadrant bounded by the line $3x + 2y = 7$ and the coordinate axes is rotated about the x-axis. What is the volume of the resulting figure?

(A) 90
(B) 20
(C) 30
(D) 120
(E) 8

17. Three tennis balls just fit in a cylindrical tennis ball can. If each ball is 2.5 inches in diameter, what is the volume of air (in cubic inches) left between the balls and the can?

(A) 98.2
(B) 122.7
(C) 8.2
(D) 12.3
(E) 65.4

5.6 VARIATION

In a *direct variation* the ratio of the variables is a constant. The first variable mentioned is in the numerator, and all others form a product in the denominator. Thus, as the first variable increases (or decreases), the second variable (or product of variables) must also increase (or decrease) in order to maintain a constant value.

EXAMPLE 1: Give a formula for the statement "x varies directly as y, the square of z, and the square root of a."

$$\frac{x}{yz^2\sqrt{a}} = K, \quad \text{where } K \text{ is a constant.}$$

In an *inverse variation* the product of all variables is equal to a constant. Thus, as the first variable increases (or decreases), the second variable (or product of variables) must decrease (or increase) in order to maintain a constant value.

EXAMPLE 2: Give a formula for the statement "x varies inversely as the square of y and the cube of z."

$$xy^2z^3 = K, \quad \text{where } K \text{ is a constant.}$$

In any variation that combines both direct and inverse variation, the formula is put together using the procedure of a direct variation (a ratio) and then an inverse variation (a product). The result is equal to a constant.

EXAMPLE 3: Give a formula for the statement "z varies directly as x and inversely as y."

$$\frac{z \cdot y}{x} = K, \quad \text{where } K \text{ is a constant.}$$

EXAMPLE 4:   Give a formula for the statement "a varies as b and the square of c and inversely as x and the square root of y."

$$\frac{ax\sqrt{y}}{bc^2} = K, \quad \text{where } K \text{ is a constant.}$$

In general, the formula for a *combined variation* is set up as a ratio (direct variation) until there is some indication that what follows is an inverse variation (usually just the word *inversely*). From that point on a product is formed.

EXAMPLE 5:   Give a formula for the statement "T varies jointly as L, P, and the square of D and inversely as R and Q."

$$\frac{T \cdot RQ}{LPD^2} = K, \quad \text{where } K \text{ is a constant.}$$

In all these examples K is called the *constant of variation* or the *constant of proportionality*.

EXAMPLE 6:   If x varies as y and inversely as z, and $x = 2$ when $y = 4$ and $z = 3$, find (A) the constant of variation, and (B) the value of z when $x = 8$ and $y = 2$.

The formula is $\dfrac{xz}{y} = K$.

(A) $\dfrac{2 \cdot 3}{4} = K = \dfrac{3}{2} =$ the constant of variation.

(B) $\dfrac{8z}{2} = K = \dfrac{3}{2}$

$8z = 3$

Therefore, $z = \dfrac{3}{8}$.

EXAMPLE 7:   If x varies as y and z^2, and inversely as the square root of w, what is the effect on y when x is doubled, z is halved, and w is multiplied by 4?

The formula is $\dfrac{x\sqrt{w}}{yz^2} = K$.

For all practical purposes, the quickest way to solve a problem of this type is to arbitrarily choose a value for each variable and compute K. For example, let $x = 1$, $y = 3$, $z = 2$, and $w = 4$ (a perfect square since $\sqrt{w}$ is needed).

$$\frac{1\sqrt{4}}{3 \cdot 2^2} = K = \frac{1 \cdot 2}{3 \cdot 4} = \frac{1}{6}$$

The new values of the variables are $x = 2$, $z = 1$, and $w = 16$.

Let $y = y_2$ just to emphasize a new value of y.

$$\frac{2\sqrt{16}}{y_2 \cdot 1} = \frac{1}{6}$$

$$\frac{2 \cdot 4}{y^2} = \frac{1}{6}$$

$$y_2 = 48$$

The original value of y was 3. The new value of y is 48.

Therefore, for any values of x, y, z, and w, when x is doubled, z is halved, and w is multiplied by 4, y is multiplied by 16.

EXERCISES

1. If x varies directly as y, which of the following statements must be true?

   I. Their product is a constant.
   II. Their sum is a constant.
   III. Their quotient is a constant.

   (A) only I
   (B) only II
   (C) only III
   (D) only I and II
   (E) only II and III

2. If $\{(x,y) : (4,3),(-2,a)\}$ consists of pairs of numbers that belong to the relationship "y varies inversely as x^2," what does a equal?

   (A) $-\dfrac{3}{2}$

   (B) -6

   (C) $-\dfrac{2}{3}$

   (D) 12

   (E) $\dfrac{3}{4}$

3. D varies as R and inversely as the square of M. If R is divided by 3 and M is doubled, what is the effect on D?

   (A) D is unchanged.
   (B) D is divided by 12.
   (C) D is multiplied by 12.
   (D) D is divided by 6.
   (E) D is multiplied by 6.

5.7   LOGIC

There are three major statements in logic:

I. A *conjunction* is a statement of the form "A and B" ($A \wedge B$). It is considered to be true if A and B are both true. The *negation* of a conjunction, denoted by $(A \wedge B)'$, or $\sim(A \wedge B)$, is equivalent to the statement "the negation of A *or* the negation of B," which is denoted by $A' \vee B'$ *or* $(\sim A) \vee (\sim B)$.

II. A *disjunction* is a statement of the form "A or B" ($A \vee B$). It is considered to be true if either A or B or both are true. The *negation* of a disjunction, denoted by $(A \vee B)'$ or $\sim(A \vee B)$, is equivalent to the statement "the negation of A *and* the negation of B," which is denoted by $A' \wedge B'$ or $(\sim A) \wedge (\sim B)$.

III. An *implication* is a statement of the form "if A, then B" ($A \rightarrow B$). It is considered to be true *except* when A is true and B is false. The negation of an implication, denoted by $(A \rightarrow B)'$ or $\sim(A \rightarrow B)$, is equivalent to the statement "A and the negation of B," which is denoted by $A \wedge B'$ or $A \wedge (\sim B)$. There are many forms of an implication that are all equivalent:

> if A, then B
> A implies B
> A only if B
> B, if A
> A is sufficient for B
> B is necessary for A

The double implication "A if and only if B," denoted by "A iff B" or $A \leftrightarrow B$, is equivalent to the statement "if A, then B and if B, then A."

Associated with every implication, $A \rightarrow B$, are three other statements:
1. The converse is $B \rightarrow A$.
2. The inverse is $A' \rightarrow B'$.
3. The contrapositive $B' \rightarrow A'$ or $(\sim B) \rightarrow (\sim A)$, which is equivalent to the original implication $A \rightarrow B$. (If $A \rightarrow B$ is true, then $B' \rightarrow A'$ is also true. If $A \rightarrow B$ is false, then $B' \rightarrow A'$ is also false.)

The negation of the statement "for all A" is "for some not-A." The negation of the statement "for some A" is "for all not-A."

A statement that is always true is called a *tautology*.

EXAMPLE 1: State the negation of each of the following:
(A) **All men are mortal.**
(B) **For some x, $x = 2$.**
(C) **Some boys play tennis.**
(D) **All cats are not dogs.**

(A) Some men are not mortal.
(B) For all x, $x \neq 2$.
(C) All boys do not play tennis.
(D) Some cats are dogs.

EXAMPLE 2: State the negation of $(p \wedge q) \rightarrow p$.
The negation is $(p \wedge q) \wedge p'$, which is always false because there is no way that p and p' can both be true.

EXAMPLE 3: Is the statement "I will drive only if I am wrong," true or false if it is known that I am always wrong?
Let $p = I$ *will drive* and $q = I$ *am wrong*. The statement is equivalent to $p \rightarrow q$, which is true for all cases except when p is true and q is false. Since it is known that q is true, the statement itself must always be true.

EXAMPLE 4: What conclusion can be drawn from the following statements?

The boy is handsome, or he is short and fat.
If he is short, then he is blond.
He is not blond.

Let $H =$ *he is handsome*, let $S =$ *he is short*, let $F =$ *he is fat*, and let $B =$ *he is blond*. The three statements become:

$$H \vee (S \wedge F)$$
$$S \rightarrow B$$
$$B'$$

Since B' is true, B is false. The only way that $S \rightarrow B$ can be true when B is false is when S is also false. Since S is false, $S \wedge F$ is false regardless of whether F is true or false. Since $S \wedge F$ is false, the only way $H \vee (S \wedge F)$ can be true is if H is true. Therefore, the conclusion is "The boy is handsome."

EXERCISES

1. The statement $(p \vee q) \rightarrow p$ is *false* if

   (A) p is true and q is true
   (B) p is true and q is false
   (C) p is false and q is true
   (D) p is false and q is false
   (E) the statement is a tautology

2. Which of the following is equivalent to the statement "Having equal radii is necessary for two circles to have equal areas"?

   I. Having equal areas is sufficient for two circles to have equal radii.
   II. Two circles have equal areas only if they have equal radii.
   III. Having equal radii implies that two circles have equal areas.

   (A) only I
   (B) only III
   (C) only I and II
   (D) only II and III
   (E) I, II, and III

3. Given the statement "If $x = 2$, then $x^2 = 4$." The negation of this statement is

   (A) $x \neq 2$, and $x^2 \neq 4$
   (B) $x = 2$, and $x^2 \neq 4$
   (C) $x \neq 2$ or $x^2 = 4$
   (D) $x \neq 2$, and $x^2 = 4$
   (E) $x \neq 2$ or $x^2 \neq 4$

4. Given these statements:

   I. Some numbers are not prime.
   II. No primes are squares.

   If *some* means "at least one," it can be concluded from I and II that

   (A) some numbers are squares
   (B) some squares are not numbers
   (C) some numbers are not squares
   (D) no numbers are squares
   (E) none of the above is a conclusion of I and II

5. In a particular town the following facts are true:

   I. Some smarties do not smoke cigars.
   II. All men smoke cigars.

   A necessary conclusion is

   (A) some smarties are men
   (B) some smarties are not men
   (C) no smartie is a man
   (D) some men are not smarties
   (E) no man is a smartie

6. Given the statement "The student will not pass the course only if he does not come to class," which one of the following can be concluded?

   (A) If the student does not pass the course, then he probably missed too many classes.
   (B) If a student comes to class, then he may pass the course.
   (C) If a student comes to class, then he will pass the course.
   (D) If a student passes the course, then he came to class.
   (E) If a student does not come to class, then he will not pass the course.

7. The contrapositive of $p \rightarrow q'$ is

   (A) $p' \rightarrow q$
   (B) $p' \rightarrow q'$
   (C) $q' \rightarrow p$
   (D) $q \rightarrow p'$
   (E) $q' \rightarrow p'$

5.8   STATISTICS

One final subject that may appear on the Math Level IIC test is statistics, but only the most elementary topics considered. Among these are measures of central tendency (averages), frequency distributions, and a simple measure of dispersion (range).

Descriptive statistics consists of methods for describing numerical information in an organized fashion. Probably the most common measure of central tendency, the arithmetic mean, can be determined regardless of whether or not the data are organized. The arithmetic mean is obtained by adding up all the items of data and dividing by the number of items. For example, the mean of 18 test scores in Table 1 is

$$\frac{\Sigma \text{ scores}}{18} = \frac{1123}{18} \approx 62.39$$

In order to draw other conclusions from the test scores in Table 1, the scores would have to be ordered into a frequency distribution (Table 2). A frequency distribution

TABLE 1				TABLE 2	
67	62	65		Data, N	Frequency, f
62	57	59		55	1
67	60	65		57	1
66	62	65		59	2
63	55	64		60	1
63	59	62		62	4
				63	2
				64	1
				65	3
				66	1
				67	2

consists of the data organized in a table (usually from smallest value to largest value) with the number of times each value occurs.

Many things about the data can be easily determined from a frequency distribution. Three of them are as follows:

1. The *range* of the data is the difference between the largest and smallest values. The range of the data in Table 2 is 12. (67 − 55 = 12).
2. The *mode* of the data is the value that occurs most often. The mode of these data is 62 (there are four 62s).
3. The *median* of the data is the middle score after the data have been ordered. (If there is an even number of scores, the mean of the two middle scores is the median.) The median of these data is

62.5. $\left(\dfrac{62 + 63}{2} = 62.5 \right)$.

Although any one of the mean, median, and mode could correctly be called the average of the data, *average* usually refers to the mean.

EXAMPLE 1: Consider this frequency distribution:

Data	Frequency
0	2
1	3
2	5
3	8
4	2

Find the values of the mode, median, and mean.

Mode $= 3$

Median $= \dfrac{2+3}{2} = 2.5$

Mean $= \dfrac{0+3+10+24+8}{20} = \dfrac{45}{20} = 2.25$

EXAMPLE 2: If the set of data 1, 2, 3, 1, 5, 7, x is to have a mode and x is equal to one of the other elements of the set, what value must x have?

Since there are two 1s and one of every other value, x must equal 1. If it were to equal any of the other numbers, there would be two values with two elements. Thus, the set of data would not have a mode.

EXAMPLE 3: Given this set of data: 15, 24, 28, 32, 35, x, where x is the largest element. If the range is 35, what is the value of x?

Since the range is the difference between the largest element and the smallest element, $x - 15 = 35$. Therefore $x = 50$.

EXAMPLE 4: Given this set of integers: 1, 2, 3, 3, 4, 1, x. If the median is 2, what is the value of x?

Since this set of data has seven elements, the median is the middle number after the data have been ordered. Since the median is 2, the value of x must be any integer ≤ 2.

EXAMPLE 5: Given this set of integers: 1, 2, 3, 3, 4, 1, x. If mean = median = 2, what is the value of x?

Mean $= \dfrac{1+2+3+3+4+1+x}{7} = \dfrac{14+x}{7} = 2$

$$14 + x = 14$$

Therefore, $x = 0$.

EXERCISES

1. In statistics, when the word *average* is mentioned, it refers to

   (A) mean
   (B) median
   (C) mode
   (D) mean or median
   (E) mean, median, or mode

2. If the range of a set of integers is 2 and the mean is 50, which of the following statements must be true?

   I. The mode is 50.
   II. The median is 50.
   III. There are exactly three items of data

   (A) only I
   (B) only II
   (C) only III
   (D) I and II
   (E) I, II, and III

3. If the range of the set of data 1, 1, 2, 2, 3, 3, 3, x is equal to the mean and x is an integer, then x must be

   (A) −1
   (B) −2
   (C) 0
   (D) 1
   (E) There are no values of x that satisfy the stated conditions.

4. In the following frequency distribution, if the mean is to be equal to one of the elements of data, how many 4s must there be?

Data	Frequency
0	1
2	3
3	2
4	?
5	1

   (A) 0
   (B) 2
   (C) 3
   (D) 4
   (E) 5

5. If the mean, median, and mode are calculated from the data in this frequency distribution, which of the following statements is true?

Data	Frequency
2	4
4	3
6	2
8	2

   (A) mode < median < mean
   (B) mean = median
   (C) mode < mean < median
   (D) mean < median < mode
   (E) median < mode < mean

5.9   ODDS AND ENDS

Each year one or two problems on the Math Level IIC examination involve topics that do not fall into any of the categories discussed above. Also, occasionally, definitions are made within problems, and then a question is asked using these definitions. Usually these questions are quite easy if you take the time to read them carefully.

EXAMPLE 1: If a 2 by 2 determinant $\begin{vmatrix} a & b \\ c & d \end{vmatrix}$ is defined to equal $ad - bc$, what does x equal if the determinant $\begin{vmatrix} 2 & 3 \\ x & 5 \end{vmatrix} = 0$?

$$2 \cdot 5 - 3x = 0$$
$$3x = 10$$
$$x = \frac{10}{3}$$

EXAMPLE 2: If the operation $*$ is defined as follows, $a * b = ab - b$, what does $3 * 5$ equal?

$$3 * 5 = 3 \cdot 5 - 5 = 15 - 5 = 10$$

EXAMPLE 3: If the operations $*$ and $\#$ are defined so that $a * b = 2a - b$ and $a \# b = \frac{a}{b} + b$, does $(3 * 2) \# 4 = 3 * (2 \# 4)$? Explain.

$$(3 * 2) \# 4 = (2 \cdot 3 - 2) \# 4 = 4 \# 4 = \frac{4}{4} + 4 = 5$$

$$3 * (2 \# 4) = 3 * \left(\frac{2}{4} + 4 \right) = 3 * 4\frac{1}{2} = 2 \cdot 3 - 4\frac{1}{2} = 6 - 4\frac{1}{2}$$
$$= 1\frac{1}{2}$$

Therefore, the expressions are not equal.

EXAMPLE 4: Following the sequence of instructions, tell what number(s) will be printed.

1. **Let $x = 2$.**
2. **Let $y = x + 2$.**
3. **If $x \cdot y < 10$, then print the value of x, replace x by $x + 3$, and return to step 2.**
   If $x \cdot y > 10$, then stop.

Starting with $x = 2$ and $y = 4$, then $x \cdot y = 8 < 10$. Print 2, replace x by 5 and $y = 7$. Then $x \cdot y = 35 \not< 10$. Stop.

Thus, the only number that is printed is 2.

EXAMPLE 5: $P(A|B)$ is the probability of event A happening after event B has already happened. Event A is "a red card is drawn from a deck of 52 cards." Event B is "a black card is drawn from a deck of 52 cards." What does $P(A|B)$ equal?

Since event B is given as having been accomplished, a black card has been drawn from the deck and only 51 cards are left in the deck: 26 red cards and 25 black cards.

Therefore, $P(A|B) = \frac{26}{51}$.

EXAMPLE 6: If $f^*(x)$ is defined to be $\dfrac{[f(x)]^2 - f(x)}{x}$ and $f(x) = x^x$, what does $f^* 2^2$ equal?

$$f * (2) = \frac{\left(2^2\right)^2 - 2^2}{2} = \frac{4^2 - 4}{2} = \frac{16 - 4}{2} = 6.$$

EXAMPLE 7: If $\begin{cases} ax + by = c \\ dx + ey = f \end{cases}$ are solved simultaneously, and $x = 5$, $y = 2$, and $\begin{vmatrix} a & b \\ d & e \end{vmatrix} = 2$, what does $\begin{vmatrix} c & b \\ f & e \end{vmatrix}$ equal?

Using determinants to solve the pair of equations gives

$$x = \frac{\begin{vmatrix} c & b \\ f & e \end{vmatrix}}{\begin{vmatrix} a & b \\ d & e \end{vmatrix}} \quad \text{and} \quad y = \frac{\begin{vmatrix} a & c \\ d & f \end{vmatrix}}{\begin{vmatrix} a & b \\ d & e \end{vmatrix}}.$$

In this case, $x = 5 = \dfrac{\begin{vmatrix} c & b \\ f & e \end{vmatrix}}{2}$.

Therefore, $\begin{vmatrix} c & b \\ f & e \end{vmatrix} = 10$.

EXAMPLE 8: At the dog pound there are 47 dogs: 16 are large, 18 are brown, and 20 are neither. How many large, brown dogs are there?

Let $L =$ the set of large dogs, let $B =$ the set of brown dogs, and let $N =$ the set of dogs that are neither large nor brown. A Venn diagram is helpful.

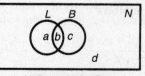

All Dogs at the Pound

Label the number of dogs in each set with a variable, a, b, c, or d. Thus,

$$a + b + c + d = 47$$
$$a + b = 16$$
$$b + c = 18$$
$$d = 20$$

Multiplying the first equation by -1 and adding all four equations results in $b = 7$.

Therefore, there are 7 large, brown dogs.

EXERCISES

1. A *harmonic sequence* is a set of numbers such that their reciprocals, taken in order, form an arithmetic sequence. If S_n = the sum of the first n terms of the harmonic sequence and the first three terms are 2, 3, and 6, then S_4 equals

(A) 11
(B) 12
(C) 1
(D) 22
(E) The value of S_4 cannot be determined.

2. If the pair of equations $\begin{cases} 2x + 3y = 4 \\ 5x + 2y = 8 \end{cases}$ is solved using determinants, the determinant appearing in the denominator of the solution has a value of

(A) −11
(B) −4
(C) −32
(D) 4
(E) 16

3. In the statement "$a = b \pmod n$," b is the remainder when a is divided by n. What is the smallest value of n such that $125 = 7 \pmod n$?

(A) 47
(B) 118
(C) 19
(D) 8
(E) 59

4. If $*$ is a binary operation defined by $a * b = \dfrac{a+b}{2}$ and $\#$ is a binary operation defined by $a \# b = \sqrt{ab}$, for what values of a and b does $a * b = a \# b$?

(A) all real numbers
(B) no real numbers
(C) 0 only
(D) 1 only
(E) only when $a = b$

5. A binary operation $*$ is defined on the set of ordered pairs of real numbers as follows: $(a,b) * (x,y) = (a + x, b - y)$. If $(1,2) * (1,1) = (p,q) * (1,2)$, then (p,q) equals

(A) (1,1)
(B) (1,2)
(C) (1,3)
(D) (0,2)
(E) $\left(2, \dfrac{1}{2}\right)$

6. Carrying out the following instructions in order, find what number is printed first.

   1. Let $a = x = 2$.
   2. Go to step 4.
   3. Replace x by the value of $a + 2$.
   4. If $a < 6$, replace a by $x + 2$ and go to step 3; otherwise print the value of x.

(A) 10
(B) 8
(C) 6
(D) 12
(E) 2

7. If darts are thrown at a target like the one in the figure (and every dart hits the figure), what is the probability that the first dart will hit outside the circle?

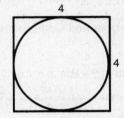

(A) 0.2
(B) 0.8
(C) 0.3
(D) 0.5
(E) 0.6

8. In a group of 100 birds, 85 had a long beak, 45 had gray feathers, and 38 had both a long beak and gray feathers. How many did not have a long beak and did not have gray feathers?

(A) 15
(B) 55
(C) 62
(D) 8
(E) 30

9. If the operation $\#$ is defined by $a \# b = \sqrt{\sin a + \sec b}$, $3 \# 5 =$

(A) 0.7
(B) 1.0
(C) 1.9
(D) 2.3
(E) 3.7

10. If $a * b$ is a binary operation defined by

$$a * b = \frac{\sqrt[3]{a} + \sqrt[3]{b}}{\sqrt{ab}}, 3 * \pi =$$

(A) 1.14
(B) 1.93
(C) 1.60
(D) 0.95
(E) 2.31

ANSWERS AND EXPLANATIONS

In these solutions the following notation is used:

- a: active—Calculator use is necessary or, at a minimum, extremely helpful.
- n: neutral—Answers can be found without a calculator, but a calculator may help.
- i: inactive—Calculator use is not helpful and may even be a hindrance.

Part 5.1 Permutations and Combinations

1. n **C** $\dfrac{(5+3)!}{5!+3!} = \dfrac{8!}{5!+3!}$

$$= \frac{8 \cdot 7 \cdot 6 \cdot 5 \cdot 4 \cdot 3 \cdot 2 \cdot 1}{(5 \cdot 4 \cdot 3 \cdot 2 \cdot 1) + (3 \cdot 2 \cdot 1)}$$

$$= \frac{40320}{120 + 6} = 320.$$

2. n **B** Number available $= 5 \cdot 8 \cdot 3 = 120$.

3. n **B** There are $\binom{6}{4} = 15$ different groups of 4 shells out of the 6 available. In each of these groups the circular permutation can be turned over. Therefore, number of bracelets $= 15 \cdot \dfrac{3!}{2} = 45$.

4. n **C** Permutation with repetitions: $\dfrac{5!}{2!2!} = 30$.

5. n **C** A combination: $\binom{52}{2} = \dfrac{52 \cdot 51}{2 \cdot 1} = 1326$.

6. i **D** The value of x must be less than 4. The only value that works is 0.

7. i **D** Only 7 can go in the units place. Any one of 4 numbers can go in the other two places. Number of numbers $= 4 \cdot 4 \cdot 1 = 16$.

8. n **C** In order to draw lines through each of 2 points, there are 8 points to be chosen 2 at a time. Number of lines $= \binom{8}{2} = \dfrac{8 \cdot 7}{2 \cdot 1} = 28$.

Part 5.2 Binomial Theorem

1. n **C** The middle term is the sixth term, which is $\binom{10}{5}x^5\left(-\dfrac{1}{x}\right)^5 = \dfrac{10 \cdot 9 \cdot 8 \cdot 7 \cdot 6}{5 \cdot 4 \cdot 3 \cdot 2 \cdot 1} = -252$.

2. n **C** The seventh term is $\binom{8}{6}(a^3)^2\left(-\dfrac{1}{a}\right)^6 = \dfrac{8 \cdot 7}{2 \cdot 1} \cdot a^6 \cdot \dfrac{1}{a^6} = 28$.

3. n **B** Since x^5 is a factor of each term, the term in the binomial expansion containing x^{12} is $-\binom{12}{6} \cdot 1^6 \cdot \left(x^2\right)^6$.

Therefore, the coefficient is $-\dfrac{12!}{6!6!} = -924$.

4. n **B** The third term is

$$\binom{\frac{1}{3}}{2} \cdot (8x)^{-5/3}(-y)^2 = \frac{\frac{1}{3} \cdot \frac{-2}{3}}{2 \cdot 1} \cdot \frac{1}{32} x^{-5/3}y^2$$

$$= -\frac{1}{9} \cdot \frac{1}{32} x^{-5/3}y^2.$$

The coefficient of the third term is $-\dfrac{1}{288}$.

Part 5.3 Probability

1. i **C** There is 1 way to get a 2, and there are 2 ways to get a 3, 4 ways to get a 5, 6 ways to get a 7, 2 ways to get an 11. Out of 36 elements in the sample space, 15 successes are possible.

$$P(\text{prime}) = \frac{15}{36} = \frac{5}{12}.$$

2. i **D** The probability of getting neither a head nor a 4 is $\dfrac{1}{2} \cdot \dfrac{5}{6} = \dfrac{5}{12}$. Therefore, probability of getting either is $1 - \dfrac{5}{12} = \dfrac{7}{12}$.

3. n **E** The probability that none of the cards was a spade $= \dfrac{39}{52} \cdot \dfrac{39}{52} \cdot \dfrac{39}{52} = \dfrac{3}{4} \cdot \dfrac{3}{4} \cdot \dfrac{3}{4} = \dfrac{27}{64}$. Probability that 1 was a spade $= 1 - \dfrac{27}{64} = \dfrac{37}{64}$.

4. i **E** The only situation when neither of these sets is satisfied occurs when three tails appear. $P(A \cup B) = \dfrac{7}{8}$.

5. n   E   If all 3 are boys, none are girls.

$$P(3B) = \frac{\binom{12}{3}\binom{4}{0}}{\binom{16}{3}},$$ where $\binom{12}{3}$ is the number of

ways 3 of 12 boys can be selected, $\binom{4}{0}$ is the number of ways 0 of 4 girls can be selected, and $\binom{16}{3}$ is the number of ways 3 of 16 students can be selected. Therefore, $P(3B) = \frac{11}{28}$.

6. i   B   Probability of both items being nondefective $= \frac{5}{8} \cdot \frac{3}{5} = \frac{3}{8}$.

7. n   B $\binom{6}{3}$ is the number of ways 3 men can be selected. $\binom{3}{2}$ is the number of ways 2 women can be selected. $\binom{9}{5}$ is the total number of ways people can be selected to fill 5 rooms.

$$P(3 \text{ men}, 2 \text{ women}) = \frac{\binom{6}{3}\binom{3}{2}}{\binom{9}{5}} = \frac{10}{21}.$$

8. a   C   There are $\binom{8}{5}$ different selections containing 5 good items. In any one of these selections, 5 are good with a probability of 0.8 each, and 3 are bad with a probability of 0.2 each. Therefore,

$$\begin{aligned}
\text{total probability} &= \binom{8}{5}(0.8)^5(0.2)^3 \\
&= \frac{(8)(7)(6)(5)(4)}{(5)(4)(3)(2)(1)}(0.8)^5(0.2)^3 \\
&= 56(0.8)^5(0.2)^3 \approx 1.47
\end{aligned}$$

Part 5.4 Sequence and Series

1. n   D $a_2 = 5$, $a_3 = 8$, $a_4 = 12$, $a_5 = 17$. Therefore, $S_5 = 45$.

2. i   A $y = x + d$, $z = y + d$. Substituting for d gives $y = x + (z - y)$. Therefore, $y = \frac{1}{2}(x + z)$.

3. n   A   The decimal $0.23\overline{37} = 0.2 + (0.037 + 0.00037 + 0.0000037 + \cdots)$, which is $0.2 +$ an infinite geometric series with a common ratio of 0.01.

$$S_n = 0.2 + \frac{0.037}{0.99} = \frac{2}{10} + \frac{37}{990} = \frac{235}{990} = \frac{47}{198}.$$

The sum of the numerator and the denominator is 245.

Alternative Solution: Let $f =$ the fraction equal to $0.23\overline{737}$ .... Since there are two digits in the repeating block, multiply through by 10^2 to get $100f = 23.73\overline{737}$ .... Subtract the equation $f = 0.23\overline{737} \ldots$ to get $99f = 23.5$. Therefore, $f = \frac{23.5}{99} = \frac{235}{990} = \frac{47}{198}$. The sum of the numerator and denominator is 245.

4. i   C   Terms are $3^{1/4}$, $3^{1/8}$, 1. Common ratio $= 3^{-1/8}$. Therefore, the fourth term is $1 \cdot 3^{-1/8} = 3^{-1/8}$ or $\frac{1}{\sqrt[8]{3}}$.

5. i   C   Arithmetic mean $= \frac{1 + 25}{2} = 13$. Geometric mean $= \sqrt{1 \cdot 25} = 5$. The difference is 8.

6. n   A   List the primes and add them until the sum approaches 100: 2,3,5,7,11,13,17,19,23. Sum equals 100.

7. i   B   Adding just units digits of $i!$ gives $1 + 2 + 6 + 4 + 0 + 0 + 0 + \cdots$. Sum of units digits for any $i!$ with $i > 4 = 13$.

8. n   D   The first few terms are $-1 + 2 - 3 + 4 - \cdots + 100$. Split up the even numbers and the odd numbers, getting $(2 + 4 + \cdots + 100) - (1 + 3 + \cdots + 99)$: 2 arithmetic series with 50 terms and a difference of 2.

$$\begin{aligned}
\text{Sum} &= \frac{50}{2}(2 + 100) - \frac{50}{2}(1 + 99) \\
&= 2550 - 2500 = 50
\end{aligned}$$

Alternative Solution: The pattern of 100 terms is $-1 + 2 - 3 + 4 - \cdots - 99 + 100$. If they are grouped in pairs, $(-1 + 2) + (-3 + 4) + \cdots + (-99 + 100)$, there are fifty 1s. Therefore, the sum is 50.

9. i   D $\frac{2}{3} = \frac{\frac{2}{7}}{1 - r}$. $2 - 2r = \frac{6}{7}$. $14 - 14r = 6$.

Therefore, $r = \frac{4}{7}$.

Part 5.5 Geometry

1. i   A   The resulting graph is the same as the given one except that it is situated to the left of the y-axis instead of to the right. Therefore, it is the graph of $f(-x)$.

2. n E Using the equation to determine y, make up a table of values for $\left(x, \sqrt{y}\right)$.

x	0	1	2	3	4	–2	–1
y	2	3	4	5	6	0	1
$\sqrt{y}$	$\sqrt{2}$	$\sqrt{3}$	$\sqrt{4}$	$\sqrt{5}$	$\sqrt{6}$	0	1

This leads to the graph in Choice E.

Graphing Calculator: Plot the graph of $y = \sqrt{x+2}$ in an $x \in [-3,3]$, $y \in [-3,3]$ window to see that the correct answer is Choice E.

3. i B Setting up a table of a few representative values leads to Choice B.

x	–1	$-\frac{1}{2}$	$-\frac{1}{2}$	0	0	0	$\frac{1}{2}$	$\frac{1}{2}$	1
y	0	0	$\frac{1}{2}$	0	$\frac{1}{2}$	1	0	$\frac{1}{2}$	0
$x+y$	–1	$-\frac{1}{2}$	0	0	$\frac{1}{2}$	1	$\frac{1}{2}$	1	1

4. i D $2\vec{U} = 2\vec{i} - 10\vec{j}$ and $3\vec{V} = 6\vec{i} + 9\vec{j}$.
$$2\vec{U} + 3\vec{V} = 8\vec{i} - \vec{j}.$$

5. i D The dot product must equal zero. Choices B and D satisfy. However, only Choice D is a unit vector.

6. i B When a plane intersects the x-axis, the y-and z-coordinates are zero. Therefore, $2x = 5$ and $x = \frac{5}{2}$ or 2.5.

7. i D $3 = \sqrt{(x-3)^2 + (-1+3)^2 + (-1-1)^2}$.
Square both sides: $9 = x^2 - 6x + 9 + 4 + 4$. $x^2 - 6x + 8 = 0$. Then $(x-4)(x-2) = 0$, and $x = 2$ or 4.

8. i E To find a trace, set one variable to zero and check to see if the result is an answer.

9. i D Direction numbers must be multiples of 2 – (–1), 4 – 5, 1 – 2 or 3, –1, –1.

10. a D If the quarter-circle is revolved about the x-axis, a hemisphere of radius 2 is formed.
$$A = \frac{2}{3}\pi r^3 = \frac{16\pi}{3} \approx 16.8.$$

11. n C The altitude is 18.
$$V = \frac{1}{3}\pi r^2 h = \frac{1}{3}\pi \cdot 144 \cdot 18 = 864\pi.$$

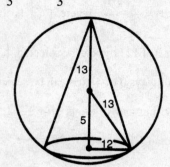

12. i C $V = \pi r^2 h$. Total area $= 2\pi r^2 + 2\pi rh$. $\pi r^2 h = \pi r(2r + 2h)$, which gives $rh = 2r + 2h$. Therefore, $h = \frac{2r}{r-2}$. Since h must be positive, the smallest integral value of r is 3.

13. n D If the base radius is 4, the side of the square base is $4\sqrt{2}$. Volume of pyramid $= \frac{1}{3}$ (area of base) $h = \frac{1}{3} \cdot 32 \cdot 9 = 96$.

14. i C In space, the set of points is the perpendicular bisector plane of the segment joining the two fixed points.

15. a B The xz-trace is obtained by letting $y = 0$ in the equation of the plane in order to get $2x + 4z = 7$. The x-intercept $= \frac{7}{2}$ and the z-intercept $= \frac{7}{4}$. The length of the segment between (0, 0, 1.75) and $(3.5, 0, 0) = \sqrt{(0-3.5)^2 + (0-0)^2 + (1.75-0)^2}$
$$= \sqrt{15.3125} \approx 3.9$$

16. a C The line intersects the y-axis at $\frac{7}{2}$ and the x-axis at $\frac{7}{3}$. When the region is rotated about the x-axis, a cone is formed with radius $\frac{7}{2}$ and height $\frac{7}{3}$.
$$V = \frac{1}{3}\pi r^2 h = \frac{1}{3}\pi \left(\frac{7}{2}\right)^2 \left(\frac{7}{3}\right) = \frac{7^3\pi}{36} \approx 30.$$

Graphing Calculator: Plot the graph of $y = \frac{7-3x}{2}$ in an $x \in [-5,5]$, $y \in [-5,5]$ window. Use the Trace and Zoom functions to see that the y-intercept ≈ 3.5 (which is r) and the x-intercept ≈ 2.3 (which is h). Since the figure is a cone, $V = \frac{1}{3}\pi r^2 h = \frac{1}{3}\pi (3.5)^2 (2.3) \approx 29.5 \approx 30$.

17. a **D** Volume of one tennis ball $= \frac{4}{3}\pi r^3 =$

$\frac{4}{3}\pi\left(\frac{2.5}{2}\right)^3 = \frac{\pi(2.5)^3}{6}$.

Volume of three tennis balls $= \frac{\pi(2.5)^3}{2}$.

Volume of can $= \pi r^2 h = \pi\left(\frac{2.5}{2}\right)^2(3)(2.5)$

$= \frac{3\pi(2.5)^3}{4}$.

Volume of air $= \frac{3\pi(2.5)^3}{4} - \frac{\pi(2.5)^3}{2}$

$= \frac{\pi(2.5)^3}{4} \approx 12.3$.

Part 5.6 Variation

1. i **C** $\frac{x}{y} = K$ by definition of direct variation.

2. i **D** $yx^2 = K$. Substitute $(4,3)$ to find $K = 48$. $a \cdot 4 = 48$, and so $a = 12$.

3. i **B** $\frac{DM^2}{R} = K$. Let $D = 1$, $M = 2$, and $R = 3$ (arbitrary choices), then $K = \frac{4}{3}$. Making the indicated changes in the values of the variables results in $R = 1$, $M = 4$, and $K = \frac{4}{3}$. Thus, $D = \frac{1}{12}$. Therefore, the original value of D (1) was divided by 12.

<u>Alternative Solution:</u> $\frac{D_1 \cdot M^2}{R} = K$. $\frac{D_2 \cdot (2M)^2}{R} = K = \frac{D_1 \cdot M^2}{R}$. Therefore, $\frac{3 \cdot 4D_2 M^2}{R} = \frac{D_1 \cdot M^2}{K}$ and $D_2 = \frac{D_1}{12}$.

Part 5.7 Logic

1. i **C** The statement is false only when $(p \vee q)$ is true and p is false. If p is false, $(p \vee q)$ is true only when q is true.

2. i **C** The statement "q is necessary for p" is equivalent to "p is sufficient for q" (I) and "p only is q" (II), but *not* "q implies p" (III).

3. i **B** The negation of "if p, then q" is "p and not q."

4. i **E** Counterexamples of each answer can be found.

5. i **B** Since "some smarties do not smoke cigars" and "all men smoke cigars," a necessary conclusion is "some smarties are not men."

6. i **C** The statement "p', only if c'" is equivalent to "if p', then c'," which is equivalent to its contrapositive, "if c, then p."

7. i **D** By definition the contrapositive is $q \rightarrow p'$.

Part 5.8 Statistics

1. i **E** Although the arithmetic mean is usually what is meant, any one of the three is considered an average.

2. i **B** Since the values are integers, the range is 2, and the mean is 50, the possible numbers in the set are 49, 50, and 51.
I. The set could consist of n 49s and n 51s, and so 50 would not even be an element of the set. Therefore, the mode is not necessarily 50, and I is false.
II. Since the mean is 50, there must be the same number of 49s as 51s. Thus, the median is 50, and II is true.
III. This is obviously false.

3. i **D** Mean $= \frac{2+4+9+x}{8} = \frac{15+x}{8}$. The range could equal $x - 1$ if $x < 3$, or $3 - x$ if $x < 1$, or 2 if $1 < x < 3$. Therefore, $\frac{15+x}{8} = x - 1$ or $\frac{15+x}{8} = 3 - x$ or $\frac{15+x}{8} = 2$; solving for x gives $x = \frac{22}{7}$ or $x = 1$ or $x = 1$. Since x is an integer, the answer can only be 1.

4. i **D** Check the mean against each of the data values. Mean $= \frac{6+6+4x+5}{7+x} = 2$; $\frac{17+4x}{7+x} = 2$; $17 + 4x = 14 + 2x$; $x = -\frac{3}{2}$. Mean $= \frac{17+4x}{7+x} = 3$; $17 + 4x = 21 + 3x$; $x = 4$; a positive integer; correct. The mean can be checked against 4 and 5 in similar fashion to show that only four 4s satisfy the condition of the problem.

5. n **A** Mode $= 2$; median $=$ middle number $= 4$; mean $= \frac{8+12+12+16}{11} = 4\frac{4}{11}$. Therefore, mode < median < mean.

Part 5.9 Odds and Ends

1. i E Since 2, 3, 6 are three terms of a harmonic sequence, $\frac{1}{2}, \frac{1}{3}, \frac{1}{6}$ are three terms of an arithmetic sequence. The fourth term of the arithmetic sequence is 0 since the difference is $\frac{1}{6}$. Because the reciprocal of zero does not exist, four terms of the harmonic sequence do not exist.

2. i A The denominator determinant is made up of the coefficients of the variables. It is
$$\begin{vmatrix} 2 & -3 \\ 5 & 2 \end{vmatrix} = 4 - (+15) = -11.$$

3. n E The division can be written in the form $n \cdot Q + 7 = 125$, and so $n \cdot Q = 118 = 2 \cdot 59$. To get a remainder of 7, n must be greater than 7. Since 59 is a prime, the answer is E.

4. i E $\frac{a+b}{2} = \sqrt{ab}$. Multiplying by 2 and squaring gives
$$a^2 + 2ab + b^2 = 4ab \quad a^2 - 2ab + b^2 = 0$$
$$(a-b)^2 = 0 \quad a = b$$

5. i C $(1,2) * (1,1) = (2,1)$ and $(p,q) * (1,2) = (p+1, q-2)$. Therefore $p + 1 = 2$ and $q - 2 = 1$, and so $p = 1, q = 3$.

6. i A Keeping track of the values of a and x, you have

Step	1	4	3	4	3
a	2	4		8	
x	2		6		10

Print 10.

7. a A The probability of hitting target is 1. The probability of hitting inside the circle = $\frac{\text{area of circle}}{\text{area of square}} = \frac{4\pi}{16}$. Probability of hitting outside the circle = $1 - \frac{4\pi}{16} \approx 0.2$.

8. i D In the Venn diagram below, a = birds that have neither long beaks nor gray feathers.

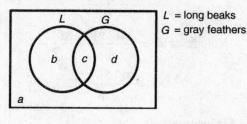

L = long beaks
G = gray feathers

$$\begin{aligned} a+b+c+d &= 100 \\ b+c &= 85 \\ c+d &= 45 \\ c &= 38 \end{aligned}$$

Substituting the value of c, and then the values of b and d, gives $a = 8$.

9. a C Put your calculator in radian mode $3 \# 5 = \sqrt{\sin 3 + \sec 5}$.
$$\sqrt{\sec 5} = \frac{1}{\cos 5} \approx \frac{1}{0.28366} \approx 3.525.$$
Therefore,
$$\sqrt{\sin 3 + \sec 5} \approx \sqrt{0.1411 + 3.525} \approx 1.9.$$

10. a D $3 * \pi = \frac{\sqrt[3]{3} + \sqrt[3]{\pi}}{\sqrt{3\pi}}$. Using your calculator to find $\sqrt[3]{3} \approx 1.4422, \sqrt[3]{\pi} \approx 1.4646$, and $\sqrt{3x} \approx 3.0699$ gives an answer of approximately 0.95.

MODEL
EXAMINATIONS
PART
3

ANSWER SHEET FOR MODEL TEST 1

Determine the correct answer for each question. Then, using a no. 2 pencil, blacken completely the oval containing the letter of your choice.

1. Ⓐ Ⓑ Ⓒ Ⓓ Ⓔ
2. Ⓐ Ⓑ Ⓒ Ⓓ Ⓔ
3. Ⓐ Ⓑ Ⓒ Ⓓ Ⓔ
4. Ⓐ Ⓑ Ⓒ Ⓓ Ⓔ
5. Ⓐ Ⓑ Ⓒ Ⓓ Ⓔ
6. Ⓐ Ⓑ Ⓒ Ⓓ Ⓔ
7. Ⓐ Ⓑ Ⓒ Ⓓ Ⓔ
8. Ⓐ Ⓑ Ⓒ Ⓓ Ⓔ
9. Ⓐ Ⓑ Ⓒ Ⓓ Ⓔ
10. Ⓐ Ⓑ Ⓒ Ⓓ Ⓔ
11. Ⓐ Ⓑ Ⓒ Ⓓ Ⓔ
12. Ⓐ Ⓑ Ⓒ Ⓓ Ⓔ
13. Ⓐ Ⓑ Ⓒ Ⓓ Ⓔ
14. Ⓐ Ⓑ Ⓒ Ⓓ Ⓔ
15. Ⓐ Ⓑ Ⓒ Ⓓ Ⓔ
16. Ⓐ Ⓑ Ⓒ Ⓓ Ⓔ
17. Ⓐ Ⓑ Ⓒ Ⓓ Ⓔ

18. Ⓐ Ⓑ Ⓒ Ⓓ Ⓔ
19. Ⓐ Ⓑ Ⓒ Ⓓ Ⓔ
20. Ⓐ Ⓑ Ⓒ Ⓓ Ⓔ
21. Ⓐ Ⓑ Ⓒ Ⓓ Ⓔ
22. Ⓐ Ⓑ Ⓒ Ⓓ Ⓔ
23. Ⓐ Ⓑ Ⓒ Ⓓ Ⓔ
24. Ⓐ Ⓑ Ⓒ Ⓓ Ⓔ
25. Ⓐ Ⓑ Ⓒ Ⓓ Ⓔ
26. Ⓐ Ⓑ Ⓒ Ⓓ Ⓔ
27. Ⓐ Ⓑ Ⓒ Ⓓ Ⓔ
28. Ⓐ Ⓑ Ⓒ Ⓓ Ⓔ
29. Ⓐ Ⓑ Ⓒ Ⓓ Ⓔ
30. Ⓐ Ⓑ Ⓒ Ⓓ Ⓔ
31. Ⓐ Ⓑ Ⓒ Ⓓ Ⓔ
32. Ⓐ Ⓑ Ⓒ Ⓓ Ⓔ
33. Ⓐ Ⓑ Ⓒ Ⓓ Ⓔ
34. Ⓐ Ⓑ Ⓒ Ⓓ Ⓔ

35. Ⓐ Ⓑ Ⓒ Ⓓ Ⓔ
36. Ⓐ Ⓑ Ⓒ Ⓓ Ⓔ
37. Ⓐ Ⓑ Ⓒ Ⓓ Ⓔ
38. Ⓐ Ⓑ Ⓒ Ⓓ Ⓔ
39. Ⓐ Ⓑ Ⓒ Ⓓ Ⓔ
40. Ⓐ Ⓑ Ⓒ Ⓓ Ⓔ
41. Ⓐ Ⓑ Ⓒ Ⓓ Ⓔ
42. Ⓐ Ⓑ Ⓒ Ⓓ Ⓔ
43. Ⓐ Ⓑ Ⓒ Ⓓ Ⓔ
44. Ⓐ Ⓑ Ⓒ Ⓓ Ⓔ
45. Ⓐ Ⓑ Ⓒ Ⓓ Ⓔ
46. Ⓐ Ⓑ Ⓒ Ⓓ Ⓔ
47. Ⓐ Ⓑ Ⓒ Ⓓ Ⓔ
48. Ⓐ Ⓑ Ⓒ Ⓓ Ⓔ
49. Ⓐ Ⓑ Ⓒ Ⓓ Ⓔ
50. Ⓐ Ⓑ Ⓒ Ⓓ Ⓔ

MODEL TEST

1

50 questions

1 hour

Tear out the preceding answer sheet. Decide which is the best choice by rounding your answer when appropriate. Blacken the corresponding space on the answer sheet. When finished, check your answers with those at the end of the test. For questions that you got wrong, note the sections containing the material that you must review. Also if you do not fully understand how you arrived at some of the correct answers, you should review the appropriate sections. Finally, fill out the self-evaluation sheet on page 139 in order to pinpoint the topics that give you the most difficulty.

OFFICIAL COLLEGE BOARD DIRECTIONS

<u>Directions</u>: For each of the following problems, decide which is the BEST of the choices given. If the exact numerical value is not one of the choices, select the choice that best approximates this value. Then fill in the corresponding oval on the answer sheet.

Notes: (1) A calculator will be necessary for answering some (but not all) of the questions in this test. For each question you will have to decide whether or not you should use a calculator. The calculator you use must be at least a scientific calculator; programmable calculators and calculators that can display graphs are permitted.

(2) For some questions in this test you may have to decide whether your calculator should be in the radian mode or the degree mode.

(3) Figures that accompany problems in this test are intended to provide information useful in solving the problems. They are drawn as accurately as possible EXCEPT when it is stated in a specific problem that the figure is not drawn to scale. All figures lie in a plane unless otherwise indicated.

(4) Unless otherwise specified, the domain of any function f is assumed to be the set of all real numbers x for which $f(x)$ is a real number.

<u>Reference Information:</u> The following information is for your reference in answering some of the questions in this test.

Volume of a right circular cone with radius r and height h: $V = \dfrac{1}{3}\pi r^2 h$

Lateral area of a right circular cone with circumference of the base c and slant height ℓ: $S = \dfrac{1}{2}c\ell$

Volume of a sphere with radius r: $V = \dfrac{4}{3}\pi r^3$

Surface area of a sphere with radius r: $S = 4\pi r^2$

Volume of a pyramid with base area B and height h: $V = \dfrac{1}{3}Bh$

---

1. The slope of a line perpendicular to the line whose equation is $\dfrac{x}{3} - \dfrac{y}{4} = 1$ is

   (A) $\dfrac{1}{4}$

   (B) $-\dfrac{4}{3}$

   (C) $-\dfrac{3}{4}$

   (D) $\dfrac{4}{3}$

   (E) -3

2. $\dfrac{\tan 15^\circ}{\cot 75^\circ} =$

   (A) 0
   (B) 1
   (C) -1
   (D) ∞
   (E) $\sqrt{3}$

3. What is the set of points in space equidistant from two vertices of an equilateral triangle and 2 inches from the third vertex?

   (A) a circle
   (B) a line segment
   (C) two points
   (D) a parabola
   (E) two parallel lines

4. If $f(x) = \sqrt{2x+3}$ and $g(x) = x^2 + 1$, then $f(g(2)) =$

   (A) 6.16
   (B) 3.61
   (C) 2.24
   (D) 3.00
   (E) 6.00

5. $\left(-\dfrac{1}{16}\right)^{2/3} =$

   (A) 0.16
   (B) -0.25
   (C) 6.35
   (D) -0.16
   (E) The value is not a real number.

6. The circumference of circle $x^2 + y^2 - 10y - 36 = 0$ is

   (A) 192
   (B) 38
   (C) 125
   (D) 54
   (E) 49

GO ON TO THE NEXT PAGE

7. What is the value of $\displaystyle\sum_{j=3}^{5} \ln j$?

    (A) 1.6
    (B) 4.8
    (C) 7.8
    (D) 4.1
    (E) 1.9

8. If $f(x) = 2$ for all real numbers x, then $f(x + 2) =$

    (A) 0
    (B) 2
    (C) 4
    (D) x
    (E) The value cannot be determined.

9. The volume of the region between two concentric spheres of radii 2 and 5 is

    (A) 66
    (B) 28
    (C) 368
    (D) 490
    (E) 113

10. The number of terms in the expansion of $(2x^2 - 3y^{1/3})^7$ is

    (A) 6
    (B) 8
    (C) 1
    (D) 7
    (E) 9

11. In right triangle ABC, $AB = 10$, $BC = 8$, $AC = 6$. The sine of $\angle A$ is

    (A) $\dfrac{4}{3}$

    (B) $\dfrac{3}{4}$

    (C) $\dfrac{4}{5}$

    (D) $\dfrac{5}{4}$

    (E) $\dfrac{3}{5}$

12. If $16^x = 4$ and $5^{x+y} = 625$, then $y =$

    (A) 2
    (B) 5
    (C) $\dfrac{25}{2}$

    (D) $\dfrac{7}{2}$

    (E) 1

GO ON TO THE NEXT PAGE

13. If the parameter is eliminated from the equations $x = t^2 + 1$ and $y = 2t$, then the relation between x and y is

(A) $y = x - 1$
(B) $y = 1 - x$
(C) $y^2 = x - 1$
(D) $y^2 = (x - 1)^2$
(E) $y^2 = 4x - 4$

14. Let $f(x)$ be a polynomial function: $f(x) = x^5 + \cdots$. If $f(1) = 0$ and $f(2) = 0$, then $f(x)$ is divisible by

(A) $x - 3$
(B) $x^2 - 2$
(C) $x^2 + 2$
(D) $x^2 - 3x + 2$
(E) $x^2 + 3x + 2$

15. $\mathrm{Sin}\left(\mathrm{Arctan}\,\dfrac{1}{3}\right)$ equals

(A) 0.95
(B) 0.32
(C) 0.33
(D) 0.35
(E) 0.50

16. Given the set of data 8, 12, 12, 15, 18, what is the range of this set?

(A) 12
(B) 18
(C) 13
(D) 15
(E) 10

17. If determinants are used to solve the equations $\begin{cases} 3x + 2y = 1 \\ x - 3y = 2 \end{cases}$ simultaneously, then y will equal

(A) $\dfrac{\begin{vmatrix} 3 & 1 \\ 1 & 2 \end{vmatrix}}{\begin{vmatrix} 3 & 2 \\ 1 & -3 \end{vmatrix}}$

(D) $\dfrac{\begin{vmatrix} 3 & 2 \\ 1 & -3 \end{vmatrix}}{\begin{vmatrix} 1 & 2 \\ 2 & -3 \end{vmatrix}}$

(B) $\dfrac{\begin{vmatrix} 3 & 2 \\ 1 & -3 \end{vmatrix}}{\begin{vmatrix} 3 & 1 \\ 1 & 2 \end{vmatrix}}$

(E) $\dfrac{\begin{vmatrix} 1 & 2 \\ 2 & -3 \end{vmatrix}}{\begin{vmatrix} 3 & 2 \\ 1 & -3 \end{vmatrix}}$

(C) $\dfrac{\begin{vmatrix} 1 & 2 \\ 3 & 1 \end{vmatrix}}{\begin{vmatrix} 3 & 2 \\ 1 & -3 \end{vmatrix}}$

GO ON TO THE NEXT PAGE

18. If $f(x) = \begin{cases} \dfrac{5}{x-2}, & \text{when } x \neq 2 \\ k, & \text{when } x = 2 \end{cases}$, what must the value of k be in order for $f(x)$ to be a continuous function?

(A) 2
(B) 5
(C) 0
(D) –2
(E) No value of k will make $f(x)$ a continuous function.

19. If $f(x) = \dfrac{2x-2}{x-1}$ and $f^2(x) = f(f(x))$, $f^3(x) = f(f^2(x))$, ..., $f^n(x) = f(f^{n-1}(x))$, where n is an integer greater than 1, for what values of n is $f^n(x) = f(x)$?

(A) all values of n
(B) all even values of n
(C) all odd values of n
(D) no values of n
(E) $\{n : n = 3k, \text{ where } k \text{ is a positive integer}\}$

20. The ellipse $4x^2 + 8y^2 = 64$ and the circle $x^2 + y^2 = 9$ intersect at points where the y-coordinate is

(A) ± 1.41
(B) ± 2.24
(C) ± 10.00
(D) ± 2.45
(E) ± 2.65

21. Each term of a sequence, after the first, is inversely proportional to the term preceding it. If the first two terms are 2 and 6, what is the twelfth term?

(A) 2
(B) 6
(C) $2 \cdot 3^{11}$
(D) 46
(E) The twelfth term cannot be determined.

22. A company offers you the use of its computer for a fee. Plan A costs $6 to join and then $9 per hour to use the computer. Plan B costs $25 to join and then $2.25 per hour to use the computer. After how many minutes of use would the cost of plan A be the same as the cost of plan B?

(A) 18,052
(B) 173
(C) 169
(D) 165
(E) 157

GO ON TO THE NEXT PAGE

USE THIS SPACE FOR SCRATCH WORK

23. If the probability that the Giants will win the NFC championship is p and if the probability that the Raiders will win the AFC championship is q, what is the probability that only one of these teams will win its respective championship?

(A) pq
(B) $p + q - 2pq$
(C) $|p - q|$
(D) $1 - pq$
(E) $2pq - p - q$

24. If a geometric sequence begins with the terms $\frac{1}{3}, 1, \ldots$, what is the sum of the first 10 terms?

(A) $9841\frac{1}{3}$
(B) 6561
(C) $3280\frac{1}{3}$
(D) $33\frac{1}{3}$
(E) 6

25. The value of $\dfrac{453!}{450!\,3!}$ is

(A) greater than 10^{100}
(B) between 10^{10} and 10^{100}
(C) between 10^5 and 10^{10}
(D) between 10 and 10^5
(E) less than 10

26. If A is the angle formed by the line $2y = 3x + 7$ and the x-axis, then $\angle A$ equals

(A) $72°$
(B) $56°$
(C) $215°$
(D) $0°$
(E) $-45°$

27. What is the smallest positive x-intercept of the graph of $y = 3\sin 2\left(x + \dfrac{2\pi}{3}\right)$?

(A) 0
(B) 2.09
(C) 1.05
(D) 0.52
(E) 1.31

28. If $(x - 4)^2 + 4(y - 3)^2 = 16$ is graphed, the sum of the distances from any fixed point on the curve to the two foci is

 (A) 4
 (B) 8
 (C) 12
 (D) 16
 (E) 32

29. In the equation $x^2 + kx + 54 = 0$, one root is twice the other root. The value(s) of k is (are)

 (A) ± 5.2
 (B) 15.6
 (C) −5.2
 (D) ± 15.6
 (E) 22.0

30. The remainder obtained when $3x^4 + 7x^3 + 8x^2 - 2x - 3$ is divided by $x + 1$ is

 (A) 5
 (B) 0
 (C) −3
 (D) 3
 (E) 13

31. If $f(x) = e^x$ and $g(x) = f(x) + f^{-1}(x)$, what does $g(2)$ equal?

 (A) 8.1
 (B) 7.5
 (C) 8.3
 (D) 5.1
 (E) 7.4

32. $(x + 2)^3 - 3(x + 2)^2 + 3(x + 2) - 1 =$

 (A) $(x + 1)^3$
 (B) $(x - 1)^3$
 (C) $(x + 2)^3$
 (D) x^3
 (E) $(x + 3)^3$

33. For what values of k does the graph of $\dfrac{(x - 2k)^2}{1} - \dfrac{(y - 3k)^2}{3} = 1$ pass through the origin?

 (A) only 0
 (B) only 1
 (C) ±1
 (D) ±√5
 (E) no value

34. If $\dfrac{1 - \cos\theta}{\sin\theta} = \dfrac{\sqrt{3}}{3}$, then $\theta =$

(A) 15°
(B) 30°
(C) 45°
(D) 60°
(E) 75°

35. If $x^2 + 3x + 2 < 0$ and $f(x) = x^2 - 3x + 2$, then

(A) $0 < f(x) < 6$
(B) $f(x) \geq \dfrac{3}{2}$
(C) $f(x) > 12$
(D) $f(x) > 0$
(E) $6 < f(x) < 12$

36. If $f(x) = |x| + [x]$, the value of $f(-2.5) + f(1.5)$ is

(A) 3
(B) 1
(C) –2
(D) 1.5
(E) 2

37. The figure at the right could be the graph of

(A) $y = \sin\dfrac{1}{4}x$

(B) $y = \cos\left(4x - \dfrac{\pi}{2}\right)$

(C) $y = \sin 2x \cdot \cos 2x$

(D) $y = -\sin 4x$

(E) $y = \cos\left(\dfrac{1}{4}x - 2\pi\right)$

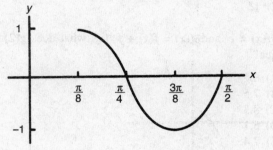

38. At the end of a meeting all participants shook hands with each other. Twenty-eight handshakes were exchanged. How many people were at the meeting?

(A) 14
(B) 7
(C) 8
(D) 28
(E) 56

39. If the values of the function $g(x)$ represent the slope of the line tangent to the graph of the function $f(x)$, shown at the right, at each point (x,y), which of the following could be the graph of $g(x)$?

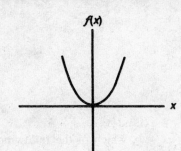

(A)

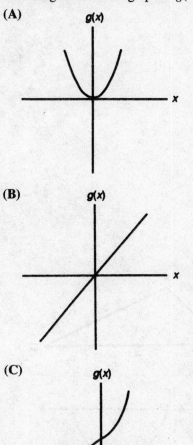

(B)

(C)

(D)

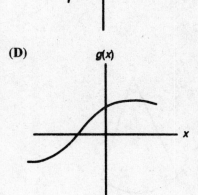

(E)

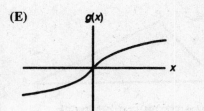

40. What is the smallest positive angle that will make $5 - \sin\left(x + \dfrac{\pi}{6}\right)$ a maximum?

(A) 1.05
(B) 2.09
(C) 1.57
(D) 4.19
(E) 5.24

41. If $f(x) = ax + b$, which of the following make(s) $f(x) = f^{-1}(x)$?

   I. $a = -1$, b = any real number
   II. $a = 1$, $b = 0$
   III. a = any real number, $b = 0$

(A) only I
(B) only II
(C) only III
(D) only I and II
(E) only I and III

42. In the figure, $\angle A = 110°$, $a = \sqrt{6}$, and $b = 2$. What is the value of $\angle C$?

(A) 50°
(B) 25°
(C) 20°
(D) 15°
(E) 10°

43. If vector $\vec{v} = \left(1, \sqrt{3}\right)$ and vector $\vec{u} = (3, -2)$, find the value of $\left|3\vec{v} - \vec{u}\right|$.

(A) 52
(B) $2 + 3\sqrt{3}$
(C) 6
(D) $0.2 + 3\sqrt{3}$
(E) 7

44. A sector of a circle, AOB, with a central angle of $\dfrac{2\pi}{5}$ and a radius of 5 is bent to form a cone with vertex at O. What is the volume of the cone that is formed?

(A) 8.17
(B) 6.04
(C) 4.97
(D) 5.13
(E) 12.31

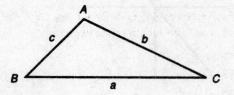

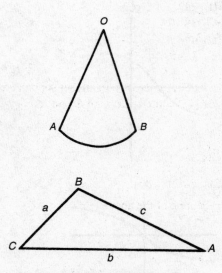

45. In $\triangle ABC$, $a = 2x$, $b = 3x + 2$, $c = \sqrt{12}$, and $\angle C = 60°$. Find x.

(A) 0.50
(B) 0.64
(C) 0.77
(D) 1.64
(E) 1.78

GO ON TO THE NEXT PAGE

46. If point $P(a, a\sqrt{3})$ is 6 units from line $5x + 3y = 12$, then a equals

   (A) only 4.6
   (B) only –2.3
   (C) 2.3 or –4.6
   (D) only 2.3
   (E) –2.3 or 4.6

47. If $f(x) = 3x^2 + 4x + 5$, what must the value of k equal so that the graph of $f(x - k)$ will be symmetric to the y-axis?

   (A) $\dfrac{2}{3}$

   (B) $-\dfrac{2}{3}$

   (C) 0

   (D) –4

   (E) $-\dfrac{4}{3}$

48. If $f(x) = \cos x$ and $g(x) = 2x + 1$, which of the following is an even function (are even functions)?

   I. $f(x) \cdot g(x)$
   II. $f(g(x))$
   III. $g(f(x))$

   (A) only I
   (B) only II
   (C) only III
   (D) only I and II
   (E) only II and III

49. A cylinder whose base radius is 3 is inscribed in a sphere of radius 5. What is the difference between the volume of the sphere and the volume of the cylinder?

   (A) 354
   (B) 297
   (C) 88
   (D) 448
   (E) 1345

50. If $f(x) = i$, where i is an integer such that $i \le x < i + 1$, and $g(x) = f(x) - 2x$, then the period of $g(x)$ is

   (A) $\dfrac{1}{2}$

   (B) 1
   (C) 2
   (D) –2
   (E) none of the above

USE THIS SPACE FOR SCRATCH WORK

ANSWER KEY

1. **C**	18. **E**	35. **E**
2. **B**	19. **A**	36. **E**
3. **A**	20. **E**	37. **B**
4. **B**	21. **B**	38. **C**
5. **A**	22. **C**	39. **B**
6. **E**	23. **B**	40. **D**
7. **D**	24. **A**	41. **D**
8. **B**	25. **C**	42. **C**
9. **D**	26. **B**	43. **C**
10. **B**	27. **C**	44. **D**
11. **C**	28. **B**	45. **A**
12. **D**	29. **D**	46. **E**
13. **E**	30. **D**	47. **A**
14. **D**	31. **A**	48. **C**
15. **B**	32. **A**	49. **B**
16. **E**	33. **C**	50. **E**
17. **A**	34. **D**	

ANSWER EXPLANATIONS

In these solutions the following notation is used:

a: active—Calculator use is necessary or, at a minimum, extremely helpful.

n: neutral—Answers can be found without a calculator, but a calculator may help.

i: inactive—Calculator use is not helpful and may even be a hindrance.

1. i C Solve for y. $y = \frac{4}{3}x - 4$. Slope $= \frac{4}{3}$. Slope of perpendicular $= -\frac{3}{4}$ [2.2].

2. n B Tan $15° = $ cot $75°$. [3.2].

Calculator (in degree mode): cot $75° = \frac{1}{\tan 75°}$, and so $\frac{\tan 15°}{\cot 75°} = \tan 15° \cdot \tan 75° = 1$.

> **TIP:** Cofunctions of complementary angles are equal.

3. i A The set of points equidistant from two vertices is the perpendicular bisecting plane of the segment joining them. The set of points 2 inches from the third vertex is a sphere with center at the third vertex and radius 2. The plane and sphere intersect in a circle. [5.5].

4. a B $g(2) = 5$. $f(g(2)) = f(5) = \sqrt{13} \approx 3.61$. [1.2].

5. a A $\left[\left(-\frac{1}{16}\right)^2\right]^{1/3} = \left(\frac{1}{256}\right)^{1/3} = \sqrt[3]{\frac{1}{256}} \approx 0.16$. [4.2].

6. a E Complete the square to get $x^2 + (y-5)^2 = 61$. Radius $= \sqrt{61}$. $C = 2\pi r = 2\pi\sqrt{61} \approx 49$. [4.1].

7. a D $\sum_{j=3}^{5} \ln j = \ln 3 + \ln 4 + \ln 5 \approx -4.1$ [5.4].

8. i B Regardless of what is substituted for x, $f(x)$ still equals 2. [1.2].

Alternative Solution: $f(x+2)$ causes the graph of $f(x)$ to be shifted 2 units to the left. Since $f(x) = 2$ for all x, $f(x+2)$ will also equal 2 for all x.

9. a D Volume of sphere $= \frac{4}{3}\pi r^3$. Volume of region $= \frac{4}{3} \cdot \pi \cdot 5^3 - \frac{4}{3} \cdot \pi \cdot 2^3 = \frac{4}{3} \cdot \pi \cdot (125 - 8) = 156\pi \approx 490$. [5.5].

10. i B The number of terms is always 1 more than the exponent of the binomial if the exponent is a positive integer. Number of terms $= 8$. [5.2].

11. i C $\sin A = \frac{8}{10} = \frac{4}{5}$. [3.1].

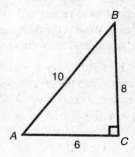

12. n D $\left(4^2\right)^x - 4^1$, and so $x = \frac{1}{2}$. $5^{x+y} = 5^4$, and so $x + y = 4$. $y = \frac{7}{2}$ [4.2].

Calculator: $16^x = 4$ is equivalent to $x \cdot \log 16 = \log 4$, and so $x = \frac{\log 4}{\log 16} = 0.5$. $5^{x+y} = 5^{0.5+y} = 625$, which is equivalent to $(0.5 + y) \cdot \log 5 = \log 625$, and so $y + 0.5 = \frac{\log 625}{\log 5} = 4$. Therefore, $y = 3.5$.

13. i   **E** $t = \dfrac{y}{2}$. Eliminate the parameter and get $x = \dfrac{y^2}{4} + 1$ or $y^2 = 4x - 4$. [4.6].

14. i   **D** $f(1) = 0$ and $f(2) = 0$ imply that $x - 1$ and $x - 2$ are factors of $f(x)$. Their product, $x^2 - 3x + 2$, is also a factor. [2.4].

15. a   **B**   Let $\theta = \text{Arctan}\dfrac{1}{3}$. Thus, $\tan \theta = \dfrac{1}{3}$. $\sin \theta =$ $\sin \theta = \dfrac{\sqrt{10}}{10} \approx 0.32$. [3.6].

Alternative Solution: Use your calculator to find the angle represented by $\text{Tan}^{-1}\left(\dfrac{1}{3}\right) \approx 18.43°$ and $\sin 18.43° \approx 0.32$.

16. i   **E**   Range = largest value − smallest value = $18 - 8 = 10$. [4.7].

17. i   **A**   The denominator determinant is $\begin{vmatrix} 3 & 2 \\ 1 & -3 \end{vmatrix}$, and so it looks like Choices B and D are ruled out. The numerator determinant is the same with the y-coefficients replaced by 1 and 2. Thus, $y = \begin{vmatrix} 3 & 1 \\ 1 & 2 \end{vmatrix}$. [5.9].

18. n   **E**   Since there is no way to reduce the fraction to eliminate $x - 2$ in the denominator, $f(x)$ has an asymptote when x approaches 2. Therefore, there is no way to define k to make f continuous. [4.5].

Graphing calculator: Plot the graph of $y = \dfrac{5}{x - 2}$ in an $x \in [1 \times 3]$, $y \in [-100 \times 100]$ window to see that there is an asymptote at $x = 2$. Thus, no value of k can make $f(x)$ continuous.

19. i   **A**   Reduce $f(x)$ to 2 for all $x \neq 1$. Therefore, $f^n(f(x)) = 2$ for all values of n. [1.2, 5.9].

20. a   **E**   Substituting for x and solving for y gives $4(9 - y^2) + 8y^2 = 64$. $4y^2 = 28$, and so $y^2 = 7$ and $y = \pm\sqrt{7} \approx \pm 2.65$. [4.1].

21. i   **B** $t_n \cdot t_{n+1} = K$. $2 \cdot 6 = K = 12$. Therefore, $6 \cdot t_3 = 12$, and so $t_3 = 2$. Continuing this process gives all odd terms to be 2 and all even terms to be 6. [5.6, 5.4].

22. a   **C**   If h = number of hours using the computer, the cost of Plan A = $6 + 9h$ and the cost of Plan B = $25 + 2.25h$. Thus, $6 + 9h = 25 + 2.25h$. Therefore, $h = \dfrac{19}{6.75} \approx 2.815$ hours ≈ 169 minutes. [5.9].

23. i   **B**   The probability that both teams will win is pq. The probability that both will lose is $(1 - p)(1 - q)$. The probability that only one will win is $1 - [pq + (1 - p)(1 - q)] = 1 - (pq + 1 - p - q + pq) = p + q - 2pq$. [5.3].

Alternative Solution: The probability that the Giants will win and the Raiders will lose is $p(1 - q)$. The probability that the Raiders will win and the Giants will lose is $q(1 - p)$. Therefore, the probability that either one of these results will occur is $p(1 - q) + q(1 - p) = p + q - 2pq$.

24. a   **A** $S_{10} = \dfrac{t_1(1 - r^n)}{1 - r} = \dfrac{\frac{1}{3}(1 - 3^{10})}{1 - 3} = \dfrac{1 - 3^{10}}{-6}$ ≈ 9841.33333. [5.4].

25. n   **C** $\dfrac{453!}{450! \cdot 3!} = \dfrac{453 \cdot 452 \cdot 451 \cdot \cancel{450!}}{3 \cdot 2 \cdot 1 \cdot \cancel{450!}}$ $\approx 2 \times 10^2 \cdot 2 \times 10^2 \cdot 5 \times 10^2$ $= 2 \times 10^7$. [5.1].

Calculator: $\dfrac{453 \cdot 452 \cdot 451}{3 \cdot 2 \cdot 1} = \dfrac{92344956}{6} =$ $15390826 \approx 1.5 \times 10^7$, which indicates that Choice C is the answer.

26. a   **B**   Solve for y: $y = \dfrac{3}{2}x + \dfrac{7}{2}$. Slope $= \dfrac{\Delta y}{\Delta x} = \dfrac{3}{2}$. Tan A also equals $\dfrac{\Delta y}{\Delta x}$. Therefore, $\tan A = \dfrac{3}{2}$. $\text{Tan}^{-1}\left(\dfrac{3}{2}\right) = \angle A \approx 56°$. [2.2].

27. a   **C**   Put your calculator in radian mode. An x-intercept occurs when $y = 0$. Thus, $3 \sin 2\left(x + \dfrac{2\pi}{3}\right) = 0$ occurs when $x + \dfrac{2\pi}{3} = 0$ or π or 2π. $x + \dfrac{2\pi}{3} = 0$ means that $x = -\dfrac{2\pi}{3}$. Ignore this since x must be positive. $x + \dfrac{2\pi}{3} = \pi$ means that $x = \pi - \dfrac{2\pi}{3} = \dfrac{\pi}{3} \approx 1.05$. [3.5].

Alternative Solution: Since the coefficient is 2, the sine curve has a period of π. Since the graph of $y = \sin x$ goes through the origin and $\left(x + \dfrac{2\pi}{3}\right)$ shifts the graph $\dfrac{2\pi}{3}$ to the left, the smallest positive value of x for which the graph is zero occurs when $x = \dfrac{\pi}{3} \approx 1.05$.

Graphing calculator: Plot the graph of $y = 3 \sin 2\left(x + \dfrac{2\pi}{3}\right)$ in an $x \in [-2\pi, 2\pi]$, $y \in [-4, 4]$ window. Use the Trace or Root function to find that the smallest positive x-intercept is $\dfrac{\pi}{3} \approx 1.05$.

28. i　**B**　Divide the equation through by 16 to get $\dfrac{(x-4)^2}{16} + \dfrac{(y-3)^2}{4} = 1$. This is the equation of an ellipse with $a^2 = 16$. The sum of the distances to the foci $= 2a = 8$. [4.1].

29. a　**D**　If the roots are r and $2r$, their sum $= -\dfrac{b}{a} = 3r = -\dfrac{k}{1}$ and their product $= \dfrac{c}{a} = 2r^2 = \dfrac{54}{1}$. Therefore, $r = \pm\sqrt{27}$ and $k = \pm 3\sqrt{27} \approx \pm 15.6$. [2.3].

Alternative Solution: If the roots are r and $2r$, $(x - r)(x - 2r) = 0$. Multiply to obtain $x^2 - 3r + 2r^2 = 0$, which represents $x^2 + kx + 54 = 0$. Thus, $-3r = k$ and $2r^2 = 54$. Since $r = -\dfrac{k}{3}$, then $2\left(-\dfrac{k}{3}\right) = 54$ and $k = \pm 3\sqrt{27} \approx 15.6$.

30. i　**D**　Substituting -1 for x gives 3. [2.4].

Alternative Solution: Using synthetic division gives

$-1\rfloor$	3	7	8	-2	-3
		-3	-4	-4	6
	3	4	4	-6	$\lfloor 3$ = remainder

31. a　**A**　The inverse of $f(x) = e^x$ is $f^{-1}(x) = \ln x$. $g(2) = e^2 + \ln 2 \approx 8.1$. [4.2].

32. i　**A**　This expression is of the form $A^3 - 3A^2 + 3A - 1$, which equals $(A - 1)^3$. Substituting $x + 2$ for A gives Choice A. [5.2].

33. i　**C**　If the graph passes through the origin, $x = 0$ and $y = 0$, then $\dfrac{4k^2}{1} - \dfrac{9k^2}{3} = 1$. $k^2 = 1$, and so $k = \pm 1$. [4.1].

34. n　**D**　$\mathrm{Tan}\,\dfrac{\theta}{2} = \dfrac{\sqrt{3}}{3}$. Therefore, $\dfrac{\theta}{2} = 30°$ or $210°$, and so $\theta = 60°$ or $420°$. [3.5].

Graphing calculator (in degree mode): Plot the graphs of $y = \dfrac{1 - \cos x}{\sin x}$ and $y = \dfrac{\sqrt{3}}{3}$ in an $x \in [0° \times 90°]$, $y \in [0 \times 1]$ window. Use the Trace function or the Intersect function to see that the graphs intersect at approximately $60°$. Thus, the answer is Choice D.

35. n　**E**　The solution set of $x^2 + 3x + 2 < 0$ is $-2 < x < -1$. $f(-2) = 12$, and $f(-1) = 6$. Intermediate values of x indicate that $f(x)$ is always between 6 and 12 when $-2 < x < -1$. [4.3, 2.3].

Graphing calculator: Plot the graph of $y = x^2 + 3x + 2$ in an $x \in [-5 \times 5]$, $y \in [-2 \times 2]$ window. Use the Trace function to see that the graph is below the x-axis on the interval $-2 < x < -1$. Then plot the graph of $y = x^2 - 3x + 2$ in an $x \in [-2 \times -1]$, $y \in [0 \times 20]$ window. (Choose the window based on the answer choices.) Use the Trace function to see that $6 < f(x) < 12$ when $-2 < x < -1$.

> **TIP:** If you are not sure what to do, try to draw a sketch. Very often a sketch can give you the answer or an insight that will lead you to a solution.

36. i　**E**　$f(-2.5) = 2.5 - 3 = -0.5$ and $f(1.5) = 1.5 + 1 = 2.5$. Therefore, $f(-2.5) + f(1.5) = 2$. [4.3, 4.4].

> **TIP:** $[x]$ represents the greatest integer function.
> $[x] = \begin{cases} x \text{ if } x \text{ is an integer} \\ \text{the integer that precedes } x \text{ if } x \text{ is not an integer.} \end{cases}$

37. n　**B**　The period is $\dfrac{\pi}{2}$, and so Choices A and E are ruled out. Choice C is the same as $\dfrac{1}{2}\sin 4x$ and is ruled out because the amplitude is $\dfrac{1}{2}$. Choice D is ruled out because $y < 0$ when $x < \dfrac{\pi}{4}$. [3.4].

Graphing calculator: Plot the graph of the answer choices to see that Choice B produces the only graph that looks like the one given.

38. i C $\left(\begin{array}{c} x \text{ people} \\ 2 \end{array}\right) = 28.$ $\dfrac{x(x-1)}{2\cdot 1} = 28.$ $x^2 - x = 56.$ $x = 8.$ [5.1].

39. i B As x increases from negative to positive, the slope increases from very negative to zero at $(0,0)$ to very positive. The only graph that has these characteristics is [B]. [5.5, 5.9].

Alternative Solution: Those who know a little calculus can use this method. The graph of $f(x)$ looks like the graph of $y = ax^2$. The slope function is the derivative, and so $g(x) = f'(x) = 2ax$, whose graph is a straight line through the origin. Thus, Choice B satisfies the conditions of the problem, and, by inspection, the other choices can be ruled out.

TIP: If you don't know how to do a general problem, think of one or two specific cases. This approach may lead you to a feasible answer choice.

40. n D This expression will be a maximum when $\sin\left(x + \dfrac{\pi}{6}\right) = -1$. $x + \dfrac{\pi}{6} = \dfrac{3\pi}{2}$. Therefore, $x = \dfrac{4\pi}{3} \approx 4.19$. [3.4].

Graphing calculator: Plot the graph of $y = 5 - \sin\left(x + \dfrac{\pi}{6}\right)$ in an $x \in [0 \times 6]$, $y \in [-1 \times 6]$ window. Use the Trace function or the Max function to see that the maximum occurs when $x \approx 4$. Therefore, Choice D is correct.

41. a D The graph of f must be symmetric about the line $y = x$. In I, f becomes $y = -1x + b$, which is symmetric about $y = x$. In II, f becomes $y = x$, which is symmetric about $y = x$ since it is $y = x$. In III, f becomes $y = ax$, which is not necessarily symmetric about $y = x$. [1.3].

42. a C Law of sines: $\dfrac{\sin 110°}{\sqrt{6}} = \dfrac{\sin B}{2}$; $\sin B = \dfrac{2 \sin 110°}{\sqrt{6}} \approx 0.7673$. $\text{Sin}^{-1}(0.7673) = \angle B = 50°$. Therefore, $\angle C = 180° - 110° - 50° = 20°$. [3.7].

43. a C $\left|3\vec{v} - \vec{u}\right| = \left|(3, \sqrt{3}) - (3, -2)\right| = \left|(0, 3\sqrt{3} + 2)\right| = \sqrt{0^2 + \left(3\sqrt{3} + 2\right)^2} = \sqrt{3\sqrt{3} + 2} \approx 7.$ [5.5].

44. a D Circumference of base of cone = length of arc $AB = 5$. $\dfrac{2\pi}{5} = 2\pi$. Circumference $= 2\pi r = 2\pi$. Therefore, radius of base = 1. Height of cone $= \sqrt{24}$. Therefore, volume $= \dfrac{1}{3}\pi r^2 h = \dfrac{1}{3}\pi \cdot 1 \cdot \sqrt{24} \approx 5.13$. [5.5, 3.2].

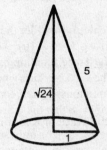

45. a A Law of cosines:
$12 = (2x)^2 + (3x+2)^2 - 2 \cdot 2x \cdot (3x+2)\cos 60°$.
$12 = 4x^2 + 9x^2 + 12x + 4 - (12x^2 + 8x) \cdot \dfrac{1}{2}$.
$7x^2 + 8x - 8 = 0$. Solving gives
$x = \dfrac{-8 \pm \sqrt{64 + 224}}{14} = \dfrac{-8 \pm \sqrt{288}}{14}$
Since a side of a triangle must be positive, x can equal only $\dfrac{-8 + \sqrt{288}}{14} \approx 0.64$. [3.7].

46. a E $\dfrac{\left|5a + 3(3\sqrt{3})a - 12\right|}{\sqrt{5^2 + 3^2}} = 6.$ $\left|5a + 3\sqrt{3}a - 12\right| = 6\sqrt{34}$. Thus, $5a + 3\sqrt{3}a - 12 = 6\sqrt{34}$ or $5a + 3\sqrt{3}a - 12 = -6\sqrt{34}$, and $(5 + 3\sqrt{3})a = 12 + 6\sqrt{34}$ or $(5 + 3\sqrt{3})a = 12 - 6\sqrt{34}$. Therefore, $a = \dfrac{12 + 6\sqrt{34}}{5 + 3\sqrt{3}} \approx 4.6$ or $a = \dfrac{12 - 6\sqrt{34}}{5 + 3\sqrt{3}} \approx -2.3$. [1.1].

47. n A Complete the square:
$$f(x) = 3\left(x^2 + \dfrac{4}{3}x + \dfrac{4}{9}\right) + 6 - \dfrac{4}{3}$$
$$= 3\left(x + \dfrac{2}{3}\right)^2 + \dfrac{11}{3}$$
Substitute $x - k$ for x in this equation in an attempt to get an equation of the form $3x^2 + \dfrac{11}{3}$, which is symmetric about the y-axis. This form is obtained if $k = \dfrac{2}{3}$. [2.3].

<u>Alternative Solution</u>: Since the first coordinate of the vertex of the general quadratic equation, $ax^2 + bx + c = 0$, is equal to $\dfrac{-b}{2a}$, $x = \dfrac{-b}{2a} = 0$ if the graph is to be symmetric about the y-axis.

Therefore, $0 - k = \dfrac{-b}{2a} = \dfrac{-4}{6}$ and $k = \dfrac{2}{3}$.

Graphing calculator: Plot the graph of $y = 3x^2 + 4x + 5$ in an $x \in [-10 \times 10]$, $y \in [-10 \times 10]$ window. Use the Trace function or the Min function to see that the vertex occurs when $x \approx -0.6$. Therefore, the vertex must be moved approximately 0.6 unit to the right so that the graph will be symmetric about the y-axis. The only answer choice close to 0.6 is $\dfrac{2}{3}$ (Choice A).

48. n   C Although f is an even function, g is not; therefore, (I) $f \cdot g$ is not even. Also, $f(g(x)) = \cos(2x + 1)$, which is a cosine curve shifted less than π to the left. Thus, $f(g(x))$ (II) is not even. However, $g(f(x)) = 2 \cos x + 1$ is a cosine curve with period 2π, amplitude 2, shifted 1 unit up. Thus, $g(f(x))$ (III) is even. [1.4].

Graphing calculator: Plot the graphs of $y = (\cos x) \cdot (2x + 1)$, $y = \cos(2x + 1)$, and $y = 2(\cos x) + 1$ to see that only the third graph is symmetric about the y-axis and thus represents an even function.

49. a   B Height of cylinder is 8.

Volume of sphere $= \dfrac{4}{3}\pi r^3 = \dfrac{4}{3}\pi(125) = \dfrac{500\pi}{3}$.

Volume of cylinder $= \pi r^2 h = \pi(9)8$.

Difference $= 166\dfrac{2}{3}\pi - 72\pi \approx 523.6 - 226.7$

≈ 297.

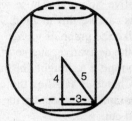

50. n   E The graph never repeats itself. Each piece of the graph extends lower than the preceding one. [4.4].

Graphing calculator: Plot the graph of $y = \text{int}(x) - 2x$ in an $x \in [-2 \times 2]$, $y \in [-2 \times 2]$ window to see that $g(x)$ is not periodic.

SELF-EVALUATION CHART FOR MODEL TEST 1

SUBJECT AREA	QUESTIONS	NUMBER OF
		RIGHT WRONG OMITTED

Mark correct answers with C, wrong answers with X, and omitted answers with O.

Algebra
(9 questions)
Review section

5	7	12	22	24	29	30	32	35
4.2	5.4	4.2	5.9	5.4	2.3	2.4	5.2	4.3

____ ____ ____

Solid Geometry
(4 questions)
Review section

3	9	44	49
5.5	5.5	5.5	5.5

____ ____ ____

Coordinate Geometry
(6 questions)
Review section

1	6	20	28	33	46
2.2	4.1	4.1	4.1	4.1	2.2

____ ____ ____

Trigonometry
(10 questions)
Review section

2	11	15	26	27	34	37	40	42	45
3.1	3.1	3.6	2.2	3.5	3.5	3.4	3.4	3.7	3.7

____ ____ ____

Functions
(12 questions)
Review section

4	8	14	18	19	31	36	39	41	47	48	50
1.2	1.2	2.4	4.5	1.2	4.2	4.3	5.5	1.3	2.3	1.4	4.4

____ ____ ____

Miscellaneous
(9 questions)
Review section

10	13	16	17	21	23	25	38	43
5.2	4.6	5.8	5.9	5.6	5.3	5.1	5.1	5.5

____ ____ ____

TOTALS   ____ ____ ____

Raw score = (number right) − $\frac{1}{4}$ (number wrong) = ____

Round your raw score to the nearest whole number = ____

Evaluate Your Performance
Model Test 1

Rating	Number Right
Excellent	41–50
Very Good	33–40
Above Average	25–32
Average	15–24
Below Average	Below 15

ANSWER SHEET FOR MODEL TEST 2

Determine the correct answer for each question. Then, using a no. 2 pencil, blacken completely the oval containing the letter of your choice.

1. Ⓐ Ⓑ Ⓒ Ⓓ Ⓔ	18. Ⓐ Ⓑ Ⓒ Ⓓ Ⓔ	35. Ⓐ Ⓑ Ⓒ Ⓓ Ⓔ
2. Ⓐ Ⓑ Ⓒ Ⓓ Ⓔ	19. Ⓐ Ⓑ Ⓒ Ⓓ Ⓔ	36. Ⓐ Ⓑ Ⓒ Ⓓ Ⓔ
3. Ⓐ Ⓑ Ⓒ Ⓓ Ⓔ	20. Ⓐ Ⓑ Ⓒ Ⓓ Ⓔ	37. Ⓐ Ⓑ Ⓒ Ⓓ Ⓔ
4. Ⓐ Ⓑ Ⓒ Ⓓ Ⓔ	21. Ⓐ Ⓑ Ⓒ Ⓓ Ⓔ	38. Ⓐ Ⓑ Ⓒ Ⓓ Ⓔ
5. Ⓐ Ⓑ Ⓒ Ⓓ Ⓔ	22. Ⓐ Ⓑ Ⓒ Ⓓ Ⓔ	39. Ⓐ Ⓑ Ⓒ Ⓓ Ⓔ
6. Ⓐ Ⓑ Ⓒ Ⓓ Ⓔ	23. Ⓐ Ⓑ Ⓒ Ⓓ Ⓔ	40. Ⓐ Ⓑ Ⓒ Ⓓ Ⓔ
7. Ⓐ Ⓑ Ⓒ Ⓓ Ⓔ	24. Ⓐ Ⓑ Ⓒ Ⓓ Ⓔ	41. Ⓐ Ⓑ Ⓒ Ⓓ Ⓔ
8. Ⓐ Ⓑ Ⓒ Ⓓ Ⓔ	25. Ⓐ Ⓑ Ⓒ Ⓓ Ⓔ	42. Ⓐ Ⓑ Ⓒ Ⓓ Ⓔ
9. Ⓐ Ⓑ Ⓒ Ⓓ Ⓔ	26. Ⓐ Ⓑ Ⓒ Ⓓ Ⓔ	43. Ⓐ Ⓑ Ⓒ Ⓓ Ⓔ
10. Ⓐ Ⓑ Ⓒ Ⓓ Ⓔ	27. Ⓐ Ⓑ Ⓒ Ⓓ Ⓔ	44. Ⓐ Ⓑ Ⓒ Ⓓ Ⓔ
11. Ⓐ Ⓑ Ⓒ Ⓓ Ⓔ	28. Ⓐ Ⓑ Ⓒ Ⓓ Ⓔ	45. Ⓐ Ⓑ Ⓒ Ⓓ Ⓔ
12. Ⓐ Ⓑ Ⓒ Ⓓ Ⓔ	29. Ⓐ Ⓑ Ⓒ Ⓓ Ⓔ	46. Ⓐ Ⓑ Ⓒ Ⓓ Ⓔ
13. Ⓐ Ⓑ Ⓒ Ⓓ Ⓔ	30. Ⓐ Ⓑ Ⓒ Ⓓ Ⓔ	47. Ⓐ Ⓑ Ⓒ Ⓓ Ⓔ
14. Ⓐ Ⓑ Ⓒ Ⓓ Ⓔ	31. Ⓐ Ⓑ Ⓒ Ⓓ Ⓔ	48. Ⓐ Ⓑ Ⓒ Ⓓ Ⓔ
15. Ⓐ Ⓑ Ⓒ Ⓓ Ⓔ	32. Ⓐ Ⓑ Ⓒ Ⓓ Ⓔ	49. Ⓐ Ⓑ Ⓒ Ⓓ Ⓔ
16. Ⓐ Ⓑ Ⓒ Ⓓ Ⓔ	33. Ⓐ Ⓑ Ⓒ Ⓓ Ⓔ	50. Ⓐ Ⓑ Ⓒ Ⓓ Ⓔ
17. Ⓐ Ⓑ Ⓒ Ⓓ Ⓔ	34. Ⓐ Ⓑ Ⓒ Ⓓ Ⓔ	

MODEL TEST

2

50 questions   1 hour

Tear out the preceding answer sheet. Decide which is the best choice by rounding your answer when appropriate. Blacken the corresponding space on the answer sheet. When finished, check your answers with those at the end of the test. For questions that you got wrong, note the sections containing the material that you must review. Also if you do not fully understand how you arrived at some of the correct answers, you should review the appropriate sections. Finally, fill out the self-evaluation sheet on page 161 in order to pinpoint the topics that give you the most difficulty.

OFFICIAL COLLEGE BOARD DIRECTIONS

Directions: For each of the following problems, decide which is the BEST of the choices given. If the exact numerical value is not one of the choices, select the choice that best approximates this value. Then fill in the corresponding oval on the answer sheet.

Notes: (1) A calculator will be necessary for answering some (but not all) of the questions in this test. For each question you will have to decide whether or not you should use a calculator. The calculator you use must be at least a scientific calculator; programmable calculators and calculators that can display graphs are permitted.

(2) For some questions on this test you may have to decide whether your calculator should be in the radian mode or the degree mode.

(3) Figures that accompany problems in this test are intended to provide information useful in solving the problems. They are drawn as accurately as possible EXCEPT when it is stated in a specific problem that the figure is not drawn to scale. All figures lie in a plane unless otherwise indicated.

(4) Unless otherwise specified, the domain of any function f is assumed to be the set of all real numbers x for which $f(x)$ is a real number.

Reference Information: The following information is for your reference in answering some of the questions in this test.

Volume of a right circular cone with radius r and height h: $V = \dfrac{1}{3}\pi r^2 h$

Lateral area of a right circular cone with circumference of the base c and slant height ℓ: $S = \dfrac{1}{2}c\ell$

Volume of a sphere with radius r: $V = \dfrac{4}{3}\pi r^3$

Surface area of a sphere with radius r: $S = 4\pi r^2$

Volume of a pyramid with base area B and height h: $V = \dfrac{1}{3}Bh$

---

1. If $f(x) = \dfrac{x-2}{x^2-4}$, for what value(s) of x does the graph of $f(x)$ have a vertical asymptote?

   (A) -2, 0, and 2
   (B) -2 and 2
   (C) 2
   (D) 0
   (E) -2

2. If a regular square pyramid has x pairs of parallel edges, then x equals

   (A) 1
   (B) 2
   (C) 4
   (D) 8
   (E) 12

3. Log $(a^2 - b^2) =$

   (A) $\log a^2 - \log b^2$
   (B) $\log \dfrac{a^2}{b^2}$
   (C) $\log \dfrac{a+b}{a-b}$
   (D) $2 \cdot \log a - 2 \cdot \log b$
   (E) $\log(a+b) + \log(a-b)$

4. The sum of the roots of the equation $\left(x - \sqrt{2}\right)^2 \left(x + \sqrt{3}\right)\left(x - \sqrt{5}\right) = 0$ is

   (A) 3.3
   (B) 1.9
   (C) 2.2
   (D) 6.8
   (E) 2.5

5. If the graph of $x + 2y + 3 = 0$ is perpendicular to the graph of $ax + 3y + 2 = 0$, then a equals

   (A) $\dfrac{3}{2}$
   (B) $-\dfrac{3}{2}$
   (C) 6
   (D) -6
   (E) $\dfrac{2}{3}$

6. The maximum value of $6 \cdot \sin x \cdot \cos x$ is

   (A) $\dfrac{1}{3}$
   (B) 1
   (C) 3
   (D) 6
   (E) $\dfrac{3\sqrt{3}}{2}$

GO ON TO THE NEXT PAGE

7. If $f(r,\theta) = r\cos\theta$, then $f(2,3) =$

   (A) −3.00
   (B) −1.98
   (C) 0.10
   (D) 2.00
   (E) 1.25

8. The sum of the zeros of $f(x) = x^3 - 3x^2 - 4x + 12$ is

   (A) 3
   (B) −3
   (C) 7
   (D) −7
   (E) 12

9. $i^{14} + i^{15} + i^{16} + i^{17} =$

   (A) 1
   (B) $2i$
   (C) $1 - i$
   (D) 0
   (E) $2 + 2i$

10. When the graph of $y = \sin 2x$ is drawn for all values of x between $10°$ and $350°$, it crosses the x-axis

   (A) zero time
   (B) one time
   (C) two times
   (D) three times
   (E) six times

11. When $\left(1 - \dfrac{1}{x}\right)^{-6}$ is expanded, the sum of the last three coefficients is

   (A) 10
   (B) 11
   (C) 16
   (D) −11
   (E) The sum cannot be determined.

12. A particular sphere has the property that its surface area has the same numerical value as its volume. What is the length of the radius of this sphere?

   (A) 1
   (B) 2
   (C) 3
   (D) 4
   (E) 6

USE THIS SPACE FOR SCRATCH WORK

GO ON TO THE NEXT PAGE

13. If the domain of $f(x) = 3x^2 + 2$ is $\{x: -2 \le x \le 2\}$, then $f(x)$ has a minimum value when $x =$

(A) −2

(B) 0

(C) 2

(D) $\dfrac{\sqrt{6}}{3}$

(E) $-\dfrac{\sqrt{6}}{3}$

14. The pendulum on a clock swings through an angle of 1 radian, and the tip sweeps out an arc of 12 inches. How long is the pendulum?

(A) 6 inches

(B) 12 inches

(C) 24 inches

(D) $\dfrac{12}{\pi}$ inches

(E) $\dfrac{24}{\pi}$ inches

15. What is the domain of the function $f(x) = 4 - \sqrt{3x^3 - 7}$?

(A) $x \le -1.33$ or $x \ge 1.33$
(B) $x \ge 2.33$
(C) $x \ge 1.33$
(D) $x \ge 1.53$
(E) $x \le -2.33$ or $x \ge 2.33$

16. If $x + y = 90°$, which of the following must be true?

(A) $\cos x = \cos y$
(B) $\sin x = -\sin y$
(C) $\tan x = \cot y$
(D) $\sin x + \cos y = 1$
(E) $\tan x + \cot y = 1$

17. The graph of the equation $y = x^3 + 5x + 1$

(A) does not intersect the x-axis
(B) intersects the x-axis at one and only one point
(C) intersects the x-axis at exactly three points
(D) intersects the x-axis at more than three points
(E) intersects the x-axis at exactly two points

18. The length of the radius of the sphere $x^2 + y^2 + z^2 + 2x - 4y = 10$ is

(A) 3.16
(B) 3.38
(C) 3.87
(D) 3.74
(E) 3.46

19. If the roots of the equation $x^2 + bx + c = 0$ are r and s, the value of $\dfrac{(r+s)^2}{rs}$ in terms of b and c is

(A) $\dfrac{b^2}{c^2}$

(B) $\dfrac{c^2}{b}$

(C) $\dfrac{b^2}{c}$

(D) $-\dfrac{b}{c}$

(E) $-\dfrac{b^2}{c}$

20. Which of the following is the solution set for $x(x - 3)(x + 2) > 0$?

(A) $x < -2$
(B) $-2 < x < 3$
(C) $-2 < x < 3$ or $x > 3$
(D) $x < -2$ or $0 < x < 3$
(E) $-2 < x < 0$ or $x > 3$

21. Which of the following is the equation of the circle that has its center at the origin and is tangent to the line with equation $3x - 4y = 10$?

(A) $x^2 + y^2 = 2$
(B) $x^2 + y^2 = 4$
(C) $x^2 + y^2 = 3$
(D) $x^2 + y^2 = 5$
(E) $x^2 + y^2 = 10$

22. If $f(x) = 3 - 2x + x^2$, then $\dfrac{f(x+t) - f(x)}{t} =$

(A) $t^2 + 2xt - 2t$
(B) $x^2t^2 - 2xt + 3$
(C) $t + 2x - 2$
(D) $2x - 2$
(E) none of the above

23. If $f(x) = x^3$ and $g(x) = x^2 + 1$, which of the following is an odd function (are odd functions)?

   I. $f(x) \cdot g(x)$
  II. $f(g(x))$
 III. $g(f(x))$

(A) only I
(B) only II
(C) only III
(D) only II and III
(E) I, II, and III

24. In how many ways can a committee of four be selected from nine men so as to always include a particular man?

(A) 84
(B) 70
(C) 48
(D) 56
(E) 126

25. When $f(x) = \sin x$ and $g(x) = \cos x$ over the interval $(0,2\pi)$, and $M(f,g)$ is defined to be the maximum of f and g, the graph of $M(f,g)$ looks like which one of the following?

(A)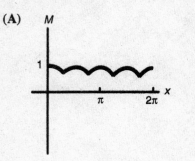

(B)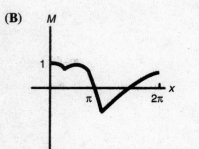

(C)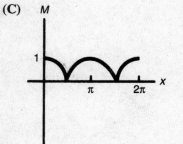

(D)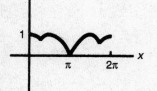

GO ON TO THE NEXT PAGE

(E)

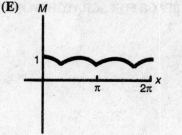

26. If the mean of the set of data 1, 2, 3, 1, 2, 5, x is $3.\overline{27}$, what is the value of x?

(A) 8.9
(B) −10.7
(C) 5.6
(D) 2.5
(E) 7.4

27. In $\triangle JKL$, $\sin L = \dfrac{1}{3}$, $\sin J = \dfrac{3}{5}$, and $JK = \sqrt{5}$ inches. The length of KL, in inches, is

(A) 3.0
(B) 3.9
(C) 3.5
(D) 1.7
(E) 4.0

28. If L varies inversely as the square of D, what is the effect on D when L is multiplied by 4?

(A) It is multiplied by $\dfrac{3}{2}$.
(B) It is multiplied by 4.
(C) It is multiplied by 2.
(D) It is divided by 2.
(E) None of the above effects occurs.

29. The contrapositive of $(p \vee q) \to q$ is

(A) $q' \to (p \wedge q)'$
(B) $(p \vee q)' \to q'$
(C) $q' \to (p' \wedge q')$
(D) $q \to (p' \vee q')$
(E) $q' \to (p' \vee q')$

30. If $f(x, y, z) = \sqrt{2}x + \sqrt{3}y - z$ and $f(a, b, 0) = f(0, a, b)$, then $\dfrac{b}{a} =$

(A) 0.32
(B) 2.7
(C) 8.6
(D) 0.12
(E) 1.18

GO ON TO THE NEXT PAGE

31. In $\triangle ABC$, $a = 1$, $b = 4$, and $\angle C = 30°$. The length of c is

(A) 4.6
(B) 3.6
(C) 3.2
(D) 2.9
(E) 2.3

32. The set of points satisfying the inequalities $y > |x| - 3$ and $2y > x + 6$ lies entirely in quadrants

(A) I and II
(B) II and III
(C) III and IV
(D) I and IV
(E) II and IV

33. Which of the following could represent the inverse of the function graphed on the right?

(A)

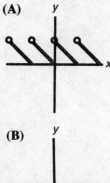

(B)

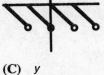

(C)

(D)

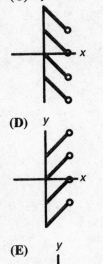

(E)

34. If f is a linear function and $f(-2) = 11$, $f(5) = -2$, and $f(x) = 4.3$, what is the value of x?

(A) 3.2
(B) −1.9
(C) 2.9
(D) 1.6
(E) −3.1

35. Which of the following could be a term in the expansion of $(p - q)^{18}$?

(A) $816p^{15}q^3$
(B) $-816p^{15}q^3$
(C) $816p^{16}q^2$
(D) $-816p^{16}q^2$
(E) $-816p^4q^{14}$

36. The range of the function $y = x^{-2/3}$ is

(A) $y < 0$
(B) $y > 0$
(C) $y \geq 0$
(D) $y \leq 0$
(E) all real numbers

37. If $\dfrac{\sin x + \cos\dfrac{\pi}{5}}{\cos\dfrac{5\pi}{6} - \sin 270°} = 0$ and $90° < x \leq 270°$, then

$x =$

(A) $54°$
(B) $144°$
(C) $126°$
(D) $234°$
(E) $216°$

38. A coin is tossed three times. Given that at least one head appears, what is the probability that exactly two heads will appear?

(A) $\dfrac{3}{8}$

(B) $\dfrac{3}{7}$

(C) $\dfrac{3}{4}$

(D) $\dfrac{5}{8}$

(E) $\dfrac{7}{8}$

GO ON TO THE NEXT PAGE

39. A unit vector parallel to vector $\vec{V} = (2, -3, 6)$ is vector

(A) $(-2, 3, -6)$
(B) $(6, -3, 2)$
(C) $(-0.29, 0.43, -0.86)$
(D) $(0.29, 0.43, -0.86)$
(E) $(-0.36, -0.54, 1.08)$

40. If the values of the function $g(x)$ represent the slope of the line tangent to the graph of the function $f(x)$, shown on the right, at each point (x, y), which of the following could be the graph of $g(x)$?

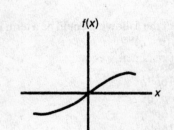

(A)   (B)

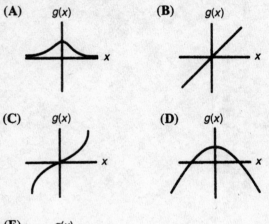

(C)   (D)

(E)

41. If $f(x) = \dfrac{x}{x-1}$ and $f^2(x) = f(f(x))$, $f^3(x) = f(f^2(x))$, $\ldots, f^n(x) = f(f^{n-1}(x))$, where n is a positive integer greater than 1, what is the smallest value of n such that $f^n(x) = f(x)$?

(A) 2
(B) 3
(C) 4
(D) 6
(E) No value of n works.

42. If $\vec{V} = (3, -5)$ and $\vec{U} = (-7, -4)$, what is the magnitude of the resultant of $\vec{V}$ and $\vec{U}$?

(A) $(-4, -9)$
(B) 9.7
(C) 9.8
(D) $(-21, 20)$
(E) 10.0

GO ON TO THE NEXT PAGE

43. Three consecutive terms, in order, of an arithmetic sequence are $x + \sqrt{2}$, $2x + \sqrt{3}$, and $5x - \sqrt{5}$. Then x equals

(A) 2.46
(B) 3.56
(C) 2.14
(D) 2.45
(E) 3.24

USE THIS SPACE FOR SCRATCH WORK

44. The graph of $xy - 4x - 2y - 4 = 0$ can be expressed as a set of parametric equations. If $y = \dfrac{4t}{t-3}$ and $x = f(t)$, then $f(t) =$

(A) $t + 1$
(B) $t - 1$
(C) $3t - 3$
(D) $\dfrac{t-3}{4t}$
(E) $\dfrac{t-3}{2}$

45. If $f(x) = ax^2 + bx + c$, how must a and b be related so that the graph of $f(x - 3)$ will be symmetric about the y-axis?

(A) $a = b$
(B) $b = 0$, a is any real number
(C) $b = 3a$
(D) $b = 6a$
(E) $a = \dfrac{1}{9} b$

46. The graph of $y = \log_5 x$ and $y = \ln 0.5x$ intersect at a point where x equals

(A) 6.24
(B) 1.14
(C) 1.69
(D) 1.05
(E) 5.44

47. Which of the following is equivalent to $\sin (A + 30°) + \cos (A + 60°)$ for all values of A?

(A) $\sin A$
(B) $\cos A$
(C) $\sqrt{3} \cdot \sin A + \cos A$
(D) $\sqrt{3} \cdot \sin A$
(E) $\sqrt{3} \cdot \cos A$

GO ON TO THE NEXT PAGE

48. The area of the region enclosed by the graph of the polar curve $r = \dfrac{1}{\sin\theta + \cos\theta}$ and the x- and y-axes is
   (A) 0.48
   (B) 0.50
   (C) 0.52
   (D) 0.98
   (E) 1.00

49. A rectangular box has dimensions of length = 6, width = 4, and height = 5. The angle formed by a diagonal of the box with the base of the box contains
   (A) 27°
   (B) 35°
   (C) 40°
   (D) 44°
   (E) 55°

50. If (x, y) represents a point on the graph of $y = 2x + 1$, which of the following could be a portion of the graph of the set of points (x, y^2)?

(A)

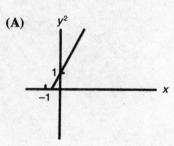

(B)

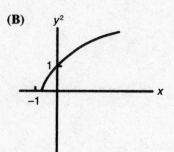

(C)

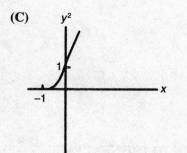

GO ON TO THE NEXT PAGE

(D)

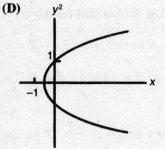

(E)

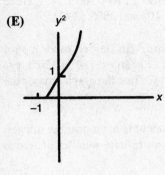

ANSWER KEY

1. **E**	18. **C**	35. **B**
2. **B**	19. **C**	36. **B**
3. **E**	20. **E**	37. **D**
4. **A**	21. **B**	38. **B**
5. **D**	22. **C**	39. **C**
6. **C**	23. **A**	40. **A**
7. **B**	24. **D**	41. **B**
8. **A**	25. **B**	42. **C**
9. **D**	26. **A**	43. **C**
10. **D**	27. **E**	44. **B**
11. **E**	28. **D**	45. **D**
12. **C**	29. **C**	46. **A**
13. **B**	30. **D**	47. **B**
14. **B**	31. **C**	48. **B**
15. **C**	32. **A**	49. **B**
16. **C**	33. **D**	50. **C**
17. **B**	34. **D**	

ANSWER EXPLANATIONS

In these solutions the following notation is used:

a: active—Calculator use is necessary or, at a minimum, extremely helpful.

n: neutral—Answers can be found without a calculator, but a calculator may help.

i: inactive—Calculator use is not helpful and may even be a hindrance.

1. n　E　$f(x) = \dfrac{\cancel{x-2}}{\cancel{(x-2)}(x+2)} = \dfrac{1}{x+2} \cdot f(x)$ is undefined at $x = 2$ and at $x = -2$. Since $x - 2$ divides out, there is a hole in the graph at $x = 2$. The only vertical asymptote occurs when $x + 2 = 0$. [4.5].

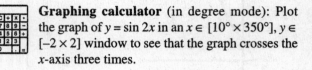

Graphing calculator: Plot the graph of $y = \dfrac{x-2}{x^2-4}$ in an $x \in [-10 \times 10]$, $y \in [-10 \times 10]$ window. Use the Trace function to see that there is a vertical asymptote when $x = -2$.

2. i　B　The only pairs of parallel edges are the opposite sides of the square base. [5.5].

3. i　E　$\text{Log}(a^2 - b^2) = \log(a + b)(a - b) = \log(a + b) + \log(a - b)$. [4.2].

4. a　A　The sum of the roots is $\sqrt{2} + \sqrt{2} + (-\sqrt{3}) + \sqrt{5} \approx 1.414 + 1.414 - 1.732 + 2.236 \approx 3.3$. [2.4].

5. a　D　The slope of the first line is $-\dfrac{1}{2}$, and the slope of the second line is $-\dfrac{a}{3}$. To be perpendicular, $-\dfrac{1}{2} = \dfrac{3}{a}$. Then $a = -6$. [2.2].

6. n　C　$6 \cdot \sin x \cdot \cos x = 3 \cdot \sin 2x$, whose amplitude is 3. [3.5].

Graphing calculator (in radian mode): Plot the graph of $y = 6 \cdot \sin x \cdot \cos x$ in an $x \in [-10 \times 10]$, $y \in [-5 \times 5]$ window. Use the Trace function or the Max function to see that the maximum occurs when $x \approx 3$. Therefore, Choice C is correct.

7. a　B　Put your calculator in radian mode. $f(2,3) = 2 \cdot \cos 3 \approx 2 \cdot (-0.98999) \approx -1.98$. [4.7].

8. i　A　Sum of zeros $= -\dfrac{b}{a} = 3$. [2.4].

Alternative Solution: Group and factor $f(x) = x^2(x - 3) - 4(x - 3) = (x - 3)(x^2 - 4) = (x - 3)(x - 2)(x + 2)$. The sum of the zeros $= 3 + 2 + (-2) = 3$.

9. i　D　$i^{14}(1 + i + i^2 + i^3)$. $i^2 = -1$ and $i^3 = -i$. $i^{14}(1 + i - 1 - i) = 0$. [4.7].

10. n　D　$y = \sin 2x$ has a period of $\dfrac{2\pi}{2} = \pi$. Since $\sin 2x = 0$ when $2x = 0°, 180°, 360°, 540°, 720°, \ldots$, $x = 0°, 90°, 180°, 270°, 360°, \ldots$. Three values lie between $10°$ and $350°$. [3.4].

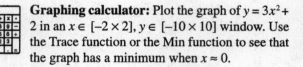

Graphing calculator (in degree mode): Plot the graph of $y = \sin 2x$ in an $x \in [10° \times 350°]$, $y \in [-2 \times 2]$ window to see that the graph crosses the x-axis three times.

11. i　E　When the exponent is not a positive integer, the expansion has an infinite number of terms. [5.2].

12. i　C　Surface area $= 4\pi r^2$. Volume $= \dfrac{4}{3}\pi r^3$. $4\pi r^2 = \dfrac{4}{3}\pi r^3$. $r = 3$. [5.5]

13. n　B　This is a parabola that opens up with vertex at $(0,2)$. The minimum value of 2 occurs when $x = 0$. [2.3].

Graphing calculator: Plot the graph of $y = 3x^2 + 2$ in an $x \in [-2 \times 2]$, $y \in [-10 \times 10]$ window. Use the Trace function or the Min function to see that the graph has a minimum when $x \approx 0$.

14. i　B　$s = r\theta$. $12 = r$. [3.2].

15. a　C　The domain consists of all numbers that make $3x^3 - 7 \geq 0$. Therefore, $x^3 \geq \dfrac{7}{3}$ and $x \geq 1.33$. [1.1, 2.5].

16. n　C　Cofunctions of complementary angles are equal. Since x and y are complementary, tan and cot are cofunctions [3.1].

Calculator (in degree mode): Choose any values of x and y such that their sum is $90°$. (For example, $x = 40°$ and $y = 50°$). Test the answer choices to see that only Choice C is true.

17. n　B　By Descartes' rule of signs, the graph does not intersect the positive x-axis but it does intersect the negative x-axis once. [2.4].

Graphing calculator: Plot the graph of $y = x^3 + 5x + 1$ in an $x \in [-10 \times 10]$, $y \in [-10 \times 10]$ window to see that it crosses the x-axis only once. To make sure you are not missing anything, you should also plot the equation in an $x \in [-1 \times 1]$, $y \in [-1 \times 1]$ window and in an $x \in [-100 \times 100]$, $y \in [-100 \times 100]$ window.

18. a   C   Complete the square: $(x^2 + 2x + 1) + (y^2 - 4y + 4) + z^2 = 10 + 1 + 4 = 15$. Therefore, $r = \sqrt{15} \approx 3.87$. [5.5].

19. i   C   In any quadratic equation the sum of the roots $= -\dfrac{b}{a}$ and the product of the roots $= \dfrac{c}{a}$. Also, $r + s = -b$, $(r + s)^2 = b^2$, $rs = c$. Therefore, $\dfrac{(r+s)^2}{rs} = \dfrac{b^2}{c}$. [2.3].

Alternative Solution: If the roots are r and s, $(x - r)(x - s) = 0$. Multiply to obtain $x^2 + (-r - s)r + rs = 0$, which in the form of $x^2 + bx + c = 0$. Thus, $(-r - s) = b$ and $rs = c$. Thus, $(r + s)^2 = b^2$ and $\dfrac{(r+s)^2}{rs} = \dfrac{b^2}{c}$.

20. n   E   Consider the associated equation, $x(x - 3)(x + 2) = 0$, which is solved when $x = 0$, 3, or -2:

   Check numbers in the inter-

vals in the original inequality. Numbers between -2 and 0 or greater than 3 satisfy the inequality. [2.5].

Graphing calculator: Plot the graph of $y = x(x - 3)(x + 2)$ in an $x \in [-10 \times 10]$, $y \in [-10 \times 10]$ window. Use the Trace function to see that the graph is above the x-axis when $-2 < x < 0$ or $x > 3$.

21. i   B   Distance from origin to the line equals the radius of the circle.

$$\text{Distance} = \frac{|3 \cdot 0 - 4 \cdot 0 - 10|}{\sqrt{3^2 + 4^2}} = \frac{10}{5} = 2.$$

Equation is $x^2 + y^2 = 4$. [4.1].

22. i   C

$$\frac{f(x+t) - f(x)}{t}$$

$$= \frac{(3-2)(x+t) + (x+t)^2 - (3 - 2x + x^2)}{t}$$

$$= \frac{3 - 2x - 2t + x^2 + 2xt + t^2 - 3 + 2x - x^2}{t}$$

$$= 2x - 2 + t. \quad [1.2].$$

TIP: For calculus students only: This difference quotient looks like the definition of the derivative. However, no limit is taken, so don't jump at $f'(x)$, which is Choice D.

23. n   A $f(x) \cdot g(x) = x^5 + x^3$; I is an odd function because $-F(x) = F(-x)$. $f(g(x)) = (x^2 + 1)^3$; II is not an odd function because $-F(x) \neq F(-x)$. $g(f(x)) = x^6 + 1$; III is not an odd function because $-F(x) \neq F(-x)$. [1.4].

Graphing calculator: Plot the graphs of $y = (x^3) \cdot (x^2 + 1)$, $y = (x^2 + 1)^3$, and $y = x^6 + 1$ to see that only I is symmetric about the origin and is thus an odd function.

24. n   D   Since one particular man must be on the committee, the problem changes to "Form a committee of 3 from 8 men." $\dbinom{8}{3} = \dfrac{8 \cdot 7 \cdot 6}{3 \cdot 2 \cdot 1} = 56$. [5.1].

   Calculator: $\dbinom{8}{3} = \dfrac{8!}{5! \cdot 3!} = \dfrac{40,320}{120 \cdot 6} = 56$.

25. n   B   A sketch of $y = \sin x$ and $y = \cos x$ on the same axes gives Choice B. [3.4].

Alternative Solution: Since $\sin x$ and $\cos x$ are both negative in quadrant III, $M(f,g)$ must be negative somewhere. Therefore, the only possible graph is Choice B.

Graphing calculator: Plot the graphs of $y = \sin x$ and $y = \cos x$ in the same $x \in [-10 \times 10]$, $y \in [-2 \times 2]$ window. Follow the path of the higher of the two functions to see that the answer is Choice B.

26. a   A   Mean $= \dfrac{1 + 2 + 3 + 1 + 2 + 5 + x}{7} = \dfrac{14 + x}{7} = 3.\overline{27}$. Therefore, $x = 8.9$. [5.8].

27. a   E   Law of sines: $\dfrac{\frac{1}{3}}{\sqrt{5}} = \dfrac{\frac{3}{5}}{KL}$; $\dfrac{1}{3} KL = \dfrac{3\sqrt{5}}{5}$.

Therefore, $KL = \dfrac{9\sqrt{5}}{5} \approx 4.0$. [3.7].

Alternative Solution: Drop a perpendicular, KM, to LJ.

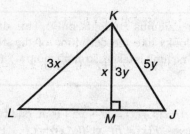

In a right triangle, $\sin x = \dfrac{\text{opposite side}}{\text{hypotenuse}}$, and so $\sin L = \dfrac{1}{3}$.

Label $KM = x$ and $KL = 3x$. Similarly, $\sin J = \dfrac{3}{5}$, so label $KM = 3y$ and $JK = 5y$. Therefore, from the diagram, since $JK = \sqrt{5}$, $y = \dfrac{\sqrt{5}}{5}$. Then $x = \dfrac{3\sqrt{5}}{5}$, and $KL = \dfrac{9\sqrt{5}}{5} \approx 4.0$.

28. i   D $LD^2 = K$. If D is divided by 2 and then squared, the 4 in the denominator will cancel out the 4 times L. [5.6].

29. i   C   Contrapositive is $q' \rightarrow (p \vee q)'$, which is equivalent to $q' \rightarrow (p' \wedge q')$. [5.7].

30. a   D $f(a,b,0) = \sqrt{2}a + \sqrt{3}b = f(0,a,b) = \sqrt{3}a - b$. $(\sqrt{3}+1)b = (\sqrt{3}-\sqrt{2})a$. Dividing both sides by $(\sqrt{3}+1)a$ gives $\dfrac{b}{a} = \dfrac{\sqrt{3}-\sqrt{2}}{\sqrt{3}+1} \approx 0.12$. [1.5].

31. a   C   Law of cosines: $c^2 = 16 + 1 - 8 \cdot \dfrac{\sqrt{3}}{2} = 17 - 4\sqrt{3} \approx 10.07$. Therefore, $c \approx 3.2$. [3.7].

32. n   A   See the figure. [4.3].

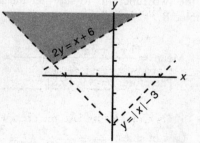

 Graphing calculator: Plot the graph of $y = $ abs$(x) - 3$ and $y = 0.5x + 3$ in an $x \in [-10 \times 10]$, $y \in [-10 \times 10]$ window. Substitute $(0,0)$ into both of the inequalities. Since this point satisfies the first inequality, the set of points above the absolute value graph are in the solution set. Since this point does not satisfy the second inequality, the set of points *below* that line are *not* in the solution

set. Therefore, the solution set is in the region above both lines, which puts it in only quadrants I and II.

33. i   D   Fold the graph about the line $y = x$, and the resulting graph will be Choice D. [1.3].

34. a   D   Since these points are on a line, all slopes must be equal. Slope $= \dfrac{-2-11}{5-(-2)} = \dfrac{-13}{7} = \dfrac{4.3-11}{x-(-2)}$. Cross-multiplying gives $-13(x + 2) = 7 \cdot (-6.7)$ and $x \approx 1.6$. [2.2].

 Graphing calculator: Draw the line that passes through points $(-2,11)$ and $(5,-2)$. Move the cursor to the point on the line where $y \approx 4.3$ to see that the x-coordinate of that point is about 1.6.

35. i   B   If the term is even it must be negative, and if it is odd it must be positive. Therefore, the answer must be Choice B or C. The coefficient of B comes from $\dbinom{18}{3} = 816$. [5.2].

36. n   B $x^{-2/3} = \dfrac{1}{x^{2/3}}$. Since all values of x are squared and $x \neq 0$, $y > 0$. [1.1, 4.2].

Graphing calculator: Plot the graph of $y = x^{-2/3}$ in an $x \in [-10 \times 10]$, $y \in [-10 \times 10]$ window. Use the Trace function to see that the graph always appears to be above the x-axis. Therefore, the range of $y = x^{-2/3}$ is $y > 0$.

TIP: It is very likely that when you sketched this graph, you got only the portion that lies in quadrant I. This occurred because many graphing (and scientific) calculators have trouble raising a negative number to a fractional power. To see the whole graph, try plotting $y = (x^{-2})^{1/3}$.

37. a   D   Calculator (in radian mode): Multiply through to get rid of the fraction and obtain $\sin x + \cos \dfrac{\pi}{5} = 0$. Sin $x - \cos \dfrac{\pi}{5} \approx -\cos 0.6283 \approx -0.8090$. Now put your calculator in degree mode, and find Sin^{-1} ($+ 0.8090$) $\approx 54°$, which is the reference angle for $\angle x$. Since $\sin x < 0$, $180° < x < 360°$. Therefore, $x = 180° + 54° = 234°$. [3.3].

TIP: If an equation contains fractions, multiply both sides by a common denominator (preferably the lowest common denominator) to remove all fractions from the problem. Also, note any values of the variable(s) that would have made any denominator equal to zero and remove them from the solution set.

38. i **B** There are 8 elements in the sample space of a coin being flipped 3 times. Of these elements, 7 contain 1 head and 3 (HHT, HTH, THH) contain 2 heads. Probability $= \dfrac{3}{7}$. [5.3].

39. a **C** A unit vector parallel to $\vec{V} = \dfrac{\vec{V}}{|\vec{V}|} \cdot |\vec{V}| = \sqrt{2^2 + (-3)^2 + 6^2} = 7$. A unit vector is either $\left(\dfrac{2}{7}, -\dfrac{3}{7}, \dfrac{6}{7}\right)$, which is parallel to and in the same direction as $\vec{V}$, or $\left(-\dfrac{2}{7}, \dfrac{3}{7}, -\dfrac{6}{7}\right)$, which is parallel to and in the direction opposite to $\vec{V}$. Using your calculator, you find that $-\dfrac{2}{7} \approx -0.29$, which indicates that the correct answer is Choice C. [5.5].

40. n **A** The slope of a tangent line at any point on the graph of f is a positive number. Therefore, every point on the graph of g must be positive. [5.5, 5.9].

 Alternative Solution (Graphing Calculator): Those who know a little calculus can use this method. The graph of $f(x)$ looks like the graph of $y = y^{1/3}$ (or $y = \text{Tan}^{-1} x$). The slope function is the derivative, and so $g(x) = f'(x) = \dfrac{1}{3} x^{-2/3}$ $\left(\text{or } g(x) = f'(x) = \dfrac{1}{1+x^2}\right)$, whose graph looks like Choice A.

> **TIP:** If you don't know how to do a general problem, think of one or two specific cases. This may lead you to a feasible answer choice.

41. i **B** $f^2(x) = f(f(x)) = f\left(\dfrac{x}{x-1}\right) = \dfrac{\frac{x}{x-1}}{\frac{x}{x-1}-1} = x$

$f^3(x) = f(f^2(x)) = f(x) = \dfrac{x}{x-1}$. [1.2, 5.9].

42. a **C** $\vec{V} + \vec{U} = (-4, -9)$.

$|\vec{V} + \vec{U}| = \sqrt{(-4)^2 + (-9)^2} = \sqrt{97} \approx 9.8$. [5.5].

43. a **C** $2x + \sqrt{3} = (x + \sqrt{2}) + d$, and $5x - \sqrt{5} = (2x + \sqrt{3}) + d$. Eliminate d, and $x + \sqrt{3} - \sqrt{2} = 3x - \sqrt{5} - \sqrt{3}$. Thus, $x = \dfrac{2\sqrt{3} - \sqrt{2} + \sqrt{5}}{2} \approx 2.14$. [5.4].

44. i **B** Substituting for y gives $x\left(\dfrac{4t}{t-3}\right) - 4x - 2\left(\dfrac{4t}{t-3}\right) - 4 = 0$, which simplifies to $12x - 12t + 12 = 0$. Then $x = t - 1$. [4.7].

45. i **D** Complete the square: $a\left(x^2 + \dfrac{b}{a}x + \dfrac{b^2}{4a^2}\right) + c - \dfrac{b^2}{4a} = a\left(x + \dfrac{b}{2a}\right)^2 - \dfrac{b^2 - 4ac}{4a}$. To have symmetry about the y-axis, $\left(x - 3 + \dfrac{b}{2a}\right)^2 = x^2$. Therefore, $b = 6a$. [2.3, 5.5].

Alternative Solution: The first coordinate of the vertex of a parabola is $\dfrac{-b}{2a}$, and so, in vertex form, $f(x) = a\left(x + \dfrac{b}{2a}\right)^2 + \mathbf{L}$ For $f(x - 3)$ to be symmetric about the y-axis, $f\left(x - \dfrac{b}{2a}\right) = f(x - 3)$. Therefore, $x - \dfrac{b}{2a} = x - 3$, which gives $b = 6a$.

46. a **A** Convert to exponential form: $x = 5^y$ and $\dfrac{1}{2}x = e^y$. Solving for x and substituting gives $5^y = 2e^y$. Taking the natural log of both sides gives $y \cdot \ln 5 = \ln 2 + y$. Therefore, $y = \dfrac{\ln 2}{\ln 5 - 1} \approx 1.14$. Substituting gives $5^{1.14} = x \approx 6.24$. [4.2].

> **TIP:** Remember the definition that converts logarithms to exponentials:
> $$y = \log_b x \text{ is equivalent to } x = b^y$$
> and the theorem:
> $$\log_b p^x = x \cdot \log_b p$$
> and the change of base theorem:
> $$\log_b x = \dfrac{\log_c x}{\log_c b}$$
> where c represents any convenient base

Graphing Calculator: Use the change-of-base theorem in order to convert $y = \log_5 x$ to $y = \dfrac{\log x}{\log 5}$ so that you can plot its graph in an $x \in [0,10]$, $y \in [0,2]$ window. Plot the graph of $y = \ln 0.5x$ in the same window. Use the Trace or Intersect function to see that the graphs intersect when $x \approx 6.24$.

Graphing Calculator: <u>Alternative Solution</u>:
Combine the two equations to get $y = \dfrac{\ln x}{\ln 5} - \ln$

$0.5x$. Plot its graph in an $x \in [0,10]$, $y \in [-1,1]$ window. Use the Trace, Root, Zero, or Solve function to see that $x \approx 6.24$.

47. i   B $\text{Sin}\,(A + 30°) = \sin A \cdot \cos 30° + \cos A \cdot$

$\sin 30° = \dfrac{\sqrt{3}}{2} \cdot \sin A + \dfrac{1}{2} \cdot \cos A$. $\text{Cos}(A + 60) =$

$\cos A \cdot \cos 60° - \sin A \cdot \sin 60° = \dfrac{1}{2} \cdot \cos A$

$-\dfrac{\sqrt{3}}{2} \cdot \sin\ A$. Adding the two equations gives

$\sin(A + 30°) + \cos(A + 60°) = \cos A$. [3.3].

48. n   B   Multiply the equation through by $\sin \theta + \cos \theta$ to get $r \sin \theta + r \cos \theta = 1$. $x = r \cos \theta$ and $y = r \sin \theta$, and so the equation becomes $y + x = 1$, a straight line with intercepts at $(0,1)$ and $(1,0)$. Therefore, the region is a right triangle with area $= 0.50$. [4.7]

Graphing Calculator: Sketch the graph in an $x \in [-4, 4]$, $y \in [-4,4]$ window to see that the polar graph appears to be a straight line. Evaluate the function when $\theta = 0$ to get $x = 1$, and when $L = \dfrac{\pi}{2}$ to get $y = 1$. The area of the triangle is 0.50.

49. a   B   The diagonal of the base is $\sqrt{6^2 + 4^2} = \sqrt{52}$. The diagonal of the box is the hypotenuse of a right triangle with one leg $\sqrt{52}$ and the other leg 5. Let θ be the angle formed by the diagonal of the base and the diagonal of the box. Tan $\theta =$

$\dfrac{5}{\sqrt{52}} \approx 0.6337$, and so $\theta = \tan^{-1} 0.69337 \approx 35°$.
[3.1]

50. n   C   A table of values indicates that the graph is Choice C. [5.5].

x	−0.5	0	1	2	3
y	0	1	3	5	7
y^2	0	1	9	25	49

<u>Alternative Solution</u>: Since $y = 2x + 1$, the set of points $(x, y^2) = (x, (2x + 1)^2)$. The graph of $f(x) = (2x + 1)^2$ is a parabola, with vertex at $\left(-\dfrac{1}{2}, 0\right)$, that opens up. Therefore, the only possible graph is Choice C. [2.3].

Graphing calculator: Plot the graph of $y_1 = 2x + 1$ and of $y_2 = (y_1)^2$ in the same $x \in [-10 \times 10]$, $y \in [-10 \times 10]$ window to see that the graph of y_2 is a parabola positioned similarly to the graph of Choice C.

SELF-EVALUATION CHART FOR MODEL TEST 2

SUBJECT AREA	QUESTIONS	NUMBER OF RIGHT WRONG OMITTED

Mark correct answers with C, wrong answers with X, and omitted answers with O.

Algebra
(9 questions)
Review section

3	4	8	9	19	20	28	36	46
4.2	2.4	2.4	4.7	2.3	2.5	5.6	1.1	4.2

___ ___ ___

Solid geometry
(4 questions)
Review section

2	12	18	39
5.5	5.5	5.5	5.5

___ ___ ___

Coordinate geometry
(6 questions)
Review section

5	17	21	32	40	50
2.2	2.4	4.1	4.3	5.5	5.5

___ ___ ___

Trigonometry
(10 questions)
Review section

6	10	14	16	25	27	31	37	47	49
3.5	3.4	3.2	3.1	3.4	3.7	3.7	3:3	3.3	3.1

___ ___ ___

Functions
(12 questions)
Review section

1	7	13	15	22	23	30	33	34	41	44	45
4.5	4.7	2.3	2.5	1.2	1.4	1.5	1.3	2.2	1.2	4.7	2.3

___ ___ ___

Miscellaneous
(9 questions)
Review section

11	24	26	29	35	38	42	43	48
5.2	5.1	5.8	5.7	5.2	5.3	5.5	5.4	4.7

___ ___ ___

TOTALS   ___ ___ ___

Raw score = (number right) – $\frac{1}{4}$ (number wrong) = _____

Round your raw score to the nearest whole number = _____

Evaluate Your Performance
Model Test 2

Rating	Number Right
Excellent	41–50
Very Good	33–40
Above Average	25–32
Average	15–24
Below Average	Below 15

ANSWER SHEET FOR MODEL TEST 3

Determine the correct answer for each question. Then, using a no. 2 pencil, blacken completely the oval containing the letter of your choice.

1. (A) (B) (C) (D) (E)
2. (A) (B) (C) (D) (E)
3. (A) (B) (C) (D) (E)
4. (A) (B) (C) (D) (E)
5. (A) (B) (C) (D) (E)
6. (A) (B) (C) (D) (E)
7. (A) (B) (C) (D) (E)
8. (A) (B) (C) (D) (E)
9. (A) (B) (C) (D) (E)
10. (A) (B) (C) (D) (E)
11. (A) (B) (C) (D) (E)
12. (A) (B) (C) (D) (E)
13. (A) (B) (C) (D) (E)
14. (A) (B) (C) (D) (E)
15. (A) (B) (C) (D) (E)
16. (A) (B) (C) (D) (E)
17. (A) (B) (C) (D) (E)

18. (A) (B) (C) (D) (E)
19. (A) (B) (C) (D) (E)
20. (A) (B) (C) (D) (E)
21. (A) (B) (C) (D) (E)
22. (A) (B) (C) (D) (E)
23. (A) (B) (C) (D) (E)
24. (A) (B) (C) (D) (E)
25. (A) (B) (C) (D) (E)
26. (A) (B) (C) (D) (E)
27. (A) (B) (C) (D) (E)
28. (A) (B) (C) (D) (E)
29. (A) (B) (C) (D) (E)
30. (A) (B) (C) (D) (E)
31. (A) (B) (C) (D) (E)
32. (A) (B) (C) (D) (E)
33. (A) (B) (C) (D) (E)
34. (A) (B) (C) (D) (E)

35. (A) (B) (C) (D) (E)
36. (A) (B) (C) (D) (E)
37. (A) (B) (C) (D) (E)
38. (A) (B) (C) (D) (E)
39. (A) (B) (C) (D) (E)
40. (A) (B) (C) (D) (E)
41. (A) (B) (C) (D) (E)
42. (A) (B) (C) (D) (E)
43. (A) (B) (C) (D) (E)
44. (A) (B) (C) (D) (E)
45. (A) (B) (C) (D) (E)
46. (A) (B) (C) (D) (E)
47. (A) (B) (C) (D) (E)
48. (A) (B) (C) (D) (E)
49. (A) (B) (C) (D) (E)
50. (A) (B) (C) (D) (E)

MODEL TEST

Tear out the preceding answer sheet. Decide which is the best choice by rounding your answer when appropriate. Blacken the corresponding space on the answer sheet. When finished, check your answers with those at the end of the test. For questions that you got wrong, note the sections containing the material that you must review. Also, if you do not fully understand how you arrived at some of the correct answers, you should review the appropriate sections. Finally, fill out the self-evaluation sheet on page 182 in order to pinpoint the topics that give you the most difficulty.

OFFICIAL COLLEGE BOARD DIRECTIONS

<u>Directions</u>: For each of the following problems, decide which is the BEST of the choices given. If the exact numerical value is not one of the choices, select the choice that best approximates this value. Then fill in the corresponding oval on the answer sheet.

Notes: (1) A calculator will be necessary for answering some (but not all) of the questions in this test. For each question you will have to decide whether or not you should use a calculator. The calculator you use must be at least a scientific calculator; programmable calculators and calculators that can display graphs are permitted.

(2) For some questions in this test you may have to decide whether your calculator should be in the radian mode or the degree mode.

(3) Figures that accompany problems in this test are intended to provide information useful in solving the problems. They are drawn as accurately as possible EXCEPT when it is stated in a specific problem that the figure is not drawn to scale. All figures lie in a plane unless otherwise indicated.

(4) Unless otherwise specified, the domain of any function f is assumed to be the set of all real numbers x for which $f(x)$ is a real number.

<u>Reference Information:</u> The following information is for your reference in answering some of the questions in this test.

Volume of a right circular cone with radius r and height h: $V = \dfrac{1}{3}\pi r^2 h$

Lateral area of a right circular cone with circumference of the base c and slant height ℓ: $S = \dfrac{1}{2}c\ell$

Volume of a sphere with radius r: $V = \dfrac{4}{3}\pi r^3$

Surface area of a sphere with radius r: $S = 4\pi r^2$

Volume of a pyramid with base area B and height h: $V = \dfrac{1}{3}Bh$

---

1. If $f(x) = 3x - 5$ and $g(y) = y^2 - 1$, then $f(g(z)) =$

   (A) $(3z - 5)^2 - 1$
   (B) $3z^2 - 8$
   (C) $3z^3 - 5z^2 - 3z + 5$
   (D) $z^2 + 3z - 6$
   (E) $9z^2 - 30z - 26$

2. A sphere is tangent to two distinct parallel planes. The set of all points equidistant from the two planes that intersect the sphere is

   (A) a circle
   (B) two points
   (C) a plane
   (D) a straight line segment
   (E) the empty set

3. If x and y are real numbers and $y = \sqrt[3]{4 - x^2}$, what is the maximum value of y?

   (A) 2
   (B) 1.59
   (C) ∞
   (D) 1.41
   (E) 0

4. A cone is inscribed in a hemisphere of radius r so that the base of the cone coincides with the base of the hemisphere. What is the ratio of the volume of the cone to the volume of the hemisphere?

   (A) $\dfrac{r}{2}$

   (B) $\dfrac{r}{3}$

   (C) $\dfrac{2r}{3}$

   (D) $\dfrac{1}{2}$

   (E) $\dfrac{1}{3}$

5. If $\log(\cos \theta) = p$, then $\log(\sec \theta) =$

   (A) $-p$
   (B) $1 - p$
   (C) $\dfrac{1}{p}$
   (D) $-\dfrac{1}{p}$
   (E) p

6. If the parabola $ay^2 + by + c = x$ passes through points $(-4,17)$, $(5,11)$, and $(8,1)$, the value of $a + b + c$ equals

(A) $\dfrac{17}{43}$

(B) $\dfrac{5}{2}$

(C) $\dfrac{14}{27}$

(D) 8

(E) −11

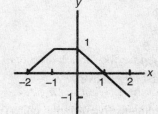

7. If, in the figure on the right, θ is the angle between segment PQ and the x-axis, then θ equals

(A) 23°
(B) 54°
(C) 25°
(D) 71°
(E) 67°

8. If the graph on the right represents the function f defined on interval $[-2,2]$, which of the following could represent the graph of $y = f(2x)$?

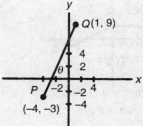

(A)

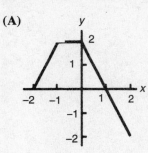

(B)

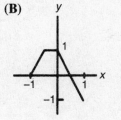

(C)

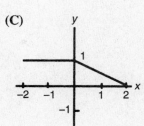

GO ON TO THE NEXT PAGE

(D)

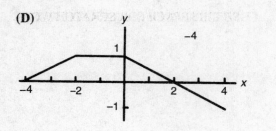

(E)

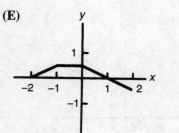

9. For each value of θ, $\sin(90° + \theta)$ equals

  (A) $\sin\theta$
  (B) $\cos\theta$
  (C) $-\sin\theta$
  (D) $-\cos\theta$
  (E) none of the above

10. A purse contains five different coins (penny, nickel, dime, quarter, half-dollar). How many different sums of money can be made using one or more coins?

  (A) 5
  (B) 10
  (C) 32
  (D) 120
  (E) none of the above

11. If $3x^3 - x^2 + 12x - 4 = (x - 2i)(3x - 1)Q(x)$ for all numbers x, then $Q(x) =$

  (A) $x - 2$
  (B) $x + 2$
  (C) $x - 2i$
  (D) $x + 2i$
  (E) $x + i$

GO ON TO THE NEXT PAGE

12. A point in space has coordinates $(7, -3, 8)$. How far is the point from the x-axis?

(A) 8.5
(B) 7
(C) 8.1
(D) 11
(E) 7.6

13. If $P(x)$ is a sixth-degree polynomial, $P(1) = 3$, and $P(-1) = -2$, what is the value of the remainder when $P(x)$ is divided by $x - 1$?

(A) −2
(B) 2
(C) −3
(D) 3
(E) The value cannot be determined.

14. $\operatorname{Sec}\left(\sin^{-1}\dfrac{\sqrt{5}}{5}\right)$ equals

(A) 2.15
(B) 1.12
(C) 0.89
(D) 0.98
(E) 1.10

15. An equation in polar form equivalent to $x^2 + y^2 - 4x + 2 = 0$ is

(A) $r = 4\cos\theta + 2$
(B) $r^2 = 4\cos\theta + 2$
(C) $4r = \cos\theta$
(D) $r^2 - 4r\cos\theta + 2 = 0$
(E) $r^2 = 4r\cos\theta$

16. Which of the following represents the y-intercept(s) of the graph of the equation $y = (x^3 - 2) \cdot \ln(x^2 + 2)$?

(A) 1.26 and 0.69
(B) −1.39
(C) 0.69
(D) 0
(E) −1.26

17. Which of the following could be a possible root of $4x^3 - px^2 + qx - 6 = 0$?

(A) $\dfrac{1}{6}$

(B) 4

(C) $\dfrac{3}{2}$

(D) $\dfrac{2}{3}$

(E) $\dfrac{4}{3}$

GO ON TO THE NEXT PAGE

18. The expression $\dfrac{1 - \cos 4x}{2}$ is equal to

   (A) $\sin^2 6x$
   (B) $\sin^2 2x$
   (C) $\cos^2 8x$
   (D) $\cos^2 4x$
   (E) $\sin^2 8x$

19. If $\log_b A = 0.2222$ and $\log_b B = 0.3333$, then the value of $\log_b\left(\sqrt{A} \cdot B^2\right)$ is

   (A) 0.0741
   (B) 0.1111
   (C) 0.5555
   (D) 0.7777
   (E) 0.9999

20. If $f(x) = x^2 + bx + c$ for all x, and if $f(-3) = 0$ and $f(1) = 0$, then $b + c =$

   (A) -5
   (B) -1
   (C) 1
   (D) 5
   (E) 0

21. If $f(x) = \sqrt[3]{4x + 2}$ for all x, then $f^{-1}\left(\dfrac{1}{2}\right) =$

   (A) 0.53
   (B) -0.30
   (C) 0.29
   (D) -0.47
   (E) -0.38

22. The sides of a triangle are 2 inches, 3 inches, and 4 inches. The value of the angle opposite the 3-inch side is

   (A) $43°$
   (B) $47°$
   (C) $64°$
   (D) $137°$
   (E) $133°$

23. The set of points (x, y) that satisfy $(x - 3)(y + 2) > 0$ lies in quadrant(s)

   (A) only I and IV
   (B) only II
   (C) only III and IV
   (D) only I, III, and IV
   (E) I, II, III, and IV

24. If $ax^3 + bx^2 + cx + 3 = 0$ when $x = -1$, what is the value of $ax^3 - bx^2 + cx + 3$ when $x = 1$?

(A) -6
(B) -3
(C) 0
(D) 3
(E) 6

25. If the operation @ is defined so that $a \, @ \, b = \dfrac{a}{1 + \dfrac{\pi}{b}}$,

what is the value of $(1 @ 2) @ 3$?

(A) 1.43
(B) 5.26
(C) 0.19
(D) 0.70
(E) 1.26

26. If h varies as V and inversely as the square of r, which of the following is true?

(A) If r is increased by 2, V is increased by 4.
(B) If both r and h are doubled, then V is doubled.
(C) If r is doubled and h is divided by 4, then V remains unchanged.
(D) If r is doubled and h is divided by 2, then V remains unchanged.
(E) None of the above is true.

27. If $\begin{cases} x = t^3 + 9 \\ y = \dfrac{3}{4}t^3 + 7 \end{cases}$ represents a line, what is the y-intercept?

(A) $\dfrac{3}{4}$
(B) 9
(C) 16
(D) $-\dfrac{27}{4}$
(E) $\dfrac{1}{4}$

28. Arcsec 0.8 + Arccsc 0.8 equals

(A) $74°$
(B) $16°$
(C) $90°$
(D) $0°$
(E) $39°$

29. What is the mean of this set of data: $\sqrt{1}, \sqrt{2}, \sqrt{3}, \sqrt{4},$ $\sqrt{5}, \sqrt{6}, \sqrt{7}$?

   (A) 2
   (B) 1.65
   (C) 2.14
   (D) 0.76
   (E) 1.93

30. Which of the following functions has (have) an inverse that is also a function?

   I. $y = x^2 - 2x + 4$
   II. $y = |x + 1|$
   III. $y = \sqrt{40 - 9x^2}$

   (A) only I
   (B) only II
   (C) only III
   (D) I, II, and III
   (E) none of the above

31. The sum of all the numerical coefficients of $(x - y)^{17}$ is

   (A) $\binom{17}{8}$
   (B) $2 \cdot \binom{17}{9}$
   (C) 1
   (D) 0
   (E) 17

32. The absolute value of the difference between the roots of the equation $1.4x^2 + 2.3x - 5 = 0$ is

   (A) 4.12
   (B) 1.64
   (C) 3.57
   (D) 2.17
   (E) 3.40

33. If $f(x) = x^7 - 97x^6 - 199x^5 + 99x^4 - 2x + 190$, then $f(99) =$

   (A) 16
   (B) 10
   (C) 4
   (D) –2
   (E) –8

34. If $2x + 3y - 4 - |2x + 3y - 4| = 0$ for all values of x and y belonging to the set $\{(x,y):p$ is true$\}$, then p must be the statement

    (A) $2x + 3y > 4$
    (B) $2x + 3y = 4$
    (C) $2x + 3y < 4$
    (D) $2x + 3y \geq 4$
    (E) $x = 0$ and $y = 0$

35. If $f(x) = 2^x$, then $f(\log_5 2) =$

    (A) 5
    (B) 2.32
    (C) 0.43
    (D) 0.19
    (E) 1.35

36. If $f(x) = \sqrt{x - 1}$ and $g(x) = \sin x$, then $g^{-1}\left(f\left(\sqrt{3}\right)\right) =$

    (A) 0.75
    (B) 1.41
    (C) 0.99
    (D) 1.12
    (E) 1.03

37. A basket contains 10 apples, of which 5 are rotten. What is the probability that a person who buys 4 apples will get none that are rotten?

    (A) $\dfrac{1}{2}$

    (B) $\dfrac{2}{5}$

    (C) $\dfrac{2}{25}$

    (D) $\dfrac{1}{4032}$

    (E) $\dfrac{1}{42}$

38. The smallest positive value of x satisfying the equation $\tan 5x = -2$ is

    (A) $13°$
    (B) $31°$
    (C) $23°$
    (D) $49°$
    (E) $63°$

GO ON TO THE NEXT PAGE

39. If f represents an even function, which of the following is also an even function (are also even functions)?

   I. $g(x) = f(x + 1)$
   II. $h(x) = f(x) + 1$
   III. $k(x) = f^{-1}(x)$

   (A) only I
   (B) only II
   (C) only III
   (D) II and III
   (E) I and III

40. Two cards are drawn from a regular deck of 52 cards. What is the probability that the cards will be an ace and a 10?

   (A) 0.157
   (B) 0.012
   (C) 0.077
   (D) 0.0004
   (E) 0.009

41. If the slope of line l_1 is $x + 1$, the slope of line l_2 is $x - 2$, and l_1 is perpendicular to l_2, x equals

   (A) 1.62 or –0.62
   (B) 0.62 or –1.62
   (C) only –0.62
   (D) only 1.62
   (E) only –1.62

42. A particle travels in a circular path at 50 centimeters per minute. If it traverses an arc of 30° in 30 seconds, what is the radius of the circular path?

   (A) 2865 centimeters
   (B) 48 centimeters
   (C) 24 centimeters
   (D) 50 centimeters
   (E) 95 centimeters

43. If the line passing through point (a,b) forms a right isosceles triangle with the x- and y-axes, the area of the triangle is

   (A) $\dfrac{(a+b)^2}{2}$

   (B) $\dfrac{a^2 - b^2}{2}$

   (C) $\dfrac{a^2 + b^2}{2}$

   (D) $\dfrac{1}{2}ab$

   (E) The area cannot be determined.

44. A cube is inscribed in a sphere, and a smaller sphere is inscribed in the cube. What is the ratio of the volume of the small sphere to the volume of the large sphere?

(A) 0.50 : 1
(B) 0.33 : 1
(C) 0.58 : 1
(D) 0.19 : 1
(E) 0.71 : 1

45. If $[x]$ is defined to represent the greatest integer less than or equal to x, and $f(x) = \left| x - [x] - \dfrac{1}{2} \right|$, the graph of $f(x)$ is discontinuous at

(A) no values of x
(B) all integer values of x
(C) all even integer values of x
(D) all odd integer values of x
(E) all odd multiples of $\dfrac{1}{2}$

46. If (x, y) represents a point on the graph of $y = x + 2$, which of the following could be a portion of the graph of the set of points $\left(\sqrt{x}, y \right)$?

(A)

(B)

(C)

(D)

(E)

GO ON TO THE NEXT PAGE

47. If $x_0 = 1$, then $\sum_{i=1}^{n}\left(x_{i-1} + \frac{1}{2}\right) =$

   (A) $\dfrac{n+2}{2}$

   (B) $\dfrac{n-1}{2}$

   (C) $\dfrac{n^2-1}{4}$

   (D) $\dfrac{n^2+5n}{4}$

   (E) $\dfrac{n^2+3n}{4}$

48. If $f(ab) = f(a) + f(b)$ for all real numbers in the domain of f, $f(x)$ equals which of the following?

   I. $\dfrac{1}{x}$

   II. e^x

   III. $\log x$

   (A) only I
   (B) only II
   (C) only III
   (D) only I and II
   (E) only II and III

49. The sum of the reciprocals of the roots of $x^3 + ax^2 + bx + c = 0$ is

   (A) $\dfrac{a}{b}$

   (B) $\dfrac{a}{c}$

   (C) $-\dfrac{a}{c}$

   (D) $-\dfrac{b}{c}$

   (E) $\dfrac{1}{a+c}$

50. What is the amplitude of the graph of $y = a\cos x + b\sin x$?

   (A) $\dfrac{a+b}{2}$

   (B) $a+b$

   (C) $\sqrt{ab}$

   (D) $\sqrt{a^2+b^2}$

   (E) $(a+b)\sqrt{2}$

USE THIS SPACE FOR SCRATCH WORK

ANSWER KEY

1. **B**	6. **D**	11. **D**	16. **B**	21. **D**	26. **C**	31. **D**	36. **E**	41. **A**	46. **A**
2. **A**	7. **E**	12. **A**	17. **C**	22. **B**	27. **E**	32. **A**	37. **E**	42. **B**	47. **D**
3. **D**	8. **B**	13. **D**	18. **B**	23. **D**	28. **C**	33. **E**	38. **C**	43. **A**	48. **C**
4. **D**	9. **B**	14. **B**	19. **D**	24. **E**	29. **E**	34. **D**	39. **B**	44. **D**	49. **D**
5. **A**	10. **E**	15. **D**	20. **B**	25. **C**	30. **E**	35. **E**	40. **B**	45. **A**	50. **D**

ANSWER EXPLANATIONS

In these solutions the following notation is used:

a: active—Calculator use is necessary or, at a minimum, extremely helpful.

n: neutral—Answers can be found without a calculator, but a calculator may help.

i: inactive—Calculator use is not helpful and may even be a hindrance.

1. i   B $f(g(z)) = f(z^2 - 1) = 3(z^2 - 1) - 5 = 3z^2 - 8.$ [1.2].

2. i   A   The set of points equidistant from two parallel planes is a plane parallel to both planes and halfway between them. This plane cuts the sphere through its center. The intersection is a circle. [5.5].

3. a   B   The maximum value of $\sqrt[3]{4 - x^2}$ occurs when $x = 0$. Therefore, maximum value = $\sqrt[3]{4} \approx 1.59$. [2.3, 4.1].

Graphing calculator: Plot the graph of $y = \sqrt[3]{4 - x^2}$ in an $x \in [-10 \times 10], y \in [-10 \times 10]$ window. Use the Trace and Zoom functions or the Max function to see that $y \approx 1.59$ when $x = 0$.

4. i   D   Volume of cone = $\frac{1}{3}\pi r^2 h = \frac{1}{3}\pi(r^2)r = \frac{1}{3}r^3\pi$. Volume of hemisphere = $\frac{2}{3}\pi r^3$. $V_c : V_h = 1 : 2$. [5.5].

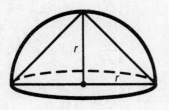

5. n   A $\text{Log}(\sec\theta) = \log\left(\dfrac{1}{\cos\theta}\right)$

$= \log 1 - \log(\cos\theta) = 0 - p.$

Alternative Solution: Let θ = any angle, say 60°. Thus, the problem becomes $\log(\cos\theta) = \log(\cos 60°)$

$= \log 0.5 \approx -0.3010 = p$. Therefore, $\log(\sec 60°)$

$= \log\left(\dfrac{1}{\cos 60°}\right) = \log 2 \approx 0.3010 = -p.$ [4.2].

6. i   D   Substitute point $(8,1)$ into the equation to get $a + b + c = 8$. [4.1].

7. a   E   Drop a vertical line from Q and a horizontal line through P to form a right triangle with sides 5, 12, and 13. $\sin\theta = \dfrac{12}{13} \approx 0.9231$. Therefore, $\theta = \text{Sin}^{-1}(0.9231) \approx 67°$. [3.1, 3.7].

8. i   B   Substituting $2x$ in place of x leads to the graph in Choice B. [5.5].

9. n   B $\sin(90° + x) = \sin 90° \cdot \cos x + \cos 90° \cdot \sin x = \cos x$ [3.1].

Graphing calculator: Plot the graph of $y = \sin(90° + x)$ in an $x \in [-10 \times 10], y \in [-2 \times 2]$ window. Then plot the graph of each answer choice to see that Choice B is correct.

10. n   E   Using 1 coin, $\binom{5}{1}$; using 2 coins, $\binom{5}{2}$; using 3 coins, $\binom{5}{3}$; using 4 coins $\binom{5}{4}$; using 5 coins, $\binom{5}{5}$. Total = $5 + 10 + 10 + 5 + 1 = 31$. [5.1].

Alternative Solution: Use the alternate notation, $_nC_r$, for $\binom{n}{r}$. Using your calculator evaluate $_5C_1 + {}_5C_2 + {}_5C_3 + {}_5C_4 + {}_5C_5$ to get $5 + 10 + 10 + 5 + 1 = 31$.

11. i   D   Since the coefficients are all real numbers, the complex factors must come in conjugate pairs: $x - 2i$ and $x + 2i$. [2.4].

12. a   A   The point is -3 from the x-axis in the y-direction and 8 in the z-direction. Therefore, the distance from the point to the x-axis is the hypotenuse of a right triangle with legs 3 and 8. Distance $= \sqrt{3^2 + 8^2} = \sqrt{73} \approx 8.5$. [5.5].

13. i   D   By the remainder theorem, the remainder when $P(x)$ is divided by $x - 1$ is $P(1) = 3$. [2.4].

14. a   B   Put your calculator in radian mode because the answer choices are not in degrees:

$$\text{Sin}^{-1}\left(\frac{\sqrt{5}}{5}\right) \approx 0.4636^R. \ \text{Sec}(0.4636) \approx$$

$$\frac{1}{\cos(0.4636)} \approx \frac{1}{0.8944} \approx 1.12. \ [3.6].$$

<u>Alternative Solution</u>: $\text{Sin}^{-1}\left(\dfrac{\sqrt{5}}{5}\right) \approx \theta$, and so $\sin \theta = \dfrac{\sqrt{5}}{5}$. Use the Pythagorean theorem to label the sides of the right triangle, as shown below.

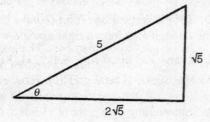

Therefore, $\sec \theta = \dfrac{5}{2\sqrt{5}} = \dfrac{\sqrt{5}}{5} = 1.12$. [3.6, 3.5].

15. i   D $x^2 + y^2 = r^2$ and $x = r \cdot \cos \theta$ give the equation $r^2 - 4r \cos \theta + 2 = 0$. [4.7].

16. a   B   The y-intercept occurs when $x = 0$, and so the y-intercept equals $-2 \cdot \ln 2 \approx -1.39$. [2.2, 4.2].

Graphing calculator: Plot the graph of $y = (x^3 - 2) \cdot \ln(x^2 + 2)$ in an $x \in [-10 \times 10]$, $y \in [-10 \times 10]$ window. Use the Trace and Zoom functions or the Table function to see that $y \approx -1.39$ when $x = 0$.

17. i   C $\dfrac{3}{2}$ is the only possibility for a root because 3 is a factor of 6 and 2 is a factor of 4. [2.4].

18. n   B   Let $A = 2x$ in the double-angle formula. Then $\cos 2A = 1 - 2 \sin^2 A$.

$$\frac{1 - \cos 4x}{2} = \frac{1 - \cos 2A}{2} = \frac{2 \sin^2 A}{2} = \sin^2 A$$
$$= \sin^2 2x. \ [3.5].$$

<u>Alternative Solution</u>: Using the half-angle formula with $A = 4x$, $\sin^2 \dfrac{1}{2} A = \dfrac{1 - \cos A}{2}$, gives $\sin^2 \dfrac{1}{2}(4x) = \dfrac{1 - \cos 4x}{2} = \sin^2 x$.

Graphing calculator: Plot the graph of $y = \dfrac{1 - \cos 4x}{2}$ in an $x \in [-10 \times 10]$, $y \in [-2 \times 2]$ window. Then plot the graph of each answer choice to see that Choice B is correct.

19. n   D
$$\log_b\left(\sqrt{A} \cdot B^2\right) = \frac{1}{2} \cdot \log_b A + 3 \cdot \log B_b$$
$$= \frac{1}{2}(0.2222) + 2(0.3333) = 0.7777$$
[4.2].

Calculator: Since the base is not given, choose any convenient base (e.g., base 10). $A = 10^{0.2222} \approx 1.668$, and $B = 10^{0.3333} \approx 2.154$. Thus, $\sqrt{A} \cdot B^2 \approx 5.994$. Therefore, $\log\left(\sqrt{A} \cdot B^2\right) = \log 5.994 \approx 0.7777$.

20. i   B -3 and 1 are zeros. Sum of zeros $= -b = -3 + 1 = -2$, and so $b = 2$. Product of zeros $= c = (-3)(1) = -3$. $b + c = -1$. [2.3].

<u>Alternative Solution</u>: Substitute points $(-3,0)$ and $(1,0)$ to get $9 - 3b + c = 0$ and $1 + b + c = 0$. Subtract the equations to get $8 - 4b = 0$, which implies that $b = 2$ and $c = -3$. Therefore, $b + c = -1$.

21. a   D $f^{-1}\left(\dfrac{1}{2}\right) =$ the value of x for which $f(x) = \dfrac{1}{2}$. Therefore, $\sqrt[3]{4x + 2} = \dfrac{1}{2}$, which implies that $4x + 2 = \dfrac{1}{8}$ and $x \approx -0.47$. [1.3].

<u>Alternative Solution</u> : Since the function, f, is $y = 4x + 2$, the inverse, $f^{-1}(x)$, is obtained by interchanging the x and the y and then solving for y:

$x = \sqrt[3]{4y + 2}; \quad 4y = x^3 - 2; y = \dfrac{x^3 - 2}{4}$. Thus,

$f^{-1}(x) = \dfrac{x^3 - 2}{4} \quad$ and $\quad f^{-1}\left(\dfrac{1}{2}\right) = \dfrac{\left(\dfrac{1}{2}\right) - 2}{4} =$

$\dfrac{\dfrac{1}{8} - 2}{4} = -\dfrac{15}{32} \approx -0.47$.

Graphing calculator: Plot the graphs of $y = \sqrt[3]{4x + 2}$ and [since you are looking for $f^{-1}\left(\frac{1}{2}\right)$] $y = \frac{1}{2}$ in an $x \in [-10 \times 10]$, $y \in [-2 \times 2]$ window. Use the Trace and Zoom functions or the Intersect function to see that the graphs intersect when x is approximately -0.47.

22. a   B   Put your calculator in degree mode because the answer choices are in degrees: By the law of cosines, $9 = 4 + 16 - 2 \cdot 2 \cdot 4 \cdot \cos x$. Then $\cos x = \dfrac{-11}{-16} = \dfrac{11}{16}$. Therefore, $\text{Cos}^{-1}\left(\dfrac{11}{16}\right) \approx 47°$. [3.7].

23. i   D   Sketch the graph and check points in the different regions. [2.5].

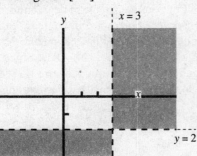

24. i   E   Substituting -1 for x gives $-a + b - c + 3 = 0$. Substituting 1 for x gives $a - b + c + 3 = k$. Adding the two equations gives $k = 6$. [2.4].

25. a   C $1 @ 2 = \dfrac{1}{1 + \dfrac{\pi}{2}} = \dfrac{1}{2.5708} \approx 0.38898$

$(1 @ 2) @ 3 \approx \dfrac{0.38898}{1 + \dfrac{\pi}{2}} \approx \dfrac{0.38898}{2.0472} \approx 0.19.$ [5.9].

26. i   C   The formula for the variation is $\dfrac{hr^2}{V} = K$. Testing the conditions of the selections indicates that the only valid answer is Choice C. [5.6].

27. n   E   Eliminating t^3 gives

$$y = \frac{3}{4}(x - 9) + 7 = \frac{3}{4}x - \frac{27}{4} + 7$$
$$= \frac{3}{4}x + \frac{1}{4}$$

Therefore, the y-intercept is $\dfrac{1}{4}$. [4.6].

<u>Alternative Solution:</u> The y-intercept occurs when $x = 0$. When $x = 0$, $t^3 = -9$ from the first equation. Substituting -9 for t^3 in the second equation gives $y = \dfrac{1}{4}$.

 Graphing calculator (in parametric mode): Plot the graphs of $x = t^3 + 9$ and $y = \dfrac{3}{4}t^3 + 7$ in a $t \in [-10 \times 10]$, $x \in [-10 \times 10]$, $y \in [-10 \times 10]$ window. Use the Trace and Zoom functions or the Table function to see that the y-intercept ≈ 0.25, which leads to Choice E.

28. n   C   Let $\text{Arcsec } 1.8 = A$ and $\text{Arccsc } 1.8 = B$. These expressions convert to $\sec A = 1.8$ and $\csc B = 1.8$, respectively. Since cofunctions of complementary angles are equal, A and B must be complementary angles. Therefore, $\text{Arcsec } 1.8 + \text{Arccsc } 1.8 = 90°$. [3.6][3.1]

Calculator: Put your calculator in degree mode because the answer choices are in degrees. $\text{Arcsec } 1.8 = \text{Arccos } \dfrac{1}{1.8} \approx 56.25°$, $\text{Arccsc } 1.8 = \text{Arcsin } \dfrac{1}{1.8} \approx 33.75°$. Therefore, $\text{Arcsec } 1.8 + \text{Arccsc } 1.8 = 90°$.

29. a   C   Convert the square roots to decimals, add to get 13.48 (approximately), and divide by 7 (the number of numbers you added) to get the mean, which is approximately 1.93. [5.8].

30. n   E   The graph of I is a parabola. The graph of II is a "V." The graph of III is the top half of an ellipse. If any one of these graphs is reflected about the line $y = x$, the resulting graph will not be a function. [1.3].

Graphing calculator: Plot the graphs of $y = x^2 - 2x + 4$, $y = \text{abs}(x + 1)$, and $y = \sqrt{40 - 9x^2}$ in an $x \in [-10 \times 10]$, $y \in [-10 \times 10]$ window. In each case, for some value of y in the range, there are two values of x in the domain that will give that y-value. Therefore, none of the three functions has an inverse that is also a function.

31. i   D   Since the signs alternate, the coefficients are symmetric about the middle terms, there is an even number of terms, and the sum of all the coefficients is zero. [5.2].

TIP: If the numbers in a problem are big or awkward, try considering a similar problem with smaller numbers to see whether a pattern shows up. In this case try expanding $(x - y)^3 = x^3 - 3x^2y + 3xy^2 - y^3$, where the sum of the numerical coefficients = 0.

32. a **A** $x = \dfrac{-2.3 + \sqrt{(2.3)^2 + 28}}{2.8} \approx 1.239$ or

$x = \dfrac{-2.3 - \sqrt{(2.3)^2 + 28}}{2.8} \approx -2.882$.

Therefore $|1.239 - (-2.882)| \approx 4.12$. [2.3].

33. n **E** Solve by synthetic division. [2.4].

$$
\begin{array}{r|rrrrrrr|r}
1 & -97 & -199 & 99 & 0 & 0 & -2 & 190 & \underline{99} \\
  & 99 & 198 & -99 & 0 & 0 & 0 & -198 & \\
\hline
1 & 2 & -1 & 0 & 0 & 0 & -2 & \boxed{-8} \\
\end{array}
$$

 Calculator: If you try to evaluate $99^7 - 97 \cdot 99^6 - 199 \cdot 99^5 + 99^4 - 2 \cdot 99 + 190$, the numbers get so big that your calculator must use scientific notation. This causes it to lose significant digits and does not give you the correct answer. Rewrite the polynomial to get $x^4(x^3 - 97x^2 - 199x + 99) - 2x + 190$. Substitute 99 for x and evaluate within the parentheses first. In this case the value is 0. Thus, the value of $f(99) = 0 + 2 \cdot 99 + 190 = -8$. (This procedure is just a special case of "nesting," described in the following tip.)

> **TIP:** You can often avoid the problem encountered here by rewriting the polynomial in "nested" form before evaluating. To obtain a polynomial in nested form you factor x's out of as many terms as possible until the innermost parentheses contain only a linear function. For example, $ax^3 + bx^2 + cx + d$ would be rewritten as $x[x(ax + b) + c] + d$. Now, if you evaluate the polynomial from the innermost parentheses, the numbers remain relatively small.

34. i **D** $2x + 3y - 4 - |2x + 3y - 4| = 0$ implies that $2x + 3y - 4 = |2x + 3y - 4|$, which is true only when $2x + 3y - 4 \geq 0$. [4.4].

35. a **E** By the change-of-base theorem, $\log_5 2 = \dfrac{\log_{10} 2}{\log_{10} 5} \approx 0.4307$. Therefore, $2^{0.4307} \approx 1.35$. [4.2].

36. a **E** $f(\sqrt{3}) = \sqrt{\sqrt{3} - 1} \approx \sqrt{0.7321} \approx 0.8556$.
$g^{-1}(f(\sqrt{3})) = g^{-1}(0.8556) = \text{Sin}^{-1}(0.8556) \approx 1.03$. [1.3].

37. n **E** To get 4 good apples, a person must make 1 of $\binom{5}{4} = 5$ selections of good apples and $\binom{5}{0} = 1$ selection of bad apples. There can be $\binom{10}{4}$

selections of 4 apples from the total of 10. Probability of 4 good apples $= \dfrac{\binom{5}{4}\binom{5}{0}}{\binom{10}{4}} = \dfrac{1}{42}$. [5.2.]

Alternative Solution: Since there are 5 good apples in the basket, P(getting a good apple on first pick) $= \dfrac{5}{10}$. On the second pick only 9 apples are left in the basket and 4 of them are good, so P(getting a good apple on second pick) $= \dfrac{4}{9}$. Continuing until 4 good apples are picked gives P(4 good apples) $= \dfrac{5}{10} \cdot \dfrac{4}{9} \cdot \dfrac{3}{8} \cdot \dfrac{2}{7} = \dfrac{1}{42}$.

38. a **C** Put your calculator in degree mode because the answer choices are in degrees: Tan $5x = -2$ implies that $5x = \text{Tan}^{-1}(-2)$. Find that the reference angle for $5x = \text{Tan}^{-1}(+2) \approx 63°$. Since tan $5x$ is negative, $5x$ must be in quadrant II (because you are looking for the smallest positive angle). Thus, $5x = 180° - 63° = 117°$. Therefore, $x = \dfrac{117}{5} \approx 23°$. [3.5].

Graphing calculator: Plot the graphs of $y = \tan 5x$ and $y = -2$ in an $x \in [0 \times 180°]$, $y \in [-3 \times 3]$ window. Use the Trace function or the Intersect function to see that the smallest positive value of x where the two graphs intersect is approximately 23°.

39. i **B** Since f is an even function, $f(-x) = f(x)$. Since the inverse of an even function is not an even function, $h(-x) = f(-x) + 1 = f(x) + 1$. Therefore, $h(x)$ (II) is the only even function. [1.4].

40. n **B** There are $\binom{4}{1}$ ways to draw 1 of the four aces, $\binom{4}{1}$ ways to draw 1 of the four 10s, and $\binom{52}{2}$ ways to draw any 2 cards from the deck.

P(getting one ace and one 10) $= \dfrac{\binom{4}{1}\binom{4}{1}}{\binom{52}{2}} = \dfrac{8}{663} \approx 0.012$. [5.3].

Alternative Solution: On the first draw 8 acceptable cards (four aces and four 10s) are available from the 52 cards in the deck. On the second draw only 4 acceptable cards (either the four aces or the four 10s, whichever were not picked on the first draw) are available from the remaining 51 cards. Therefore, P(a 10 and an ace) $=$ $\dfrac{8}{52} \cdot \dfrac{4}{51} = \dfrac{8}{663} \approx 0.012.$

41. n A Two lines are perpendicular if the product of their slopes equals -1; $(x + 1)(x - 2) = -1$. $x^2 - x - 1 = 0$; $x = \dfrac{1 \pm \sqrt{1+4}}{2} = \dfrac{1 \pm \sqrt{5}}{2}$. $x = \dfrac{1 + \sqrt{5}}{2} \approx$ 1.62 or $x = \dfrac{1 - \sqrt{5}}{2} \approx -0.62$. [2.2].

42. a B The particle travels 25 centimeters in 30 seconds. $s = r\theta$. $\theta = 30° = \dfrac{\pi}{6}$. $\dfrac{\pi}{6} \cdot 25 = r \cdot \dfrac{\pi}{6} \cdot r = \dfrac{150}{\pi} \approx 48$. [3.2].

43. i A The line must cut the axes at two points, $(c,0)$ and $(0,c)$. $\dfrac{b-0}{a-c} = \dfrac{b-c}{a-0} = $ slope. Therefore, $c = a + b$. Area $= \dfrac{1}{2}(a+b)^2$. [2.2].

44. a D The diameter of the small sphere equals the side of the cube, say s. The diameter of the large sphere equals the diagonal of the cube, which is $s\sqrt{3}$.

$\dfrac{\text{Small volume}}{\text{Large volume}} = \dfrac{s^3}{\left(s\sqrt{3}\right)^3} = \dfrac{1}{3\sqrt{3}} = \dfrac{\sqrt{3}}{9}$

$\approx \dfrac{1.732}{9} \approx \dfrac{0.19}{1}$

(i.e., volumes of similar figures are to one another as the cubes of linear corresponding parts). [5.5].

45. n A Sketch a portion of the graph to see that it is continuous. [4.5, 4.6, 4.4].

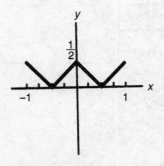

Graphing calculator: Plot the graph of $y =$ abs(x – int(x) – 0.5) in an $x \in [-2 \times 2]$, $y \in [-1 \times 1]$ window to see that the graph is continuous.

46. i A From the table of values below, the point (x,y) lies on the graph of $y = x + 2$ and the set of points $\left(\sqrt{x}, y\right)$ lies on the graph that you are looking for. A rough sketch indicates that the answer is Choice A. [5.5].

x	0	1	2	3	4
$\sqrt{x}$	0	1	$\sqrt{2}$	$\sqrt{3}$	2
y	2	3	4	5	6

47. i D Listing the first few terms indicates that the series is arithmetic with first term $\dfrac{3}{2}$ and a common difference of $\dfrac{1}{2}$. $S_n = \dfrac{n}{2}\left[3 + (n-1)\dfrac{1}{2}\right] = \dfrac{n}{2}\left(\dfrac{5}{2} + \dfrac{n}{2}\right) = \dfrac{n^2 + 5n}{4}$. [5.4].

48. i C By inspection: If $f(x) = \dfrac{1}{x}$, $f(ab) = \dfrac{1}{ab} = \dfrac{1}{a} \cdot \dfrac{1}{b} = f(a) \cdot f(b)$. False.
If $f(x) = e^x$, $f(ab) = e^{ab} = e^a \cdot e^b = f(a) \cdot f(b)$. False.
If $f(x) = \log x$, $f(ab) = \log ab = \log a + \log b = f(a) + f(b)$. True.   [4.2]

49. i D If p, q, and r are the three roots, the sum of the reciprocals is $\dfrac{1}{p} + \dfrac{1}{q} + \dfrac{1}{r} = \dfrac{qr + pr + pq}{pqr}$. $qr + pr + pq = b$, and $pqr = -c$. [2.4].

50. i D Multiply the expression by $\dfrac{\sqrt{a^2 + b^2}}{\sqrt{a^2 + b^2}}$ to

get $y = \sqrt{a^2 + b^2}\left(\dfrac{a}{\sqrt{a^2 + b^2}}\cos x\right.$

$\left. + \dfrac{b}{\sqrt{a^2 + b^2}}\sin x\right)$. Since $\left(\dfrac{a}{\sqrt{a^2 + b^2}}\right)^2 +$

$\left(\dfrac{b}{\sqrt{a^2 + b^2}}\right)^2 = 1$, $\dfrac{a}{\sqrt{a^2 + b^2}}$ could represent

$\sin \theta$ and $\dfrac{b}{\sqrt{a^2 + b^2}}$ could represent $\cos \theta$. Thus,

$y = \sqrt{a^2 + b^2}\ (\sin \theta \cos x + \cos \theta \sin x) = \sqrt{a^2 + b^2}\ \sin(\theta + x)$, which has an amplitude of $\sqrt{a^2 + b^2}$. [3.4, 3.5]

SELF-EVALUATION CHART FOR MODEL TEST 3

SUBJECT AREA	QUESTIONS	NUMBER OF
		RIGHT WRONG OMITTED

Mark correct answers with C, wrong answers with X, and omitted answers with O.

Algebra
(9 questions)

3	17	19	23	24	26	32	34	49
4.1	2.4	4.2	2.5	2.4	5.6	2.3	4.4	2.4

Review section   ___   ___   ___

Solid geometry
(4 questions)

2	4	12	44
5.5	5.5	5.5	5.5

Review section   ___   ___   ___

Coordinate geometry
(6 questions)

6	16	41	43	45	46
4.1	2.2	2.2	2.2	4.5	5.5

Review section   ___   ___   ___

Trigonometry
(10 questions)

5	7	9	14	18	22	28	38	42	50
4.2	3.1	3.1	3.6	3.5	3.7	3.6	3.5	3.2	3.4

Review section   ___   ___   ___

Functions
(12 questions)

1	8	11	13	20	21	30	33	35	36	39	48
1.2	5.5	2.4	2.4	2.3	1.3	1.3	2.4	4.2	1.3	1.4	4.2

Review section   ___   ___   ___

Miscellaneous
(9 questions)

10	15	25	27	29	31	37	40	47
5.1	4.6	5.9	4.6	5.8	5.2	5.2	5.3	5.4

Review section   ___   ___   ___

TOTALS   ___   ___   ___

Raw score = (number right) − ¼ (number wrong) = _____

Round your raw score to the nearest whole number = _____

Evaluate Your Performance
Model Test 3

Rating	Number Right
Excellent	41–50
Very good	33–40
Above average	25–32
Average	15–24
Below average	Below 15

ANSWER SHEET FOR MODEL TEST 4

Determine the correct answer for each question. Then, using a no. 2 pencil, blacken completely the oval containing the letter of your choice.

1. Ⓐ Ⓑ Ⓒ Ⓓ Ⓔ	18. Ⓐ Ⓑ Ⓒ Ⓓ Ⓔ	35. Ⓐ Ⓑ Ⓒ Ⓓ Ⓔ
2. Ⓐ Ⓑ Ⓒ Ⓓ Ⓔ	19. Ⓐ Ⓑ Ⓒ Ⓓ Ⓔ	36. Ⓐ Ⓑ Ⓒ Ⓓ Ⓔ
3. Ⓐ Ⓑ Ⓒ Ⓓ Ⓔ	20. Ⓐ Ⓑ Ⓒ Ⓓ Ⓔ	37. Ⓐ Ⓑ Ⓒ Ⓓ Ⓔ
4. Ⓐ Ⓑ Ⓒ Ⓓ Ⓔ	21. Ⓐ Ⓑ Ⓒ Ⓓ Ⓔ	38. Ⓐ Ⓑ Ⓒ Ⓓ Ⓔ
5. Ⓐ Ⓑ Ⓒ Ⓓ Ⓔ	22. Ⓐ Ⓑ Ⓒ Ⓓ Ⓔ	39. Ⓐ Ⓑ Ⓒ Ⓓ Ⓔ
6. Ⓐ Ⓑ Ⓒ Ⓓ Ⓔ	23. Ⓐ Ⓑ Ⓒ Ⓓ Ⓔ	40. Ⓐ Ⓑ Ⓒ Ⓓ Ⓔ
7. Ⓐ Ⓑ Ⓒ Ⓓ Ⓔ	24. Ⓐ Ⓑ Ⓒ Ⓓ Ⓔ	41. Ⓐ Ⓑ Ⓒ Ⓓ Ⓔ
8. Ⓐ Ⓑ Ⓒ Ⓓ Ⓔ	25. Ⓐ Ⓑ Ⓒ Ⓓ Ⓔ	42. Ⓐ Ⓑ Ⓒ Ⓓ Ⓔ
9. Ⓐ Ⓑ Ⓒ Ⓓ Ⓔ	26. Ⓐ Ⓑ Ⓒ Ⓓ Ⓔ	43. Ⓐ Ⓑ Ⓒ Ⓓ Ⓔ
10. Ⓐ Ⓑ Ⓒ Ⓓ Ⓔ	27. Ⓐ Ⓑ Ⓒ Ⓓ Ⓔ	44. Ⓐ Ⓑ Ⓒ Ⓓ Ⓔ
11. Ⓐ Ⓑ Ⓒ Ⓓ Ⓔ	28. Ⓐ Ⓑ Ⓒ Ⓓ Ⓔ	45. Ⓐ Ⓑ Ⓒ Ⓓ Ⓔ
12. Ⓐ Ⓑ Ⓒ Ⓓ Ⓔ	29. Ⓐ Ⓑ Ⓒ Ⓓ Ⓔ	46. Ⓐ Ⓑ Ⓒ Ⓓ Ⓔ
13. Ⓐ Ⓑ Ⓒ Ⓓ Ⓔ	30. Ⓐ Ⓑ Ⓒ Ⓓ Ⓔ	47. Ⓐ Ⓑ Ⓒ Ⓓ Ⓔ
14. Ⓐ Ⓑ Ⓒ Ⓓ Ⓔ	31. Ⓐ Ⓑ Ⓒ Ⓓ Ⓔ	48. Ⓐ Ⓑ Ⓒ Ⓓ Ⓔ
15. Ⓐ Ⓑ Ⓒ Ⓓ Ⓔ	32. Ⓐ Ⓑ Ⓒ Ⓓ Ⓔ	49. Ⓐ Ⓑ Ⓒ Ⓓ Ⓔ
16. Ⓐ Ⓑ Ⓒ Ⓓ Ⓔ	33. Ⓐ Ⓑ Ⓒ Ⓓ Ⓔ	50. Ⓐ Ⓑ Ⓒ Ⓓ Ⓔ
17. Ⓐ Ⓑ Ⓒ Ⓓ Ⓔ	34. Ⓐ Ⓑ Ⓒ Ⓓ Ⓔ	

MODEL TEST

4

50 questions   1 hour

Tear out the preceding answer sheet. Decide which is the best choice by rounding your answer when appropriate. Blacken the corresponding space on the answer sheet. When finished, check your answers with those at the end of the test. For questions that you got wrong, note the sections containing the material that you must review. Also, if you do not fully understand how you arrived at some of the correct answers, you should review the appropriate sections. Finally, fill out the self-evaluation sheet on page 202 in order to pinpoint the topics that give you the most difficulty.

OFFICIAL COLLEGE BOARD DIRECTIONS

<u>Directions</u>: For each of the following problems, decide which is the BEST of the choices given. If the exact numerical value is not one of the choices, select the choice that best approximates this value. Then fill in the corresponding oval on the answer sheet.

Notes: (1) A calculator will be necessary for answering some (but not all) of the questions in this test. For each question you will have to decide whether or not you should use a calculator. The calculator you use must be at least a scientific calculator; programmable calculators and calculators that can display graphs are permitted.

(2) For some questions in this test you may have to decide whether your calculator should be in the radian mode or the degree mode.

(3) Figures that accompany problems in this test are intended to provide information useful in solving the problems. They are drawn as accurately as possible EXCEPT when it is stated in a specific problem that the figure is not drawn to scale. All figures lie in a plane unless otherwise indicated.

(4) Unless otherwise specified, the domain of any function f is assumed to be the set of all real numbers x for which $f(x)$ is a real number.

Reference Information: The following information is for your reference in answering some of the questions in this test.

Volume of a right circular cone with radius r and height h: $V = \frac{1}{3}\pi r^2 h$

Lateral area of a right circular cone with circumference of the base c and slant height ℓ: $S = \frac{1}{2}c\ell$

Volume of a sphere with radius r: $V = \frac{4}{3}\pi r^3$

Surface area of a sphere with radius r: $S = 4\pi r^2$

Volume of a pyramid with base area B and height h: $V = \frac{1}{3}Bh$

---

1. The plane whose equation is $3x + 4y - 5z = 60$ intersects the xy-plane in the line whose equation is

   (A) $3x + 4y = 60$
   (B) $x = 20$
   (C) $y = 15$
   (D) $3x - 4y = 0$
   (E) $z = -12$

2. If 5 and $3 + \sqrt{2}$ are zeros of the integral polynomial $P(x) = ax^4 + bx^3 - cx + d$, which of the following must also be a zero?

   I. -5
   II. $3 - \sqrt{2}$
   III. 0

   (A) only I
   (B) only II
   (C) only III
   (D) only I and II
   (E) only II and III

3. If $3x + 4 = 2(y + 2)$, the $y{:}x$ ratio is

   (A) 2:3
   (B) 3:2
   (C) 1:1
   (D) 7:4
   (E) 4:7

4. The value of $\log_7 \sqrt{3}$ is

   (A) 0.24
   (B) 0.26
   (C) 0.28
   (D) 0.30
   (E) 0.32

5. If $f(x) = \sin x$ and $g(x) = e^x$, then $f(g(\pi)) =$

   (A) 0.39
   (B) -0.91
   (C) -0.73
   (D) 1
   (E) 0.91

6. In the figure, $r \sin \theta$ equals

   (A) a
   (B) b
   (C) $-a$
   (D) $-b$
   (E) $a + b$

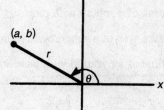

GO ON TO THE NEXT PAGE

7. What is the y-intercept of $y = \sqrt{5} \cos\left(x + \dfrac{\pi}{5}\right)$?

(A) 2.24
(B) 1.81
(C) 0.94
(D) 0.81
(E) 1.63

8. If three noncolinear points determine a plane, how many planes are determined by 10 points, no 3 of which are colinear?

(A) 3
(B) 120
(C) 45
(D) 90
(E) 720

9. If $f(x,y) = \tan x + \tan y$ and $g(x,y) = 1 - \tan x \cdot \tan y$, then $\dfrac{f(1,2)}{g(1,2)} =$

(A) 0
(B) −0.14
(C) 0.58
(D) 0.05
(E) −0.20

10. If the graph on the right represents the function $f(x)$, which of the following could represent the graph of $y = \dfrac{1}{f(x)}$?

(A)

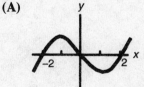

(B)

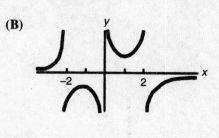

(C)

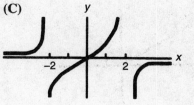

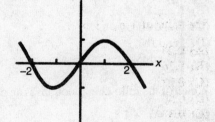

GO ON TO THE NEXT PAGE

(D)

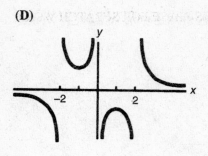

(E)

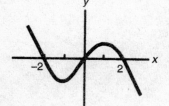

11. Given the following four equations, where $a \neq b \neq 0$:

 I. $ax + by = c$
 II. $ax - by = c$
 III. $-ax + by = c$
 IV. $bx - ay = c$

 Which pair represents perpendicular lines?

 (A) I and IV
 (B) II and IV
 (C) II and III
 (D) I and II
 (E) III and IV

12. Which of the following functions is an odd function?

 (A) $f(x) = x^3 + 1$
 (B) $f(x) = \dfrac{x}{x-1}$
 (C) $f(x) = x^3 + x$
 (D) $f(x) = 2x^4$
 (E) $f(x) = \cos x$

13. If $f(x) = \dfrac{x^2 - 1}{x + 1}$, what does $f(i)$ equal, where $i = \sqrt{-1}$?

 (A) 0
 (B) $\dfrac{2}{i+1}$
 (C) $i - 1$
 (D) -2
 (E) $i + 1$

GO ON TO THE NEXT PAGE

14. In order for the inverse of $f(x) = 2 \sin x$ to be a function, the domain of f must be limited to

(A) $0° \le x \le 180°$
(B) $90° \le x \le 270°$
(C) $135° \le x \le 315°$
(D) $45° \le x \le 135°$
(E) $180° \le x \le 360°$

15. $\displaystyle \lim_{x \to a} \frac{2x^2 - 3ax + a^2}{x^2 - a^2} =$

(A) $\dfrac{1}{2}$
(B) 0
(C) $\dfrac{3}{2}$
(D) a
(E) The value is undefined.

16. The domain of $f(x) = \dfrac{x^2 - 1}{x^2 - x}$ is

(A) all real numbers
(B) all reals except $x = 1$
(C) all reals except $x = 0$
(D) all reals except $x = -1$
(E) all reals except $x = 0$ or $x = 1$

17. If the ratio of $\sin x$ to $\cos x$ is 1 to 2, then the ratio of $\tan x$ to $\cot x$ is

(A) 1:4
(B) 1:2
(C) 1:1
(D) 2:1
(E) 4:1

18. If $\sin A = 0.4321$, what is the tangent of the supplement of $\angle A$?

(A) 0.3965
(B) −0.4791
(C) 2.087
(D) −0.3965
(E) 0.4791

19. The shaded area in the figure is represented by which of the following?

(A) $(A \cap B) \cap C$
(B) $A \cup (B \cup C)$
(C) $(A \cap B) \cup C$
(D) $A \cap (B \cup C)$
(E) $(A \cup B) \cap C$

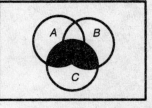

GO ON TO THE NEXT PAGE

20. If $\dfrac{x+3}{x} < 5$, then the solution set is

(A) $x > \dfrac{3}{4}$

(B) $x \neq \dfrac{3}{4}$

(C) $x > \dfrac{4}{3}$

(D) $x < 0$ or $x > \dfrac{3}{4}$

(E) none of these

21. The function defined by $f(x) = \sqrt{3}\,\cos x + 3\sin x$ has an amplitude of

(A) 1.27
(B) 1.73
(C) 3.46
(D) 4.73
(E) 5.20

22. What is the equation of the set of points situated in a plane so that the distance between any point and (0,0) is twice the distance between that point and the x-axis?

(A) $3x^2 - y^2 = 0$
(B) $x^2 - 3y^2 = 0$
(C) $x^2 + y^2 - 2y = 0$
(D) $x^2 + y^2 - 2x = 0$
(E) $4x^2 + 3y^2 = 0$

23. If p_1 and p_2 are the points of intersection of two circles whose equations are $x^2 + y^2 = 4$ and $(x-2)^2 + (y-2)^2 = 4$, what is the slope of the line perpendicular to the line that passes through p_1 and p_2?

(A) 0
(B) 1
(C) −1
(D) 2
(E) The slope is undefined.

24. When $5x^{13} + 3x^{10} - K$ is divided by $x + \sqrt{2}$, the remainder is 20. The value of K, to the nearest whole number, is

(A) 357
(B) −529
(C) −357
(D) −377
(E) 417

GO ON TO THE NEXT PAGE

25. If the equation $x^3 + 9x^2 - ax - b = 0$ has three equal roots, then

    (A) $a = 27$
    (B) $ab = 0$
    (C) $b = 27$
    (D) each root equals 3
    (E) each root equals -3

26. In a race involving several people, the probability that Bob will win is $\dfrac{1}{5}$ and the probability that Sarah will win is $\dfrac{1}{4}$. What is the probability that either Bob or Sarah will win the race alone?

    (A) $\dfrac{1}{20}$
    (B) $\dfrac{9}{20}$
    (C) $\dfrac{3}{5}$
    (D) $\dfrac{7}{20}$
    (E) $\dfrac{2}{5}$

27. In a triangle with sides of 6, 5, and 7, the measure of the largest angle is

    (A) $11.5°$
    (B) $101.5°$
    (C) $78.5°$
    (D) $66.5°$
    (E) $168.5°$

28. If $\sin A = 0.8364$ and $\tan A = -1.5258$, $\angle A =$

    (A) 0.99
    (B) 4.13
    (C) 2.56
    (D) 2.15
    (E) 5.29

29. The graph of the curve represented by $\begin{cases} x = 3\sin\theta \\ y = 3\sin\theta \end{cases}$ is

    (A) a line
    (B) a horizontal line segment
    (C) a circle
    (D) a line segment 3 units long
    (E) a line segment with slope 1

USE THIS SPACE FOR SCRATCH WORK

GO ON TO THE NEXT PAGE

30. If the zeros of the function $f(x)$ are 3, –2, and 1, what are the zeros of $f(x - 3)$?

   (A) 0,–5,–2
   (B) 6,1,4
   (C) 9,–6,3
   (D) –9,6,–3
   (E) $1, -\dfrac{2}{3}, \dfrac{1}{3}$

31. If the following steps are followed in order, what sequence of numbers will be printed?

   1. Let $x = A = 2$.
   2. If $x \geq 5$, stop.
      If $x < 5$, print the value of x.
   3. Replace x by $x + 1$.
   4. Replace A by $2A - 1$.
   5. If $A \leq x$, print the value of A.
      If $A > x$, go back to step 2.
   6. Stop.

   (A) 2,3,4
   (B) 2,3,4,5
   (C) 2,3,3,4
   (D) 2,3
   (E) 2,3,3,4,5

32. There are n integers in the solution set of $x(x - 2)(x + 3)(x + 5) < 0$. Therefore, n equals

   (A) 2
   (B) 6
   (C) 4
   (D) 3
   (E) more than 6

33. $(2 \text{ cis } 50°)^3$ written in rectangular form is

   (A) $6.9 + 4i$
   (B) $4 - 6.9i$
   (C) $6.9 - 4i$
   (D) $-6.9 + 4i$
   (E) $-4 + 6.9i$

34. If $A = e^{kt}$, what is the value of k when $A = 10,000$ and $t = 12$?

   (A) 0.06
   (B) 0.58
   (C) 0.33
   (D) 0.77
   (E) 0.82

GO ON TO THE NEXT PAGE

35. For what positive values of $x \le 2\pi$ does $\sin^2 x \cdot \cos^2 x + \sin^2 x + \cos^4 x = 1$?

(A) only $\dfrac{\pi}{2}, \dfrac{3\pi}{2}$

(B) only $\pi, 2\pi$

(C) only $\dfrac{\pi}{4}, \dfrac{3\pi}{4}, \dfrac{5\pi}{4}, \dfrac{7\pi}{4}$

(D) all values of x

(E) no values of x

36. What is the length of the radius of the sphere whose equation is $x^2 + y^2 + z^2 - 4x - 5y + 6z = 0$?

(A) 6.75
(B) 4.39
(C) 2.60
(D) 19.25
(E) 3.46

37. If $f(x) = x^2 + 1$ and $f(g(x)) = 4x - 3$, then $g(x) =$

(A) $2\sqrt{x} - 1$

(B) $2\sqrt{x-1}$

(C) $\sqrt{x} - 4$

(D) $\sqrt{4x+4}$

(E) $\dfrac{\sqrt{x-1}}{4}$

38. What are the coordinates of the point on the line $7x - 3y = 11$ that is closest to the origin?

(A) (1.57,0)
(B) (1.37,0.47)
(C) (1.33,–0.57)
(D) (1.43,–0.47)
(E) (1.27,–0.67)

39. If $f(x) = x + \sqrt{3x + 7}$, on what interval is $f(x) \le 7$?

(A) $(-\infty, 3]$
(B) $(-\infty, 3], [14, \infty)$
(C) $[-2.\overline{3}, 3]$
(D) $[-2.\overline{3}, 3], [14, \infty)$
(E) $[3, 14]$

40. If a square prism is inscribed in a right circular cylinder of radius 4 and height 10, to the nearest whole number, what is the total surface area of the prism?

(A) 192
(B) 88
(C) 226
(D) 290
(E) 320

GO ON TO THE NEXT PAGE

41. The lines $4x - 7y - 3 = 0$ and $8x - 14y + 11 = 0$ are parallel. The perpendicular distance between them is

(A) 1.05
(B) 2.11
(C) 0.95
(D) 1.11
(E) 2.05

42. A point at which two branches of a curve meet and stop and have different tangents is called a *salient* point. Which of the following has (have) salient points?

   I. $y = |x|$
   II. $y = x^{2/3}$
   III. $x^2 - y^2 = 1$

(A) only I
(B) only II
(C) only III
(D) only I and II
(E) only II and III

43. For all positive angles less than 360°, if $\csc(2x + 30°) = \cos(3y - 15°)$, the sum of x and y is

(A) 185°
(B) 65°
(C) 35°
(D) 215°
(E) 95°

44. The lines $3x - 7y = -15$ and $4x + 2y = 9$ and the x-axis intersect to form a triangle. How many degrees are in the angle of the triangle where the two lines intersect?

(A) 116.6°
(B) 93.4°
(C) 139.8°
(D) 40.2°
(E) 86.6°

45. The rate of growth of a certain organism varies jointly as the warmth of the sun and the square of the available food, and inversely as the number of enemies. If the growth rate remains constant when the warmth of the sun is cut in half and the number of enemies doubles, what can be said about the quantity of available food?

(A) It is doubled.
(B) It is 4 times as great.
(C) It is cut in half.
(D) It is divided by 4.
(E) It remains the same.

GO ON TO THE NEXT PAGE

46. If $f(x) = |x| + 2$, $g(y) = 3y - 2$, and $h(z) = f(g(z)) + g(z)$, the least value of $h(z)$ is

(A) 0
(B) 2
(C) 4
(D) –4
(E) A minimum value does not exist.

47. If x, $3x + 3$, $5x + 5$ are three consecutive terms of a geometric sequence, the sum of these three terms is

(A) –2.25
(B) –12.25
(C) –14.85
(D) –4.75
(E) –10

48. In the figure on the right, S is the set of points in the shaded region. Which of the following represents the set T consisting of all points $(x - y, y)$, where (x, y) is a point in S?

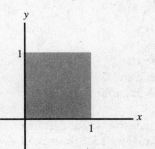

(A)

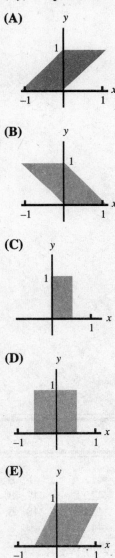

(B)

(C)

(D)

(E)

GO ON TO THE NEXT PAGE

49. If $p(x) = 3x^2 + 4x + 1$ and $p(a) = 9$, then $a =$

(A) $-0.67 \pm 1.49i$
(B) -0.82 or 2.66
(C) 2.43 or -1.10
(D) 0.82 or -2.16
(E) -2.43 or 1.10

50. Mary, John, and Fran are on a trip. Mary drives during the first hour at an average speed of 50 miles per hour. John drives during the next 2 hours at an average speed of 48 miles per hour. Fran drives for the next 3 hours at an average speed of 52 miles per hour. They reach their destination after exactly 6 hours. Their mean speed (in miles per hour) was

(A) 52
(B) 50
(C) $51\dfrac{1}{3}$
(D) $50\dfrac{1}{3}$
(E) $50\dfrac{2}{3}$

USE THIS SPACE FOR SCRATCH WORK

ANSWER KEY

1. A	6. B	11. A	16. E	21. C	26. D	31. D	36. B	41. A	46. B
2. B	7. B	12. C	17. A	22. B	27. C	32. A	37. B	42. D	47. B
3. B	8. B	13. C	18. B	23. B	28. D	33. D	38. C	43. A	48. B
4. C	9. B	14. B	19. D	24. D	29. E	34. D	39. C	44. B	49. E
5. B	10. B	15. A	20. D	25. E	30. B	35. D	40. D	45. A	50. D

ANSWER EXPLANATIONS

In these solutions the following notation is used:

a: active—Calculator use is necessary or, at a minimum, extremely helpful.

n: neutral—Answers can be found without a calculator, but a calculator may help.

i: inactive—Calculator use is not helpful and may even be a hindrance.

1. i A The xy-plane is intersected when $z = 0$, and so the equation of the line is $3x + 4y = 60$. [5.5].

2. i B When coefficients are rational, the irrational roots come in conjugate pairs, but no relationship between the other roots is necessary. [2.4].

3. i B $3x + 4 = 2y + 4$. $\dfrac{3x}{2x} = \dfrac{2y}{2x}$. Therefore, $\dfrac{2y}{2x} \cdot$ $\dfrac{y}{x} = \dfrac{3}{2}$. [5.6].

4. a C Use the change-of-base theorem to get $\log_7 \sqrt{3} = \dfrac{\log_{10} \sqrt{3}}{\log_{10} 7} \approx \dfrac{0.2386}{0.8451} \approx 0.28$. [4.2].

5. a B $g(\pi) = e^\pi \approx 23.14$. $f(g(\pi)) \approx f(23.14) \approx \sin 23.14 \approx -0.91$. [1.2]

 Graphing calculator: Plot the graph of $y = \sin e^x$ in an $x \in [2 \times 4]$, $y \in [-2 \times 2]$ window. Use the Trace and Zoom functions to see that, when x is approximately equal to π, y is approximately -0.9.

6. i B Sin $\theta = \dfrac{b}{r}$. Therefore, $r \sin \theta = b$. [3.1].

7. a B Put your calculator in radian mode because of the π in the problem: The y-intercept occurs when $x = 0$. Therefore, y-intercept $= \sqrt{5} \cos \dfrac{\pi}{5} \approx 1.81$. [3.4].

Graphing calculator: Plot the graph of $y = \sqrt{5} \cos\left(x + \dfrac{\pi}{5}\right)$ in an $x \in [-10 \times 10]$, $y \in [-10 \times 10]$ window. Use the Trace and Zoom functions to see that the graph crosses the y-axis at approximately 1.81.

8. n B From the 10 points, 3 must be chosen each time. Therefore, $\dbinom{10}{3} = \dfrac{10!}{3!\,7!} = 120$. [5.1].

9. a B Put your calculator in radian mode:
$$\frac{f(1,2)}{g(1,2)} = \frac{\tan 1 + \tan 2}{1 - \tan 1 \cdot \tan 2} \approx \frac{-0.6276}{4.4030} \approx -0.1425.$$
[1.5, 3.5].

Alternative Solution:
$$\frac{f(1,2)}{g(1,2)} = \frac{\tan 1 + \tan 2}{1 - \tan 1 \cdot \tan 2} = \tan 3 \approx -0.1425.$$

10. n B Wherever $f(x) = 0$, $\dfrac{1}{f(x)}$ is undefined, and so asymptotes occur. Choices A, C, and E are ruled out. The answer is B because $\dfrac{1}{f(x)}$ is positive when $f(x)$ is positive, and negative when $f(x)$ is negative. [5.5]

 Graphing calculator: Since the given graph looks like a cubic with zeros of 0, –2, and 2, a reasonable equation to represent it could be $y = -x(x + 2)(x - 2)$. Plot the graph of $y = \dfrac{1}{-x(x + 2)(x - 2)}$ in an $x \in [-5,5]$, $y \in [-5,5]$ window to see that the graph looks like answer Choice B.

11. i A Slope of I is $-\dfrac{a}{b}$; slope of II is $\dfrac{a}{b}$; slope of III is $\dfrac{a}{b}$; slope of IV is $\dfrac{b}{a}$. I and IV are negative reciprocals. [2.2].

12. n C With an odd function, $f(-x) = -f(x)$. Of the choices given, $f(x) = x^3 + x$ is the only possible odd function since $f(-x) = (-x)^3 + (-x) = -x^3 - x = -(x^3 + x) = -f(-x)$. [1.4].

Graphing calculator: Plot the graphs of the answer choices to see that only Choice C is symmetric about the origin and thus is an odd function.

13. i C $f(x)$ reduces to $x - 1$ with the restriction $x \neq -1$. Therefore, $f(i) = i - 1$. [1.2].

14. i B In order for $f^{-1}(x)$ to be a function, the domain of f must be such that for each value of y there is only one value of x. This occurs when $90° \leq x \leq 270°$. [1.3, 3.6].

15. n A Factor and reduce and then take the limit: $\dfrac{(2x - a)(x - a)}{(x + a)(x - a)}$. Limit $= \dfrac{a}{2a} = \dfrac{1}{2}$. [4.5].

Graphing calculator: Since a can be any number except 0, let $a = 1$ and plot the graph of $y = \dfrac{2x^2 - 3x + 1}{x^2 - 1}$ in an $x \in [-10, 10]$, $y \in [-10, 10]$ window. Use the Trace and Zoom functions to see that y approaches $\dfrac{1}{2}$ as x approaches 1 (the value of a that we chose).

16. n   E $f(x) = \dfrac{x^2 - 1}{x(x - 1)}$. Since division by zero is undefined, $x \neq 0$ or 1. Therefore, the domain is all real numbers except 0 or 1. [1.1].

17. i   A $\dfrac{\tan x}{\cot x} = \dfrac{\dfrac{\sin x}{\cos x}}{\dfrac{\cos x}{\sin x}} = \dfrac{\sin^2 x}{\cos^2 x} = \dfrac{1^2}{2^2} = \dfrac{1}{4}$. [3.1].

18. a   B   Put your calculator in degree mode: Sin A + 0.4321 implies that $\mathrm{Sin}^{-1}(0.4321) \approx 25.6°$ The supplement of $\angle A \approx 180° - 25.6° \approx 154.4°$. Therefore, tan $154.4° \approx -0.4791$. [3.1].

19. i   E   The shaded region is the intersection of C and the union of A and B. [5.9].

20. n   D   If $x > 0$, $x + 3 < 5x$ and $x > \dfrac{3}{4}$. If $x < 0$, $x + 3 > 5x$ and $x < \dfrac{3}{4}$. Therefore, $x > \dfrac{3}{4}$ or $x < 0$. [2.5].

Alternative Solution: Consider the equation $\dfrac{x + 3}{x} = 5$, which gives the boundary points of the regions indicated by the inequality. $x \neq 0$ and $x = \dfrac{3}{4}$:

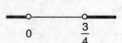

Choose a number in one of the regions. For example, choose 1 and check it in the original inequality. It makes the inequality true, and so the region to the right of $\dfrac{3}{4}$ is part of the solution set. In a similar manner the region to the left of zero also is found to be part of the solution set. Thus, the answer is Choice D.

Graphing calculator: Plot the graphs of $y = \dfrac{x + 3}{x}$ and $y = 5$ in an $x \in [-10 \times 10]$, $y \in [-10 \times 10]$ window and notice that there appears to be a vertical asymptote at $x = 0$. Use the Trace and Zoom functions or the Intersect function to

see that the graphs intersect when $x \approx 0.75$. Therefore, the graph of $y = \dfrac{x + 3}{x}$ is below the line $y = 5$ when $x < 0$ or $x > 0.75$.

21. a   C   Multiply and divide by $2\sqrt{3}$, making the coefficients of sin x and cos x trig values of familiar angles (e.g., 30°, 45°, 60°).

$$f(x) = 2\sqrt{3}\left(\frac{1}{2}\cos x + \frac{\sqrt{3}}{2}\sin x\right)$$
$$= 2\sqrt{3}(\sin 30° \cdot \cos x + \cos 30° \cdot \sin x)$$
$$= 2\sqrt{3}\sin(30° + x)$$

Therefore, the amplitude is $2\sqrt{3} \approx 3.46$. [3.4].

Graphing calculator: Plot the graph of $y = \sqrt{3}\cos x + 3\sin x$ in an $x \in [-10 \times 10]$, $y \in [-10 \times 10]$ window. Use the Trace and Zoom functions (or the Min and Max functions) to find that the minimum value is approximately -3.46 and the maximum value is $+3.46$. Therefore, amplitude $\approx \dfrac{3.46 - (-3.46)}{2} \approx 3.46$.

22. i   B   If (x, y) represents any such point, $|y|$ represents the distance between that point and the x-axis. $d = \sqrt{(x - 0)^2 + (y - 0)^2} = \sqrt{x^2 + y^2}$. Therefore, $\sqrt{x^2 + y^2} = 2|y|$. Squaring both sides and simplifying gives $x^2 - 3y^2 = 0$. [4.1].

23. i   B   Substituting gives $x^2 + y^2 = x^2 - 4x + 4 + y^2 - 4y + 4$. Simplifying gives the equation of the line through p_1 and p_2: $x + y = 2$. The slope of this line is -1, and so the slope of the perpendicular is $+1$. [4.1].

24. a   D   By the remainder theorem, substituting $-\sqrt{2}$ for x gives $5(-\sqrt{2})^{13} + 3(-\sqrt{2})^{10} - K = 20$. Thus, $-452.5 + 96 - K \approx 20$. Therefore, $K \approx -377$. [2.4].

Graphing calculator: Rearrange the terms in the equation and let y represent K. Then plot the graph of $y = 5x^{13} + 3x^{10} - 20$ in an $x \in [-2 \times 2]$, $y \in [-1000 \times 1000]$ window. Since $-\sqrt{2} \approx -1.414$, use the Trace and Zoom functions to find that $y \approx -377$ when $x \approx -1.414$. Thus, $K \approx -377$.

25. i   E $r + r + r = -9$, and so $r = -3$. [2.4].

26. i   D   The probability that neither Bob nor Sara will win is $\dfrac{4}{5} \cdot \dfrac{3}{4} = \dfrac{3}{5}$. Probability that both will win (a tie) is $\frac{1}{5} \cdot \frac{1}{4} = \frac{1}{20}$. Probability that one of these events will happen is $\frac{13}{20}$, and so the probability that either Bob or Sarah will win is $1 - \frac{13}{20} = \frac{7}{20}$. [5.20]

Alternative Solution: P(Bob wins and Sarah loses) $= \frac{1}{5} \cdot \frac{3}{4} = \frac{3}{20}$. P(Sarah wins and Bob loses) $= \frac{1}{4} \cdot \frac{4}{5} = \frac{4}{20}$. Therefore, P(Bob wins or Sarah wins) $= \frac{3}{20} + \frac{4}{20} = \frac{7}{20}$.

27. a **C** Put your calculator in degree mode because the answer choices are in degrees. Law of cosines: $49 = 36 + 25 - 2 \cdot 6 \cdot 5 \cdot \cos C$. Therefore, $\cos C = 0.2$, which implies that $C = \text{Cos}^{-1}(0.2) \approx 78.5°$. [3.7].

28. a **D** Put your calculator in radian mode. Since $\sin A > 0$ and $\tan A < 0$, $\angle A$ must be in quadrant II. Reference angle for $\angle A = \text{Sin}^{-1} 0.8364 \approx 0.9907$. Therefore, $\angle A \approx \pi - 0.9907 \approx 2.15$. [3.5].

29. n **E** Removing the parameter results in $y = x$. However, x and y are both limited between -3 and 3 by $3 \sin \theta$. [4.6].

TIP: When you eliminate the parameter, you might be discarding restrictions that the parameter put on the value of x and y. Always check for restrictions on x and y in the original problem. Also, always look at all the answer choices to see possibilities that you had not thought of.

 Graphing calculator (in parametric mode): Plot the graphs of $x = 3 \sin t$ and $y = 3 \sin t$ in a $t \in [-10 \times 10]$, $x \in [-10 \times 10]$, $y \in [-10 \times 10]$ window in order to see that the graph is a line segment with a slope of 1.

30. i **B** $f(x - 3) = 0$ when $x - 3 = 3, -2,$ or 1. Therefore, $x = 6, 1,$ or 4. [2.4].

31. i **D** Keeping track of the values of A and x gives

Step	1	2	3	5	6
A	2		3		
x	2		3		
Printed		2		3	Stop

[5.9].

32. n **A** Consider the equality $x(x - 2)(x + 3)(x + 5) = 0$ to find four points of separation of the inequalities $(0, 2, -3, -5)$. The regions satisfying the inequality contain only two integers. [2.5].

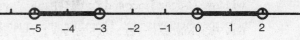

 Graphing calculator: Plot the graph of $y = x(x - 2)(x + 3)(x + 5)$ in an $x \in [-10 \times 10]$, $y \in [-10 \times 10]$ window. Since the graph crosses the x-axis at $-5, -3, 0, 2$ and is below it on the intervals $(-5, -3)$ and $(0, 2)$, only two integers, -4 and 1, lie in the solution set.

33. a **D** $(2 \text{ cis } 50°)^3 = 8 \text{ cis } 150°$
$$= 8(\cos 150° + i \cdot \sin 150°)$$
$$= 8\left(-\frac{\sqrt{3}}{2} + \frac{1}{2}i\right)$$
$$= -4\sqrt{3} + 4i \approx -6.9 + 4i \quad [4.7].$$

34. a **D** Substituting gives $10{,}000 = e^{12k}$. Thus, $\ln 10{,}000 = 12k \cdot \ln e$. Therefore, $k = \frac{\ln 10{,}000}{12} \approx 0.77$. [4.2].

 Graphing calculator: Plot the graphs of $y = e^{12x}$ and $y = 10{,}000$ in an $x \in [0 \times 1]$, $y \in [0 \times 20{,}000]$ window. Use the Trace and Zoom functions or the Intersect function to see that the graphs intersect when $x \approx 0.77$.

35. n **D** Factoring the first and third terms makes the equation $\cos^2 x(\sin^2 x + \cos^2 x) + \sin^2 x = 1$, which becomes $\cos^2 x \cdot (1) + \sin^2 x = 1$, which again simplifies $1 = 1$. [3.5].

 Graphing calculator (in radian mode because of π in the answers): Plot the graph of $y = \sin^2 x \cdot \cos^2 x + \sin^2 x + \cos^4 x$ in an $x \in [0 \times 6.28]$, $y \in [-2 \times 2]$ window and notice that the graph is a horizontal line at $y = 0$ (which you cannot see unless the axes are turned off). Therefore, Choice D is the answer.

36. a **B** Complete the square:
$x^2 - 4x + y^2 - 5y + 6.25 + z^2 - 6z + 9 = 4 + 6.25 + 9 = 19.25$. Therefore, radius $= \sqrt{19.25} \approx 4.39$ [5.5].

37. i **B** $f(x) = x^2 + 1$, $f(g(x)) = (g(x))^2 + 1 = 4x - 3$, $(g(x))^2 = 4x - 4$, $g(x) = \pm\sqrt{4x - 4} = \pm 2\sqrt{x - 1}$. Therefore, $2\sqrt{x - 1}$ is an expression for $g(x)$. [1.2].

38. a   C   The point closest to (0,0) is on the line through the origin, perpendicular to the given line. The slope of the given line is $\frac{7}{3}$, and so the slope of the perpendicular is $-\frac{3}{7}$. Therefore, the equation of the perpendicular line is $y = -\frac{3}{7}x$. To find the point of intersection, substitute in the original equation, $7x - 3\left(-\frac{3}{7}x\right) = 11$. Thus, $x = \frac{77}{58} \approx$ 1.33 and $y = \frac{-33}{40} \approx -0.57$. Therefore, (1.33, –0.57) is the point on the line closest to the origin. [2.2].

 Graphing calculator: Plot the graphs of $y = \frac{7x - 11}{3}$ and $y = -\frac{3}{7}x$ in an $x \in [-10 \times 10]$, $y \in [-10 \times 10]$ window. Use the Trace and Zoom functions or the Intersect function to see that the graphs intersect at approximately (1.33,–0.57).

39. n   C $x + \sqrt{3x + 7} = 7$ and $\sqrt{3x + 7} = 7 - x$. Square both sides to get $3x + 7 = 49 - 14x + x^2$. Thus, $x^2 - 17x + 42 = 0$. Therefore, $(x - 14)(x - 3) = 0$, which gives boundary points ($x = 3$ and $x = 14$) for the regions indicated by the inequality. Checking points in each region indicates that the inequality is satisfied only when $x < 3$ (values of $x > 14$ are extraneous because they do not check in the original inequality). Also, $3x + 7 \geq 0$ to keep the expression under the square root nonnegative. Therefore, $f(x) \leq 7$ when $[-2.\overline{3}, 3]$.   [2.5].

Graphing calculator: Plot the graphs of $y = x + \sqrt{3x + 7}$ and $y = 7$ in an $x \in [-10, 10]$, $y \in [-10, 10]$ window. Use the Trace and Zoom functions to see that the graph of $f(x)$ seems to start when $x \approx -2.3$. Also, use the Trace and Zoom functions or the Intersect function to see that the graphs intersect when $x = 3$. Therefore, $f(x) < 7$ on the interval $[-2.\overline{3}, 3]$.

40. a   D   The diameter of the cylinder is the diagonal of the square. Therefore, a side of the square base is $4\sqrt{2}$. The area of the two square bases is 64, and the area of each of the four sides is $40\sqrt{2}$. Total surface area = $160\sqrt{2} + 64 \approx 290$. [5.5].

41. a   A   Choose any point on one of the lines, such as (1,–1) on the first line. The distance between this point and the other line equals $\frac{|8 \cdot (-1) - 14 \cdot (-1) + 11|}{\sqrt{8^2 + 14^2}} = \frac{17}{\sqrt{260}} \approx 1.05$. [2.2].

42. n   D   As x approaches zero from the left, the slope of I is –1 and the slope of II approaches ∞. As x approaches zero from the right, the slope of I is 1 and the slope of II approaches $-\infty$. The branches of III do not meet. Therefore, only I and II have salient points. [5.9].

 Graphing calculator: Plot the graph of each of the functions in an $x \in [-2 \times 2]$, $y \in [-2 \times 2]$ window. Use the Trace and Zoom functions to see that only the graphs of I and II have salient points.

> **TIP:** To see both branches of the graph of $y = x^{2/3}$, you may have to enter the equation into the calculator as $y = (x^2)^{1/3}$. To see the whole graph of $x^2 + y^2 = 1$, solve for y and plot $y = \sqrt{x^2 - 1}$ and $y = -\sqrt{x^2 - 1}$.

43. i   A ± 1 are the only numbers that are both within the range of csc and cos. If each equals 1, $2x + 30 = 90°$ and $3y - 15 = 0°$. This is not allowed since $0°$ is not positive. If each equals –1, $2x + 30 = 270°$ and $3y - 15 = 180°$. Thus, $x + y = 185°$. [3.3].

44. a   B   The slope of a line equals the tangent of the angle, α, formed by the line and the positive x-axis. Thus, $\tan \angle 2 = \frac{3}{7}$, which implies that $\angle 2 = \text{Tan}^{-1}\left(\frac{3}{7}\right) \approx 23.2°$. Since $\tan \angle \alpha = -2$, $\tan \angle 1 = +2$, which implies that $\angle 1 = \text{Tan}^{-1}(2) \approx 63.4°$. Therefore, $\angle 3 = 180° - 23.2° - 63.4° \approx 93.4°$. [3.5].

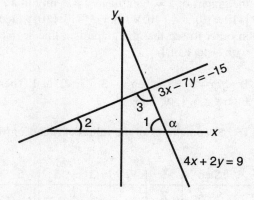

45. i   A $\frac{RE}{WF^2} = K$. Let $R = 5$, $E = 2$, $W = 4$, $F = 1$

(arbitrary choices to make the arithmetic easy).

$K = \dfrac{5 \cdot 2}{4 \cdot 1} = \dfrac{5}{2}$. Changing the variables as indicated gives $\dfrac{5 \cdot 4}{2F^2} = \dfrac{5}{2} \cdot F^2 = 4$. Since F is the amount of food, $F = 2$ only. The original value of F was doubled. [5.6].

Alternative Solution: $\dfrac{RE}{WF^2} = K$. With the changes, the formula becomes $\dfrac{R \cdot 2E}{\frac{1}{2}W \cdot F^2} = K$.

Simplifying gives $\dfrac{4RE}{WF^2} = K$.

Therefore, F^2 must be 4 times as large as it was originally in order for the fraction to remain equal to K. Thus, the original value of F must be doubled.

46. n **B** Since $f(g(z)) = f(3z - 2) = |3z - 2| + 2$, $h(z) = |3z - 2| + 3z$. When $3z - 2 \geq 0$, $h(z) = 6z - 2$, which is ≥ 2. When $3z - 2 < 0$, $h(z) = 2$. [1.2, 4.3].

 Graphing calculator: After finding that $h(z) = |3z - 2| + 3z$, plot the graph of $y = \text{abs}(3x - 2) + 3x$ in an $x \in [-10 \times 10]$, $y \in [-10 \times 10]$ window. Use the Trace and Zoom functions or the Min function to see that the minimum value of the graph is 2.

47. a **B** $3x + 3 = rx$ and $\dfrac{5(x + 1)}{3(x + 1)} = r$. Therefore, $3x + 3 = \dfrac{5}{3}x$, and so $x = -\dfrac{9}{4}$. Sum $= 9x + 8 = 9\left(-\dfrac{9}{4}\right) + 8 = -\dfrac{49}{4} \approx -12.25$. [5.4].

48. i **B** Setting up a table of a few representative values leads to Choice B. [5.5].

x	0	0	0	$\frac{1}{2}$	$\frac{1}{2}$	$\frac{1}{2}$	1	1	1
y	0	$\frac{1}{2}$	1	0	$\frac{1}{2}$	1	0	$\frac{1}{2}$	1
$x - y$	0	$-\frac{1}{2}$	-1	$\frac{1}{2}$	0	$-\frac{1}{2}$	1	$\frac{1}{2}$	0

49. a **E** Substituting gives $3a^2 + 4a + 1 = 9$; thus, $3a^2 + 4a - 1 = 0$. Therefore, $a = \dfrac{-4 + \sqrt{16 + 96}}{6} = \dfrac{-4 + \sqrt{112}}{6} \approx 1.10$ or $a = \dfrac{-4 + \sqrt{112}}{6} \approx -2.34$. [2.3].

Graphing calculator: Plot the graphs of $y = 3x^2 + 4x + 1$ and $y = 9$ in an $x \in [-10 \times 10]$, $y \in [-10 \times 10]$ window. Use the Trace and Zoom functions or the Intersect function to find that the values of x where the two graphs intersect are approximately -2.43 and 1.10.

50. i **D** Mary drove for $1 \times 50 = 50$ miles.
John drove for $2 \times 48 = 96$ miles.
Fran drove for $3 \times 52 = 156$ miles.

Average (mean) speed $= \dfrac{\text{total distance}}{\text{total time}}$

$= \dfrac{302}{6} = 50\dfrac{1}{3}$ miles per hour.

[5.8].

SELF-EVALUATION CHART FOR MODEL TEST 4

SUBJECT AREA	QUESTIONS				NUMBER OF
					RIGHT　WRONG　OMITTED

Mark correct answers with C, wrong answers with X, and omitted answers with O.

Algebra
(9 questions)
Review section

3	4	20	24	25	32	34	41	45
5.6	4.2	2.5	2.4	2.4	2.5	4.2	2.2	5.6

_____ _____ _____

Solid geometry
(4 questions)
Review section

1	8	36	40
5.5	5.1	5.5	5.5

_____ _____ _____

Coordinate geometry
(6 questions)
Review section

10	11	22	23	38	48
5.5	2.2	4.1	4.1	2.2	5.5

_____ _____ _____

Trigonometry
(10 questions)
Review section

6	7	17	18	21	27	28	35	43	44
3.1	3.4	3.1	3.1	3.4	3.7	3.5	3.5	3.3	3.5

_____ _____ _____

Functions
(12 questions)
Review section

2	5	9	12	13	14	16	30	37	39	46	49
2.4	1.2	1.5	1.4	1.2	1.3	1.1	2.4	1.2	2.5	1.2	2.3

_____ _____ _____

Miscellaneous
(9 questions)
Review section

15	19	26	29	31	36	42	47	50
4.5	5.9	5.2	4.6	5.9	4.7	5.9	5.4	5.8

_____ _____ _____

TOTALS　_____ _____ _____

Raw score = (number right) – $\frac{1}{4}$ (number wrong) = _____

Round your raw score to the nearest whole number = _____

Evaluate Your Performance
Model Test 4

Rating	Number Right
Excellent	41–50
Very good	33–40
Above average	25–32
Average	15–24
Below average	Below 15

ANSWER SHEET FOR MODEL TEST 5

Determine the correct answer for each question. Then, using a no. 2 pencil, blacken completely the oval containing the letter of your choice.

1. Ⓐ Ⓑ Ⓒ Ⓓ Ⓔ	18. Ⓐ Ⓑ Ⓒ Ⓓ Ⓔ	35. Ⓐ Ⓑ Ⓒ Ⓓ Ⓔ
2. Ⓐ Ⓑ Ⓒ Ⓓ Ⓔ	19. Ⓐ Ⓑ Ⓒ Ⓓ Ⓔ	36. Ⓐ Ⓑ Ⓒ Ⓓ Ⓔ
3. Ⓐ Ⓑ Ⓒ Ⓓ Ⓔ	20. Ⓐ Ⓑ Ⓒ Ⓓ Ⓔ	37. Ⓐ Ⓑ Ⓒ Ⓓ Ⓔ
4. Ⓐ Ⓑ Ⓒ Ⓓ Ⓔ	21. Ⓐ Ⓑ Ⓒ Ⓓ Ⓔ	38. Ⓐ Ⓑ Ⓒ Ⓓ Ⓔ
5. Ⓐ Ⓑ Ⓒ Ⓓ Ⓔ	22. Ⓐ Ⓑ Ⓒ Ⓓ Ⓔ	39. Ⓐ Ⓑ Ⓒ Ⓓ Ⓔ
6. Ⓐ Ⓑ Ⓒ Ⓓ Ⓔ	23. Ⓐ Ⓑ Ⓒ Ⓓ Ⓔ	40. Ⓐ Ⓑ Ⓒ Ⓓ Ⓔ
7. Ⓐ Ⓑ Ⓒ Ⓓ Ⓔ	24. Ⓐ Ⓑ Ⓒ Ⓓ Ⓔ	41. Ⓐ Ⓑ Ⓒ Ⓓ Ⓔ
8. Ⓐ Ⓑ Ⓒ Ⓓ Ⓔ	25. Ⓐ Ⓑ Ⓒ Ⓓ Ⓔ	42. Ⓐ Ⓑ Ⓒ Ⓓ Ⓔ
9. Ⓐ Ⓑ Ⓒ Ⓓ Ⓔ	26. Ⓐ Ⓑ Ⓒ Ⓓ Ⓔ	43. Ⓐ Ⓑ Ⓒ Ⓓ Ⓔ
10. Ⓐ Ⓑ Ⓒ Ⓓ Ⓔ	27. Ⓐ Ⓑ Ⓒ Ⓓ Ⓔ	44. Ⓐ Ⓑ Ⓒ Ⓓ Ⓔ
11. Ⓐ Ⓑ Ⓒ Ⓓ Ⓔ	28. Ⓐ Ⓑ Ⓒ Ⓓ Ⓔ	45. Ⓐ Ⓑ Ⓒ Ⓓ Ⓔ
12. Ⓐ Ⓑ Ⓒ Ⓓ Ⓔ	29. Ⓐ Ⓑ Ⓒ Ⓓ Ⓔ	46. Ⓐ Ⓑ Ⓒ Ⓓ Ⓔ
13. Ⓐ Ⓑ Ⓒ Ⓓ Ⓔ	30. Ⓐ Ⓑ Ⓒ Ⓓ Ⓔ	47. Ⓐ Ⓑ Ⓒ Ⓓ Ⓔ
14. Ⓐ Ⓑ Ⓒ Ⓓ Ⓔ	31. Ⓐ Ⓑ Ⓒ Ⓓ Ⓔ	48. Ⓐ Ⓑ Ⓒ Ⓓ Ⓔ
15. Ⓐ Ⓑ Ⓒ Ⓓ Ⓔ	32. Ⓐ Ⓑ Ⓒ Ⓓ Ⓔ	49. Ⓐ Ⓑ Ⓒ Ⓓ Ⓔ
16. Ⓐ Ⓑ Ⓒ Ⓓ Ⓔ	33. Ⓐ Ⓑ Ⓒ Ⓓ Ⓔ	50. Ⓐ Ⓑ Ⓒ Ⓓ Ⓔ
17. Ⓐ Ⓑ Ⓒ Ⓓ Ⓔ	34. Ⓐ Ⓑ Ⓒ Ⓓ Ⓔ	

MODEL TEST
5

50 questions   1 hour

Tear out the preceding answer sheet. Decide which is the best choice by rounding your answer when appropriate. Blacken the corresponding space on the answer sheet. When finished, check your answers with those at the end of the test. For questions that you got wrong, note the sections containing the material that you must review. Also, if you do not fully understand how you arrived at some of the correct answers, you should review the appropriate sections. Finally, fill out the self-evaluation sheet on page 223 in order to pinpoint the topics that give you the most difficulty.

OFFICIAL COLLEGE BOARD DIRECTIONS

<u>Directions</u>: For each of the following problems, decide which is the BEST of the choices given. If the exact numerical value is not one of the choices, select the choice that best approximates this value. Then fill in the corresponding oval on the answer sheet.

Notes: (1) A calculator will be necessary for answering some (but not all) of the questions in this test. For each question you will have to decide whether or not you should use a calculator. The calculator you use must be at least a scientific calculator; programmable calculators and calculators that can display graphs are permitted.

(2) For some questions in this test you may have to decide whether your calculator should be in the radian mode or the degree mode.

(3) Figures that accompany problems in this test are intended to provide information useful in solving the problems. They are drawn as accurately as possible EXCEPT when it is stated in a specific problem that the figure is not drawn to scale. All figures lie in a plane unless otherwise indicated.

(4) Unless otherwise specified, the domain of any function f is assumed to be the set of all real numbers x for which $f(x)$ is a real number.

<u>Reference Information:</u> The following information is for your reference in answering some of the questions in this test.

Volume of a right circular cone with radius r and height h: $V = \frac{1}{3}\pi r^2 h$

Lateral area of a right circular cone with circumference of the base c and slant height ℓ: $S = \frac{1}{2}c\ell$

Volume of a sphere with radius r: $V = \frac{4}{3}\pi r^3$

Surface area of a sphere with radius r: $S = 4\pi r^2$

Volume of a pyramid with base area B and height h: $V = \frac{1}{3}Bh$

---

1. The amplitude of function $f(x) = -\sin x \cdot \cos x$ is

    (A) 1
    (B) 2
    (C) $\dfrac{1}{2}$
    (D) $-\dfrac{1}{2}$
    (E) -1

2. What is the remainder when $3x^4 - 2x^3 - 20x^2 - 12$ is divided by $x + 2$?

    (A) -4
    (B) -28
    (C) -6
    (D) -36
    (E) -60

3. $\text{Log}_2 (\cos 325°) =$

    (A) -0.500
    (B) 2.70
    (C) -0.288
    (D) 0.301
    (E) -0.087

4. The lines $3x - 4y + 8 = 0$ and $8x + 6y - 4 = 0$ intersect at point P. One angle formed at point P contains

    (A) $30°$
    (B) $45°$
    (C) $60°$
    (D) $90°$
    (E) Point P does not exist because the lines are parallel.

5. The domain of $f(x) = \log_{10} (\sin x)$ contains which of the following intervals?

    (A) $0 \le x \le \pi$
    (B) $-\dfrac{\pi}{2} \le x \le \dfrac{\pi}{2}$
    (C) $0 < x < \pi$
    (D) $-\dfrac{\pi}{2} < x < \dfrac{\pi}{2}$
    (E) $\dfrac{\pi}{2} < x < \dfrac{3\pi}{2}$

GO ON TO THE NEXT PAGE

6. Which of the following is the ratio of the surface area of the sphere with radius r to its volume?

(A) $\dfrac{4}{\pi}$

(B) $\dfrac{r}{\pi}$

(C) $\dfrac{3}{r}$

(D) $\dfrac{r}{4}$

(E) $\dfrac{4}{r}$

7. If the two solutions of $x^2 - 9x + c = 0$ are complex conjugates, which of the following describes all possible values of c?

(A) $c = 0$

(B) $c \neq 0$

(C) $c > \dfrac{81}{4}$

(D) $c > 81$

(E) $c < 9$

8. If $\tan x = 3$, the numerical values of $\sqrt{\csc x}$ is

(A) 0.97
(B) 1.03
(C) 1.78
(D) 3.16
(E) 0.32

9. In the figure, the graph of $f(x)$ has two transformations performed on it. First it is rotated 180° about the origin, and then it is reflected about the x-axis. Which of the following is the equation of the resulting curve?

(A) $y = -f(x)$
(B) $y = f(x + 2)$
(C) $x = f(y)$
(D) $y = f(x)$
(E) none of the above

10. $\displaystyle \lim_{x \to \infty} \frac{3x^3 - 7x^2 + 2}{4x^2 - 3x - 1} =$

(A) $\dfrac{3}{4}$

(B) 0
(C) 3
(D) 1
(E) ∞

11. As x increases from $-\dfrac{\pi}{4}$ to $\dfrac{3\pi}{4}$, the value of $\cos x$

(A) always increases
(B) always decreases
(C) increases and then decreases
(D) decreases and then increases
(E) does none of the above

12. The vertical distance between the minimum and maximum values of the function $y = \left| -\sqrt{2}\, \sin \sqrt{3}x \right|$ is

(A) 1.414
(B) 2.828
(C) 1.732
(D) 3.464
(E) 2.094

13. If the domain of $f(x) = -|x| + 2$ is $\{x\colon -1 \le x \le 3\}$, $f(x)$ has a minimum value when x equals

(A) 0
(B) −1
(C) 1
(D) 3
(E) There is no minimum value.

14. If $f(x, y) = \dfrac{\log x}{\log y}$, $f(4, 2) =$

(A) 0
(B) $\dfrac{1}{2}$
(C) 1
(D) 2
(E) $\log 2$

15. A positive rational root of the equation $4x^3 - x^2 + 16x - 4 = 0$ is

(A) $\dfrac{1}{2}$
(B) 1
(C) $\dfrac{1}{4}$
(D) 2
(E) $\dfrac{3}{4}$

16. The norm of vector $\vec{V} = 3\vec{i} - \sqrt{2}\,\vec{j}$ is

(A) 4.24
(B) 2.45
(C) 3.61
(D) 3.32
(E) 1.59

GO ON TO THE NEXT PAGE

17. If five coins are flipped and all the different ways they could fall are listed, how many elements of this list will contain more than three heads?

   (A) 16
   (B) 10
   (C) 5
   (D) 6
   (E) 32

USE THIS SPACE FOR SCRATCH WORK

18. The negation of the statement "For all sets, there is one subset" is

   (A) for all sets, there is not one subset
   (B) for no sets, there is one subset
   (C) for some sets, there is not one subset
   (D) for some sets, there is one subset
   (E) for no sets, there is not one subset

19. The graph of the curve represented by $\begin{Bmatrix} x = \sec\theta \\ y = \cos\theta \end{Bmatrix}$ is

   (A) a line
   (B) a hyperbola
   (C) an ellipse
   (D) a line segment
   (E) a portion of a hyperbola

20. Point (3,2) lies on the graph of the inverse of $f(x) = 2x^3 + x + A$. The value of A is

   (A) 15
   (B) –15
   (C) 18
   (D) 54
   (E) –54

21. If $f(x) = ax^2 + bx + c$ and $f(1) = 3$ and $f(-1) = 3$, then $a + c$ equals

   (A) –3
   (B) 0
   (C) 3
   (D) 6
   (E) 2

22. In $\triangle ABC$, $\angle B = 42°$, $\angle C = 30°$, and $AB = 100$. The length of BC is

   (A) 47.6
   (B) 66.9
   (C) 190.2
   (D) 133.8
   (E) none of the above

GO ON TO THE NEXT PAGE

23. The value of $\cos 10° \cdot \cos 20° - \sin 10 \cdot \sin 20$ is

    (A) 0.87
    (B) 0.43
    (C) 1.87
    (D) 1.42
    (E) 0.15

24. The primary period of the function $f(x) = 2 \cdot \cos^2 3x$ is

    (A) 2π
    (B) $\dfrac{\pi}{3}$
    (C) π
    (D) $\dfrac{\pi}{2}$
    (E) 3π

25. In $a + bi$ form, the reciprocal of $2 + 6i$ is

    (A) $-\dfrac{1}{16} + \dfrac{3}{16}i$
    (B) $\dfrac{1}{16} + \dfrac{3}{16}i$
    (C) $\dfrac{1}{20} - \dfrac{3}{20}i$
    (D) $\dfrac{1}{20} + \dfrac{3}{20}i$
    (E) none of the above

26. A central angle of two concentric circles is $\dfrac{3\pi}{14}$. The area of the large sector is twice the area of the small sector. What is the ratio of the lengths of the radii of the two circles?

    (A) 0.50:1
    (B) 0.71:1
    (C) 0.25:1
    (D) 1:1
    (E) 0.67:1

27. If the region bounded by the lines $y = -\dfrac{4}{3}x + 4$, $x = 0$, and $y = 0$ is rotated about the y-axis, the volume of the figure formed is

    (A) 18.8
    (B) 37.7
    (C) 56.5
    (D) 84.8
    (E) 113.1

USE THIS SPACE FOR SCRATCH WORK

GO ON TO THE NEXT PAGE

28. If there are known to be 4 broken transistors in a box of 12, and 3 transistors are drawn at random, what is the probability that none of the 3 is broken?

(A) 0.375
(B) 0.255
(C) 0.250
(D) 0.750
(E) 0.556

29. In order for the inverse of $f(x) = \sin 2x$ to be a function, the domain of f can be limited to

(A) $-\dfrac{\pi}{2} \le x \le \dfrac{\pi}{2}$

(B) $0 \le x \le \dfrac{\pi}{2}$

(C) $\dfrac{\pi}{4} \le x \le \dfrac{3\pi}{4}$

(D) $\dfrac{\pi}{2} \le x \le \pi$

(E) $0 \le x \le \pi$

30. R varies as the square of z and inversely as the cube of T. If z is tripled and T is doubled, the value of R is

(A) multiplied by 3
(B) multiplied by $\dfrac{9}{8}$
(C) multiplied by 8
(D) divided by 3
(E) divided by $\dfrac{2}{3}$

31. Two roots of $x^3 + 3x^2 + Kx - 12 = 0$ are unequal but have the same absolute value. The value of K is

(A) 4
(B) –4
(C) 6
(D) –6
(E) –9

32. If n is an integer, what is the remainder when $3x^{2n+3} - 4x^{2n+2} + 5x^{2n+1} - 8$ is divided by $x + 1$?

(A) –4
(B) –10
(C) 0
(D) –20
(E) The remainder cannot be determined.

USE THIS SPACE FOR SCRATCH WORK

GO ON TO THE NEXT PAGE

33. Four men, A, B, C, and D, line up in a row. What is the probability that man A is at either end of the row?

(A) $\dfrac{1}{2}$

(B) $\dfrac{1}{3}$

(C) $\dfrac{1}{4}$

(D) $\dfrac{1}{6}$

(E) $\dfrac{1}{12}$

34. $\displaystyle\sum_{n=1}^{\infty} \log\left(\dfrac{1}{n}\right) =$

(A) 0
(B) 1
(C) $-\infty$
(D) ∞
(E) The value cannot be determined.

35. The graph of $y^4 - 3x^2 + 7 = 0$ is symmetric with respect to which of the following?

I. the x-axis
II. the y-axis
III. the origin

(A) only I
(B) only II
(C) only III
(D) only I and II
(E) I, II, and III

36. In a group of 30 students, 20 take French, 15 take Spanish, and 5 take neither language. How many students take both French and Spanish?

(A) 0
(B) 5
(C) 10
(D) 15
(E) 20

37. If $f(x) = \dfrac{x+1}{x^2+1}$ and $g(x) = \dfrac{x^2+1}{x+1}$, find the slope of the line that passes through points $\left(\sqrt{5}, g\left(\sqrt{5}\right)\right)$ and $\left(\sqrt{2}, f\left(\sqrt{2}\right)\right)$.

(A) 0.06
(B) 2.13
(C) −0.63
(D) −1.26
(E) 1.28

GO ON TO THE NEXT PAGE

38. The plane whose equation is $2x + 3y + 5z = 35$ forms a pyramid in the first octant with the coordinate planes. Its volume is

    (A) 190.6
    (B) 238.2
    (C) 285.8
    (D) 381.1
    (E) 566.8

USE THIS SPACE FOR SCRATCH WORK

39. Solve the equation $\sin 15x + \cos 15x = 0$. What is the sum of the three smallest positive solutions?

    (A) $\dfrac{\pi}{20}$

    (B) $\dfrac{\pi}{3}$

    (C) $\dfrac{7\pi}{20}$

    (D) $\dfrac{21\pi}{20}$

    (E) $\dfrac{21\pi}{4}$

40. Given the set of data 1, 1, 2, 2, 2, 3, 3, x, y, where x and y represent two different integers. If the mode is 2, which of the following statements must be true?

    (A) If $x = 1$ or 3, then y must = 2.
    (B) Both x and y must be > 3.
    (C) Either x or y must = 2.
    (D) It does not matter what values x and y have.
    (E) Either x or y must = 3, and the other must = 1.

41. If $f(x) = \sqrt{2x + 3}$ and $g(x) = x^2$, for what value(s) of x does $f(g(x)) = g(f(x))$?

    (A) 5.45
    (B) −0.55
    (C) 0.46
    (D) −0.55 and 5.45
    (E) 0.46 and 6.46

42. If $3x - x^2 \geq 2$ and $y^2 + y \leq 2$, then

    (A) $-1 \leq xy \leq 2$
    (B) $-2 \leq xy \leq 2$
    (C) $-4 \leq xy \leq 4$
    (D) $-4 \leq xy \leq 2$
    (E) 1, 2, and 4 only

43. In $\triangle ABC$, if $\sin A = \dfrac{1}{3}$ and $\sin B = \dfrac{1}{4}$, $\sin C =$

    (A) 0.14
    (B) 0.58
    (C) 0.56
    (D) 3.15
    (E) 2.51

GO ON TO THE NEXT PAGE

44. The solution set of $\dfrac{|x-1|}{x} > 2$ is

   (A) $0 < x < \dfrac{1}{3}$

   (B) $x < \dfrac{1}{3}$

   (C) $x > \dfrac{1}{3}$

   (D) $\dfrac{1}{3} < x < 1$

   (E) $x > 0$

45. If (x,y) represents a point on the graph of $y = 2x + 1$, which of the following could be a portion of the graph of the set of points (x^2,y)?

   (A)

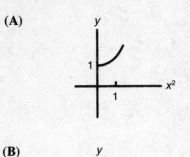

   (B)

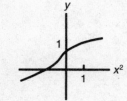

   (C)

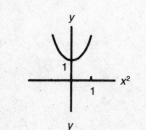

   (D)

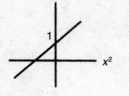

   (E)

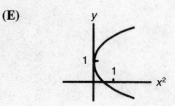

46. In the figure, the bases, *ABC* and *DEF*, of the right prism are equilateral triangles of side *s*. The altitude of the prism *BE* is *h*. If a plane cuts the figure through points *A, C,* and *E*, two solids, *EABC,* and *EACFD,* are formed. What is the ratio of the volume of *EABC* to the volume of *EACFD*?

(A) $\dfrac{1}{2}$

(B) $\dfrac{1}{3}$

(C) $\dfrac{\sqrt{3}}{3}$

(D) $\dfrac{\sqrt{3}}{4}$

(E) $\dfrac{1}{4}$

47. If $x + 3y = 6$ and $2x - y = 3$, then $\dfrac{x}{y} =$

(A) $\dfrac{5}{3}$

(B) $\dfrac{3}{7}$

(C) $\dfrac{3}{5}$

(D) $\dfrac{15}{7}$

(E) $\dfrac{9}{7}$

48. The length of the major axis of the ellipse $3x^2 + 2y^2 - 6x + 8y - 1 = 0$ is

(A) $\sqrt{3}$

(B) $2\sqrt{3}$

(C) $\sqrt{6}$

(D) $2\sqrt{6}$

(E) 4

49. If a coordinate system is devised so that the positive *y*-axis makes an angle of 60° with the positive *x*-axis, what is the distance between the points with coordinates (4,−3) and (5,1)?

(A) 4.12

(B) 4.58

(C) 3.87

(D) 3.61

(E) 7.14

USE THIS SPACE FOR SCRATCH WORK

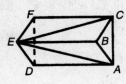

GO ON TO THE NEXT PAGE

50. What is the distance between the *x*- and *y*-intercepts of the graph of $f(x) = 5x^3 - x^2 + 5x - 1$?

(A) $\dfrac{4}{5}$

(B)   1

(C) $\dfrac{2\sqrt{6}}{5}$

(D) $\dfrac{\sqrt{26}}{5}$

(E) $\dfrac{5\sqrt{2}}{7}$

USE THIS SPACE FOR SCRATCH WORK

ANSWER KEY

1. C	6. C	11. C	16. D	21. C	26. B	31. B	36. C	41. B	46. A
2. B	7. C	12. A	17. D	22. C	27. B	32. D	37. E	42. D	47. A
3. C	8. B	13. D	18. C	23. D	28. B	33. A	38. B	43. C	48. D
4. D	9. D	14. D	19. E	24. B	29. C	34. C	39. C	44. A	49. B
5. C	10. E	15. C	20. B	25. C	30. B	35. E	40. A	45. E	50. D

ANSWER EXPLANATIONS

In these solutions the following notation is used:

a: active—Calculator use is necessary or, at a minimum, extremely helpful.

n: neutral—Answers can be found without a calculator, but a calculator may help.

i: inactive—Calculator use is not helpful and may even be a hindrance.

1. n C $f(x) = -\sin x \cos x = -\dfrac{1}{2}(2 \sin x \cos x) = -\dfrac{1}{2}\sin 2x$. Amplitude $= \left| -\dfrac{1}{2} \right| = \dfrac{1}{2}$. [3.4].

Graphing calculator (in radian mode): Plot the graph of $y = -\sin x \cdot \cos x$ in an $x \in [-3 \times 3]$, $y \in [-2 \times 2]$ window. Use the Trace function to see that the graph goes from –0.5 to 0.5. Therefore, the amplitude is 0.5.

2. n B Substituting –2 for x gives $48 + 16 - 80 - 12 = -28$. [2.4].

<u>Alternative Solution</u>: Using synthetic division gives

$$
\begin{array}{r|rrrrr}
-2 & 3 & -2 & -20 & 0 & -12 \\
   &   & -6 & 16 & 8 & -16 \\
\hline
   & 3 & -8 & -4 & 8 & \underline{-28} \\
\end{array} = \text{remainder}
$$

Graphing calculator: Plot the graph of $y = 3^4 - 2x^3 - 20x^2 - 12$ in an $x \in [-10 \times 10]$, $y \in [-50 \times 50]$ window. Use the Trace function to see that $y \approx -28$ when $x \approx -2$.

3. a C Put your calculator in degree mode: Use the change-of-base theorem. $\log_2 (\cos 325°) \approx \log_2 (0.819) \approx -0.288$. [3.3, 4.2].

4. i D The slope of the first line is $\dfrac{3}{4}$, and of the second line is $-\dfrac{4}{3}$. Slopes are negative reciprocals, and so lines are perpendicular. [2.2].

5. n C The domain of $y = \log_{10} x$ consists of only positive numbers. Therefore, $\sin x > 0$. $\sin x > 0$ in quadrants I and II, and so $0 < x < \pi$. [1.1, 3.4, 4.2].

Graphing calculator: Plot the graph of $y = \log(\sin x)$ in an $x \in [-10 \times 10]$, $y \in [-10 \times 10]$ window. Use the Trace and Zoom functions to see that the domain could be the interval from 0 to π. Since

the calculator is ambiguous about the endpoints, 0 and π, you must check them yourself. In both cases the sine is 0 and log 0 is not defined. Therefore, the domain is $0 < x < \pi$.

6. i C $\dfrac{\text{Surface area of sphere}}{\text{Volume of sphere}} = \dfrac{4\pi r^2}{\dfrac{4}{3}\pi r^2} = \dfrac{4 \cdot 3}{\dfrac{4}{3} r \cdot 3}$
$= \dfrac{12}{4r} = \dfrac{3}{r}$. [5.5].

7. n C $b^2 - 4ac = 81 - 4(1)(c) < 0$. Therefore, $c > \dfrac{81}{4}$. [2.3].

Graphing calculator: Plot the graph of $y = x^2 - 9x$ in an $x \in [-10 \times 10]$, $y \in [-50 \times 50]$ window. In order for the solutions of the equation to be complex conjugates, the horizontal line $y = -c$ cannot intersect the graph. Use the Trace and Zoom functions or the Min function to see that the minimum point occurs when $y \approx -20$. Therefore, c must be greater than $\dfrac{81}{4}$.

8. a B Put your calculator in degree mode: Tan $x = 3$ implies that $\text{Tan}^{-1} 3 = x \approx 71.6°$. Therefore, $\sqrt{\csc 71.6°} = \sqrt{\dfrac{1}{\sin 71.6°}} \approx \sqrt{\dfrac{1}{0.949}} \approx \sqrt{1.054} \approx 1.03$. [3.1].

9. i D The two transformations put the graph right back where it started. [5.5].

10. n E Divide the numerator and denominator through by x^3 and then let $x \to \infty$. The numerator approaches 3, and the denominator approaches 0, and so the whole fraction approaches ∞ [4.5].

Graphing calculator: Plot the graph of $y = \dfrac{3x^3 - 7x^2 + 2}{4x^2 - 3x - 1}$ in an $x \in [-10 \times 10]$, $y \in [-10 \times 10]$ window. Keep increasing the size of the window until you are convinced that the function approaches ∞ as x approaches ∞.

11. n C Sketch the graph to see that the answer is Choice C. [3.4].

Graphing calculator (in degree mode since $-\dfrac{\pi}{4} = -45°$ and $\dfrac{3\pi}{4} = 135°$): Plot the graph of $y = \cos x$ in an $x \in [-45° \times 135°]$, $y \in [-2 \times 2]$ window to see that the graph increases and then decreases.

12. n **A** The amplitude is $\sqrt{2}$, and so the maximum value is $\sqrt{2}$. Because of the absolute value, the minimum value is 0. Therefore, the vertical distance is $\sqrt{2} - 0 \approx 1.414$. [3.4].

 Graphing calculator: Plot the graph of $y =$ abs($-\sqrt{2} \sin \sqrt{3}x$) in an $x \in [0 \times 6.28]$, $y \in [-2 \times 2]$ window. Use the Trace and Zoom functions or the Min and Max functions to see that the maximum occurs when $x \approx 1.414$ and the minimum occurs when $x = 0$. Therefore, the vertical distance is $\sqrt{2} - 0 \approx 1.414$.

13. n **D** Plot a few points. The minimum occurs when $x = 3$. [4.3].

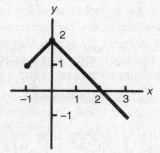

Graphing calculator: Plot the graph of $y =$ abs(x) + 2 in an $x \in [-1 \times 3]$, $y \in [-2 \times 2]$ window. Use the Trace and Zoom functions or the Min function to see that the minimum occurs when $x = 3$.

14. i **D** $f(4,2) = \dfrac{\log 4}{\log 2} = \dfrac{\log 2^2}{\log 2} = \dfrac{2 \cdot \log 2}{\log 2} = 2$.
[4.2].

15. n **C** The possible rational roots are ± 1, ± 2, ± 4, $\pm\dfrac{1}{4}$, $\pm\dfrac{1}{2}$. Synthetic division yields $\dfrac{1}{4}$ as a positive rational root. [2.4].

Alternative Solution: $4x^3 - x^2 + 16x - 4 = 0$ can be factored. $x^2(4x - 1) + 4(4x - 1) = 0$, which gives $(4x - 1)(x^2 + 4) = 0$. Thus, $x = \dfrac{1}{4}$ is the only real zero.

Graphing calculator: Plot the graph of $y = 4x^3 - x^2 + 16x - 4$ in an $x \in [-5 \times 5]$, $y \in [-5 \times 5]$ window. Use the Trace and Zoom functions or the Root, Zero, or Solve function to see that the graph crosses the x-axis only when $x = 0.25$.

16. a **D** $|\vec{V}| = \sqrt{3^2 + \left(-\sqrt{2}\right)^2} = \sqrt{9 + 2} = \sqrt{11} \approx 3.32$.
[5.5].

17. n **D** "More than 3" implies 4 or 5, and so the number of elements is $\dbinom{5}{4} + \dbinom{5}{5} = 6$. [5.1].

Calculator : $\dbinom{5}{4} = \dfrac{5!}{4!1!} = \dfrac{120}{24} = 5$

$\dbinom{5}{5} = \dfrac{5!}{5!0!} = \dfrac{120}{120} = 1$

Therefore, $\dbinom{5}{4} + \dbinom{5}{5} = 5 + 1 = 6$.

18. i **C** By the definition of negation, the negation of the given statements is Choice C. [5.7].

19. n **E** $x = \sec \theta = \dfrac{1}{\cos \theta} = \dfrac{1}{y}$. A portion of the hyperbola $xy = 1$ because $y = \cos \theta$ limits the values of y to the interval $[-1,1]$. [4.6].

Graphing calculator (in parametric mode): Since $\sec \theta = \dfrac{1}{\cos \theta}$, plot the graph of $x = \dfrac{1}{\cos t}$ and $y = \cos t$ in a $t \in [0 \times 6.28]$, $x \in [-10 \times 10]$, $y \in [-2 \times 2]$ window to see that the graph looks like a portion of a hyperbola.

20. i **B** If (3,2) lies on the inverse of f, (2,3) lies on f. Substituting in f gives $2 \cdot 2^3 + 2 + A = 3$. Therefore, $A = -15$. [1.3].

21. i **C** Substitute 1 for x to get $a + b + c = 3$. Substitute -1 for x to get $a - b + c = 3$. Add these two equations to get $a + b = 3$. [2.3].

22. a **C** $\angle A = 108°$. Law of sines: $\dfrac{a}{\sin 108°} = \dfrac{100}{\sin 30°}$. Therefore, $a = 200 \sin 108° = 200 \sin 72° \approx 190.2$. [3.7].

23. a **D** Put your calculator in degree mode: Find that $\cos 10° \cdot \cos 20° \approx 0.9254$. Switch to radian mode and find that $\sin 10 \cdot \sin 20 \approx -0.4967$. Therefore, $0.9254 - (-0.4967) \approx 1.42$. [3.5].

24. n **B** $f(x) = 2 \cdot \cos^2 3x = (2 \cdot \cos^2 3x - 1) + 1 = \cos 6x + 1$ (using the double-angle formula). Period $= \dfrac{2\pi}{6} = \dfrac{\pi}{3}$. [3.5].

Alternative Solution: Sketch the graph of $y = \sqrt{2} \cos 3x$, which has a period of $\dfrac{2\pi}{3}$. Square the y values to get the graph of $y = 2 \cos^2 3x$. This graph looks somewhat like the graph of $y = \sqrt{2} \cos 3x$ except that the negative values are reflected above the x-axis. This should indicate that the period is one-half the period of $y = \sqrt{2} \cos 3x$. Thus, the answer is Choice B.

 Graphing calculator: Plot the graph of $y = 2\cos^2 3x$ in an $x \in [0 \times 6.28]$, $y \in [-2 \times 2]$ window. Use the Trace and Zoom functions to see that the primary period is about 1. The only answer choice that is approximately 1 is $\dfrac{\pi}{3}$.

25. i   C $\dfrac{1}{2+6i} \cdot \dfrac{2-6i}{2-6i} = \dfrac{2-6i}{4-(-36)} = \dfrac{1}{20} - \dfrac{3}{20}i$.
[4.7].

26. a   B   The central angle $\dfrac{3\pi}{14}$ is not necessary.

$\dfrac{1}{2}R^2\theta = \dfrac{1}{2}r^2\theta \cdot 2$, and so $\dfrac{1}{2} = \dfrac{r^2}{R^2}$. Therefore,

$\dfrac{r}{R} = \dfrac{\sqrt{2}}{2} \approx \dfrac{1.414}{2} \approx 0.71{:}1$.   [3.2].

TIPS: (1) Volumes of similar figures are proportional to the cube of corresponding linear measures.
(2) Areas of similar figures are proportional to the square of corresponding linear measures.

---

27. a   B   The line cuts the x-axis at 3 and the y-axis at 4 to form a right triangle that, when rotated about the y-axis, forms a cone with radius 3 and altitude 4. Volume $= \dfrac{1}{3}\pi r^2 h = \dfrac{1}{3}\pi(9)(4) = 12\pi \approx 37.7$. [5.5].

28. a   B   There are $\dbinom{8}{3} = 56$ ways to select 3 good transistors. There are $\dbinom{12}{3} = 220$ ways to select any 3 transistors. $P(3 \text{ good ones}) = \dfrac{56}{220} = \dfrac{14}{55} \approx 0.255$. [5.3].

<u>Alternative Solution</u>: Since there are 4 broken transistors, there must be 8 good ones. $P(\text{first pick is good}) = \dfrac{8}{12}$. Of the remaining 11 transistors, 7 are good, and so $P(\text{second pick is good}) = \dfrac{7}{11}$. Finally, $P(\text{third pick is good}) = \dfrac{6}{10}$. Therefore, $P(\text{all three are good}) = \dfrac{8}{12} \cdot \dfrac{7}{11} \cdot \dfrac{6}{10} = \dfrac{14}{55} \approx 0.255$.

29. n   C   In order for $f^{-1}(x)$ to be a function, the domain of f must be such that, for each value of y, there is only one value of x. The period of the graph is $\dfrac{2\pi}{2} = \pi$, and the figure below shows that the necessary interval occurs when $\dfrac{\pi}{4} \leq x \leq \dfrac{3\pi}{4}$. [1.3,3.4,3.6]

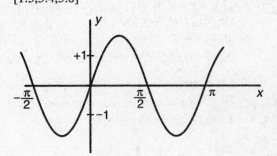

 Graphing calculator: In order for an inverse to exist, a horizontal line can cross $f(x)$ at only one point. Put your calculator in degree mode and plot the graph of $y = \sin 2x$ in an $x \in [-90 \times 180°]$, $y \in [-2 \times 2]$ window. Use the Trace function and check the intervals listed in the answer choices to see that a horizontal line crosses $f(x)$ only once, in the interval $[45°, 135°]$. Therefore, Choice C is the correct answer.

30. i   B $\dfrac{RT^3}{Z^2} = K$. Let $R = 1$, $T = 2$, $Z = 3$ (arbitrary choices) to get $K = \dfrac{8}{9}$. The new values are $Z = 9$, $T = 4$, and so $\dfrac{R(64)}{81} = \dfrac{8}{9}$. Therefore, $R = \dfrac{9}{8}$, and the original value of R has been multiplied by $\dfrac{9}{8}$. [4.5].

<u>Alternative Solution</u>: Taking the original equation, $\dfrac{RT^3}{Z^2} = K$, make the indicated changes; $\dfrac{R(2T)^3}{(3Z)^2} = \dfrac{8RT^3}{9Z^2}$. In order for this fraction to remain equal to K, the value of R must be multiplied by $\dfrac{9}{8}$.

31. i   B   The sum of the roots, $r + (-r) + p$, equals $-\dfrac{3}{1} = -3$. Therefore, the third root, p, equals -3. Substituting -3 for x in the equation gives $-27 + 27 + 3K - 12 = 0$. $K = -4$. [2.4].

32. i   D   Substitute -1 for x. -1 to an even exponent $= 1$, and to an odd exponent $= -1$. $3(-1) - 4(1) + 5(-1) - 8 = -20$. [2.4].

33. i   A   In half of the arrangements man A is at one end. Therefore, P(man A is in an end seat) = $\frac{1}{2}$. [5.4].

Alternative Solution: There are $_4P_4 = 24$ ways the four men can be arranged in a line. If A is at the front of the row, there are $_3P_3 = 6$ ways the remaining 3 men can be arranged. Similarly, if A is at the end of the row, the other 3 men can be arranged in 6 ways. Therefore, A is at one end of the row for 12 of the arrangements. Thus, the probability that A is at one of the ends is $\frac{12}{24} = \frac{1}{2}$.

34. i   C   Listing the first few terms gives

$$\log 1 + \log \frac{1}{2} + \log \frac{1}{3} + \log \frac{1}{4} + \cdots$$

$$= \log\left(1 \cdot \frac{1}{2} \cdot \frac{1}{3} \cdot \frac{1}{4} \cdots\right).$$

As $n \to \infty$, this product approaches zero and log approaches $-\infty$. [4.2].

35. n   E   If y is replaced by $-y$, the original equation is unchanged, and so the graph is symmetric with respect to the x-axis (I). If x is replaced by $-x$, the original equation is unchanged, and so the graph is symmetric with respect to the y-axis (II). If x is replaced by $-x$ and y is replaced by $-y$, the equation is unchanged, and so the graph is symmetric with respect to the origin (III). [1.4].

Graphing calculator: Plot the graphs of $y = \sqrt[4]{3x^2 + 7}$ and $y = -\sqrt[4]{3x^2 + 7}$ in an $x \in [-10 \times 10]$, $y \in [-10 \times 10]$ window to see that the graph of $y^4 - 3x^2 + 7 = 0$ is symmetric about the x-axis, the y-axis, and the origin.

36. i   C   From the Venn diagram below you get the following equations:

$$
\begin{array}{ll}
a + b + c + d = 30 & (1) \\
b + c \qquad\quad = 20 & (2) \\
\quad\;\; c + d = 15 & (3) \\
a \qquad\qquad\;\; = 5
\end{array}
$$

Subtract equation (2) from equation (1): $a + d = 10$. Since $a = 5$, $d = 5$. Substituting 5 for d in equation (3) leaves $c = 10$. [5.9].

All students

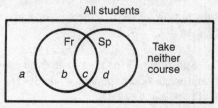

37. a   E $g(\sqrt{5}) = \frac{6}{\sqrt{5} + 1} \approx 1.854$. $f(\sqrt{2}) = \frac{\sqrt{2} + 1}{3} \approx 0.805$. Therefore, slope $\approx \frac{1.854 - 0.805}{\sqrt{5} - \sqrt{2}} \approx \frac{1.049}{0.8219} \approx 1.28$. [1.2, 2,2].

38. a   B   The plane cuts the x-axis at 17.5, the y-axis at 11.7, and the z-axis at 7. The base is a right triangle with area $\approx \frac{1}{2}(17.5)(11.7) \approx 102.1$. $V = \frac{1}{3}Bh \approx \frac{1}{3}(102.1)(7) \approx 238.2$. [5.5].

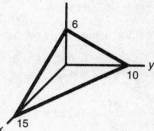

39. n   C $\sin 15x = -\cos 15x$ converts to $\tan 15x = -1$. Thus, the three smallest positive values of $15x = \frac{3\pi}{4}, \frac{7\pi}{4}, \frac{11\pi}{4}$, leading to $x = \frac{3\pi}{60}, \frac{7\pi}{60}, \frac{11\pi}{60}$. Their sum $= \frac{21\pi}{60} = \frac{7\pi}{20}$. [3.5].

Graphing calculator: Sketch the graph of $\sin 15x + \cos 15x$ in an $x \in [0, \frac{\pi}{2}]$, $y \in [-4, 4]$ window. Use the Trace and Zoom functions (or the Root, Zero, or Solve function) to get decimal values of the three smallest positive roots whose sum is about 1.1. Evaluate the answer choices to see that $\frac{7\pi}{20}$ is the correct answer.

40. i   A   The number of 2s must exceed the number of other values. Some of the choices can be eliminated. B: one integer could be 2. C: x or y could be 2, but not necessarily. D and E: if $x = 3$ and $y = 1$, there will be no mode. Therefore, Choice A is the answer. [5.9].

41. a   B $f(g(x)) = \sqrt{2x^2 + 3}$, and $g(f(x)) = 2x + 3$. Thus, $\sqrt{2x^2 + 3} = 2x + 3$. Square both sides to get $2x^2 + 3 = 4x^2 + 12x + 9$, which leads to $x^2 + 6x + 3 = 0$. Thus, $x = \frac{-6 \pm \sqrt{36 - 12}}{2}$. Therefore, $x = -3 - \sqrt{6}$ (which is extraneous) or $x = -3 + \sqrt{6} \approx -0.55$. [1.2].

Graphing calculator: Plot the graphs of $y = f(g(x)) = \sqrt{2x^2 + 3}$ and $y = g(f(x)) = 2x + 3$ in an $x \in [-10 \times 10]$, $y \in [-10 \times 10]$ window. Use the Trace and Zoom functions or the Intersect function to see that the graphs intersect only once, when $x \approx -0.55$.

42. i **D** Solve the first inequality to get $1 \leq x \leq 2$. Solve the second inequality to get $-2 \leq y \leq 1$. The smallest product xy possible is -4, and the largest product xy possible is $+2$. [2.5].

43. a **C** $\text{Sin } C = \sin(180° - (A + B)) = \sin(A + B) =$

$\sin A \cdot \cos B + \cos A \cdot \sin B = \dfrac{1}{3} \cdot \dfrac{\sqrt{15}}{4} + \dfrac{\sqrt{8}}{3} \cdot \dfrac{1}{4}$

$= \dfrac{\sqrt{15} + 2\sqrt{2}}{12} \approx$

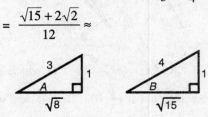

Alternative Solution: Draw $\triangle ABC$ and drop a perpendicular, CM, from C to side AB. Since, in a right triangle, $\sin A = \dfrac{\text{opposite side}}{\text{hypotenuse}} = \dfrac{1}{3}$ and $\sin B = \dfrac{1}{4}$, the lengths of segments AC, CM, and CB are indicated. Using the Pythagorean theorem gives $AM = \sqrt{8}$ and $MB = \sqrt{15}$, and so $AB = \sqrt{8} + \sqrt{15}$. By the law of sines in $\triangle ABC$,

$\dfrac{\sin C}{\sqrt{8} + \sqrt{15}} = \dfrac{\sin A}{4} = \dfrac{\frac{1}{3}}{4}$. Therefore,

$\sin C = \dfrac{1}{12}\left(\sqrt{8} + \sqrt{15}\right) \approx \dfrac{2\sqrt{2} + \sqrt{15}}{12} \approx 0.56$.

[Triangle ABC with altitude CM, sides 3 and 4, height 1]

TIP: Always look at the answer choices. You may find a clue as you work through your solution. In this case, when you find that $AB = \sqrt{8} + \sqrt{15}$, which equals $2\sqrt{2} + \sqrt{15}$, you might conclude that Choice C is the correct answer, thus saving much work.

44. n **A** If $x \geq 1$, the inequality becomes $x - 1 > 2x$ and $x < -1$. Therefore, no points are possible. If $0 < x < 1$, the inequality becomes $-x + 1 > 2x$ and $x < \dfrac{1}{3}$. Therefore, $0 < x < \dfrac{1}{3}$. If $x < 0$, the inequality becomes $-x + 1 < 2x$ and $x < \dfrac{1}{3}$, which contains no points. [4.3, 2.5].

Alternative Solution: Consider the equation, $\dfrac{|x - 1|}{x} = 2$, associated with the inequality. Noting that $x \neq 0$, solve the equation $|x - 1| = 2x$. From the definition of absolute value, if $x - 1 \geq 0$, $x - 1 = 2x$ and $x = -1$. But this gives a contradiction: $x > 1$ and $x = -1$. Therefore, if $x - 1 \geq 0$, there are no solutions. If $x - 1 < 0$, $x - 1 = -2x$ and $x = \dfrac{1}{3}$. Therefore, if $x < 1$, x must equal $\dfrac{1}{3}$. The boundary points for the inequality are 0 and $\dfrac{1}{3}$:

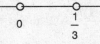

Test points in each of the intervals to find which intervals are included in the solution set of the original inequality. The answer is Choice A.

 Graphing calculator: Plot the graphs of $y = [\text{abs}(x - 1)]/x$ and $y = 2$ in an $x \in [-10 \times 10]$, $y \in [-10 \times 10]$ window. Use the Trace and Zoom functions to see that the function is above $y = 2$ only when $0 < x < \dfrac{1}{3}$.

45. i **E** From the table of values below, point (x,y) can be seen to lie on the graph of $y = 2x + 1$, and the set of points (x^2,y) lies on the graph we are looking for. Plotting a few points gives a rough sketch that indicates the answer is Choice E. [5.5].

x	-2	-1	0	1	2	3
x^2	4	1	0	1	4	9
y	-3	-1	1	3	5	7

46. i **A** The volume of the prism is area of base times height. The figure $EABC$ is a pyramid with base triangle ABC and height BE, the same as the base and height of the prism. The volume of the pyramid is $\dfrac{1}{3}$ (base times height), $\dfrac{1}{3}$ the volume of the prism. Therefore, the other solid, $EACFD$, is $\dfrac{2}{3}$ the volume of the prism. The ratio of the volumes is $\dfrac{1}{2}$. [5.5].

47. i   A   Multiply the second equation by -2 and add to the first equation to get $-3x + 5y = 0$. Then $3x = 5y$, and $\dfrac{x}{y} = \dfrac{5}{3} \approx 1.67$. [5.9]

48. n   D   Get the center axis form of the equation by completing the square: $3x^2 - 6x + 2y^2 + 8y = 1$
$3(x^2 - 2x + 1) + 2(y^2 + 4y + 4) = 1 + 3 + 8 = 12$,

which leads to $\dfrac{3(x-1)^2}{12} + \dfrac{2(y+2)^2}{12} = 1$ and

finally to $\dfrac{(x-1)^2}{4} + \dfrac{(y+2)^2}{6} = 1$. Thus, half the

major axis is $\sqrt{6}$, making the major axis $2\sqrt{6}$. [4.1]

 Graphing calculator: After completing the square (see above) solve for y to get

$$y = \pm\sqrt{\dfrac{12 - 3(x-1)^2}{2}} - 2.$$ Graph $y =$

$+\sqrt{\dfrac{12 - 3(x-1)^2}{2}} - 2$ to get the upper half of

the ellipse and graph $y = -\sqrt{\dfrac{12 - 3(x-1)^2}{2}} - 2$

to get the lower half. Use the Trace and Zoom functions to find that the vertical axis is the major axis with a length of about 4.9. Evaluate the answer choices to see that $2\sqrt{6}$ is the correct answer.

49. a   B   From the figure it can be seen that the lines drawn parallel to the axes and the line through the two points form a triangle with one angle of 120°

and adjacent sides of 4 and 1. From the law of cosines,

$$d^2 = 1 + 16 - 2 \cdot 1 \cdot 4 \cos 120°$$
$$= 17 + 4$$

Thus, the distance between the two points $d = \sqrt{21} \approx 4.58$. [5.9].

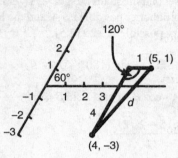

50. n   D   Factor $f(x) = (5x - 1)(x^2 + 1)$, which has only one x-intercept at $(\frac{1}{5}, 0)$. $f(0) = -1$, and so the y-intercept is at $(0, -1)$. The distance between them

is $\sqrt{(\frac{1}{5} - 0)^2 + (0+1)^2} = \dfrac{\sqrt{26}}{5}$. [2.4]

 Graphing calculator: Sketch the graph of $f(x)$ in an $x \in [0,2]$, $y \in [-4,4]$ window. Use the Trace and Zoom functions to get decimal values of the intercepts. Use the distance formula to find that the distance between the intercepts is about 1.02. Evaluate the answer choices to see that $\dfrac{\sqrt{26}}{5}$ is the correct answer.

SELF-EVALUATION CHART FOR MODEL TEST 5

		NUMBER OF		
SUBJECT AREA	QUESTIONS	RIGHT	WRONG	OMITTED

Mark correct answers with C, wrong answers with X, and omitted answers with O.

Algebra
(9 questions)
Review section

3	4	7	25	30	31	42	44	47
4.2	2.2	2.3	4.7	4.5	2.4	2.5	4.3	5.9

___   ___   ___

Solid geometry
(4 questions)
Review section

6	27	38	46
5.5	5.5	5.5	5.5

___   ___   ___

Coordinate geometry
(6 questions)
Review section

9	19	35	45	48	49
5.5	4.6	1.4	5.5	4.1	5.9

___   ___   ___

Trigonometry
(10 questions)
Review section

1	8	11	12	22	23	24	26	39	43
3.4	3.1	3.4	3.4	3.7	3.5	3.5	3.2	3.5	3.8

___   ___   ___

Functions
(12 questions)
Review section

2	5	13	14	15	20	21	29	32	37	41	50
2.4	1.1	4.3	4.2	2.4	1.3	2.3	1.3	2.4	1.2	1.2	2.4

___   ___   ___

Miscellaneous
(9 questions)
Review section

10	16	17	18	28	33	34	36	40
4.5	5.5	5.1	5.7	5.3	5.4	4.2	5.9	5.9

___   ___   ___

TOTALS   ___   ___   ___

Raw score = (number right) − $\frac{1}{4}$ (number wrong) = _____

Round your raw score to the nearest whole number = _____

Evaluate Your Performance
Model Test 5

Rating	Number Right
Excellent	41–50
Very good	33–40
Above average	25–32
Average	15–24
Below average	Below 15

ANSWER SHEET FOR MODEL TEST 6

Determine the correct answer for each question. Then, using a no. 2 pencil, blacken completely the oval containing the letter of your choice.

1. Ⓐ Ⓑ Ⓒ Ⓓ Ⓔ
2. Ⓐ Ⓑ Ⓒ Ⓓ Ⓔ
3. Ⓐ Ⓑ Ⓒ Ⓓ Ⓔ
4. Ⓐ Ⓑ Ⓒ Ⓓ Ⓔ
5. Ⓐ Ⓑ Ⓒ Ⓓ Ⓔ
6. Ⓐ Ⓑ Ⓒ Ⓓ Ⓔ
7. Ⓐ Ⓑ Ⓒ Ⓓ Ⓔ
8. Ⓐ Ⓑ Ⓒ Ⓓ Ⓔ
9. Ⓐ Ⓑ Ⓒ Ⓓ Ⓔ
10. Ⓐ Ⓑ Ⓒ Ⓓ Ⓔ
11. Ⓐ Ⓑ Ⓒ Ⓓ Ⓔ
12. Ⓐ Ⓑ Ⓒ Ⓓ Ⓔ
13. Ⓐ Ⓑ Ⓒ Ⓓ Ⓔ
14. Ⓐ Ⓑ Ⓒ Ⓓ Ⓔ
15. Ⓐ Ⓑ Ⓒ Ⓓ Ⓔ
16. Ⓐ Ⓑ Ⓒ Ⓓ Ⓔ
17. Ⓐ Ⓑ Ⓒ Ⓓ Ⓔ

18. Ⓐ Ⓑ Ⓒ Ⓓ Ⓔ
19. Ⓐ Ⓑ Ⓒ Ⓓ Ⓔ
20. Ⓐ Ⓑ Ⓒ Ⓓ Ⓔ
21. Ⓐ Ⓑ Ⓒ Ⓓ Ⓔ
22. Ⓐ Ⓑ Ⓒ Ⓓ Ⓔ
23. Ⓐ Ⓑ Ⓒ Ⓓ Ⓔ
24. Ⓐ Ⓑ Ⓒ Ⓓ Ⓔ
25. Ⓐ Ⓑ Ⓒ Ⓓ Ⓔ
26. Ⓐ Ⓑ Ⓒ Ⓓ Ⓔ
27. Ⓐ Ⓑ Ⓒ Ⓓ Ⓔ
28. Ⓐ Ⓑ Ⓒ Ⓓ Ⓔ
29. Ⓐ Ⓑ Ⓒ Ⓓ Ⓔ
30. Ⓐ Ⓑ Ⓒ Ⓓ Ⓔ
31. Ⓐ Ⓑ Ⓒ Ⓓ Ⓔ
32. Ⓐ Ⓑ Ⓒ Ⓓ Ⓔ
33. Ⓐ Ⓑ Ⓒ Ⓓ Ⓔ
34. Ⓐ Ⓑ Ⓒ Ⓓ Ⓔ

35. Ⓐ Ⓑ Ⓒ Ⓓ Ⓔ
36. Ⓐ Ⓑ Ⓒ Ⓓ Ⓔ
37. Ⓐ Ⓑ Ⓒ Ⓓ Ⓔ
38. Ⓐ Ⓑ Ⓒ Ⓓ Ⓔ
39. Ⓐ Ⓑ Ⓒ Ⓓ Ⓔ
40. Ⓐ Ⓑ Ⓒ Ⓓ Ⓔ
41. Ⓐ Ⓑ Ⓒ Ⓓ Ⓔ
42. Ⓐ Ⓑ Ⓒ Ⓓ Ⓔ
43. Ⓐ Ⓑ Ⓒ Ⓓ Ⓔ
44. Ⓐ Ⓑ Ⓒ Ⓓ Ⓔ
45. Ⓐ Ⓑ Ⓒ Ⓓ Ⓔ
46. Ⓐ Ⓑ Ⓒ Ⓓ Ⓔ
47. Ⓐ Ⓑ Ⓒ Ⓓ Ⓔ
48. Ⓐ Ⓑ Ⓒ Ⓓ Ⓔ
49. Ⓐ Ⓑ Ⓒ Ⓓ Ⓔ
50. Ⓐ Ⓑ Ⓒ Ⓓ Ⓔ

MODEL TEST

50 questions   1 hour

Tear out the preceding answer sheet. Decide which is the best choice by rounding your answer when appropriate. Blacken the corresponding space on the answer sheet. When finished, check your answers with those at the end of the test. For questions that you got wrong, note the sections containing the material that you must review. Also, if you do not fully understand how you arrived at some of the correct answers, you should review the appropriate sections. Finally, fill out the self-evaluation sheet on page 243 in order to pinpoint the topics that give you the most difficulty.

OFFICIAL COLLEGE BOARD DIRECTIONS

<u>Directions</u>: For each of the following problems, decide which is the BEST of the choices given. If the exact numerical value is not one of the choices, select the choice that best approximates this value. Then fill in the corresponding oval on the answer sheet.

Notes: (1) A calculator will be necessary for answering some (but not all) of the questions in this test. For each question you will have to decide whether or not you should use a calculator. The calculator you use must be at least a scientific calculator; programmable calculators and calculators that can display graphs are permitted.

(2) For some questions in this test you may have to decide whether your calculator should be in the radian mode or the degree mode.

(3) Figures that accompany problems in this test are intended to provide information useful in solving the problems. They are drawn as accurately as possible EXCEPT when it is stated in a specific problem that the figure is not drawn to scale. All figures lie in a plane unless otherwise indicated.

(4) Unless otherwise specified, the domain of any function f is assumed to be the set of all real numbers x for which $f(x)$ is a real number.

<u>Reference Information:</u> The following information is for your reference in answering some of the questions in this test.

Volume of a right circular cone with radius r and height h: $V = \frac{1}{3}\pi r^2 h$

Lateral area of a right circular cone with circumference of the base c and slant height ℓ: $S = \frac{1}{2}c\ell$

Volume of a sphere with radius r: $V = \frac{4}{3}\pi r^3$

Surface area of a sphere with radius r: $S = 4\pi r^2$

Volume of a pyramid with base area B and height h: $V = \frac{1}{3}Bh$

---

1. If point (a,b) lies on the graph of function f, which of the following points must lie on the graph of the inverse f?

   (A) (a,b)
   (B) $(-a,b)$
   (C) $(a,-b)$
   (D) (b,a)
   (E) $(-b,-a)$

2. Harry had grades of 70, 80, 85, and 80 on his quizzes. If all quizzes have the same weight, what grade must he get on his next quiz so that his average will be 80?

   (A) 85
   (B) 90
   (C) 95
   (D) 100
   (E) more than 100

3. Which of the following is an asymptote of $f(x) = \dfrac{x^2+3x+2}{x+2}\cdot \tan \pi x$?

   (A) $x = 2$
   (B) $x = 1$
   (C) $x = -2$
   (D) $x = -1$
   (E) $x = \dfrac{1}{2}$

4. A trace of the plane $5x - 2y + 3z = 10$ is

   (A) $5x + 2y = 10$
   (B) $3z = 2y$
   (C) $2y + 3z = 10$
   (D) $5x + 3z = 10$
   (E) $2y = 5x + 10$

5. The sum of the roots of $3x^3 + 4x^2 - 4x = 0$ is

   (A) $\dfrac{4}{3}$
   (B) 0
   (C) $-\dfrac{4}{3}$
   (D) 4
   (E) $-\dfrac{3}{4}$

6. If $f(x) = x - \dfrac{1}{x}$, then $f(a) + f\left(\dfrac{1}{a}\right) =$

   (A) 0

   (B) $2a - \dfrac{2}{a}$

   (C) $a - \dfrac{1}{a}$

   (D) $\dfrac{a^4 - a^2 + 1}{a(a^2 - 1)}$

   (E) 1

7. If $f(x) = x^4 - 4x^3 + 6x^2 - 4x + 2$, then $f(2) - f(\sqrt{2}) =$

   (A) 0.97
   (B) 1.42
   (C) 0.86
   (D) 1.73
   (E) 1.03

8. If $f(x) \geq 0$ for all x, then $f(2 - x)$ is

   (A) ≥ 0
   (B) ≥ 2
   (C) ≥ -2
   (D) ≤ 2
   (E) ≤ 0

9. How many four-digit numbers can be formed from the numbers 0, 2, 4, 8 if no digit is repeated?

   (A) 24
   (B) 18
   (C) 64
   (D) 36
   (E) 27

10. If $x - 1$ is a factor of $x^2 + ax - 4$, then a has the value

    (A) 4
    (B) 3
    (C) 2
    (D) 1
    (E) none of the above

11. If 10 coins are to be flipped and the first 5 all come up heads, what is the probability that exactly 3 more heads will be flipped?

    (A) 0.3125
    (B) 0.0439
    (C) 0.6000
    (D) 0.1172
    (E) 0.1250

USE THIS SPACE FOR SCRATCH WORK

GO ON TO THE NEXT PAGE

12. If $i = \sqrt{-1}$ and n is a positive integer, which of the following statements is FALSE?

(A) $i^{4n} = 1$
(B) $i^{4n+1} = -i$
(C) $i^{4n+2} = -1$
(D) $i^{n+4} = i^n$
(E) $i^{4n+3} = -i$

13. If $f(x) = x^2 + 3x - 4$ and $g(x) = x - 4$, then $f(g(\ln 2)) =$

(A) −4.67
(B) 16.86
(C) 8.43
(D) −8.43
(E) −2.99

14. If $f(x) = 4x^2$ and $g(x) = f(\sin x) + f(\cos x)$, then $g(23°)$ is

(A) 1
(B) 4
(C) 4.29
(D) 5.37
(E) 8

15. What is the sum of the roots of the equation $\left(x - \sqrt{2}\right)\left(x^2 - \sqrt{3}x + \pi\right) = 0$?

(A) 0.318
(B) 3.15
(C) −0.318
(D) −0.315
(E) 4.56

16. Which of the following equations has (have) graphs consisting of two perpendicular lines?

  I. $xy = 0$
 II. $|y| = |x|$
III. $|xy| = 1$

(A) only I
(B) only II
(C) only III
(D) only I and II
(E) I, II, and III

17. A line, m, is parallel to a plane, X, and is 6 inches from X. The set of points that are 6 inches from m and 1 inch from X form

(A) a line parallel to m
(B) two lines parallel to m
(C) four lines parallel to m
(D) one point
(E) the empty set

GO ON TO THE NEXT PAGE

18. The angle that the line $5x + 12y = 13$ makes with the y-axis could be

    (A) 56.4°
    (B) 22.6°
    (C) 33.6°
    (D) 78.6°
    (E) 67.4°

19. A cylindrical bar of metal has a base radius of 2 and a height of 9. It is melted down and reformed into a cube. A side of the cube is

    (A) 2.32
    (B) 4.84
    (C) 97.21
    (D) 3.84
    (E) 113.10

20. The graph of $y = (x + 2)(2x - 3)$ can be expressed as a set of parametric equations. If $x = 2t - 2$ and $y = f(t)$, the $f(t) =$

    (A) $2t(4t - 5)$
    (B) $(2t - 2)(4t - 7)$
    (C) $2t(4t - 7)$
    (D) $(2t - 2)(4t - 5)$
    (E) $2t(4t + 1)$

21. If points $\left(\sqrt{2}, y_1\right)$ and $\left(-\sqrt{2}, y_2\right)$ lie on the graph of $y = x^3 + ax^2 + bx + c$, and $y_1 - y_2 = 3$, then $b =$

    (A) 1.473
    (B) −0.939
    (C) −2.167
    (D) −0.354
    (E) 1.061

22. Which one of the following is NOT a fifth root of 1?

    (A) $1(\cos 0 + i \cdot \sin 0)$
    (B) $1(\cos 72° + i \cdot \sin 72°)$
    (C) $1(\cos 154° + i \cdot \sin 154°)$
    (D) $1(\cos 216° + i \cdot \sin 216°)$
    (E) $1(\cos 288° + i \cdot \sin 288°)$

23. If a and b are real numbers, with $a > b$ and $|a| < |b|$, then

    (A) $a > 0$
    (B) $a < 0$
    (C) $b > 0$
    (D) $b < 0$
    (E) none of the above

GO ON TO THE NEXT PAGE

24. If [x] is defined to represent the greatest integer less than or equal to x, and $f(x) = \left| x - [x] - \dfrac{1}{2} \right|$, the maximum value of $f(x)$ is

(A) 1
(B) 2
(C) 0
(D) $\dfrac{1}{2}$
(E) −1

25. $\displaystyle \lim_{x \to 2} \frac{x^3 - 8}{x^2 - 4} =$

(A) 0
(B) 2
(C) 3
(D) 1
(E) ∞

26. A right circular cone whose base radius is 4 is inscribed in a sphere of radius 5. What is the ratio of the volume of the cone to the volume of the sphere?

(A) 0.333 : 1
(B) 0.864 : 1
(C) 0.222 : 1
(D) 0.288 : 1
(E) 0.256 : 1

27. The negation of the statement "If a dog is hungry, then he will howl" is

(A) If a dog is not hungry, then he will not howl.
(B) If a dog does not howl, then he is not hungry.
(C) The dog is hungry and he does not howl.
(D) The dog is not hungry and he howls.
(E) None of the above is the negation.

28. The y-intercept of $y = \left| \sqrt{2} \csc 3\left(x + \dfrac{\pi}{5} \right) \right|$ is

(A) 0.22
(B) 1.49
(C) 4.58
(D) 0.67
(E) 1.41

29. If the center of the circle $x^2 + y^2 + ax + by + 2 = 0$ is point (4,−8), then $a + b =$

(A) −4
(B) 4
(C) 8
(D) −8
(E) 24

GO ON TO THE NEXT PAGE

30. If $p(x) = 3x^2 + 9x + 7$ and $p(a) = 2$, then $a =$

    (A) only 0.736
    (B) only -2.264
    (C) 0.736 or 2.264
    (D) 0.736 or -2.264
    (E) -0.736 or -2.264

31. If i is a root of $x^4 + 2x^3 - 3x^2 + 2x - 4 = 0$, the product of the real roots is

    (A) 0
    (B) -2
    (C) 2
    (D) 4
    (E) -4

32. If $\sin A = \dfrac{3}{5}, 90° \le A \le 180°, \cos B = \dfrac{1}{3},$ and $270° \le B \le 360°$, $\sin(A + B) =$

    (A) -0.333
    (B) 0.733
    (C) -0.832
    (D) 0.954
    (E) -0.554

33. If x varies directly as t and t varies inversely as the square of y, what is the relationship between x and y?

    (A) x varies as y^2
    (B) x varies inversely as y^2
    (C) y varies as x^2
    (D) y varies inversely as x^2
    (E) No variation between x and y can be determined.

34. If $\sec 1.4 = x$, find the value of $\csc(2 \operatorname{Arctan} x)$.

    (A) 0.33
    (B) 3.03
    (C) 1.00
    (D) 1.06
    (E) 0.87

35. The graph of $|y - 1| = |x + 1|$ forms an X. The two branches of the X intersect at a point whose coordinates are

    (A) (1,1)
    (B) (−1,1)
    (C) (1,−1)
    (D) (−1,−1)
    (E) (0,0)

36. For what value of x between $0°$ and $360°$ does $\cos 2x = 2 \cos x$?

   (A) $68.5°$ or $291.5°$
   (B) only $68.5°$
   (C) $103.9°$ or $256.1°$
   (D) $90°$ or $270°$
   (E) $111.5°$ or $248.5°$

37. For what value(s) of x will the graph of the function $f(x) = \sin \sqrt{B - x^2}$ have a maximum?

   (A) $\dfrac{\pi}{2}$

   (B) $\sqrt{B - \dfrac{\pi}{2}}$

   (C) $\sqrt{B - \left(\dfrac{\pi}{2}\right)^2}$

   (D) $\pm\sqrt{B - \dfrac{\pi}{2}}$

   (E) $\pm\sqrt{B - \left(\dfrac{\pi}{2}\right)^2}$

38. For each positive integer n, let S_n = the sum of all positive integers less than or equal to n. Then S_{51} equals

   (A) 50
   (B) 1326
   (C) 1275
   (D) 1250
   (E) 51

39. If the graphs of $3x^2 + 4y^2 - 6x + 8y - 5 = 0$ and $(x - 2)^2 = 4(y + 2)$ are drawn on the same coordinate system, at how many points do they intersect?

   (A) 0
   (B) 1
   (C) 2
   (D) 3
   (E) 4

40. $\text{Log}_x 2 = \log_3 x$ is satisfied by two values of x. Their sum equals

   (A) 0
   (B) 1.73
   (C) 2.35
   (D) 2.81
   (E) 3.14

GO ON TO THE NEXT PAGE

41. In the expansion of $(2b^2 - 3b^{-3})^n$, if the fifth term does not contain a factor of b, what is the value of n?

   (A) 6
   (B) 10
   (C) $\dfrac{15}{2}$
   (D) $\dfrac{25}{2}$
   (E) 9

42. If $\dfrac{3 \sin 2\theta}{1 - \cos 2\theta} = \dfrac{1}{2}$ and $0° \le \theta \le 180°$, then $\theta =$

   (A) $0°$
   (B) $0°$ or $180°$
   (C) $80.5°$
   (D) $0°$ or $80.5°$
   (E) $99.5°$

43. If $f(x,y) = 2x^2 - y^2$ and $g(x) = 2^x$, which one of the following is equal to 2^{2x}?

   (A) $f(x, g(x))$
   (B) $f(g(x), x)$
   (C) $f(g(x), g(x))$
   (D) $f(g(x), 0)$
   (E) $g(f(x, x))$

44. Two positive numbers, a and b, are in the sequence 4, a, b, 12. The first three numbers form a geometric sequence, and the last three numbers form an arithmetic sequence. The difference $b - a$ equals

   (A) 1
   (B) $1\dfrac{1}{2}$
   (C) 2
   (D) $2\dfrac{1}{2}$
   (E) 3

45. A sector of a circle has an arc length of 2.4 feet and an area of 14.3 square feet. How many degrees are in the central angle?

   (A) $63.4°$
   (B) $20.2°$
   (C) $14.3°$
   (D) $11.5°$
   (E) $12.9°$

46. $\displaystyle\sum_{k=1}^{250}\left(\frac{1}{k+1}-\frac{1}{k}\right)=$

(A) $\dfrac{1}{251}$

(B) $\dfrac{250}{251}$

(C) $-\dfrac{250}{251}$

(D) $\dfrac{252}{251}$

(E) $-\dfrac{252}{251}$

47. In the figure, $ABCD$ is a square. M is the point one-third of the way from B to C. N is the point one-half of the way from D to C. Then $\theta =$

(A) 36.9°
(B) 45.0°
(C) 50.8°
(D) 30.0°
(E) 36.1°

48. For what positive value(s) of $x \le 180°$ does tan $2x =$ 2 cot $2x$?

(A) 54.7°
(B) 25° and 155°
(C) 27.4° and 117.4°
(D) 27.4°, 62.6°, 117.4°, and 152.6°
(E) none of the above

49. If (x,y) represents a point on the graph of $y = x^2 + 1$, which of the following could be a portion of the graph of the set of points (x^2,y)?

(A)

(B)

(C)

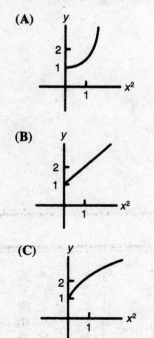

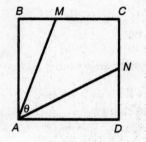

(D)

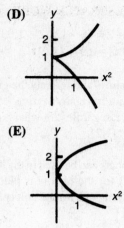

(E)

y

2 ⊢
1

x²
1

USE THIS SPACE FOR SCRATCH WORK

50. The binary operation * is defined over the set of real

numbers to be $a * b = \begin{cases} a\sin\dfrac{b}{a} & \text{if } a > b \\ b\cos\dfrac{a}{b} & \text{if } a < b \end{cases}$. What is the

value of 2 * (5 * 3)?

(A) 4.01
(B) 3.65
(C) 1.84
(D) 2.79
(E) 2.14

ANSWER KEY

1. D	6. A	11. A	16. D	21. B	26. E	31. E	36. E	41. B	46. C
2. A	7. A	12. B	17. B	22. C	27. C	32. D	37. E	42. C	47. B
3. E	8. A	13. E	18. E	23. D	28. B	33. B	38. B	43. C	48. D
4. D	9. B	14. B	19. B	24. D	29. C	34. B	39. C	44. E	49. B
5. C	10. B	15. B	20. C	25. C	30. E	35. B	40. D	45. D	50. E

ANSWER EXPLANATIONS

In these solutions the following notation is used:

a: active—Calculator use is necessary or, at a minimum, extremely helpful.

n: neutral—Answers can be found without a calculator, but a calculator may help.

i: inactive—Calculator use is not helpful and may even be a hindrance.

1. i D Since inverse functions are symmetric about the line $y = x$, if point (a,b) lies on f, point (b,a) must lie on f^{-1}. [1.3].

2. n A Average $= \dfrac{70 + 80 + 85 + 80 + x}{5} = 80.$
Therefore, $x = 85$. [5.8].

3. i E $f(x) = \dfrac{(x+2)(x+1)}{(x+2)} \cdot \tan \pi x.$ Since $x + 2$ divides out, the only asymptote occurs because of $\tan \pi x$. Since tan has an asymptote at $\dfrac{\pi}{2}$, $x = \dfrac{1}{2}$. [4.5].

4. i D The equation of a trace of a plane can be found by letting one of the variables $= 0$. By inspection, only Choice D is a trace. [5.5].

5. n C Factor out an x, getting 0 as one root. The sum of the roots of the remaining quadratic, $3x^2 + 4x - 4 = 0$, equal $-\dfrac{b}{a} = -\dfrac{4}{3}$. Then, $-\dfrac{4}{3} + 0 = -\dfrac{4}{3}$. [2.3].

Alternative Solution: In any polynomial, sum of roots $=$
$$-\dfrac{\text{coefficient of 2nd-highest-degree term}}{\text{coefficient of highest-degree term}} = -\dfrac{4}{3}.$$
[2.4].

Graphing calculator: Plot the graph of $y = 3x^3 + 4x^2 - 4x$ in an $x \in [-10 \times 10]$, $y \in [-10 \times 10]$ window. Use the Trace and Zoom functions or the Root, Zero, or Solve functions to see that the 3 roots are approximately 0, 0.67, and -2. Therefore, the sum ≈ 1.33, so Choice C is the answer.

6. i A $f(a) = a - \dfrac{1}{a} \cdot f\left(\dfrac{1}{a}\right) = \dfrac{1}{a} - a.$ Therefore, $f(a) + f\left(\dfrac{1}{a}\right) = 0.$ [1.2].

7. a A $f(2) = 16 - 32 + 24 - 8 + 2 = 2$, and $f\left(\sqrt{2}\right) = 4 - 8\sqrt{2} + 12 - 4\sqrt{2} + 2 = 18 - 12\sqrt{2} \approx 1.03.$ Therefore, $f(2) - f\left(\sqrt{2}\right) \approx 0.97.$ [1.2].

8. i A The $f(2 - x)$ just shifts and reflects the graph horizontally; it does not have any vertical effect on the graph. Therefore, regardless of what is substituted for x, $f(x) \geq 0$. [1.2].

9. i B Only 3 of the numbers can be used in the thousands place, 3 are left for the hundreds place, 2 for the tens place, and only one for the units place. $3 \cdot 3 \cdot 2 \cdot 1 = 18$. [5.1].

10. i B Substituting 1 for x gives $1 + a - 4 = 0$, and so $a = 3$. [2.3].

11. a A The first 5 flips have no effect on the last 5 flips, so the problem becomes "What is the probability of getting exactly 3 heads in the flip of 5 coins?" $\binom{5}{3} = 10$ outcomes contain 3 heads out of a total of $2^5 = 32$ possible outcomes. $P(3H) = \dfrac{5}{16} \approx 0.3125.$ [5.3].

12. i B $i^{4n} = 1; i^{4n+1} = i; i^{4n+2} = -1; i^{4n+3} = -i; i^{4n+4} = (i^{4n})(i^4) = (1)(1).$ [4.7, 4.2].

13. a E $g(\ln 2) = \ln 2 - 4 \approx -3.307.$ $f(g(\ln 2)) \approx (-3.307)^2 + 3(-3.307) - 4 \approx -2.99.$ [1.2, 4.2].

14. n B $g(x) = f(\sin x) + f(\cos x) = 4\sin^2 x + 4\cos^2 x = 4(\sin^2 x + \cos^2 x) = 4(1) = 4.$ [1.2, 3.5]

Calculator: Put your calculator in degree mode: $g(23°) = f(\sin 23°) + f(\cos 23°) \approx f(0.3901) + f(0.9205) \approx 0.611 + 3.389 \approx 4.$

15. a B The sum of the roots of the quadratic factor is $-\dfrac{\sqrt{3}}{1} \approx 1.732$, and the root of the linear factor is $\sqrt{2} \approx 1.414$. Therefore, the sum of all the roots is $1.732 + 1.414 \approx 3.15.$ [2.3].

16. n D I: Graph consists of lines $x = 0$ and $y = 0$ (the x-axis and the y-axis), which are perpendicular. II: Graph consists of two lines, $y = x$ and $y = -x$, which are perpendicular. III: Graph consists of two rectangular hyperbolas, one branch in each quadrant, with the axes as asymptotes, not lines. [4.3].

Graphing calculator: Graph I: $x \cdot y = 0$ implies that $x = 0$ or $y = 0$, which are the equations of the y-axis and the x-axis. Graph II: $y = \pm|x|$ gives both branches. Graph III: $y = \dfrac{\pm 1}{x}$ gives both branches. Plot the graphs of $y = \text{abs}(x)$, $y = -\text{abs}(x)$, and $y = \dfrac{1}{x}$, $y = \dfrac{-1}{x}$, in an $x \in [-10 \times 10]$, $y \in [-10 \times 10]$ window to see that the first two equations produce perpendicular lines but the last two do not. Therefore, Choice D is the answer.

17. i   B   Points 6 in. from m form a cylinder, with m as axis, which is tangent to plane X. Points 1 in. from X are two planes parallel to X, one above and one below X. The cylinder intersects only one of the planes in two lines parallel to m. [5.5].

18. a   E   Put your calculator in degree mode because the answer choices are in degrees: Slope of line $= -\dfrac{5}{12} = \tan \alpha$. Therefore, $\alpha = \text{Tan}^{-1}\left(-\dfrac{5}{12}\right) \approx$ 157.4°. Since $157.4° \approx \angle 1 + \angle 2$, $\angle 2 \approx 157.4° - 90° = 67.4°$. [3.1].

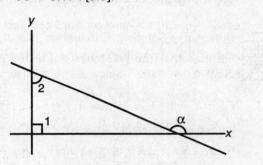

19. a   B   Volume of cylinder $= \pi r^2 h = 36\pi =$ volume of cube $= s^3$. Therefore, $s = \sqrt[3]{36\pi} \approx 4.84$. [5.5].

20. i   C   Substitute $2t - 2$ for x. [4.6].

21. a   B $y_1 = 2^{3/2} + 2a + \sqrt{2}b + c$ and $y_2 = -(2)^{3/2} + 2a - 2\sqrt{2}b + c$. So, $y_1 - y_2 = (2^{3/2} + 2^{3/2}) + 2\sqrt{2}b = 3$. Therefore, $5.65685 + 2.828b \approx 3$ and $b \approx \dfrac{3 - 5.65685}{2.8284} \approx -0.939$. [2.4].

22. n   C $1 = 1[\cos (0 + 360k)° + i \cdot \sin (0 + 360k)°]$. $\sqrt[5]{1} = \sqrt[5]{1}\left[\cos \dfrac{1}{5}(0 + 360k)° + i \cdot \sin \dfrac{1}{5}(0 + 360k)°\right]$ as $k = 0, 1, 2, 3, 4$. $\sqrt[5]{1} = \cos 0° + i \cdot \sin 0°$ or $\cos 72° + i \cdot \sin 72°$ or $\cos 144° + i \cdot \sin 144°$ or $\cos 216° + i \cdot \sin 216°$ or $\cos 288° + i \cdot \sin 288°$. [4.7].

<u>Alternative Solution</u>: The n nth roots of any complex number can be represented by n vectors symmetrically drawn about the origin $\dfrac{360°}{n}$ apart.

The vectors for the fifth roots of any complex number should be $\dfrac{360°}{5} = 72°$ apart. The only answer that disrupts this pattern is Choice C.

23. i   D   Here, a could be either positive or negative. However, b must be negative. [4.3, 2.5].

24. n   D   Sketch a portion of the graph. The maximum is $\dfrac{1}{2}$. [4.3, 4.4].

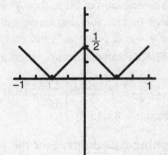

Graphing calculator: Plot the graphs of $y = \text{abs}(x - \text{int}(x) - 0.5)$ in an $x \in [-1 \times 1]$, $y \in [-1 \times 1]$ window to see that the maximum value is approximately 0.5.

25. n   C $\lim\limits_{x \to 2} \dfrac{x^3 - 8}{x^2 - 4} = \lim\limits_{x \to 2} \dfrac{(x - 2)(x^2 + 2x + 4)}{(x - 2)(x + 2)}$ $= \dfrac{4 + 4 + 4}{2 + 2} = 3$. [4.5].

Graphing calculator: Plot the graph of $y = \dfrac{x^3 - 8}{x^2 - 4}$ in an $x \in [-10 \times 10]$, $y \in [-10 \times 10]$ window. Use the Trace and Zoom functions to see that although y is not defined at 2, as $x \to 2$ from the left and the right the value of the function approaches 3.

TIP: For calculus students only: Use l'Hôpital's rule to see that $\lim\limits_{x \to 2} \dfrac{x^3 - 8}{x^2 - 4} = \lim\limits_{x \to 2} \dfrac{3x^2}{2x} = \lim\limits_{x \to 2} \dfrac{3x}{2} = \dfrac{3 \cdot 2}{2} = 3$.

26. a   E   Height of cone $= 8$. Volume of cone $= \dfrac{1}{3}\pi r^2 = \dfrac{1}{3}\pi(16)(8) = \dfrac{128\pi}{3}$. Volume of sphere $= \dfrac{4}{3}\pi r^3 = \dfrac{4}{3}\pi(125) = \dfrac{500\pi}{3}$. $V_c : V_s = 32:125 = 0.256 : 1$. [5.5].

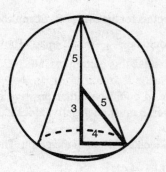

27. i **C** The negation of "If p, then q" is "p and $\sim q$." [5.7].

28. a **B** The y-intercept occurs when $x = 0$. Therefore, $y = \left| \sqrt{2} \csc \dfrac{3\pi}{5} \right| = \left| \dfrac{\sqrt{2}}{\sin \dfrac{3\pi}{5}} \right| \approx 1.49$. [3.4].

Graphing calculator: Plot the graph of $y = \left| \dfrac{\sqrt{2}}{\sin 3\left(x + \dfrac{\pi}{5}\right)} \right|$ in an $x \in [-1 \times 1]$, $y \in [-5 \times 5]$ window. Use the Trace and Zoom functions to see that the y-intercept is approximately 1.49.

29. i **C** The equation of the circle is $(x - 4)^2 + (y + 8)^2 = r^2$. Multiplying out indicates that $a = -8$ and $b = 16$, and so $a + b = 8$. [4.1].

30. a **E** Since $p(a) = 3a^2 + 9a + 7 = 2$, then $3a^2 + 9a + 5 = 0$, and thus $a = \dfrac{-9 \pm \sqrt{81 - 60}}{6} = \dfrac{-9 \pm \sqrt{21}}{6}$. Therefore, $a \approx -0.736$ or -2.264. [2.3].

Graphing calculator: Plot the graphs of $y = 3x^2 + 9x + 7$ and $y = 2$ in an $x \in [-10 \times 10]$, $y \in [-10 \times 10]$ window. Use the Trace and Zoom functions or the Intersect function to see that the graphs intersect when x is approximately -0.74 or -2.3. Thus, Choice E is correct.

31. i **E** Product of roots = $(-1)^n \cdot \dfrac{\text{constant term}}{\text{leading coefficient}} = \dfrac{-4}{1}$. Since $-i$ is also a root (because i is a root), their product is $-i^2 = 1$. Descartes' rule of signs indicates that the other roots are real, and so their product is -4. [2.4].

Alternative Solution: Since i is a root, $-i$ is also a root. Using synthetic division twice gives

$$
\begin{array}{r|ccccc}
i & 1 & 2 & -3 & 2 & -4 \\
  &   & i & -1+2i & -2-4i & 4 \\
\hline
-i & 1 & 2+i & -4+2i & -4i & 0 \\
   &   & -i & -2i & 4i & \\
\hline
   & 1 & 2 & -4 & 0 &
\end{array}
$$

Therefore, the final quotient represents the quadratic equation, $x^2 + 2x - 4 = 0$. The roots of this equation give the two real roots of the original equation. In a quadratic the product of the roots equals $\dfrac{c}{a} = \dfrac{-4}{1} = -4$. [2.3].

32. a **D** From $\sin^2 x + \cos^2 x = 1$, $\sin A = \dfrac{3}{5}$ implies that $\cos A = -\dfrac{4}{5}$, and $\cos B = \dfrac{1}{3}$ implies that $\sin B = -\dfrac{2\sqrt{2}}{3}$. $\sin(A + B) = \sin A \cdot \cos B + \cos A \cdot \sin B = \dfrac{3 + 8\sqrt{2}}{15} \approx 0.954$. [3.5].

Alternative Solution: Calculator: $\sin A = \dfrac{3}{5}$ implies that the reference angle for $\angle A = \sin^{-1} 0.6 \approx 36.87°$. Since $\angle A$ is in quadrant II, $\angle A \approx 180° - 36.87° \approx 143.13°$. $\cos B = \dfrac{1}{3}$ implies that the reference angle for $\angle B = \cos^{-1} \dfrac{1}{3} \approx 70.53°$. Since $\angle B$ is in quadrant IV, $\angle B \approx 360° - 70.53° \approx 289.47°$. Therefore, $\sin(A + B) \approx \sin(143.13° + 289.47°) \approx \sin 432.60° \approx 0.954$.

33. i **B** $\dfrac{x}{t} = K$ and $ty^2 = C$, where K and C are constants. Solve the first equation for t: $t = \dfrac{x}{K}$. Substituting for t in the second equation gives $\dfrac{xy^2}{K} = C$. Thus, $xy^2 = CK$, which indicates that x varies inversely as y^2. [5.6].

34. a **B** Put your calculator in radian mode: $\sec 1.4 = x$ implies that $\dfrac{1}{\cos 1.4} = x \approx 5.883$. $\csc(2\,\text{Arctan}\,x) \approx \csc(2\,\text{Arctan}\,5.883) \approx \csc 2 (1.4024) \dfrac{1}{\sin 2.8048} \approx 3.03$. [3.6].

35. n **B** The important point of an absolute value problem occurs where the expression within the absolute value sign equals zero. The important point of this absolute value problem occurs when $y - 1 = 0$ and $x + 1 = 0$. Therefore, the pieces of the graph intersect at $(-1, 1)$. [4.3].

Graphing calculator: Plot the graphs of $y =$ abs$(x +1) + 1$ and $y = -$abs$(x + 1) + 1$ in an $x \in$ $[-1 \times 1]$, $y \in [-10 \times 10]$ window to get both branches of the graph. Use the Trace and Zoom functions or the Intersect function to see that the point of intersection is approximately $(-1,1)$. Therefore, Choice B is the answer.

36. a **E** Cos $2x = 2 \cos x$ implies that $2 \cos^2 x - 1 =$ $2 \cos x$, and thus, $2 \cos^2 x - 2 \cos x - 1 = 0$. Cos $x = \dfrac{2 \pm \sqrt{4+8}}{4} = \dfrac{1 \pm \sqrt{3}}{2}$. $\dfrac{1+\sqrt{3}}{2}$ is not in the range of cos x because it is greater than 1. Therefore, $\cos x = \dfrac{1-\sqrt{3}}{2} \approx -0.3660$, which implies that $x = \text{Cos}^{-1}(-0.3660)$. To get the reference angle for x, find $\text{Cos}^{-1}(+0.3660)$, which is approximately $68.5°$. Therefore, since cosine is negative in quadrants II and III, $x \approx 180° \pm 68.5° \approx 111.5°$ or $248.5°$. [3.5].

Alternative Solution: Using your calculator, just plug the various answer choices into the equation to see that Choice E is the answer.

37. i **E** Since sin θ has a maximum at $\theta = \dfrac{\pi}{2}$, $\sqrt{B - x^2} = \dfrac{\pi}{2}$. Thus, $B - x^2 = \left(\dfrac{\pi}{2}\right)^2$ and $x^2 = B - \left(\dfrac{\pi}{2}\right)^2$. Therefore, $x = \pm\sqrt{B - \left(\dfrac{\pi}{2}\right)^2}$. [3.4].

38. n **B** This is an arithmetic series with $t_1 = 1$, $d = 1$. $S_{51} = \dfrac{51}{2}(2 + 50 \cdot 1) = 51 \cdot 26 = 1326$. [5.4].

39. a **C** Complete the square on the first equation: $3(x^2 - 2x + 1) + 4(y^2 + 2y + 1) = 5 + 3 + 4$. $3(x-1)^2 + 4(y+1)^2 = 12$. $\dfrac{(x-1)^2}{4} + \dfrac{(y+1)^2}{3} = 1$. From the sketch it is apparent that the graphs intersect at two points. [4.1].

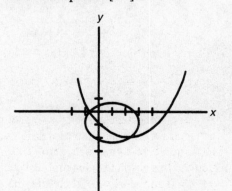

Graphing calculator: Complete the square and solve for y: $y = \pm\sqrt{\dfrac{12 - 3(x-1)^2}{4}} - 1$. Solve the second equation for y: $y = \dfrac{1}{4}(x - 2)^2 - 2$. Plot the graphs of $y = \sqrt{\dfrac{12 - 3(x-1)^2}{4}} - 1$, $y = -\sqrt{\dfrac{12 - 3(x-1)^2}{4}} - 1$, and $y = \dfrac{1}{4}(x - 2)^2 - 2$ in an $x \in [-4 \times 4]$, $y \in [-4 \times 4]$ window to see that the graphs intersect at two points.

40. a **D** Let $y = \log_x 2 = \log_3 x$. Converting to exponential form gives $x^y = 2$ and $3^y = x$. Substitute to get $3^{y^2} = 2$, which can be converted into $y^2 = \dfrac{\log 2}{\log 3} \approx 0.6309$. Thus, $y \approx \pm 0.7943$. Therefore, $3^{0.7943} = x \approx 2.393$ or $3^{-0.7943} = x \approx 0.4178$. Therefore, the sum of two x's is 2.81. [4.2].

41. i **B** The exponent on $(-3b^{-3})$ in the fifth term is 4. The exponent on $(2b^2)$ in the fifth term is $n - 4$. $(b^2)^{n-4} \cdot (b^{-3})^4 = b^0$. $2(n-4) + (-3)4 = 0$. $2n - 8 - 12 = 0$, $2n = 20$, and $n = 10$. [5.2].

42. a **C** $\dfrac{3 \sin 2\theta}{1 - \cos 2\theta} = \dfrac{1}{2}$ leads to $6 \sin 2\theta = 1 - \cos 2\theta$ and to $12 \cdot \sin \theta \cdot \cos \theta = 1 - (1 - 2 \sin^2 \theta)$ and to $6 \cdot \sin \theta \cdot \cos \theta - \sin^2 \theta = 0$. Solve to get $\sin \theta(6 \cos \theta - \sin \theta) = 0$, which implies that $\sin \theta = 0$ or $\tan \theta = 6$. Therefore, $\theta = 0°$, $180°$, or $80.5°$. Since $0°$ and $180°$ do not check back in the original equation, the only value of x is approximately $80.5°$. [3.5].

Graphing calculator (in degree mode because the answer choices are in degrees): Plot the graphs of $y = \dfrac{3 \sin 2x}{1 - \cos 2x}$ and $y = \dfrac{1}{2}$ in an $x \in [0 \times 180°]$, $y \in [-3 \times 3]$ window. Use the Trace and Zoom functions or the Intersect function to see that the graphs intersect only when $x \approx 80°$.

43. i **C** To get 2^{2x}, either one term must be zero in $f(x,y)$ or both must contain 2^x. Choice D gives $2 \cdot 2^{2x}$, which is wrong. The only other possibility is Choice C: $f(g(x), g(x)) = 2(2^x)^2 - (2^x)^2 = 2^{2x}$. [1.2, 1.5, 4.2].

44. i **A** From the geometric sequence, $b = a\left(\dfrac{a}{4}\right)$. From the arithmetic sequence, $2b - a = 12$ since $r = \dfrac{a}{4}$ and $d = b - a$. Substituting gives $2\left(\dfrac{a^2}{4}\right) -$

$a = 12$. Solving gives $a = 6$ or -4. Eliminate -4 since a is given to be positive. Substituting the 6 gives $2b - 6 = 12$, giving $b = 9$. Therefore, $b - a = 3$. [5.4].

45. a   D   Since $s = r\theta^R$, then $2.4 = r\theta$, which implies that $r = \dfrac{2.4}{\theta}$. $A = \dfrac{1}{2} r^2 \theta$, and so $14.3 = \dfrac{1}{2} r^2 \theta$, which implies that $r^2 = \dfrac{28.6}{\theta}$. Therefore, $\left(\dfrac{2.4}{\theta} \right)^2 = \dfrac{28.6}{\theta}$, which implies that $2.4^2 = 28.6\theta$. Therefore, $\theta = \dfrac{5.76}{28.6} \approx 0.2014^R \approx 11.5°$. [3.2].

46. i   C   List the first few terms:
$\dfrac{1}{2} - \dfrac{1}{1} + \dfrac{1}{3} - \dfrac{1}{2} + \dfrac{1}{4} - \dfrac{1}{3} + \cdots + \dfrac{1}{251} - \dfrac{1}{250}$. Every positive term pairs with a negative term except -1 and $\dfrac{1}{251}$, leaving a total of $\dfrac{250}{251}$. [5.4].

47. a   B   Because you are bisecting one side and trisecting another side, it is convenient to let the length of the sides be a number divisible by both 2 and 3. Let $AB = AD = 6$. Thus $BM = 2$, $MC = 4$, and $CN = ND = 3$. Let $\angle NAD = x$, so that, using right triangle NAD, $\tan x = \dfrac{3}{6} = 0.5$, which implies that $x = \tan^{-1} 0.5 \approx 26.6°$. Let $\angle MAB = y$, so that, using right triangle MAB, $\tan y = \dfrac{2}{6}$, which implies that $y = \text{Tan}^{-1} \dfrac{1}{3} \approx 18.4°$. Therefore, $\theta \approx 90° - 26.6° - 18.4° \approx 45°$. [3.7].

48. a   D $\text{Tan } 2x = \dfrac{2}{\tan 2x}$, which implies that $\tan^2 2x = 2$, $\tan 2x = \pm \sqrt{2}$, and thus $2x = \arctan \pm \sqrt{2}$. The reference angle for $2x \approx 54.7°$. Therefore, $2x = 54.74°$, $125.26°$, $234.74°$, $305.26°$, and so $x = 27.4°$, $62.6°$, $117.4°$, $152.6°$. [3.5].

TIP: Remember that, when solving an equation for a multiple angle ($2x$, $3x$, etc.), you must consider enough solutions (e.g., "extra" solutions $234.74°$ and $305.26°$) so that you will get all the values of x in the domain (e.g., $0° \leq x \leq 180°$).

Graphing calculator (in degree mode because the answer choices are in degrees): Plot the graph of $y = \tan 2x$ and $y = \dfrac{2}{\tan 2x}$ in an $x \in [0° \times 180°]$, $y \in [-3 \times 3]$ window. Use the Trace and Zoom functions or the Intersect function to see that there are four solutions: $27.4°$, $62.6°$, $117.4°$, $152.6°$.

49. i   B   If $z = x^2$, $y = x^2 + 1$ becomes $y = z + 1$. The graph of $y = z + 1$ will be a straight line, which rules out all answers but Choice B. [5.5, 2.2, 2.3].

Alternative Solution: From the table of values below, point (x, y) lies on the graph of $y = x^2 + 1$, and the set of points (x^2, y) lies on the graph we are looking for. Plotting a few points gives a straight line that indicates the answer is Choice B. [5.5].

x	0	1	2	3
x^2	0	1	4	9
y	1	2	5	10

50. a   E   Put your calculator in radian mode:
$5 * 3 = 5 \sin \dfrac{3}{5} \approx 2.823$. $2 * (5 * 3) = 2 * 2.823 \approx$ $2.823 \cos \dfrac{2}{2.823} \approx 2.14$. [5.9].

SELF-EVALUATION CHART FOR MODEL TEST 6

SUBJECT AREA	QUESTIONS	NUMBER OF RIGHT WRONG OMITTED

Mark correct answers with C, wrong answers with X, and omitted answers with O.

Algebra
(9 questions)
Review section

5	12	15	20	21	23	25	33	40
2.3	4.7	2.3	4.6	2.4	4.3	4.5	5.6	4.2

_____ _____ _____

Solid geometry
(4 questions)
Review section

4	17	19	26
5.5	5.5	5.5	5.5

_____ _____ _____

Coordinate geometry
(6 questions)
Review section

16	18	29	35	39	49
4.3	3.1	4.1	4.3	4.1	5.5

_____ _____ _____

Trigonometry
(10 questions)
Review section

22	28	32	34	36	37	42	45	47	48
4.7	3.4	3.5	3.6	3.5	3.4	3.5	3.2	3.7	3.5

_____ _____ _____

Functions
(12 questions)
Review section

1	3	6	7	8	10	13	14	24	30	31	43
1.3	4.5	1.2	1.2	1.2	2.3	1.2	1.2	4.3	2.3	2.4	1.2

_____ _____ _____

Miscellaneous
(9 questions)
Review section

2	9	11	27	38	41	44	46	50
5.8	5.1	5.3	5.7	5.4	5.2	5.4	5.4	5.9

_____ _____ _____

TOTALS   _____ _____ _____

Raw score = (number right) – $\frac{1}{4}$ (number wrong) = _____

Round your raw score to the nearest whole number = _____

Evaluate Your Performance
Model Test 6

Rating	Number Right
Excellent	41–50
Very good	33–40
Above average	25–32
Average	15–24
Below average	Below 15

ANSWER SHEET FOR MODEL TEST 7

Determine the correct answer for each question. Then, using a no. 2 pencil, blacken completely the oval containing the letter of your choice.

1. (A) (B) (C) (D) (E)
2. (A) (B) (C) (D) (E)
3. (A) (B) (C) (D) (E)
4. (A) (B) (C) (D) (E)
5. (A) (B) (C) (D) (E)
6. (A) (B) (C) (D) (E)
7. (A) (B) (C) (D) (E)
8. (A) (B) (C) (D) (E)
9. (A) (B) (C) (D) (E)
10. (A) (B) (C) (D) (E)
11. (A) (B) (C) (D) (E)
12. (A) (B) (C) (D) (E)
13. (A) (B) (C) (D) (E)
14. (A) (B) (C) (D) (E)
15. (A) (B) (C) (D) (E)
16. (A) (B) (C) (D) (E)
17. (A) (B) (C) (D) (E)

18. (A) (B) (C) (D) (E)
19. (A) (B) (C) (D) (E)
20. (A) (B) (C) (D) (E)
21. (A) (B) (C) (D) (E)
22. (A) (B) (C) (D) (E)
23. (A) (B) (C) (D) (E)
24. (A) (B) (C) (D) (E)
25. (A) (B) (C) (D) (E)
26. (A) (B) (C) (D) (E)
27. (A) (B) (C) (D) (E)
28. (A) (B) (C) (D) (E)
29. (A) (B) (C) (D) (E)
30. (A) (B) (C) (D) (E)
31. (A) (B) (C) (D) (E)
32. (A) (B) (C) (D) (E)
33. (A) (B) (C) (D) (E)
34. (A) (B) (C) (D) (E)

35. (A) (B) (C) (D) (E)
36. (A) (B) (C) (D) (E)
37. (A) (B) (C) (D) (E)
38. (A) (B) (C) (D) (E)
39. (A) (B) (C) (D) (E)
40. (A) (B) (C) (D) (E)
41. (A) (B) (C) (D) (E)
42. (A) (B) (C) (D) (E)
43. (A) (B) (C) (D) (E)
44. (A) (B) (C) (D) (E)
45. (A) (B) (C) (D) (E)
46. (A) (B) (C) (D) (E)
47. (A) (B) (C) (D) (E)
48. (A) (B) (C) (D) (E)
49. (A) (B) (C) (D) (E)
50. (A) (B) (C) (D) (E)

MODEL TEST

7

50 questions   1 hour

Tear out the preceding answer sheet. Decide which is the best choice by rounding your answer when appropriate. Blacken the corresponding space on the answer sheet. When finished, check your answers with those at the end of the test. For questions that you got wrong, note the sections containing the material that you must review. Also, if you do not fully understand how you arrived at some of the correct answers, you should review the appropriate sections. Finally, fill out the self-evaluation sheet on page 262 in order to pinpoint the topics that give you the most difficulty.

OFFICIAL COLLEGE BOARD DIRECTIONS

<u>Directions</u>: For each of the following problems, decide which is the BEST of the choices given. If the exact numerical value is not one of the choices, select the choice that best approximates this value. Then fill in the corresponding oval on the answer sheet.

Notes: (1) A calculator will be necessary for answering some (but not all) of the questions in this test. For each question you will have to decide whether or not you should use a calculator. The calculator you use must be at least a scientific calculator; programmable calculators and calculators that can display graphs are permitted.

(2) For some questions in this test you may have to decide whether your calculator should be in the radian mode or the degree mode.

(3) Figures that accompany problems in this test are intended to provide information useful in solving the problems. They are drawn as accurately as possible EXCEPT when it is stated in a specific problem that the figure is not drawn to scale. All figures lie in a plane unless otherwise indicated.

(4) Unless otherwise specified, the domain of any function f is assumed to be the set of all real numbers x for which $f(x)$ is a real number.

<u>Reference Information:</u> The following information is for your reference in answering some of the questions in this test.

Volume of a right circular cone with radius r and height h: $V = \dfrac{1}{3}\pi r^2 h$

Lateral area of a right circular cone with circumference of the base c and slant height ℓ: $S = \dfrac{1}{2}c\ell$

Volume of a sphere with radius r: $V = \dfrac{4}{3}\pi r^3$

Surface area of a sphere with radius r: $S = 4\pi r^2$

Volume of a pyramid with base area B and height h: $V = \dfrac{1}{3}Bh$

---

1. $2^{2/3} + 2^{4/3} =$

    (A) 1.6
    (B) 1.9
    (C) 3.2
    (D) 4.0
    (E) 4.1

2. In three dimensions, what is the set of all points for which $x = 0$?

    (A) the origin
    (B) a line parallel to the x-axis
    (C) the yz-plane
    (D) a plane containing the x-axis
    (E) the x-axis

3. Expressed with positive exponents only, $\dfrac{ab^{-1}}{a^{-1} - b^{-1}}$ is equivalent to

    (A) $\dfrac{a^2}{a - b}$

    (B) $\dfrac{a^2}{a - 1}$

    (C) $\dfrac{b - a}{ab}$

    (D) $\dfrac{a^2}{b - a}$

    (E) $\dfrac{1}{a - b}$

4. If $f(x) = \sqrt[3]{x}$ and $g(x) = x^3 + 8$, find $f \circ g(3)$.

    (A) 5
    (B) 3.3
    (C) 50.5
    (D) 11
    (E) 35

5. $x > \sin x$ for

    (A) all $x > 0$
    (B) all $x < 0$
    (C) all x for which $x \neq 0$
    (D) all x
    (E) all x for which $-\dfrac{\pi}{2} < x < 0$

6. The sum of the zeros of $f(x) = 3x^2 - 5$ is

    (A) 1.3
    (B) 1.8
    (C) 1.7
    (D) 3.3
    (E) 0

GO ON TO THE NEXT PAGE

7. If x varies inversely as the cube root of y, and if $x = 3$ and $y = 4$, the constant of variation is

   (A) 1.9
   (B) 4.8
   (C) 0.04
   (D) 192
   (E) 0.53

8. In the figure, c equals

   (A) 1
   (B) xy
   (C) $\dfrac{x}{y}$
   (D) $\dfrac{y}{x}$
   (E) -1

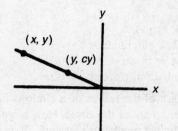

9. The plane $ax + by + cz = 12$ intersects the x-axis at $(2,0,0)$, the y-axis at $(0,-3,0)$, and the z-axis at $(0,0,-4)$. $a + b + c =$

   (A) 13
   (B) 7
   (C) 6
   (D) 0
   (E) -1

10. $P(x) = x^5 + x^4 - 2x^3 - x - 1$ has at most n positive zeros. Then $n =$

   (A) 0
   (B) 1
   (C) 2
   (D) 3
   (E) 5

11. Evaluate: $\left(\dfrac{64}{27}\right)^{-(2/3)}$.

   (A) 0.27
   (B) 0.56
   (C) 1.8
   (D) 2.7
   (E) 3.6

GO ON TO THE NEXT PAGE

12. If $f(x)$ is a linear function and $f(2) = 1$ and $f(4) = -2$, then $f(x) =$

   (A) $-\dfrac{3}{2}x + 4$

   (B) $\dfrac{3}{2}x - 2$

   (C) $-\dfrac{3}{2}x + 2$

   (D) $\dfrac{3}{2}x - 4$

   (E) $-\dfrac{2}{3}x + \dfrac{7}{3}$

13. The length of the radius of a circle is one-half the length of an arc of the circle. How large is the central angle that intercepts that arc?

   (A) $60°$
   (B) $120°$
   (C) π^R
   (D) 1^R
   (E) 2^R

14. If $f(x) = 2^x + 1$, then $f^{-1}(7) =$

   (A) 2.8
   (B) 3
   (C) 3.6
   (D) 2.4
   (E) 2.6

15. The statement "If it is green, then it is a turkey" is true. Which of the following is (are) also true?

   I. It is not green; therefore it is not a turkey.
   II. It is a turkey; therefore it is green.
   III. It is not a turkey; therefore it is not green.

   (A) only I
   (B) only II
   (C) only III
   (D) only I and III
   (E) only II and III

16. The 71st term of 30, 27, 24, 21, . . . , is

   (A) 180
   (B) −183
   (C) −180
   (D) 240
   (E) 5325

GO ON TO THE NEXT PAGE

17. If $0 < x < \dfrac{\pi}{2}$ and $\tan 5x = 3$, to the nearest tenth, what is the value of $\tan x$?

(A) 0.5
(B) 0.4
(C) 0.3
(D) 0.2
(E) 0.1

18. The value of $\cos\left[2 \cdot \text{Arcsin}\left(-\dfrac{3}{5}\right)\right]$ is

(A) $\dfrac{4}{5}$

(B) $\dfrac{9}{25}$

(C) $\dfrac{7}{25}$

(D) $-\dfrac{7}{25}$

(E) $-\dfrac{4}{5}$

19. A cylinder has a base radius of 2 and a height of 9. To the nearest whole number, by how much does the lateral area exceed the sum of the areas of the two bases?

(A) 101
(B) 96
(C) 88
(D) 81
(E) 75

20. If $\cos 67° = \tan x°$, then $x =$

(A) 0.4
(B) 6.8
(C) 21
(D) 29.3
(E) 7.8

21. $P(x) = x^3 + 18x - 30$ has a zero in the interval

(A) $(0, 0.5)$
(B) $(0.5, 1)$
(C) $(1, 1.5)$
(D) $(1.5, 2)$
(E) $(2, 2.5)$

22. The lengths of the sides of a triangle are 23, 32, and 37. To the nearest degree, what is the value of the largest angle?

(A) 83°
(B) 122°
(C) 128°
(D) 142°
(E) 71°

GO ON TO THE NEXT PAGE

23. A point, p, is 5 inches from a plane, X. The set of points 13 inches from p and 2 inches from X forms

(A) a circle parallel to X with a radius <13
(B) two circles parallel to X with radii >10
(C) a sphere with radius <13
(D) two lines parallel to X
(E) two planes parallel to X

24. Two cards are drawn from a regular deck of 52 cards. What is the probability that both will be 7s?

(A) 0.149
(B) 0.012
(C) 0.005
(D) 0.009
(E) 0.04

25. If $\sqrt{y} = 3.216$, then $\sqrt{10y} =$

(A) 321.6
(B) 32.16
(C) 10.17
(D) 5.67
(E) 4.23

26. What is the domain of the function $f(x) = \log\sqrt{2x^2 - 15}$?

(A) $-7.5 < x < 7.5$
(B) $x < -7.5$ or $x > 7.5$
(C) $x < -2.7$ or $x > 2.7$
(D) $x < -3.2$ or $x > 3.2$
(E) $x < 1.9$ or $x > 1.9$

27. The sum of the roots of $3x - 7x^{-1} + 3 = 0$ is

(A) $\dfrac{7}{3}$
(B) 1
(C) $-\dfrac{7}{3}$
(D) -1
(E) $\dfrac{3}{7}$

28. Let S be the sum of the first n terms of the arithmetic sequence 3, 7, 11, . . . , and let T be the sum of the first n terms of the arithmetic sequence 8, 10, 12, ... For $n > 1$, $S = T$ for

(A) no value of n
(B) one value of n
(C) two values of n
(D) three values of n
(E) four values of n

GO ON TO THE NEXT PAGE

29. On the interval $\left[-\dfrac{\pi}{4}, \dfrac{\pi}{4}\right]$, the function $f(x) =$ $\sqrt{1 + \sin^2 x}$ has a maximum value of

(A) 0.78
(B) 1
(C) 1.1
(D) 1.2
(E) 1.4

30. A point has rectangular coordinates (3,4). The polar coordinates are $(5, \theta)$. What is the value of θ?

(A) 37°
(B) 30°
(C) 51°
(D) 53°
(E) 60°

31. If $f(x) = x^2 - 4$, for what real number values of x will $f(f(x)) = 0$?

(A) 2.4
(B) ±2.4
(C) 2 or 6
(D) ±1.4 or ±2.4
(E) no values

32. If $f(x) = x \log x$ and $g(x) = 10^x$, then $g(f(2)) =$

(A) 24
(B) 17
(C) 4
(D) 2
(E) 0.6

33. If $f(x) = x^{\sqrt{x}}$, then $f\left(\sqrt{2}\right) =$

(A) 1.6
(B) 2.7
(C) 1.5
(D) 2.0
(E) 1.4

34. If $f(x) = 7x^2 + 11x - 13$, and $f(q) = 0$, one value of q is

(A) 2.3
(B) 0.79
(C) −13
(D) −0.79 + 1.11i
(E) 0

GO ON TO THE NEXT PAGE

35. (p,q) is called a *lattice point* if p and q are both integers. How many lattice points lie in the area between the two curves $x^2 + y^2 = 9$ and $x^2 + y^2 - 6x + 5 = 0$?

    (A) 0
    (B) 1
    (C) 2
    (D) 3
    (E) 4

36. If $\sin A = \dfrac{3}{5}$, $90° < A < 180°$, $\cos B = \dfrac{1}{3}$, and $270° < B < 360°$, the value of $\sin (A + B)$ is

    (A) −0.33
    (B) 0.73
    (C) −0.83
    (D) −0.55
    (E) 0.95

37. If $f(x) = 2x + 5$ and $|f(x) - f(2)| < 1$, then $|x - 2| < L$. The smallest value of L is

    (A) 1
    (B) 7
    (C) $\dfrac{3}{2}$
    (D) $\dfrac{1}{2}$
    (E) There is no smallest value of L.

38. For what value(s) of k is $x^2 - kx + k$ divisible by $x - k$?

    (A) only 0
    (B) only 0 or $-\dfrac{1}{2}$
    (C) only 1
    (D) any value of k
    (E) no value of k

39. If the graphs of $x^2 = 4(y + 9)$ and $x + ky = 6$ intersect on the x-axis, then $k =$

    (A) 0
    (B) 6
    (C) −6
    (D) no real number
    (E) any real number

40. The length of the latus rectum of the hyperbola whose equation is $x^2 - 4y^2 = 16$ is

    (A) 1
    (B) $\sqrt{20}$
    (C) 16
    (D) $2\sqrt{20}$
    (E) 2

41. If $f_n = \begin{cases} \dfrac{f_{n-1}}{2} & \text{when } f_{n-1} \text{ is an even number} \\ 3 \cdot f_{n-1} + 1 & \text{when } f_{n-1} \text{ is an odd number} \end{cases}$

   and $f_1 = 3$, then $f_5 =$

   (A) 1
   (B) 2
   (C) 4
   (D) 8
   (E) 16

42. If the operation $*$ is defined on the set of ordered triples as follows, $(a,b,c) * (x,y,z) = (ax, b + y, cz)$, which of the following represents the identity element for this operation?

   (A) $(0,0,0)$
   (B) $(1,1,1)$
   (C) $(1,0,1)$
   (D) $(0,1,0)$
   (E) $(1,1,0)$

43. The amount of heat received by a body varies inversely as the square of its distance from the heat source. In comparison, how much heat is received by a body that is 3 times as far from the heat source?

   (A) 3 times as much
   (B) 9 times as much
   (C) $\dfrac{1}{3}$ as much
   (D) $\dfrac{1}{9}$ as much
   (E) $\dfrac{1}{6}$ as much

44. How many positive integers are there in the solution set of $\dfrac{x}{x-2} > 5$?

   (A) 0
   (B) 2
   (C) 4
   (D) 5
   (E) an infinite number

45. During the year 1995 the price of ABC Company stock increased by 125%, and during the year 1996 the price of the stock increased by 80%. Over the period from January 1, 1995, through December 31, 1996, by what percentage did the price of ABC Company stock rise?

   (A) 103%
   (B) 205%
   (C) 305%
   (D) 405%
   (E) 505%

USE THIS SPACE FOR SCRATCH WORK

GO ON TO THE NEXT PAGE

46. If $x_0 = 3$ and $x_{n+1} = x_n \sqrt{x_n + 1}$, then $x_3 =$

(A) 15.9
(B) 31.7
(C) 173.9
(D) 44.9
(E) 65.2

47. When the smaller root of the equation $3x^2 + 4x - 1 = 0$ is subtracted from the larger root, the result is

(A) 0.7
(B) 1.8
(C) 2.0
(D) 1.3
(E) −1.3

48. Each of a group of 50 students studies either French or Spanish but not both, and either math or physics but not both. If 16 students study French and math, 26 study Spanish, and 12 study physics, how many study both Spanish and physics?

(A) 5
(B) 6
(C) 8
(D) 4
(E) 10

49. What is the equation of the set of points situated in a plane so that the distance between any point and (0,0) is twice the distance between that point and the x-axis?

(A) $3x^2 - y^2 = 0$
(B) $x^2 - 3y^2 = 0$
(C) $x^2 + y^2 - 2y = 0$
(D) $x^2 + y^2 - 2x = 0$
(E) $4x^2 + 3y^2 = 0$

50. $\text{Sin}^{-1}(\cos 100°) =$

(A) 1.0
(B) 1.4
(C) 0.2
(D) −1.4
(E) −0.2

USE THIS SPACE FOR SCRATCH WORK

ANSWER KEY

1. E	6. E	11. B	16. C	21. C	26. C	31. D	36. E	41. D	46. E
2. C	7. B	12. A	17. C	22. A	27. D	32. C	37. D	42. C	47. B
3. D	8. D	13. E	18. C	23. B	28. B	33. C	38. A	43. D	48. D
4. B	9. E	14. E	19. C	24. C	29. D	34. B	39. E	44. A	49. B
5. A	10. B	15. C	20. C	25. C	30. D	35. D	40. E	45. C	50. E

ANSWER EXPLANATIONS

In these solutions the following notation is used:

a: active—Calculator use is necessary or, at a minimum, extremely helpful.

n: neutral—Answers can be found without a calculator, but a calculator may help.

i: inactive—Calculator use is not helpful and may even be a hindrance.

1. a   E $10^{2/3} \approx 1.59$. $10^{4/3} \approx 2.52$. Therefore, $10^{2/3} + 10^{4/3} \approx 1.59 + 2.52 \approx 4.1$. [4.2].

2. i   C   When $x = 0$, y and z can be any value. Therefore, any point in the yz-plane is a possible member of the set. [5.5].

3. i   D $\dfrac{\dfrac{a}{b}}{\dfrac{1}{a} - \dfrac{1}{b}} \cdot \dfrac{ab}{ab} = \dfrac{a^2}{b - a}$. [4.2].

4. a   B $f \circ g(3) = f(g(3)) = \sqrt[3]{3^3 + 8} = \sqrt[3]{35} \approx 3.27106 = 3.3$ [1.2].

5. n   A   Sketch the graph of $y = x$ and $y = \sin x$, and the answer is obvious. [3.4].

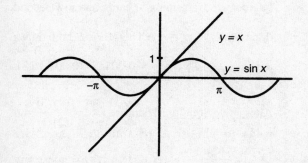

 Graphing calculator: Plot the graphs of $y = x$ and $y = \sin x$ in an $x \in [-5,5]$, $y \in [-5,5]$ window. Use the Zoom function at the origin to see that $x > \sin x$ when $x > 0$.

6. n   E $3x^2 - 5 = 0$. Then $x^2 = \dfrac{5}{3}$, and $x = \pm\sqrt{\dfrac{5}{3}}$.

Sum $= \sqrt{\dfrac{5}{3}} + \left(-\sqrt{\dfrac{5}{3}}\right) = 0$. [2.3].

Calculator: $\sqrt{\dfrac{5}{3}} \approx 1.29$

Sum $= 1.29 + (-1.29) = 0$. [2.3].

<u>Alternative Solution</u>: The sum of the zeros of a quadratic function $= -\dfrac{b}{a} = -\dfrac{0}{3} = 0$.

Graphing calculator: Plot the graph of $y = 3x^2 - 5$ in an $x \in [-5,5]$, $y \in [-5,5]$ window. Use the Trace and Zoom functions or the Root, Zero, or Solve function to see that the two zeros are symmetric about the origin; thus, their sum is 0.

7. n   B $(x)\left(\sqrt[3]{y}\right) = k$. $(3)\left(\sqrt[3]{4}\right) = k \approx 3 \cdot (1.5) = 4.5 \approx 4.8$. [5.6].

Calculator: $k = 3\sqrt[3]{4} \approx 3(1.587) \approx 4.762203 \approx 4.8$.

8. i   D   The slope of the line through (x,y) and $(0,0) = \dfrac{y}{x}$. The slope of the line through (y,cy) and $(0,0) = \dfrac{cy}{y} = c$. The two slopes are equal, and so $c = \dfrac{y}{x}$. [2.2].

9. i   E   Substituting the coordinates of the three points into the equation gives $2a = 12$, $-3b = 12$, and $-4c = 12$. $a + b + c = 6 - 4 - 3 = -1$. [5.5].

10. i   B   By Descartes' rule of signs, the one sign change in $P(x)$ implies there is exactly one positive real zero. [2.4].

11. n   B $\left(\dfrac{64}{27}\right)^{-(2/3)} = \left(\dfrac{27}{64}\right)^{2/3} = \left(\dfrac{3^3}{4^3}\right)^{2/3} = \dfrac{3^2}{4^2}$

$= \dfrac{9}{16} \approx 0.56$. [4.2].

Calculator: $\left(\dfrac{64}{27}\right)^{-2/3} \approx (2.37)^{-2/3} = 0.56.$

12. n **A** The slope of $f(x) = \dfrac{-2-1}{4-2} = \dfrac{-3}{2}$. Using the point-slope form, $f(x) - 1 = \dfrac{-3}{2}(x-2)$. Therefore,

$$f(x) = \dfrac{-3}{2}x + 4. \ [2.2].$$

13. i **E** $s = r\theta.\ 2r = r\theta.\ \theta = 2^R.\ [3.2].$

14. a **E** $f^{-1}(7)$ means "Find x when $2^x + 1 = 7$." $2^x = 6,\ x \log 2 = \log 6$. Therefore, $x = \dfrac{\log 6}{\log 2} \approx \dfrac{0.778}{0.301} \approx 2.6.\ [4.2].$

 Graphing calculator: Plot the graphs of $y = 2^x + 1$ and $y = 7$ in an $x \in [-10,10],\ y \in [-10,10]$ window. Since the value of $f^{-1}(7)$ is the same as the value of x that makes $2^x + 1 = 7$, use the Trace and Zoom functions or the Intersect function to see that x is approximately 2.6 at the point where the graphs intersect.

15. i **C** III is the contrapositive of the given true statement, and so III is true also. [5.7].

16. i **C** In an arithmetic sequence with $t_i = 30$, and $d = -3,\ t_{71} = 30 + 70(-3) = -180.\ [5.4].$

17. a **C** Put your calculator in radian mode: $5x = \text{Tan}^{-1}\ 3 \approx 1.249.\ x \approx 0.2498$. Therefore, $\tan x = 0.255139 \approx 0.3.\ [3.1].$

 Graphing calculator (in radian mode): Plot the graphs of $y = \tan 5x$ and $y = 3$ in an $x \in [0, \dfrac{\pi}{2}]$, $y \in [-5,5]$ window. Use the Trace and Zoom functions or the Intersect function to see that the graphs intersect when x is approximately 0.25. Therefore, $\tan 0.25 = 0.26 = 0.3$.

18. n **C** Let $\theta = \text{Arcsin}\left(-\dfrac{3}{5}\right)$ so that $\sin \theta = -\dfrac{3}{5}$. The problem becomes $\cos 2\theta = 1 - 2 \sin^2 \theta = 1 - 2\left(-\dfrac{3}{5}\right)^2 = \dfrac{7}{25}.\ [3.6].$

 Calculator (in degree mode):
$$\cos\left[2 \text{ Arcsin}\left(-\dfrac{3}{5}\right)\right] \approx \cos\left[2 \cdot (-36.9°)\right] \approx$$
$$\cos 73.8° \approx 0.28 = \dfrac{28}{100} = \dfrac{7}{25}.$$

19. a **C** Area of one base $= \pi r^2 = 4\pi$. Lateral area $= 2\pi r h = 36\pi$. Lateral area $-$ two bases $= 36\pi - 8\pi = 28\pi \approx 87.96 \approx 88.\ [5.5, 6.5].$

20. a **C** Put your calculator in degree mode: $\cos 67° \approx 0.3907\ \text{Tan}^{-1}\ (0.3907) \approx 21.\ [3.1].$

21. n **C** Choose integer values first because they are easier to work with. $P(0) = -30.\ P(1) = -11.$ $P(2) = 8 + 36 - 30 = 14$. Therefore, a zero lies between 1 and 2. Check $P(1.5)$ by hand or with the aid of your calculator. $P(1.5) = (1.5)^3 + 18(1.5) - 30 = 3.375 + 27 - 30 = 0.375$. Therefore, since $P(1) < 0$ and $P(1.5) > 0$, a zero lies in the interval $(1, 1.5).\ [2.4].$

 Graphing calculator: Plot the graph of $y = x^3 + 18x - 30$ in an $x \in [-5,5],\ y \in [-5,5]$ window. Use the Trace and Zoom functions to see that one of the zeros is between 1 and 1.5.

22. a **A** The angle opposite the 37 side (call it $\angle A$) is the largest angle. By the law of cosines, $37^2 = 23^2 + 32^2 - 2(23)(32) \cos A.$

$$\text{Cos } A = \dfrac{37^2 - 23^2 - 32^2}{-2(23)(32)} \approx \dfrac{-184}{-1472} = 0.125.$$
Therefore, $A = \text{Cos}^{-1}\ (0.125) \approx 83°.\ [3.7].$

23. i **B** The set of points 13 inches from p is a sphere with center at p and radius 13 inches. The set of points 2 inches from X consists of two planes parallel to X, one above and one below X. Since the radius, 13, is greater than $5 + 2$, the two sets intersect in two circles. [5.5].

24. n **C** There are four 7s in a deck, and so P(first draw is a 7) $= \dfrac{4}{52} = \dfrac{1}{13}$. There are now only three 7s among the remaining 51 cards, and so P(second draw is a 7) $= \dfrac{3}{51} = \dfrac{1}{17}$. Therefore, P(both draws are 7s) $= \dfrac{1}{13} \cdot \dfrac{1}{17} = \dfrac{1}{221} \approx 0.00452 \approx 0.005.\ [5.3].$

<u>Alternative Solution:</u> There are $\binom{4}{2} = \dfrac{(4)(3)}{(2)(1)} = 6$ ways to choose 2 of four 7s. There are $\binom{52}{2} = \dfrac{(52)(51)}{(2)(1)} = (26)(51)$ ways to choose any 2 of the 52 cards. P(both cards are 7s) $= \dfrac{6}{(26)(51)} \approx \dfrac{6}{1326} \approx 0.00452 \approx 0.005.$

25. n C Since $\sqrt{y} = 3.216$, $y \approx 10$, and $10y \approx 100$, and so $\sqrt{10y} \approx 10$. [4.2].

Calculator: $\sqrt{y} = 3.216$ implies that $y \approx 10.34$. Thus, $10y \approx 103.4$ and $\sqrt{10y} = \sqrt{103.4} \approx 10.17$.

26. n C $2x^2 - 15 > 0$. $2x^2 > 15$. $x^2 > \dfrac{15}{2}$. Therefore, $x > \sqrt{7.5}$ or $x < -\sqrt{7.5}$. Since $\sqrt{7.5} \approx 2.7$, the answer is Choice C. [2.5].

Graphing calculator: Plot the graph of $y = \log \sqrt{2x^2 - 15}$ in an $x \in [-5,5]$, $y \in [-5,5]$ window. Use the Trace and Zoom functions to see that the endpoints of the graph are at approximately ± 2.7. Therefore, Choice C is correct.

27. n D $3x - \dfrac{7}{x} + 3 = 0$ is equivalent to $3x^2 + 3x - 7 = 0$ and $x \neq 0$. The sum of the roots $= -\dfrac{b}{a} = \dfrac{-3}{3} = -1$. [2.3, 4.2].

Graphing calculator: Plot the graph of $y = 3x - 7x^{-1} + 3$ in an $x \in [-10,10]$, $y \in [-10,10]$ window. Use the Trace and Zoom functions or the Root, Zero, or Solve function to see that the zeros are approximately -2 and 1. Therefore, their sum is approximately -1.

28. i B $S = \dfrac{n}{2}[6 + (n-1)4] = T = \dfrac{n}{2}[16 + (n-1)2]$. Solving for n gives 6. [5.4].

29. a D On the interval $\left[-\dfrac{\pi}{4}, \dfrac{\pi}{4} \right]$ the maximum value of $|\sin x| = \dfrac{\sqrt{2}}{2}$. Therefore, the maximum value of $f(x) = \sqrt{1 + \dfrac{1}{2}} = \sqrt{\dfrac{3}{2}} \approx 1.2474 \approx 1.2$. [3.4].

Graphing calculator (in radian mode): Plot the graph of $y = \sqrt{1 + (\sin x)^2}$ in an $x \in \left[-\dfrac{\pi}{4}, \dfrac{\pi}{4} \right]$, $y \in [0,3]$ window. Use the Trace and Zoom functions or the Max function to see that the maximum value is approximately 1.2 at either end of the interval.

30. a D $\sin \theta = \dfrac{4}{5}$.

Therefore, $\theta = \sin^{-1}\left(\dfrac{4}{5} \right) \approx 53°$.

[4.7, 3.6].

31. n D $f(f(x)) = (f(x))^2 - 4 = (x^2 - 4)^2 - 4 = 0$. $(x^2 - 4)^2 = 4$. $x^2 - 4 = \pm 2$. $x^2 = 4 \pm 2 = 6$ or 2. $x = \pm\sqrt{6} \approx \pm 2.4$ or $\pm\sqrt{2} \approx \pm 1.4$. [1.2, 2.3].

Graphing calculator: $f(f(x)) = (x^2 - 4)^2 - 4$. Plot the graph of $y = (x^2 - 4)^2 - 4$ in an $x \in [-10,10]$, $y \in [-10,10]$ window. Use the Trace and Zoom functions or the Root, Zero, or Solve function to see that the zeros are at approximately ± 1.4 and ± 2.4.

32. n C $f(2) = 2 \log 2$. $g(f(2)) = 10^{2 \log 2} = 10^{\log 4} = 4$. [4.2].

Calculator: $f(2) = 2\log 2 \approx 0.602$. Thus, $g[f(2)] \approx g(0.602) \approx 10^{0.602} \approx 4$.

33. a C $f\left(\sqrt{2}\right) = \left(\sqrt{2}\right)^{\sqrt{2}} \approx \left(\sqrt{2}\right)^{1.19} \approx 1.5$. [4.2].

Graphing calculator: Plot the graph of $y = x^{\sqrt{x}}$ in an $x \in [-10,10]$, $y \in [-10,10]$ window. Since $\sqrt{2} \approx 1.414$, use the Trace and Zoom functions to see that the value of y is approximately 1.5 when x is approximately 1.414.

34. a B $f(q) = 7q^2 + 11q - 13 = 0$. Use the general quadratic formula to get

$$q = \frac{-11 \pm \sqrt{121 + (28)(13)}}{14} = \frac{-11 \pm \sqrt{485}}{14}$$
$$\approx \frac{-11 \pm 22.02}{14}.$$

$$q \approx \frac{-11 + 22.02}{14} \approx 0.79. \quad [2.3].$$

Graphing calculator: Plot the graph of $y = 7x^2 + 11x - 13$ in an $x \in [-10,10]$, $y \in [-10,10]$ window. Use the Trace and Zoom functions or the Root, Zero, or Solve function to see that one of the zeros is approximately 0.79.

35. n D Sketch the graphs. It is obvious that points $(2,-1)$, $(2,0)$, $(2,1)$ are within the required area. Check $(2,2)$ by substituting into each equation to see whether this point is in the region. You see that it is not because the second equation gives a value greater than zero. [5.9].

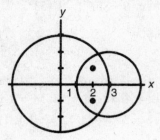

Graphing calculator: Turn on the grid points in your graphing window. Plot the graphs of $y = \sqrt{9 - x^2}$, $y = -\sqrt{9 - x^2}$, $y = \sqrt{-x^2 + 6x - 5}$, and $y = -\sqrt{-x^2 + 6x - 5}$ in an $x \in [-10,10]$, $y \in [-10,10]$ window. Use the Zoom function to examine the region of intersection to see that there are three lattice points.

36. a   E   Using $\sin^2 x + \cos^2 x = 1$ gives $\sin A = \dfrac{3}{5}$, which implies $\cos A = -\dfrac{4}{5}$, and $\cos B = \dfrac{1}{3}$, which implies $\sin B = -\dfrac{2\sqrt{2}}{3}$. $\sin(A + B) = \sin A \cdot \cos B + \cos A \cdot \sin B = \dfrac{3 + 8\sqrt{2}}{15} \approx \dfrac{14.3}{15} \approx 0.95$. [3.5].

Calculator: With your calculator in degree mode: $\sin^{-1} \dfrac{3}{5} \approx 36.87°$, and so $A \approx 180° - 36.87° = 143.13°$, and $\cos^{-1} \dfrac{1}{3} \approx 70.53°$, and so $B \approx 360° - 70.53° = 289.47°$. Therefore, $\sin(A + B) = \sin 432.60° \approx 0.95$.

37. i   D $|f(x) - f(2)| < 1$ implies $|(2x + 5) - (4 + 5)| = |2x - 4| = 2|x - 2| < 1$. Therefore, $|x - 2| < \dfrac{1}{2}$. [2.5, 4.3].

38. i   A   Using the factor theorem, substitute k for x and set the result equal to zero. Then $k^2 - k^2 + k = 0$, and $k = 0$. [2.4, 2.3].

39. i   E   If the graphs intersect on the x-axis, the value of y must be zero. Since the value of y is zero, it does not matter what k is. [2.3].

40. i   E $a^2 = 16$. $b^2 = 4$. Latus rectum $= \dfrac{2b^2}{a} = 2$. [4.1].

<u>Alternative Solution:</u> $\dfrac{x^2}{16} - \dfrac{y^2}{4} = 1$. The distance between the center and a focus $= c = \sqrt{16 + 4} = \sqrt{20}$. Substituting for x gives $20 - 4y^2 = 16$, which leads to $y^2 = 1$. Therefore, $y = \pm 1$, and the length of the latus rectum $= 2|y| = 2$.

41. i   D

n	1	2	3	4	5
f_n	3	10	5	16	8

[5.4].

42. i   C   The result $(ax, b + y, cz)$ must equal (a, b, c). Therefore, the identity element must be $(1, 0, 1)$. [5.9].

43. i   D $H_1 d_1^2 = H_2 d_2^2$. $d_2 = 3d$. $H_1 d_1^2 = H_2 (9d_1^2)$. Therefore, $H_2 = \dfrac{1}{9} H_1$. [5.6].

44. n   A   Consider the equation $\dfrac{x}{x - 2} = 5$. $x \neq 2$. $x = 5x - 10$. $x = \dfrac{5}{2}$.

Substituting numbers into the regions of the number line indicated by the equation shows the solution of the inequality contains *no* integers. [2.5].

Graphing calculator: Plot the graphs of $y = \dfrac{x}{x - 2}$ and $y = 5$ in an $x \in [-5, 5]$, $y \in [-5, 5]$ window. Use the Trace and Zoom functions or the Intersect function to see that the graphs intersect when x is approximately 2.5. Since there is a vertical asymptote at $x = 2$, there are no integer values of x in the interval where $\dfrac{x}{x - 2} > 5$.

45. n   C   Let the starting price of the stock be $100. During the first year a 125% increase means a $125 increase to $225. During the second year an 80% increase of the $225 stock price means a $180 increase to $405. Thus, over the 2-year period the price increased $305 from the original $100 starting price. Therefore, the price increased 305%. [5.9].

46. a   E   Let $n = 0$. $x_{0+1} = x_0 \sqrt{x_0 + 1} = 3\sqrt{4} = 6 = x_1$. Let $n = 1$. $x_{1+1} = x_1 \sqrt{x_1 + 1} = 6\sqrt{7} = x_2$. Let $n = 2$. $x_{2+1} = x_2 \sqrt{x_2 + 1} = 6\sqrt{7}\sqrt{6\sqrt{7} + 1} = x_3 \approx 15.87\sqrt{16.87} \approx (15.87)(4.108) \ 65.2$. [5.4].

47. n   B   Use the general quadratic formula:
$$x = \frac{-4 \pm \sqrt{16 + 12}}{6} = \frac{-2 \pm \sqrt{7}}{3}. \ \frac{-2 + \sqrt{7}}{3} - \frac{-2 - \sqrt{7}}{3} = \frac{2\sqrt{7}}{3} \approx \frac{2 \cdot (2.7)}{3} = 1.8.$$ [2.3].

48. i   **D**

	F	S
P	c	a
M	16	b

$a + b + c + 16 = 50$, $a + b = 26$, $a + c = 12$. Subtracting the first two equations and then the first and third gives $c = 8$, $b = 22$, and $a = 4$. Four students take both Spanish and physics. [5.9].

49. i   **B**   If (x, y) represents any such point, $|y|$ represents the distance between it and the x-axis.

$d = \sqrt{(x-0)^2 + (y-0)^2} = \sqrt{x^2 + y^2}$. Therefore, $\sqrt{x^2 + y^2} = 2|y|$. Squaring both sides and simplifying gives $x^2 - 3y^2 = 0$. [4.1].

50. a   **E**   Put your calculator in degree mode: $\text{Sin}^{-1}(\cos 100°) \approx \text{Sin}^{-1}(-0.1736) \approx 10°$. Convert your calculator to radian mode to get $10° \approx -0.1745 \approx -0.2$ radians. [3.6].

SELF-EVALUATION CHART FOR MODEL TEST 7

SUBJECT AREA	QUESTIONS	NUMBER OF RIGHT WRONG OMITTED

Mark correct answers with C, wrong answers with X, and omitted answers with O.

Algebra

(9 questions)

Review section

1	3	7	11	25	26	27	44	47
4.2	4.2	5.6	4.2	4.2	2.5	2.3	2.5	2.3

___ ___ ___

Solid geometry

(4 questions)

Review section

2	9	19	23
5.5	5.5	5.5	5.5

___ ___ ___

Coordinate geometry

(6 questions)

Review section

8	12	35	39	40	49
2.2	2.2	5.9	2.3	4.1	4.1

___ ___ ___

Trigonometry

(10 questions)

Review section

5	13	17	18	20	22	29	30	36	50
3.4	3.2	3.1	3.6	3.1	3.7	3.4	3.6	3.5	3.6

___ ___ ___

Functions

(12 questions)

Review section

4	6	10	14	21	31	32	33	34	37	38	46
1.2	2.3	2.4	4.2	2.4	1.2	4.2	4.2	2.3	2.5	2.4	5.4

___ ___ ___

Miscellaneous

(9 questions)

Review section

15	16	24	28	41	42	43	45	48
5.7	5.4	5.3	5.4	5.3	5.9	5.6	5.9	5.9

___ ___ ___

TOTALS   ___ ___ ___

Raw score = (number right) $-\frac{1}{4}$ (number wrong) = _____

Round your raw score to the nearest whole number = _____

Evaluate Your Performance
Model Test 7

Rating	Number Right
Excellent	41–50
Very good	33–40
Above average	25–32
Average	15–24
Below average	Below 15

ANSWER SHEET FOR MODEL TEST 8

Determine the correct answer for each question. Then, using a no. 2 pencil, blacken completely the oval containing the letter of your choice.

1. Ⓐ Ⓑ Ⓒ Ⓓ Ⓔ
2. Ⓐ Ⓑ Ⓒ Ⓓ Ⓔ
3. Ⓐ Ⓑ Ⓒ Ⓓ Ⓔ
4. Ⓐ Ⓑ Ⓒ Ⓓ Ⓔ
5. Ⓐ Ⓑ Ⓒ Ⓓ Ⓔ
6. Ⓐ Ⓑ Ⓒ Ⓓ Ⓔ
7. Ⓐ Ⓑ Ⓒ Ⓓ Ⓔ
8. Ⓐ Ⓑ Ⓒ Ⓓ Ⓔ
9. Ⓐ Ⓑ Ⓒ Ⓓ Ⓔ
10. Ⓐ Ⓑ Ⓒ Ⓓ Ⓔ
11. Ⓐ Ⓑ Ⓒ Ⓓ Ⓔ
12. Ⓐ Ⓑ Ⓒ Ⓓ Ⓔ
13. Ⓐ Ⓑ Ⓒ Ⓓ Ⓔ
14. Ⓐ Ⓑ Ⓒ Ⓓ Ⓔ
15. Ⓐ Ⓑ Ⓒ Ⓓ Ⓔ
16. Ⓐ Ⓑ Ⓒ Ⓓ Ⓔ
17. Ⓐ Ⓑ Ⓒ Ⓓ Ⓔ

18. Ⓐ Ⓑ Ⓒ Ⓓ Ⓔ
19. Ⓐ Ⓑ Ⓒ Ⓓ Ⓔ
20. Ⓐ Ⓑ Ⓒ Ⓓ Ⓔ
21. Ⓐ Ⓑ Ⓒ Ⓓ Ⓔ
22. Ⓐ Ⓑ Ⓒ Ⓓ Ⓔ
23. Ⓐ Ⓑ Ⓒ Ⓓ Ⓔ
24. Ⓐ Ⓑ Ⓒ Ⓓ Ⓔ
25. Ⓐ Ⓑ Ⓒ Ⓓ Ⓔ
26. Ⓐ Ⓑ Ⓒ Ⓓ Ⓔ
27. Ⓐ Ⓑ Ⓒ Ⓓ Ⓔ
28. Ⓐ Ⓑ Ⓒ Ⓓ Ⓔ
29. Ⓐ Ⓑ Ⓒ Ⓓ Ⓔ
30. Ⓐ Ⓑ Ⓒ Ⓓ Ⓔ
31. Ⓐ Ⓑ Ⓒ Ⓓ Ⓔ
32. Ⓐ Ⓑ Ⓒ Ⓓ Ⓔ
33. Ⓐ Ⓑ Ⓒ Ⓓ Ⓔ
34. Ⓐ Ⓑ Ⓒ Ⓓ Ⓔ

35. Ⓐ Ⓑ Ⓒ Ⓓ Ⓔ
36. Ⓐ Ⓑ Ⓒ Ⓓ Ⓔ
37. Ⓐ Ⓑ Ⓒ Ⓓ Ⓔ
38. Ⓐ Ⓑ Ⓒ Ⓓ Ⓔ
39. Ⓐ Ⓑ Ⓒ Ⓓ Ⓔ
40. Ⓐ Ⓑ Ⓒ Ⓓ Ⓔ
41. Ⓐ Ⓑ Ⓒ Ⓓ Ⓔ
42. Ⓐ Ⓑ Ⓒ Ⓓ Ⓔ
43. Ⓐ Ⓑ Ⓒ Ⓓ Ⓔ
44. Ⓐ Ⓑ Ⓒ Ⓓ Ⓔ
45. Ⓐ Ⓑ Ⓒ Ⓓ Ⓔ
46. Ⓐ Ⓑ Ⓒ Ⓓ Ⓔ
47. Ⓐ Ⓑ Ⓒ Ⓓ Ⓔ
48. Ⓐ Ⓑ Ⓒ Ⓓ Ⓔ
49. Ⓐ Ⓑ Ⓒ Ⓓ Ⓔ
50. Ⓐ Ⓑ Ⓒ Ⓓ Ⓔ

MODEL TEST

8

50 questions

Tear out the preceding answer sheet. Decide which is the best choice by rounding your answer when appropriate. Blacken the corresponding space on the answer sheet. When finished, check your answers with those at the end of the test. For questions that you got wrong, note the sections containing the material that you must review. Also, if you do not fully understand how you arrived at some of the correct answers, you should review the appropriate sections. Finally, fill out the self-evaluation sheet on page 281 in order to pinpoint the topics that give you the most difficulty.

OFFICIAL COLLEGE BOARD DIRECTIONS

<u>Directions</u>: For each of the following problems, decide which is the BEST of the choices given. If the exact numerical value is not one of the choices, select the choice that best approximates this value. Then fill in the corresponding oval on the answer sheet.

Notes: (1) A calculator will be necessary for answering some (but not all) of the questions in this test. For each question you will have to decide whether or not you should use a calculator. The calculator you use must be at least a scientific calculator; programmable calculators and calculators that can display graphs are permitted.

(2) For some questions in this test you may have to decide whether your calculator should be in the radian mode or the degree mode.

(3) Figures that accompany problems in this test are intended to provide information useful in solving the problems. They are drawn as accurately as possible EXCEPT when it is stated in a specific problem that the figure is not drawn to scale. All figures lie in a plane unless otherwise indicated.

(4) Unless otherwise specified, the domain of any function f is assumed to be the set of all real numbers x for which $f(x)$ is a real number.

<u>Reference Information:</u> The following information is for your reference in answering some of the questions in this test.

Volume of a right circular cone with radius r and height h: $V = \frac{1}{3}\pi r^2 h$

Lateral area of a right circular cone with circumference of the base c and slant height ℓ: $S = \frac{1}{2}c\ell$

Volume of a sphere with radius r: $V = \frac{4}{3}\pi r^3$

Surface area of a sphere with radius r: $S = 4\pi r^2$

Volume of a pyramid with base area B and height h: $V = \frac{1}{3}Bh$

---

1. In the diagram, the circle has a radius of 1 and center at the origin. If the point F represents a complex number, $a + bi$, which of the other points could represent the conjugate of F?

   (A) A
   (B) B
   (C) C
   (D) D
   (E) E

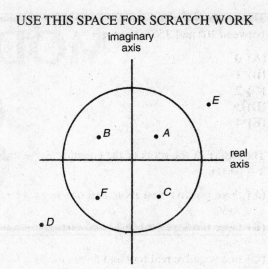

2. For what values of x and y is $|x - y| \le |y - x|$?

   (A) $x < y$
   (B) $y < x$
   (C) $x > 0$ and $y < 0$
   (D) for no value of x and y
   (E) for all values of x and y

3. If (a,b) is a solution of the system of equations $\begin{cases} 2x - y = 7 \\ x + y = 8 \end{cases}$, then the difference, $a - b$, equals

   (A) 0
   (B) 2
   (C) 4
   (D) −12
   (E) −10

4. If $f(x) = x - 1$, $g(x) = 3x$, and $h(x) = \dfrac{5}{x}$, then $f^{-1}(g(h(5))) =$

   (A) 4
   (B) 2
   (C) $\dfrac{5}{12}$
   (D) $\dfrac{5}{6}$
   (E) $\dfrac{1}{2}$

5. A sphere is inscribed in a cube. The ratio of the volume of the sphere to the volume of the cube is

   (A) 1:2
   (B) 0.52:1
   (C) 1:3.1
   (D) 0.24:1
   (E) 0.79:1

GO ON TO THE NEXT PAGE

6. The equation $\sec^2 x - \tan x - 1 = 0$ has n solutions between $10°$ and $350°$. Then $n =$

   (A) 0
   (B) 1
   (C) 2
   (D) 3
   (E) 4

7. The nature of the roots of the equation $3x^4 + 4x^3 + x - 1 = 0$ is

   (A) three positive real roots and one negative real root
   (B) three negative real roots and one positive real root
   (C) one negative real root and three complex roots
   (D) one positive real root, one negative real root, and two complex roots
   (E) two positive real roots, one negative real root, and one complex root

8. For what value(s) of k is $x^2 + 3x + k$ divisible by $x + k$?

   (A) only 0
   (B) only 0 or 2
   (C) only 0 or –4
   (D) no value of k
   (E) any value of k

9. When 99,756 is divided by 559, what is the remainder?

   (A) 0
   (B) 558
   (C) 176
   (D) 384
   (E) 254

10. What is the equation of the set of points that are 5 units from point (2,3,4)?

    (A) $2x + 3y + 4z = 5$
    (B) $x^2 + y^2 + z^2 - 4x - 6y - 8z = 25$
    (C) $(x - 2)^2 + (y - 3)^2 + (z - 4)^2 = 25$
    (D) $x^2 + y^2 + z^2 = 5$
    (E) $\dfrac{x}{2} + \dfrac{y}{3} + \dfrac{z}{4} = 5$

11. If $3x^{3/2} = 4$, then $x =$

    (A) 1.1
    (B) 1.2
    (C) 1.3
    (D) 1.4
    (E) 1.5

12. If $f(x) = x^3 - 4$, then the inverse of $f =$

   (A) $-x^3 + 4$
   (B) $\sqrt[3]{x + 4}$
   (C) $\sqrt[3]{x - 4}$
   (D) $\dfrac{1}{x^3 - 4}$
   (E) $\dfrac{4}{\sqrt[3]{x}}$

13. If f is an odd function and $f(a) = b$, which of the following must also be true?

   I. $f(a) = -b$
   II. $f(-a) = b$
   III. $f(-a) = -b$

   (A) only I
   (B) only II
   (C) only III
   (D) only I and II
   (E) only II and III

14. If $\cos (5n - 30°) = \sin 50°$ and $0° < n < 90°$, then $n =$

   (A) $2°$
   (B) $14°$
   (C) $88°$
   (D) $16°$
   (E) $40°$

15. The period of the function $f(x) = k \cos kx$ is $\dfrac{\pi}{2}$. The amplitude of f is

   (A) 2
   (B) $\dfrac{1}{2}$
   (C) 1
   (D) $\dfrac{1}{4}$
   (E) 4

16. If $f(x) = \dfrac{x + 2}{(x - 2)(x^2 - 4)}$, its graph will have

   (A) one horizontal and three vertical asymptotes
   (B) one horizontal and two vertical asymptotes
   (C) one horizontal and one vertical asymptote
   (D) zero horizontal and one vertical asymptote
   (E) zero horizontal and two vertical asymptotes

GO ON TO THE NEXT PAGE

17. At a distance of 100 feet, the angle of elevation from the horizontal ground to the top of a building is 42°. The height of the building is

   (A) 67 feet
   (B) 74 feet
   (C) 90 feet
   (D) 110 feet
   (E) 229 feet

18. A sphere has a surface area of 36π. Its volume is

   (A) 113
   (B) 339
   (C) 201
   (D) 84
   (E) 905

19. A pair of dice is tossed 10 times. What is the probability that no 7s or 11s ever appear?

   (A) 0.08
   (B) 0.09
   (C) 0.11
   (D) 0.16
   (E) 0.24

20. The lengths of two sides of a triangle are 50 inches and 63 inches. The angle opposite the 63-inch side is 66°. How many degrees are in the largest angle of the triangle?

   (A) 72°
   (B) 68°
   (C) 71°
   (D) 67°
   (E) 66°

21. If the following instructions are followed, what number will be printed in line 6?

   1. Let $A = 1$.
   2. Let $x = 4$.
   3. Let A be replaced by the sum of A and x.
   4. Increase the value of x by 3.
   5. If $x < 9$ go back to step 3.
      If $x \geq 9$ go to step 6.
   6. Print the value of A.

   (A) 7
   (B) 10
   (C) 12
   (D) 0
   (E) 9

USE THIS SPACE FOR SCRATCH WORK

GO ON TO THE NEXT PAGE

22. What is the period of the graph of the function $y = \dfrac{\sin x}{1 + \cos x}$?

(A) 2π

(B) π

(C) $\dfrac{\pi}{2}$

(D) $\dfrac{\pi}{4}$

(E) 4π

23. For what values of k are the roots of the equation $kx^2 + 4x + k = 0$ real and unequal?

(A) $0 < k < 2$

(B) $|k| < 2$

(C) $|k| > 2$

(D) $k > 2$

(E) $-2 < k < 0$ or $0 < k < 2$

24. A point moves in a plane so that its distance from the origin is always twice its distance from point $(1,1)$. All such points form

(A) a line

(B) a circle

(C) a parabola

(D) an ellipse

(E) a hyperbola

25. If $f(x) = 3x^2 + 24x - 53$, find the negative value of $f^{-1}(0)$.

(A) -58.8

(B) -9.8

(C) -1.8

(D) -8.2

(E) -0.2

26. The operation $\#$ is defined by the equation $a \# b = \dfrac{a}{b} - \dfrac{b}{a}$. What is the value of k if $3 \# k = k \# 2$?

(A) ± 2.0

(B) ± 3.0

(C) ± 6.0

(D) ± 2.4

(E) ± 5.5

27. If $7^{x-1} = 6^x$, find x.

(A) 0.08

(B) -13.2

(C) 0.22

(D) 12.6

(E) 0.52

GO ON TO THE NEXT PAGE

28. A red box contains eight items, of which three are defective, and a blue box contains five items, of which two are defective. An item is drawn at random from each box. What is the probability that one item is defective and one is not?

(A) $\dfrac{5}{8}$

(B) $\dfrac{19}{40}$

(C) $\dfrac{17}{32}$

(D) $\dfrac{17}{20}$

(E) $\dfrac{9}{40}$

29. If $(\log_3 x)(\log_5 3) = 3$, find x.

(A) 5
(B) 25
(C) 125
(D) 81
(E) 9

30. If $f(x) = \sqrt{x}$, $g(x) = \sqrt[3]{x+1}$, and $h(x) = \sqrt[4]{x+2}$, then $f(g(h(2))) =$

(A) 1.2
(B) 8.5
(C) 1.4
(D) 2.9
(E) 4.7

31. In $\triangle ABC$, $\angle A = 45°$, $\angle B = 30°$, and $b = 8$. Side $a =$

(A) 12
(B) 16
(C) 6.5
(D) 11
(E) 14

32. The equations of the asymptotes of the graph of $4x^2 - 9y^2 = 36$ are

(A) $y = x$ and $y = -x$
(B) $y = 0$ and $x = 0$
(C) $y = \dfrac{2}{3}x$ and $y = -\dfrac{2}{3}x$
(D) $y = \dfrac{3}{2}x$ and $y = -\dfrac{3}{2}x$
(E) $y = \dfrac{4}{9}x$ and $y = -\dfrac{4}{9}x$

USE THIS SPACE FOR SCRATCH WORK

GO ON TO THE NEXT PAGE

33. If $g(x-1) = x^2 + 2$, then $g(x) =$

(A) $x^2 - 2x + 3$
(B) $x^2 + 2x + 3$
(C) $x^2 + 2$
(D) $x^2 - 2$
(E) $x^2 - 3x + 2$

34. If $f(x) = 3x^3 - 2x^2 + x - 2$, then $f(i) =$

(A) $-2i - 4$
(B) $4i$
(C) $4i - 4$
(D) $-2i$
(E) 0

35. If the hour hand of a clock moves k radians in 48 minutes, $k =$

(A) 2.4
(B) 5
(C) 0.3
(D) 0.4
(E) 0.5

36. If the longer diagonal of a rhombus is 10 and the large angle is $100°$, what is the area of the rhombus?

(A) 45
(B) 40
(C) 37
(D) 42
(E) 50

37. Let $f(x) = \sqrt{x^3 - 4x}$ and $g(x) = 3x$. The sum of all values of x for which $f(x) = g(x)$ is

(A) 0
(B) 9
(C) 9.4
(D) 8
(E) -8.5

38. Given $A = \{a,b\}$ and $C = \{a,b,c,d\}$. If $A \subseteq B \subseteq C$, how many different sets, B, are there that satisfy this condition? ($A \subseteq B$ means that all the elements of set A are elements of set B.)

(A) 2
(B) 4
(C) 6
(D) 8
(E) 10

USE THIS SPACE FOR SCRATCH WORK

GO ON TO THE NEXT PAGE

39. Given the statement "All vacationers are tourists," which conclusion follows logically?

    (A) If the Browns are tourists, then they are vacationers.
    (B) If the Smiths are not tourists, then they are not vacationers.
    (C) If the Polks are not vacationers, then they are not tourists.
    (D) All tourists are vacationers.
    (E) Some tourists are not vacationers.

40. For what positive value of n are the zeros of $P(x) = 5x^2 + nx + 12$ in ratio 2:3?

    (A) 0.42
    (B) 15.8
    (C) 1.32
    (D) 4.56
    (E) 25

41. If Arcsin $x = 2$ Arccos x, then $x =$

    (A) 0.5
    (B) 0.9
    (C) 0
    (D) ±0.9
    (E) ±0.5

42. A man piles 150 toothpicks in layers so that each layer has one less toothpick than the layer below. If the top layer has three toothpicks, how many layers are there?

    (A) 15
    (B) 17
    (C) 20
    (D) 148
    (E) 11,322

43. If the circle $x^2 + y^2 - 2x - 6y = r^2 - 10$ is tangent to the line $5x + 12y = 60$, the value of r is

    (A) 3.2
    (B) 1.5
    (C) 1.1
    (D) 1.7
    (E) 13

44. $\sqrt{(12345)(12345) - (12343)(12347)} =$

    (A) 12.2
    (B) 234.7
    (C) 3.7
    (D) 464
    (E) 2

GO ON TO THE NEXT PAGE

45. The line passing through $(1,4,-2)$ and $(2,1,4)$ can be represented by the set of equations

(A) $x = -1 + 2d$
$ y = 3 + d$
$ z = 2 + 4d$

(B) $x = 1 + 2d$
$ y = 4 + d$
$ z = -2 + 4d$

(C) $x = 2 + d$
$ y = 1 + 4d$
$ z = 4 - 2d$

(D) $x = 1 + d$
$ y = 4 - 3d$
$ z = -2 + 6d$

(E) $x = 1 - d$
$ y = -3 - 4d$
$ z = 2 + 2d$

46. As $n \to \infty$, find the limit of the product
$\left(\sqrt[3]{3}\right)\left(\sqrt[6]{3}\right)\left(\sqrt[12]{3}\right)\cdots\left(\sqrt[2n]{3}\right)$.

(A) 2.3
(B) 1.9
(C) 2.2
(D) 2.0
(E) 2.1

47. The function $f(x) = 4x^3 - px^2 + qx - 2p$ crosses the x-axis at three points, 4, 7, and t. Find t.

(A) 0.73
(B) 0.93
(C) −0.79
(D) 0.64
(E) 0.85

48. If the length of the diameter of a circle is equal to the length of the major axis of the ellipse whose equation is $x^2 + 4y^2 - 4x + 8y - 28 = 0$, to the nearest whole number, what is the area of the circle?

(A) 113
(B) 64
(C) 28
(D) 254
(E) 452

GO ON TO THE NEXT PAGE

49. The force of the wind on a sail varies jointly as the area of the sail and the square of the wind velocity. On a sail of area 50 square yards, the force of a 15-mile-per-hour wind is 45 pounds. Find the force on the sail if the wind increases to 45 miles per hour.

(A) 135 pounds
(B) 405 pounds
(C) 450 pounds
(D) 225 pounds
(E) 675 pounds

50. If the riser of each step in the drawing is 6 inches and the tread is 8 inches, what is the value of |AB|?

(A) 40 inches
(B) 43.9 inches
(C) 46.6 inches
(D) 48.3 inches
(E) 50 inches

USE THIS SPACE FOR SCRATCH WORK

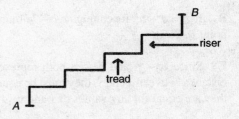

ANSWER KEY

1. B	6. D	11. B	16. C	21. C	26. D	31. D	36. D	41. B	46. E
2. E	7. D	12. B	17. C	22. A	27. D	32. C	37. C	42. A	47. E
3. B	8. B	13. C	18. A	23. E	28. B	33. B	38. B	43. B	48. A
4. A	9. E	14. B	19. A	24. B	29. C	34. D	39. B	44. E	49. B
5. B	10. C	15. E	20. B	25. B	30. A	35. D	40. B	45. D	50. B

ANSWER EXPLANATIONS

In these solutions the following notation is used:

a: active—Calculator use is necessary or, at a minimum, extremely helpful.

n: neutral—Answers can be found without a calculator, but a calculator may help.

i: inactive—Calculator use is not helpful and may even be a hindrance.

1. i B If $F = a + bi$, its conjugate $a - bi$ must be at point B. [4.7].

2. i E Since $|x - y|$ and $|y - x|$ both represent the distance between x and y, they must be equal, and they are equal for any values of x and y. [4.3].

3. n B Adding the equation gives $3x = 15$. $x = 5$ and $y = 3$. $a - b = 2$. [2.2, 5.9].

 Graphing calculator: Plot the graphs of $y = 2x - 7$ and $y = -x + 8$ in an $x \in [-10,10]$, $y \in [-10,10]$ window. Use the Trace and Zoom functions or the Intersect function to see that the coordinates of the point of intersection are approximately $(4.9, 2.9)$. Their difference is approximately 2.

4. i A $h(5) = 1$. $g(1) = 3$. Interchange x and y to find that $f^{-1}(x) = x + 1$, and so $f^{-1}(3) = 4$. [1.2, 1.3].

5. n B Diameter of sphere = side of cube.

Volume of sphere $= \dfrac{4}{3}\pi r^3$.

Volume of cube $= s^3 = (2r)^3$.

$$\frac{\text{Volume of sphere}}{\text{Volume of cube}} = \frac{\frac{4}{3}\pi r^3}{8r^3} = \frac{\pi}{6} \approx \frac{3.14}{6} \approx \frac{0.52}{1}.$$

Calculator: $\pi \div 6 = 0.523599 \approx 0.52$. [5.5].

6. n D $\sec^2 x = 1 + \tan^2 x$, and so the equation becomes $1 + \tan^2 x - \tan x - 1 = 0$; $\tan x (\tan x - 1) = 0$. $\tan x = 0$ or $\tan x = 1$. Therefore, $x = 0°, 180°, 360°$ or $x = 45°, 225°$, thus $n = 3$. [3.5].

Graphing calculator (in degree mode): Plot the graph of $y = \dfrac{1}{(\cos x)^2} - \tan x - 1$ in an $x \in [10°,350°]$, $y \in [-1,1]$ window. The graph crosses the x-axis three times; therefore, there are three solutions.

7. n D If $P(x)$ represents the polynomial, by Descartes' rule of signs there is one sign change in $P(x)$, which implies one positive real root, and one sign change in $P(-x)$, which implies one negative real root. Since there are four roots, there must be two complex roots also. [2.4].

 Graphing calculator: Plot the graphs of $y = 3x^4 + 4x^3 + x - 1$ in an $x \in [-10,10]$, $y \in [-10,10]$ window. Use the Trace and Zoom functions to see that there is one positive real root and one negative real root. Since there is a 4th degree polynomial, it must also have two complex roots.

8. i B If $P(x)$ represents the polynomial, $P(-k) = k^2 - 3k + k = 0$. $k(k - 2) = 0$. $k = 0, 2$. [2.4, 2.3].

9. n E By long division, the remainder is 254.

 Calculator: Divide 99756 by 559 to get 178.4543828. Subtract 178 and then multiply by 559 to see that the remainder is 254. [5.9].

10. i C The set of points represents a sphere with equation $(x - 2)^2 + (y - 3)^2 + (z - 4)^2 = 5^2$. [5.5].

11. a B $x^{3/2} = \dfrac{4}{3}$. $x = \left(\dfrac{4}{3}\right)^{2/3} \approx (1.333)^{2/3} \approx 1.2$. [4.2].

12. i B Let $y = f(x) = x^3 - 4$. To get the inverse, interchange x and y and solve for y. $x = y^3 - 4$. $y = \sqrt[3]{x + 4}$. [1.3].

13. i C Use the definition of an odd function. If $f(a) = b$, then $f(-a) = -b$. Only III is true. [1.4].

14. n B Cofunctions of complementary angles are equal. Therefore, $(5n - 30) + 50 = 90$, and so $n = 14°$. [3.1].

 Calculator (in degree mode): $\cos(5n - 30°) = \sin 50° \approx 0.766$. Thus, $5n - 30° \approx \cos^{-1}(0.766) \approx 40°$. Therefore, $5n = 70°$ and $n = 14°$.

 Graphing calculator (in degree mode): Plot the graphs of $y = \cos(5x - 30°)$ and $y = \sin 50°$ in an $x \in [-0°,90°]$, $y \in [-1,1]$ window. Use the Trace function or the Intersect function to see that the graphs intersect when x is approximately $14°$. (The other points of intersection are not among the answer choices.)

15. i **E** Period = $\dfrac{2\pi}{k} = \dfrac{\pi}{2}$. $k = 4$. Amplitude = 4. [3.4].

16. n **C** When $x^2 - 4$ is factored, the $x + 2$ divides out, leaving $f(x) = \dfrac{1}{(x-2)(x-2)}$, and so the only vertical asymptote is at $x = 2$. As $x \to \infty$, the numerator stays at 1 while the denominator $\to \infty$, making $f(x) \to 0$. Therefore, there is a horizontal asymptote of $y = 0$. [4.5].

Graphing calculator: Plot the graph of $y = \dfrac{x+2}{(x-2)(x^2-4)}$ in an $x \in [-10,10]$, $y \in [-10,10]$ window. Use the Trace and Zoom functions to see that there is a vertical asymptote when $x \approx 2$. As $x \to \infty$, $y \to 0$, and so there is a horizontal asymptote at $y = 0$. Therefore, Choice C is correct.

17. a **C** Tan $42° = \dfrac{x}{100}$.
$x = 100 \tan 42 \approx 90$.
[3.1].

18. n **A** $4\pi r^2 = 36\pi$. $r^2 = 9$. $r = 3$. $V = \dfrac{4}{3}\pi r^3 = 36\pi \approx 36 \cdot 3.14 \approx 113$. [5.5].

19. a **A** There are six ways to get a 7 and two ways to get an 11 on two dice, and so there are 28 ways to get anything else. Therefore, P(no 7 or 11) = P(always getting something else) = $\left(\dfrac{28}{36}\right)^{10} \approx (0.7777)^{10} \approx 0.08$. [5.3].

20. a **B** Use the law of sines: $\dfrac{\sin B}{50} = \dfrac{\sin 66°}{63}$. $\sin B = \dfrac{50 \sin 66}{63} \approx \dfrac{45.68}{63} \approx 0.725$. $B = \text{Sin}^{-1}(0.725) \approx 46°$ and $\angle A = 180 - 46 - 66 = 68°$. [3.7].

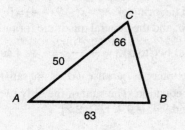

21. i **C** Keep track of the values of A and x:

Step	1	2	3	4	3	4
A	1		5		12	
x		4		7		10

Print 12 in line 6. [5.9].

22. n **A** This is a formula for $\tan \dfrac{x}{2}$. Normal tan period is π. Period = $\dfrac{\pi}{\frac{1}{2}} = 2\pi$. [3.4].

Graphing calculator (in radian mode): Plot the graph of $y = \dfrac{\sin x}{1 + \cos x}$ in an $x \in [-10,10]$, $y \in [-10,10]$ window. Use the Trace function to inspect the graph from the origin to the first asymptote. This distance is approximately 3.14 or π. Therefore, the period of the whole branch is 2π.

23. i **E** $b^2 - 4ac > 0$. $b^2 - 4ac = 16 - 4k^2 > 0$. $4 > k^2$. So $-2 < k < 2$. However, $k \neq 0$ because if $k = 0$, there would no longer be a quadratic equation. [2.3].

24. i **B** If (x,y) represents any of the points, $\sqrt{(x-0)^2 + (y-0)^2} = 2\sqrt{(x-1)^2 + (y-1)^2}$ $x^2 + y^2 = 4(x^2 - 2x + y^2 - 2y + 2)$. $3x^2 + 3y^2 - 8x - 8y + 8 = 0$. All such points form a circle. [4.1].

25. a **B** $f^{-1}(0)$ means "Find the value of x that makes $f(x) = 3x^2 + 24x - 53 = 0$." Use the general quadratic formula.

$$x = \dfrac{-24 \pm \sqrt{24^2 + (12)(53)}}{6} = \dfrac{-24 \pm \sqrt{1212}}{6}$$
$$\approx \dfrac{-24 \pm 34.8}{6}.$$

The negative value is $\dfrac{-24 - 34.8}{6} \approx -9.8$. [2.3].

Graphing calculator: Plot the graphs of $y = 3x^2 + 24x - 53$ and $y = 0$ (the x-axis) in an $x \in [-60,0]$, $y \in [-10,10]$ window (because the answer choices are between -58.8 and -0.2). Since the value of $f^{-1}(0)$ is the same as the value of x that makes $3x^2 + 24x - 53 = 0$, use the Trace and Zoom functions or the Root, Zero, or Solve function to see that the negative value of x is approximately -9.8 at the point where the graph crosses the x-axis.

26. a **D** $3 \# k = \dfrac{3}{k} - \dfrac{k}{3} = \dfrac{9 - k^2}{3k} \cdot = \dfrac{k}{2} - \dfrac{2}{k} = \dfrac{k^2 - 4}{2k}$.

$\dfrac{9 - k^2}{3k} = \dfrac{k^2 - 4}{2k}$. $18 - 2k^2 = 3k^2 - 12$.

$k^2 - 6$ and $k = \pm\sqrt{6} \approx \pm 2.4$. [5.9].

27. a **D** $(x - 1) \log 7 = x \log 6. \; x \log 7 - \log 7 = x \log$
$6. \; x \log 7 - x \log 6 = \log 7. \; x(\log 7 - \log 6) = \log 7.$

$x = \dfrac{\log 7}{\log 7 - \log 6} \approx \dfrac{0.845}{0.845 - 0.778} \approx 12.6.$ [4.2].

Graphing calculator: Although this looks like a problem that can be solved using a graphing calculator, it would take far too much time to locate an appropriate viewing window that would include the point of intersection. The graphs intersect when $x \approx 12.6$ and $y \approx 6{,}651{,}421{,}870$.

28. i **B** Probability that an item from the red box is defective and an item from the blue box is good $=$ $\dfrac{3}{8} \cdot \dfrac{3}{5} = \dfrac{9}{40}$. Probability that an item from the red box is good and that an item from the blue box is defective $= \dfrac{5}{8} \cdot \dfrac{2}{5} = \dfrac{10}{40}$. Since these are mutually exclusive events, the answer is $\dfrac{9}{40} + \dfrac{10}{40} = \dfrac{19}{40}$.
[5.3].

29. n **C** By the change-of-base theorem, $\log_3 x = \dfrac{\log_5 x}{\log_5 3}$. Therefore $\log_5 x = 3$ and $x = 5^3 = 125$.
[4.2].

Alternative Solution:

$\left(\dfrac{\log x}{\log 3}\right)\left(\dfrac{\log 3}{\log 5}\right) = \dfrac{\log x}{\log 5} = 3.$

$\log x = 3 \log 5 \approx 2.0969.$ Therefore, $x \approx 10^{2.0969} \approx 125.$

30. a **A** $h(2) = \sqrt[4]{2 + 2} = \sqrt[4]{4} = 4^{1/4} = (2^2)^{1/4} = 2^{1/2} = \sqrt{2}. \; g(h(2)) = \sqrt[3]{\sqrt{2} + 1} = \left(\sqrt{2} + 1\right)^{1/3}. \; f(g(h(2)))$
$= \sqrt{\left(\sqrt{2} + 1\right)^{1/3}} \approx \sqrt{2.414^{1/3}} \approx \sqrt{1.34} \approx 1.2.$
[4.2].

31. a **D** Use the law of sines: $\dfrac{\sin 45°}{a} = \dfrac{\sin 30°}{8}$

$\dfrac{1}{2} a = 8 \dfrac{\sqrt{2}}{2} \cdot a = 8\sqrt{2} \approx 11.$ [3.7].

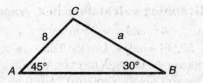

32. i **C** From this form of the equation of the hyperbola, $\dfrac{x^2}{9} - \dfrac{y^2}{4} = 1$, the equations of the asymptotes can be found from $\dfrac{x^2}{9} - \dfrac{y^2}{4} = 0$. Thus, $y = \pm\dfrac{2}{3} x$. [4.1].

33. i **B** Let $r = x - 1. \; x = r + 1. \; g(x - 1) = g(r) = x^2 + 2 = (r + 1)^2 + 2 = r^2 + 2r + 3.$ Since $g(r) = r^2 + 2r + 3, \; g(x) = x^2 + 2x + 3.$ [1.2, 2.3].

34. i **D** $f(i) = 3i^3 - 2i^2 + i - 2 = -3i + 2 + i - 2 = -2i.$
[2.4, 4.7].

35. a **D** In 1 hour, the hour hand moves $\dfrac{1}{12}$ of the way around the clock, or $\dfrac{2\pi}{12} = \dfrac{\pi}{6}$ radians.
$\dfrac{48}{60} \cdot \dfrac{\pi}{6} = \dfrac{2\pi}{15} \approx \dfrac{6.28}{15} \approx 0.4.$ [3.2].

36. a **D** Diagonals of a rhombus are perpendicular and bisect each other and the angles of the rhombus.
$\text{Tan } 40° = \dfrac{x}{5}. \quad x = 5 \tan 40°. \quad x \approx 4.195.$
$A = \dfrac{1}{2} d_1 d_2 = \dfrac{1}{2} (10)(2)(4.195) = 41.95 \approx 42.$
[3.1, 6.5].

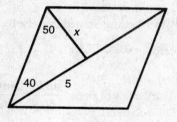

37. a **C** $\sqrt{x^3 - 4x} = 3x.$ Squaring both sides gives $x^3 - 4x = 9x^2.$ Setting this equation equal to zero and factoring gives $x(x^2 - 9x - 4) = 0.$ One root is zero, and the general quadratic formula gives the other two to be $x = \dfrac{9 \pm \sqrt{97}}{2} \approx -0.4$ and $9.4.$ -0.4 is extraneous because it does not satisfy the original equation. The sum of the only two solutions, 0 and 9.4, is 9.4. [1.2, 2.3].

Graphing calculator: Plot graphs of $y = \sqrt{x^3 - 4x}$ and $y = 3x$ in an $x \in [-20,20]$, $y \in [-50,50]$ window. Use the Trace and Zoom functions or the Intersect function to see that the graphs intersect when x is approximately 0 and 9.4. Therefore, the sum of the values is 9.4.

38. i   B   Every element of A, (a,b), must be an element of B, and every element of B must be an element of C, (a,b,c,d). Four sets satisfy this condition: $\{a,b\}$, $\{a,b,c,d\}$, $\{a,b,c\}$, and $\{a,b,d\}$. [5.9].

39. i   B   Counterexamples of Choices A, C, and D can be found. Choice E does not follow if the sets of tourists and vacationers are equal. [5.7].

40. a   B   The zeros of $P(x) = 5x^2 + nx + 12$ are the same as the zeros of $\frac{1}{5}f(x) = x^2 + \frac{n}{5} + \frac{12}{5}$. Since the zeros are in a ratio of 2:3, they can be expressed as $2a$ and $3a$. Thus, $(x + 2a)(x + 3a) = x^2 + 5ax + 6a^2 = x^2 + \frac{n}{5}x + \frac{12}{5}$. Therefore, $6a^2 = \frac{12}{5}$, making $a = \sqrt{\frac{2}{5}}$ and $5ax = \frac{n}{5}x$, making $n = 25a \approx 15.8$. [2.3].

Alternative Solution #1:

$r_1 r_2 = \frac{12}{5}$. $r_1 + r_2 = \frac{-n}{5}$. $\frac{r_1}{r_2} = \frac{2}{3}$. $r_1 = \frac{2}{3}r_2$.

$\left(\frac{2}{3}r_2\right)r_2 = \frac{12}{5}$. $(r_2)^2 = \left(\frac{12}{5}\right)\left(\frac{3}{2}\right) = \frac{36}{10}$. $r_2 = \sqrt{\frac{36}{10}}$. $r_1 = \frac{2}{3}\sqrt{\frac{36}{10}}$. $r_1 + r_2 = \frac{5}{3}\sqrt{\frac{36}{10}} = \frac{-n}{5}$.

Therefore, $n = \frac{25}{3}\sqrt{\frac{36}{10}} = \frac{25}{3} \cdot \frac{6}{\sqrt{10}} = 5\sqrt{10} \approx 5 \cdot 3.16 \approx 15.8$. [2.3].

Alternative Solution #2: From the general quadratic formula the two zeros are $\frac{-n \pm \sqrt{n^2 - 240}}{10}$. Thus, $\frac{-n + \sqrt{n^2 - 240}}{-n - \sqrt{n^2 - 240}} = \frac{2}{3}$. Cross-multiply to get $-3n + 3\sqrt{n^2 - 240} = -2n - 2\sqrt{n^2 - 240}$, which simplifies to $5\sqrt{n^2 - 240} = n$. Square both sides: $25(n^2 - 240) = n^2$. This simplifies to $n^2 = 250$. Therefore, $n = \sqrt{250} \approx 15.8$.

41. a   B   Let $A = \text{Arcsin } x$ and $B = \text{Arccos } x$. Therefore, $A = 2B$. From the diagrams, it is clear that

A and B must be complementary. Therefore, $A + B = 90°$, $2B + B = 90°$, $B = 30°$. $x = \cos 30° = \frac{\sqrt{3}}{2} \approx 0.9$. [3.6].

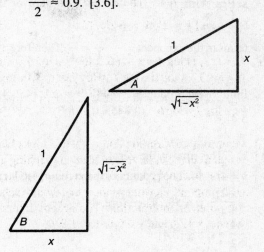

Graphing calculator (in radian mode): Plot the graphs of $y = \sin^{-1} x$ and $y = 2\cos^{-1} x$ in an $x \in [-1,1]$, $y \in [-10,10]$ window. Use the Trace and Zoom functions or the Intersect function to see that x is approximately 0.9 when the graphs intersect.

42. i   A   This is an arithmetic series with $t_1 = 3$, $d = 1$, and $S = 150$. $150 = \frac{n}{2}[6 + (n - 1) \cdot 1]$. $n = 15$. [5.4].

43. a   B   Complete the square: $(x^2 - 2x + 1) + (y^2 - 6y + 9) = r^2 - 10 + 10$. $(x - 1)^2 + (y - 3)^2 = r^2$. Center at $(1,3)$.

$r = \frac{|5 \cdot 1 + 12 \cdot 3 - 60|}{\sqrt{5^2 + 12^2}} = \frac{|5 + 36 - 60|}{13} = \frac{19}{13} \approx 1.5$. [4.1, 2.3].

44. i   E   If $x = 123456789$, the problem is of the form
$$\sqrt{x^2 - (x - 2)(x + 2)} = \sqrt{x^2 - (x^2 - 4)}$$
$$= \sqrt{x^2 - x^2 + 4} = 2.$$
[2.3, 4.2].

> **TIP:** The numbers have too many significant digits for the calculator to correctly compute the answer. Because of this, it needs to use scientific notation and drops some significant digits, leading to an incorrect answer of zero.

45. i   D   Find the direction numbers by taking the difference of the corresponding coordinates of the two points: 1, –3, 6. Choice D is the only possibility. [5.5].

46. a E The product $= (3^{1/3})(3^{1/6})(3^{1/12}) \cdots (3^{1/2n}) = 3^{(1/3+1/6+1/12+\cdots+1/2n)}$. The exponent is a geometric series with $t_1 = \dfrac{1}{3}$ and $r = \dfrac{1}{2}$. The sum of the terms in the exponent $= \dfrac{\dfrac{1}{3}}{1-\dfrac{1}{2}} = \dfrac{2}{3}$. Therefore, the limit of the product $= 3^{2/3} = \sqrt[3]{9} \approx 2.1$. [4.2, 4.5, 5.4].

47. n E The sum of the zeros $= 4 + 7 + t = -\dfrac{-p}{4}$. $p = 4t + 44$. The product of the zeros $= (4)(7)(t) = -\dfrac{-2p}{4}$. $p = 56t$. Therefore, $44 + 4t = 56t$ and $t = \dfrac{44}{52} \approx 0.85$. [2.4].

48. a A Complete the square on the ellipse formula, and put the equation in standard form: $x^2 - 4x + 4 + 4(y^2 + 2y - 1) = 28 + 4 + 4$. $\dfrac{(x-2)^2}{36} +$

$\dfrac{(y+1)^2}{9} = 1$. This leads to the length of the major axis: $2\sqrt{36} = 12$. Therefore, the radius of the circle is 6, and the area $= 36\pi \approx 36 \cdot 3.14 \approx 113$. [4.1].

49. n B $\dfrac{F}{Av^2} = K$. First case: $\dfrac{45}{(50)(15)^2} = \dfrac{1}{250} = K$. Second case: $\dfrac{F}{(50)(45)^2} = \dfrac{1}{250}$. $F = \dfrac{(50)(45)^2}{250} = \dfrac{(45)^2}{5} = 9(45) = 405$. $F = 405$.

Calculator: $F = \dfrac{50(45)^2}{250} = \dfrac{101250}{250} = 405$.

50. a B Total horizontal distance traveled $= (4)(8) = 32$. Total vertical distance traveled $= (5)(6) = 30$. If the diagram is put on a coordinate system with A at $(0,0)$, then B will be at $(32,30)$. $|AB|$ $\sqrt{(32)-0)^2 + (30-0)^2} = \sqrt{1024+900} = \sqrt{1924} \approx 43.9$. [2.2].

SELF-EVALUATION CHART FOR MODEL TEST 8

SUBJECT AREA	QUESTIONS	NUMBER OF
		RIGHT WRONG OMITTED

Mark correct answers with C, wrong answers with X, and omitted answers with O.

Algebra
(9 questions)
Review section

2	3	7	11	23	27	29	44	49
4.3	2.2	2.4	4.2	2.3	4.2	4.2	2.3	5.6

____   ____   ____

Solid geometry
(4 questions)
Review section

5	10	18	45
5.5	5.5	5.5	5.5

____   ____   ____

Coordinate geometry
(6 questions)
Review section

1	24	32	43	48	50
4.7	4.1	4.1	1.5	4.1	2.2

____   ____   ____

Trigonometry
(10 questions)
Review section

6	14	15	17	20	22	31	35	36	41
3.5	3.1	3.4	3.1	3.7	3.4	3.7	3.2	3.1	3.6

____   ____   ____

Functions
(12 questions)
Review section

4	8	12	13	16	25	30	33	34	37	40	47
1.2	2.4	1.3	1.4	4.5	2.3	4.2	1.2	2.4	1.2	2.3	2.4

____   ____   ____

Miscellaneous
(9 questions)
Review section

9	19	21	26	28	38	39	42	46
5.9	5.3	5.9	5.9	5.3	5.9	5.7	5.4	4.2

____   ____   ____

TOTALS   ____   ____   ____

Raw score = (number right) $-\frac{1}{4}$ (number wrong) = _____

Round your raw score to the nearest whole number = _____

Evaluate Your Performance
Model Test 8

Rating	Number Right
Excellent	41–50
Very good	33–40
Above average	25–32
Average	15–24
Below average	Below 15

SUMMARY OF FORMULAS

APPENDIX

CHAPTER 2:
POLYNOMIAL FUNCTIONS

Linear Functions:

General form of the equation: $Ax + By + C = 0$

Slope-intercept form: $y = mx + b$, where m represents the slope and b the y-intercept

Point-slope form: $y - y_1 = m(x - x_1)$, where m represents the slope and (x_1, y_1) are the coordinates of some point on the line

Slope: $m = \dfrac{y_1 - y_2}{x_1 - x_2}$, where (x_1, y_1) and (x_2, y_2) are the coordinates of two points

Parallel lines have equal slopes.

Perpendicular lines have slopes that are negative reciprocals.

If m_1 and m_2 are the slopes of two perpendicular lines, $m_1 \cdot m_2 = -1$.

Distance between two points with coordinates (x_1, y_1) and

$$\left(x_2, y_2\right) = \sqrt{\left(x_1 - x_2\right)^2 + \left(y_1 - y_2\right)^2}$$

Coordinates of the midpoint between two points =

$$\left(\frac{x_1 + x_2}{2}, \frac{y_1 + y_2}{2}\right)$$

Distance between a point with coordinates (x_1, y_1) and a line $Ax + By + C = 0 =$

$$\frac{\left|Ax_1 + By_1 + C\right|}{\sqrt{A^2 + B^2}}$$

If θ is the angle between two lines, $\tan\theta = \dfrac{m_1 - m_2}{1 + m_1 m_2}$,

where m_1 and m_2 are the slopes of the two lines.

Quadratic Functions:

General quadratic equation: $ax^2 + bx + c = 0$

General quadratic formula:

$$x = \frac{-b \pm \sqrt{b^2 - 4ac}}{2a}$$

General quadratic function: $y = ax^2 + bx + c$

Coordinates of vertex: $\left(-\dfrac{b}{2a}, c - \dfrac{b^2}{4a}\right)$

Axis of symmetry equation: $x = -\dfrac{b}{2a}$

Sum of zeros (roots) $= -\dfrac{b}{a}$

Product of zeros (roots) $= \dfrac{c}{a}$

Nature of zeros (roots):

If $b^2 - 4ac < 0$, two complex numbers

If $b^2 - 4ac = 0$, two equal real numbers

If $b^2 - 4ac > 0$, two unequal real numbers

CHAPTER 3:
TRIGONOMETRIC FUNCTIONS

$\sin\theta = \dfrac{\text{opposite}}{\text{hypotenuse}}$ $\cos\theta = \dfrac{\text{adjacent}}{\text{hypotenuse}}$

$\tan\theta = \dfrac{\text{opposite}}{\text{adjacent}}$ $\cot\theta = \dfrac{\text{adjacent}}{\text{opposite}}$

$\sec\theta = \dfrac{\text{hypotenuse}}{\text{adjacent}}$ $\csc\theta = \dfrac{\text{hypotenuse}}{\text{opposite}}$

$\pi^R = 180°$

Length of arc in circle of radius r and central angle θ is given by $r\theta^R$.

Area of sector of circle of radius r and central angle θ is given by $\frac{1}{2}r^2\theta^R$.

Trigonometric Reduction Formulas:

1. $\sin^2 x + \cos^2 x = 1$ ⎫
2. $\tan^2 x + 1 = \sec^2 x$ ⎬ Pythagorean identities
3. $\cot^2 x + 1 = \csc^2 x$ ⎭

4. $\sin(A+B) =$
$\sin A \cdot \cos B + \cos A \cdot \sin B$

5. $\sin(A-B) =$
$\sin A \cdot \cos B - \cos A \cdot \sin B$

6. $\cos(A+B) =$
$\cos A \cdot \cos B - \sin A \cdot \sin B$

7. $\cos(A-B) =$ sum and difference
$\cos A \cdot \cos B + \sin A \cdot \sin B$ formulas

8. $\tan(A+B) =$
$\dfrac{\tan A + \tan B}{1 - \tan A \cdot \tan B}$

9. $\tan(A-B) =$
$\dfrac{\tan A - \tan B}{1 + \tan A \cdot \tan B}$

10. $\sin 2A = 2\sin A \cdot \cos A$ ⎫
11. $\cos 2A = \cos^2 A - \sin^2 A$
12. $\quad = 2\cos^2 A - 1$ double-angle
13. $\quad = 1 - 2\sin^2 A$ formulas
14. $\tan 2A = \dfrac{2\tan A}{1 - \tan^2 A}$ ⎭

15. $\sin \dfrac{1}{2}A = \pm\sqrt{\dfrac{1 - \cos A}{2}}$

16. $\cos \dfrac{1}{2}A = \pm\sqrt{\dfrac{1 + \cos A}{2}}$

17. $\tan \dfrac{1}{2}A = \pm\sqrt{\dfrac{1 - \cos A}{1 + \cos A}}$ half-angle
  formulas

18. $\quad = \dfrac{1 - \cos A}{\sin A}$

19. $\quad = \dfrac{\sin A}{1 + \cos A}$

In any $\triangle ABC$:

Law of sines : $\dfrac{\sin A}{a} = \dfrac{\sin B}{b} = \dfrac{\sin C}{c}$

Law of cosines : $a^2 = b^2 + c^2 - 2bc \cdot \cos A$

Area $= \dfrac{1}{2}bc \cdot \sin A$

CHAPTER 4: MISCELLANEOUS RELATIONS AND FUNCTIONS

General Quadratic Equation in Two Variables:

$$Ax^2 + Bxy + Cy^2 + Dx + Ey + F = 0$$

If $B^2 - 4AC < 0$ and $A = C$, graph is a circle.
If $B^2 - 4AC < 0$ and $A \neq C$, graph is an ellipse.
If $B^2 - 4AC = 0$, graph is a parabola.
If $B^2 - 4AC > 0$, graph is a hyperbola.

Circle:

$(x - h)^2 + (y - k)^2 = r^2$
  with center at (h,k) and radius $= r$

Ellipse:

$\dfrac{(x-h)^2}{a^2} + \dfrac{(y-k)^2}{b^2} = 1$, major axis horizontal

$\dfrac{(x-h)^2}{b^2} + \dfrac{(y-k)^2}{a^2} = 1$, major axis vertical,

where $a^2 = b^2 + c^2$. Coordinates of center: (h,k).
Vertices: $\pm a$ units along major axis from center
Foci: $\pm c$ units along major axis from center
Minor axis: perpendicular to major axis at center

Length $= 2b$

Eccentricity $= \dfrac{c}{a}$

Length of latus rectum $= \dfrac{2b^2}{a}$

Hyperbola:

$\dfrac{(x-h)^2}{a^2} - \dfrac{(y-k)^2}{b^2} = 1$, transverse axis horizontal

$\dfrac{(y-k)^2}{a^2} - \dfrac{(x-h)^2}{b^2} = 1$, transverse axis vertical, where

  $c^2 = a^2 + b^2$. Coordinates of center: (h,k).

Vertices: $\pm a$ units along the transverse axis from center
Foci: $\pm c$ units along the transverse from center
Conjugate axis: perpendicular to transverse axis at center

Eccentricity $= \dfrac{c}{a}$

Length of latus rectum $= \dfrac{2b^2}{a}$

Asymptotes: Slopes $=$

  $\pm \dfrac{b}{a}$ if transverse axis is horizontal

  $\pm \dfrac{a}{b}$ if transverse axis is vertical

Parabola:

$(x - h)^2 = 4p(y - k)$ opens up or down—axis of symmetry is vertical

$(y - k)^2 = 4p(x - h)$, opens to the side—axis of symmetry is horizontal

Coordinates of vertex: (h, k)

Equation of axis of symmetry:

  $x = h$ if vertical
  $y = k$ if horizontal

Focus: p units along the axis of symmetry from vertex

Equation of directrix:

  $y = -p$ if axis of symmetry is vertical
  $x = -p$ if axis of symmetry is horizontal

Eccentricity = 1

Length of latus rectum = $4p$

Exponents:

$$x^a \cdot x^b = x^{a+b} \qquad \frac{x^a}{x^b} = x^{a-b}$$

$$(x^a)^b = x^{ab}$$

$$x^0 = 1 \qquad x^{-a} = \frac{1}{x^a}$$

Logarithms:

$$\log_b(p \cdot q) = \log_b p + \log_b q \qquad \log_b\left(\frac{p}{q}\right) = \log_b p - \log_b q$$

$$\log_b p^x = x \cdot \log_b p \qquad \log_b 1 = 0$$

$$\log_b p = \frac{\log_a p}{\log_a b} \qquad \log_b b = 1$$

$$b^{\log_b p} = p$$

$\operatorname{Log}_b N = x$ if and only if $b^x = N$

Absolute Value:

If $x \geq 0$, then $|x| = x$.

If $x < 0$, then $|x| = -x$.

Greatest Integer Function:

$[x] = i$, where i is an integer and $i \leq x < i + 1$

Polar Coordinates:

$x = r \cdot \cos \theta \qquad y = r \cdot \sin \theta$

$x^2 + y^2 = r^2$

De Moivre's Theorem:

If
$$z_1 = x_1 + y_1 i = r_1(\cos \theta_1 + i \cdot \sin \theta_1) = r_1 \operatorname{cis} \theta_1$$
and
$$z_2 = x_2 + y_2 i = r_2(\cos \theta_2 + i \cdot \sin \theta_2) = r_2 \operatorname{cis} \theta_2:$$

1. $z_1 \cdot z_2 = r_1 \cdot r_2[\cos(\theta_1 + \theta_2) + i \cdot \sin(\theta_1 + \theta_2)]$
   $= r_1 \cdot r_2 \cdot \operatorname{cis}(\theta_1 + \theta_2)$

2. $\dfrac{z_1}{z_2} = \dfrac{r_1}{r_2}[\cos(\theta_1 - \theta_2) + i \cdot \sin(\theta_1 - \theta_2)]$
   $= \dfrac{r_1}{r_2} \operatorname{cis}(\theta_1 - \theta_2)$

3. $z^n = r^n(\cos n\theta + i \cdot \sin n\theta) = r^n \operatorname{cis} n\theta$

4. $z^{1/n} = r^{1/n}\left(\cos \dfrac{\theta + 2\pi k}{n} + i \cdot \sin \dfrac{\theta + 2\pi k}{n}\right)$
   $= r^{1/n} \operatorname{cis} \dfrac{\theta + 2\pi k}{n}$, where k is an integer taking on values from 0 to $n - 1$.

CHAPTER 5: MISCELLANEOUS TOPICS

Permutations:

$_nP_r = \dfrac{n!}{(n - r)!}$, where $n! = n(n - 1)(n - 2) \cdots 3 \cdot 2 \cdot 1$

Circular permutation (e.g., around a table) of n elements = $(n - 1)!$

Circular permutation (e.g., beads on a bracelet) of n elements = $\dfrac{(n - 1)!}{2}$

Permutations of n elements with a repetitions and with b repetitions = $\dfrac{n!}{a! b!}$

Combinations:

$$_nC_r = \binom{n}{r} = \frac{n!}{(n - r)! r!} = \frac{_nP_r}{n!}$$

Binomial Theorem:

There are $n + 1$ terms in $(a + b)^n$.

The sum of the exponents in each term is n.

The exponent on b is 1 less than the number of the term.

Coefficient of each term = $\left(\begin{array}{c} n \\ \text{either exponent} \end{array}\right)$

Probability:

$$P(\text{event}) = \frac{\text{number of ways to get a successful result}}{\text{total number of ways of getting any result}}$$

Independent events: $P(A \cap B) = P(A) \cdot P(B)$

Mutually exclusive events: $P(A \cap B) = 0$
  and $P(A \cup B) = P(A) + P(B)$

Sequences and Series:

Arithmetic Sequence (or Progression)

nth term = $t_n = t_1 + (n - 1)d$

Sum of n terms $= S_n = \dfrac{n}{2}(t_1 + t_n)$

$\qquad\qquad\qquad = \dfrac{n}{2}\left[2t_1 + (n-1)d\right]$

Geometric Sequence (or Progression)

nth term $= t_n = t_1 r^{n-1}$

Sum of n terms $= S_n = \dfrac{t_1(1-r^n)}{1-r}$

If $|r| < 1$, $S_\infty = \lim\limits_{n\to\infty} S_n = \dfrac{t_1}{1-r}$

Vectors:

If $\vec{V} = (v_1, v_2)$ and $\vec{U} = (u_1, u_2)$,

$\vec{V} + \vec{U} = (v_1 + u_1, v_2 + u_2)$

$\vec{V} \cdot \vec{U} = v_1 u_1 + v_2 u_2$

Two vectors are perpendicular if and only if $\vec{V} \cdot \vec{U} = 0$.

Determinants:

$\begin{vmatrix} a & b \\ c & d \end{vmatrix} = ad - bc$

Geometry:

Distance between two points with coordinates
(x_1, y_1, z_1) and $(x_2, y_2, z_2) =$

$\sqrt{(x_1 - x_2)^2 + (y_1 - y_2)^2 + (z_1 - z_2)^2}$.

Distance between a point with coordinates (x_1, y_1, z_1) and a plane with equation $Ax + By + Cz + D = 0 =$

$$\dfrac{Ax_1 + By_1 + Cz_1 + D}{\sqrt{A^2 + B^2 + C^2}}$$

Triangle

$A = \dfrac{1}{2}bh$; $b = $ base, $h = $ height

$A = \dfrac{1}{2}ab\sin C$; a, $b = $ any two sides, $C = $ angle included between sides a and b

Heron's formula:

$A = \sqrt{s(s-a)(s-b)(s-c)}$; a, b, c are the three sides of the triangle,

$s = \dfrac{1}{2}(a+b+c)$

Rhombus

Area $= bh = \dfrac{1}{2}d_1 d_2$; $b = $ base, $h = $ height, $d = $ diagonal

Cylinder

Volume $= \pi r^2 h$
Lateral surface area $= 2\pi rh$
Total surface area $= 2\pi rh + 2\pi r^2$
In all formulas, $r = $ radius of base, $h = $ height

Cone

Volume $= \dfrac{1}{3}\pi r^2 h$

Lateral surface area $= \pi r\sqrt{r^2 + h^2}$

Total surface area $= \pi r\sqrt{r^2 + h^2} + \pi r^2$

In all formulas, $r = $ radius of base, $h = $ height

Sphere

Volume $= \dfrac{4}{3}\pi r^3$

Surface area $= 4\pi r^2$
In all formulas, $r = $ radius

INDEX

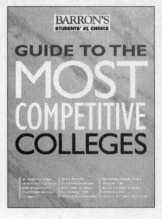